The Coffee Table Book of
ASTROLOGY

The Coffee Table Book of

ASTROLOGY

Revised edition

EDITED BY JOHN LYNCH

We are born at a given moment, in a given place
and, like vintage years of wine, we have the qualities
of the year and of the season in which we are born.
Astrology does not lay claim to anything more.
—C. G. JUNG

A Studio Book • *The Viking Press* • *New York*

ACKNOWLEDGMENTS

Thanks are gratefully extended to the publishers for permission to quote from the following works: *Astrology for All* by Alan Leo: International Publishing Company, Edinburgh; *From Pioneer to Poet* by Isabelle M. Pagan: Theosophical Publishing House London Ltd., London; *Work It Out Yourself* by Nora Wydenbruck: Sidgwick & Jackson Ltd., London.

"Written in the Stars" by Santha Rama Rau: Copyright © 1962 by The Curtis Publishing Company. This article appeared originally in the March 1962 issue of *Holiday*. By permission of William Morris Agency, Inc.

"Shakespeare's Artistic Use of Astrology" from *Tamburlaine's Malady and Other Essays on Astrology in Elizabethan Drama* by Johnstone Parr. Copyright 1953 by University of Alabama Press and reprinted by their permission.

"Palmistry as Related to Astrology" from *The History of Magic* by Kurt Seligmann. Copyright 1948 by Pantheon Books and reprinted by their permission.

"The Ephemerides of the Moon" from *Astrology for Everyone* by Edward Lyndoe. Copyright © 1959 by Edward Lyndoe. By permission of E. P. Dutton & Co., Inc., and the author.

The editor wishes to thank the many people who have assisted in the compilation of this book. Particular thanks go to the Metropolitan Museum of Art for all the reproductions from the Mediaeval Housebook, Castle Wolfegg, John Wright's Shepherd's Kalendar (1631), Sebastian Munster's Horologiographia, and many other illustrations; the Pierpont Morgan Library; and the Rare Book Room and Print Room of the New York Public Library. Credit is due to the latter for all the Hevelius, Alessandro Temini, and Hyginus illustrations, and for the reproductions from the Persian manuscript "Book of Stars and Constellations." A special vote of thanks goes to Wide World Photos, who supplied nearly all the photographs of famous contemporary personalities included. Many thanks also to Zoltan S. Mason for his professional advice on many technical details and to Karl Kup for his guidance in finding many of the illustrations, including those from books in the Spencer Collection. Thanks also to Christopher Harris, Mary Kopecky, and Beatrice Trueblood of The Viking Press for their tireless devotion to this project. And especially and above all, my gratitude and special thanks to Bryan Holme, Director of Studio Books, without whom this book could not have been done.

The sources of birth dates for the historical personalities included in this book were the Encyclopaedia Britannica, *Who's Who* and *Current Biography*. The dates given for the beginning and end of each of the twelve zodiac signs are an average based on listings in *Raphael's Astronomical Ephemeris*. Those born on the first or last two days of a sign (on the cusp) are referred to page 46.

CONTENTS

Astronomicum Caesareum. Ingolstadt, 1540.
Petrus Apianus. *Metropolitan Museum of Art*

PREFACE

Considering the enormous quantity of books that are published each year, it is extraordinary how difficult it is to find an astrology book addressed to the intelligent reader, let alone one reproducing relevant illustrations, engravings, woodcuts, etchings, drawings, and paintings by great artists. The fact is even more surprising when one considers that "let's talk about me" has always been a singularly popular topic of conversation.

The intent of this book is to present some of the best writings on the subject and leave it to the reader to decide for himself whether or not there is anything more in astrology than an amusing parlor game. In any event, anything that helps one to find out more about himself is constructive, and the selected texts on these pages continually lead to startling observations. Some are likely to give even the most skeptical reader pause for thought.

Astrology has been used, abused, exploited by charlatans for personal profit, condemned as utter nonsense, hailed as a science, accepted as a religion. The truth about it probably lies somewhere between the extremes. Sir Francis Bacon in a letter to a colleague, a mathematician who was a violent opponent of astrology, wrote: "I have practised Astrology, you have not, if I do not condemn it how can you presume to do so?" In the present century great men such as Einstein, Spengler, and the Nobel Prize winner Dr. C. G. Jung, have admitted that there is a great deal to it. Jung, particularly, has endorsed astrology, and hundreds of favorable references can be found in his collected works.

Among the classic writings included here are those of Isabelle Pagan. These form the basis for the chapters on the twelve zodiac signs and have been chosen because no one has done a more sober job of general character analysis than this pioneering author. Alan Leo's research has been used for further qualifications according to the position of the moon at the hour of one's birth. The writings of Pagan and Leo are considered by most professional astrologers to be about the most reliable in the field, and it is true that most recent texts are largely based on these authors' researches. However, before looking at the pages referring to his Sun sign, the reader should study page 45.

Also presented for the reader's enjoyment are Santha Rama Rau's "Written in the Stars," the notations of Shakespeare's artistic use of astrology by Johnstone Parr, and Kurt Seligmann's chapter on palmistry as related to astrology. Included entirely for amusement is an intriguing astrology board game, revived from the seventeenth century, in which the cast of the dice as well as the position of the constellations, with their traditional malevolent or beneficent influence, speeds the player forward or sends him back to a benign constellation. Amusing seventeenth-century French reasons are given for the forward, backward, or stay-put moves. Among these we might mention that a player who lands on Venus must pay a chip to the kitty for staying with her until someone jealous of his good fortune lands on Venus, forcing the first player to leave. If a player lands on the constellation of Noah's dove he is sent back to circle 1, the earth, to see whether or not the flood waters have receded. The game represents a combination of logic and wit so dear to the hearts and minds of the French.

Readers wishing to delve deeper into astrology should read Zoltan Mason's essay on astrology in relation to religion, and Norah Wydenbruck's excellent instructions on how to cast a horoscope. This author also gives analyses of the characters and lives of Napoleon, Churchill, and Franklin D. Roosevelt which show the fascinating way horoscope charts are professionally interpreted.

JOHN LYNCH

Augsburg Kalendar, 1484. *Metropolitan Museum of Art*

Nun saget das bůch von dēn übzigen
kǒzen der hīmel vnd jrem lauff vnd na
turen Vnd hebt an dem hīmel an·der do
ꝓʃʃet das firmament·

1. WRITTEN IN THE STARS

I have known from my childhood that there is a great difference between a qualified astrologer and the fun-fair kind of palm reader, crystal-ball viewer, or fortune teller, and I learned the lesson again at the time of the birth of my son, who, in the correct Hindu way, had to come into the world in the heart of his Indian family. So strong was my early indoctrination that it seemed to me quite natural to overrule my husband's very reasonable American objections that it cost a shocking amount to go all the way to India to have a child born *there* — simply for the sake of being born *there*. I could only think that it was only decent for a first child to be born in the home of his grandparents. We went to India.

There we found that my oldest aunt, who is now pushing ninety, was firmly established in my parents' house and was quite determined to sit out my pregnancy for me and with me. It was only right. *Someone* had to see to the accepted ceremonies. Her first words to me after the birth of my son were, "I have noted the time exactly. Now we must quickly have the chart made out."

When I laughed, rather weakly, at her fierce expression, she said coldly, "It is silly to ignore such a simple precaution. How, for instance, will you know what to name him if you don't consult an astrologer?"

We had the child's chart made out, consulted an astrologer, and learned that since my child

11

was born on the last day of the famous ten-day war between King Rama and the forces of evil — an epic story in Indian mythology — his name had to contain some version of the many Sanskrit words for victory. We had to be absolutely certain that his equivocal birth date didn't mean that he might be on the wrong side, the side of evil which lost the war. He is called Jai, the simplest form of the word for victory, so he is permanently on the side of Rama, the winner of the battle and the force for good. I have yet to find out how much this will influence him.

In this elaborate process, however, I began to wonder about precisely what a true astrologer is. It was an interesting excursion. To himself, and to most of his patrons, an astrologer is a scientist probing the mysteries of the outer reaches of human life and destiny in much the same way that a physicist probes the mysteries of outer space. He relies partly on knowledge, partly on theory, partly on guesswork. He is an Einstein in miniature, dealing with an unexplored, speculative, and to some degree philosophic field in which he is certain that some element of truth can be mined, aware of the fact that most of the world thinks him a crackpot but conscious of the idea that his knowledge and intuition can be as disastrous to human beings as the theory of atomic energy proved to be.

My astrological chart, like those of most Hindus of my age and upbringing, was plotted (with fewer sneers than my son's received from me) at the moment of my birth. The *chart*, that is, not the horoscope. There is big difference, and one that the readers of the astrology columns in the newspapers seldom recognize. Those wildly imaginative columnists ask, in effect, "Are you born between January 21 and February 19? Yes?" And they answer themselves, "All right, you're an Aquarian." Or, "Your birthday is between February 20 and March 20? You're a child of Pisces." And so on. Then they go on to give you snippets of rather mysterious advice: "By thinking objectively you can now rid yourself of any personal worries you may have." "Get into matters of policy. Go out to dinner with mate and have wonderful time." (I quote from the *Los Angeles Times*, though the column doesn't say what you do if your "mate" is advised that day to stay home and do some serious reading.)

Any Indian astrologer worth his salt would be transfixed by the logical absurdities of such a column. Does everyone born in the same month have the same life and need the same advice? Of course not. Are they even born under the same heavenly sign? No.

The aspect that seems to an Indian the most important is the sign that is ascending from the horizon at the *exact moment* of your birth; those signs change, roughly, every two hours during the course of the day, and the strength of their influence changes every few minutes. One can, for instance, be born in the month of Pisces but still be an Aquarian. You can see that we are getting into deeper waters — and this isn't even the beginning of the end.

Your astrologer must take into account, besides your zodiac birth sign, the position of the moon and sun as seen from the particular place where you were born, the separate but very telling influence of the various planets at that moment, and his own gift for interpretation. Make no mistake — the plotting of a chart is an exercise in mathematics, astronomy, research, and a number of undefined qualities. The reading of the chart and, finally, the horoscope that emerges from the reading, are an exploration of the most rarefied dimension of human thought — the element of time. It has its ridiculous aspects, as we all know. It also has its power.

My own experience with the reading of a chart and its transformation into a horoscope was rather chilling. When I was six years old I was sent to school in England, and before that no one had thought to get my chart read by an astrologer. Ten years later, when I went back to India, my mother and I, returning from a luncheon in Delhi, saw a small sign outside a narrow alley through which our car was passing, and on an impulse I said, "An astrologer! Let's stop."

The man conducted us through the normal courtesies of tea and polite conversation, and then performed a properly reverent ceremony before he was willing to read my horoscope. Naturally I hadn't my chart with me — indeed, with all our traveling around, I doubt that any member of the family could have recalled where it had been placed for safekeeping. However, the astrologer was most accommodating, willing to make a new chart. He needed to know the time, date, and place of my birth, which my mother could easily provide — except that, understandably, she couldn't remember whether the time was five minutes *to* or five minutes *past* nine in the morning. Resignedly, the astrologer said, "Well, we will have to look up both."

After consulting a number of large, well-thumbed books, he asked, "Does the girl have two brothers? No? In that case she must have one older sister. Very well. Now we know the right time." He started telling me the story of my own life by saying, "This girl will come to seek her horoscope for the first time when she is sixteen. Not because she wants to learn anything specific, but on the whim of a moment."

Sobered and rather incredulous, I listened to him recite with remarkable accuracy and elaborate detail the not very startling events of my youth, embellished with the accounts of the births, marriages, illnesses, deaths of various members of my family. I thought he could know all this only because, during our tea-drinking and preliminary formalities, possibly his servant or assistant had talked to our chauffeur and could relay all this convincing information. I couldn't imagine how there had been time, but still, hanging on to my skepticism with all my Western education, I asked to be told the future. If *that* worked out correctly, then I could be decently respectful about an occupation that seemed to me at best a denial of all good sense, or at worst an outright fraud.

"In two years you will go abroad for higher education. You will travel by a means as yet undiscovered to a country as yet unknown." It sounded a most adventurous prospect, and since space travel was not, at the time, the alarming reality it now is, I relaxed finding the whole thing rather fun and rather silly. The astrologer was chanting on, "You will be writing books and articles in the *rajabhasha*," a rare Sanskrit word meaning "the language of the ruler." There was, of course, a good deal more about the rest of my life. On the way home, puzzled by the man's use of that archaic word, I asked my mother why he hadn't simply said, "You will write in English."

"Because the English weren't rulers of India at the time that was written. English wouldn't have been the *rajabhasha*."

"When *was* my horoscope written?"

"Oh, centuries ago," she said airily, and then explained to me that the man had been reading my life story from the *Brighu Sangita*, an ancient collection of palmyra-leaf documents outlining hundreds of thousands of lives. The mythological story is that the Hindu Lord Shiva and Parvati, his consort, were sitting one starlit night on the beach. Idly, and to see how clever her husband was, Parvati asked Lord Shiva to look up at the various constellations and describe to her the assorted lives that people would live according to the stars at the moment of their birth. Miraculously, by sunrise, he had plotted out for her all the lives of all the people in the world for ever and ever. Unfortunately, we poor mortals received only a few of the notes she took.

A more convincing account, supported by history, is that in ancient times there were colleges of astrology established in India. The students were given problems to solve, were assigned past birth dates and future birth dates with instructions to work out just how, by the stars, this or that life would develop. This vast mass of homework was preserved in part, and a number of Indian astrologers are the dedicated owners of such collections.

In a voice of horror I said, "But *Mother*, that means that someone plotted my life ages ago — "

"Of course," she answered placidly. "Not everyone is so lucky. We would have had to wait while he made up a new horoscope otherwise."

Two years later, when I was on my way to Wellesley College in America, it occurred to me, in the plane, that I was traveling "by a means as yet undiscovered to a country as yet unknown." In other ways, too, my horoscope was so uncannily exact that, perhaps deliberately, I lost it.

This time in India I told myself that I was making a *scientific* inquiry. Armed with a light disdain for the girl of sixteen to twenty-five who panicked easily, who swallowed all kinds of myths, I decided to find out just how astrology worked, and what sound basis it had in fact or theory. Now, like the man who didn't believe in ghosts but was afraid of them, I don't know where I stand on the subject.

Certainly it is true that from earliest recorded history man has been trying to find a meaning in the stars and their effect on human life. The ancient Egyptians consulted astrologers before any major royal act was to be performed. Ancient Greece, the Romans ("Beware the Ides of March"), the fifteenth and sixteenth centuries (Copernicus, founder of modern astronomy, was also a student of medicine because it was accepted that the two were connected inextricably; Nostradamus, the French astrologer, wrote his famous prophecies in quatrains; Indian astrologers still prefer to write their predictions in rhyming couplets, indicating their belief that art, science, and more mundane matters are all inter-related — all these show that man's concern with the power of the stars is not without dignity.

Although there have always been skeptics (Cassius: "The fault, dear Brutus, is not in our stars but in ourselves that we are underlings"), many people have tried successfully or unsuccessfully to explain away the strength of heavenly bodies on our experience and destinies. The control of the moon, for instance, on the movement of the tides has been adequately documented and proven, and one can, with no affront to rationality, accept the fact that the movement of the tides does, to some extent, determine human life. But what about the serious economists that ask us, more fancifully, to consider the effects of sunspots on business cycles in Wall Street?

Even in modern times, such eminent heads of state as U Nu will wait for astrological advice before fixing, for example, the auspicious time for the signing of Burmese independence from colonial rule, or for the inauguration of the constitution. In fact, it was from an official high in the Indian government, a charming and brilliant man, that I got my basic information about astrology. His position as one of India's chief financial advisers and his amateur but expert interest in astrology seemed to him not to conflict at all. After hearing his explanation I began to understand the reasoning behind this calm acceptance.

Inevitably, because it is the most immediate illogicality, I asked him, "But *why* should the stars, of all things, influence us?"

"Silly question," he replied gently. "There is never an answer to 'Why should it happen?' in science. It happens. Through experiment, observation, thought, evidence, a law is discovered. Why does gravity happen? Nobody knows. We just know that it *is* a law within its conditions, and we plan accordingly, The 'why' always leads you into philosophy. Another matter altogether."

He went on to ask me to consider, for example, that people have known from very early times

Indian Miniature. Kangra School, 18th Century

that the stars moved in certain ways and obeyed certain designs. Astronomy became a science. For centuries it has been possible to predict, say, a lunar eclipse, or the appearance of a certain comet. "Isn't that an experiment in time? A penetration into the future?" Astrology, he insisted, like other sciences began with observation and empirical evidence, and moved on through experiment to turn a possible generality into a law.

I began, at once, to protest. "Of *course* stars move according to law, they can't *think*, they haven't free will, they aren't *people*, they — "

"Oh, dear," he interrupted, sounding quite depressed, "I can see we are going to get into a discussion of predestination."

Well, we did. And I realized that this aspect of astrology is what scares so many of us — particularly those with a Western education. We can't allow ourselves to believe that we are not Captains of Our Fate. We can accept the past accidents of birth, breeding, physical or mental caliber and so on, but only with the self-assurance that it can all be changed. Any boy can grow up to be President. We can't accept the "future accidents" of destiny — of predestination, in short.

Feeling thoroughly uncomfortable, I remember ending the conversation rather crossly, asking, "Well, if its all written in the stars, why don't you use the knowledge to work out India's economic policies and problems? You ought to be able to tell, very easily, what people are going to think and do."

He burst out laughing. "But I *do*. Wherever I can. It's not an exact science, you know. There are no pre-tested recipes for international affairs. I'd say roughly, eighty per cent predetermination and twenty per cent free will and action. We work to a great extent in that twenty per cent." (Any good astrology client has his horoscope re-interpreted every few months or years to clarify the particular path, out of his narrow limit of choices, that he seems to be taking.)

Other people, I later discovered, have a consuming faith in the eighty per cent. A friend of mine in Bombay, the head of a business firm, never makes an important decision for his company without first consulting his astrologer. "So you *can* avoid disaster?" I asked this commercially successful citizen.

"Not really," he said peaceably, "but you can soften the blow a bit."

Soon afterward, I went to talk to an astrologer of considerable local renown. He lived in a rather obscure part of town, but when I stopped at the corner betel-nut stand to ask directions, I grasped the extent of his fame. A small boy playing in the gutter led me at once to the house.

He was a thin old man surrounded by clients, and asked me very politely if I could wait a while. My case, he pointed out, was not urgent — after all, I had only come to ask him in a general way about the rest of my life. The others were impatient and prosperous-looking men, and I soon understood their anxiety. The following week the new Indian budget was to be presented to the Indian parliament. Naturally that would cause flurried activity on the stock exchange. These troubled gentlemen, all stockbrokers, needed specific advice right away. The broad outlines of my life could wait.

I sat in the corner of the room watching the consultations. The room itself seemed to me entirely inappropriate for matters of such moment. The walls were painted a frivolous, bedroomy pink and decorated with a couple of garish religious prints partly obscured by garlands of marigolds hung over the frames, and a large shiny calendar. There were sparrows nesting in the ceiling fan, flying in and out of the open windows. The worried stockbrokers clustered round the desk in the middle of the room. Behind it, on a straight chair, the shriveled old man sat cross-legged,

16

Brihaspati, Cingalese Divinity, Hindu form of Jupiter.

puffing thoughtfully on his hookah. His assistants dashed in and out of the room bringing reference books, charts, palmyra manuscripts, glowing charcoal, and water for the hookah.

After long deliberation, the old man would give his advice and predictions for each individual. If a client wanted the opinion in writing, one of the apprentices would be delegated to the task. And the old man never touched the money that was offered in payment (twenty-five rupees — five dollars — for a lifetime reading, ten rupees for a particular, detailed problem). Sordid transactions of that sort were handled by the most junior of assistants.

After waiting for two hours, I got up to leave, but the old man motioned me back to my chair. I said, "I can see that my life is not as important as next week's business prices"

Much amused, he replied, "You don't need an astrologer to tell you that you were born, that you live, that you will die. It is the small matters in between that are important."

Enchanted by this answer, I sat down and waited another half hour until he had time for me and my destiny. Eventually he made out my chart and asked me in formal tones whether I would like to hear first about my last life. "Yes, indeed," I said, enthralled by the idea of getting, so to speak, two for the price of one.

Scrabbling rapidly through his papers and calculations, he told me about my last Hindu incarnation. A pretty giddy report. I wish my present life were half as heady. I was an Indian girl; I married a man for his money, then ran off with some other man and assisted in the murder of my brother, who stood in the way of my departure with the handsome stranger. The punishment for that piece of adventure is that I won't have a brother either in this life or my next life. It all sounded deliciously romantic, except for the fact that in a freezing moment I remembered that it was almost identically the account of my past life given me by the astrologer in Delhi more than twenty years before.

The old man didn't work from the *Brighu Sangita*, but from the records of a different ancient college of astrologers — the *Arun Sangita*. The reading and interpretation of this requires yet another skill, a literary one. The horoscope must be presented in rhyming couplets, in Sanskrit. When I had it translated, however, I was in no mood to appreciate the poetry. The facts were too unnervingly accurate.

Still ruthlessly determined to be scientific, I consulted another astrologer from South India — not, this time, to ask about my own life. The whole matter was getting too creepy. This time I wanted to know only how it was done. I wanted methods, meanings, explanations. With entire equanimity, the man said, "There are no secrets. You could work this out for yourself."

I present herewith the Rama Rau do-it-yourself astrology scheme. First you find out the exact date, time, and place of your birth. Then you make a chart. This is easy to do in India, where pamphlets are published every month, and in greater detail every week, telling you exactly where the zodiac signs and the planets were placed within minutes of their appearance and the rate at which they move. In America, I suppose, you would have to ask an astronomer to give you these heavenly placings. Naturally, they vary from country to country and from city to city. I remember being amazed, on my first journey to South Africa, to see the Southern Cross for the first time and to realize that in the Northern Hemisphere it can never be observed. I was also rather distressed to discover that in the Southern Hemisphere the Man in the Moon is upside down. It all makes a difference.

Assuming that you have somehow managed to acquire the necessary background information, you are ready to draw your chart. In it must be placed the signs of the zodiac, the position of the planets, of the sun and the moon, and of the Heavenly Twins, called in India Rahu and Ketu. I felt that all this was a bit complicated, and asked my Southern astrologer to give me a sample chart — but this time, cagily, I offered the birthdate of a friend of mine. This is the way it looked:

7 PISCES (Jupiter)	8 ARIES	9 TAURUS	10 GEMINI (Moon, Rahu, Mercury)
6 AQUARIUS			11 CANCER (Sun)
5 CAPRICORN			12 LEO (Venus, Mars)
4 SAGITTARIUS (Ketu)	3 SCORPIO (Saturn)	2 LIBRA	1 VIRGO

The zodiac signs (in capitals) are always in the same little squares, but the numbering of the squares (or "houses") changes according to which sign dominates your birth. Since my friend was born under Virgo, that becomes her first "house" and the rest are numbered clockwise accordingly. If Capricorn was rising when you were born, you would write 1 in that house and number the rest accordingly. You would then place the relevant planets and stars in their appropriate positions in the various houses. And now you are ready to go.

Your first house, like all the others, has a specific meaning in your life. Each planet, as well as the sun, moon and the Heavenly Twins, has its own character. Each will influence the house in which it is found on your chart. Each has certain positions in which it is strong and which it is weak. What's more, each has a certain power to strengthen or soften the power of the others.

Let me list first the meanings and scope of the various houses on your chart. House number 1 controls your birth, of course, your health, personality, and appearance. Number 2 covers what money you inherit, and also your speech and eyesight. (If you think this idiotic, I would have agreed with you until, at a large party, an astrologer who was among the guests was challenged on this point. Reversing the process, he went through the entire assembly, placing each individual in his correct birth sign purely by his looks and speech. He made only one mistake.) In short, even looks are, according to astrology, determined by the stars; so are the colors you like, the diseases you are susceptible to, your taste in food, whether you have warts or not, and so on.

To continue: house number 3 controls your brothers, sisters, your family, neighbors, and (oddly enough) your short journeys and the written word — that is, letters you write or books you read, the literature that is ingested or produced, but not for profit. Number 4 influences your house, comfort, conveyance (whether you have a car, many cars, no cars, etc.), and whether the end of your life will be peaceful. Number 5 deals with children, financial speculation, entertainment and pleasures, as well as romance and the early stages of sex. House 6 controls enemies, servants, debts, and sickness, but not death. Number 7, is your partner in life or business. It is also all oppositions. This isn't as weird a combination as it sounds. Indian astrologers are convinced that only opposites marry each other and that total agreement between husband and wife is impossible. Number 8 governs the nature and details of your death, the property you acquire, and things like insurance and monetary safeguards. Number 9 will tell you about what distant journeys you may make, the foreigners in your life, as well as your education, your religious feeling, and your regard for truth. Number 10 influences your profession, your worldly recognition, honor, popularity, and credit. Number 11 watches over your friends, your hopes, and (possibly related) your gains that require little effort — gambling profits, for instance. Number 12 controls your hidden enemies (who could even, under certain circumstances, be your own children), your expenditure (including such matters as insolvency and losses), your criminal tendencies that might end in imprisonment. It also covers your future life.

One way and another the twelve zodiac houses take into account virtually every aspect of a human being's character, and influence virtually every aspect of his life.

Now that you know the meaning of your various houses, you must learn the particular influence of the signs that appear in those houses. For instance, my friend's birth sign, and consequently her first house, was Virgo, which makes for an excellent social worker but a bad wife. Anyone born under Virgo is likely to be useful, hard-working, given to public service with no sense of gain, but also argumentative to the point of hair-splitting, nagging and indulging in an interminable analysis of people and situations. This, you see, would affect her birth (refer to the characteristics of the first house), in the sense of the kind of family into which she would be born. Her health, since she is by nature hard-working, would be good. Her personality and appearance would, in turn, be influenced by Virgo. Similarly, her second house would be Libra and would cover her inherited money, her speech, and her eyesight.

So here, omitting Virgo, are the characteristics of the other signs to be considered, according to which of *your* houses they happen to fall in and their effects on those special aspects of *your* life.

Libra is balanced, sympathetic, a judicial type, generally happy in a quiet way. (My friend, therefore would probably inherit a reasonable amount of money, would moderate her instinct to nagging and quarrelsome speech, would have good eyesight.)

Scorpio is temperamental, sometimes overbearing, sometimes self-sacrificing to the point of his or her own destruction. "This," said my informant, "is the only genuinely misunderstood sign in the world. If a Scorpio does good, it will often be taken for bad. And vice versa. A scorpio will suffer, but not too deeply, because he has the emotional make-up that finds satisfaction even in that."

Sagittarius is another complicated sign. The combination of the archer and the horse makes it half-dominating, half-accepting. Such a personality can be either pliant or aggressive to the extreme of killing.

Capricorn is the most practical sign: selfish, active, assertive, materialistic, with a firm grasp of method and order, and always successful.

Aquarius, on the other hand, is the artist's sign. He is likely to be intellectual, original, unconventional, a rebel against the law (but not in a criminal way). "He is always asking himself," my Southern astrologer explained, " 'Why should the human soul be bound by all these social rules?' "

Pisces is very good, very steady, dedicated to other people, to his family, his community, and can expect a very modest life.

Aries, in contrast, is hasty, impulsive, proud, dashing, often a headlong success in life, but he has a high temper — and a high intelligence.

Taurus is steady, dependable, obstinate, down-to-earth, often more useful to others than he is to himself. He is a king-maker rather than a king.

Gemini is a double sign and a curious one. He is both male and female (or vice versa), excellent at diplomacy even when it reaches the degree of intrigue. He can appear to be yielding when he doesn't give an inch. And he is genuinely intellectual, though not necessarily creative.

Cancer is emotional, sometimes rash, but mentally both active and diligent. Solid accomplishment can back up his dotty ideas.

Leo is both arrogant and dignified. He has a great sense of position, he is likely to command with no effort to reach high office. He doesn't need to fight, because, in some way, he is born to "royalty."

Those are the basic zodiac signs, their intrinsic personality which will in some way influence the houses in which they are found on your particular chart.

Don't think that is all. We still have to consider the planets, the moon, and the sun, and their respective influences. Each has its own power, and each affects both the sign in which it is found and the house which, for this particular moment, claims it.

Look back for a moment to my friend's chart, and you will find that Saturn is placed in the box marked 3. Check back again, and you will find that number 3 concerns brothers, sisters, family, and so on. Clearly Saturn is going to influence this area of her life — and not in a pleasant way. For each planet has its own attributes and its positions of extreme and of very low power. Saturn, like Mars, is always malevolent, but, luckily for my friend, he is not in his strongest position, which is Libra; still, being only one house away, he is too close for comfort. His weakest position is in Aries, but that does her very little good. She can certainly expect trouble in her third field — letters will be misunderstood, she will have worries and disturbances within her family, difficult contretemps with her neighbors, and so on. The general pattern of her life is beginning to emerge.

With this in mind, you need to know the character of the various planets and stars that are used. Mars (a nasty number) is strongest in Capricorn, weakest in Cancer. But if either Mars or Saturn is found in conjunction with the benevolent planets, Jupiter and Venus, in one house, then the edge will be taken off their wickedness. Jupiter's strongest position is in Cancer, his weakest in Capricorn. Now, suppose you were to find both Mars and Jupiter together in Capricorn; clearly Mars would be the overpowering planet, but his wickedness would be softened, and the disasters (still taking my friend's chart as a model) to children, financial excursions, pleasures, and romances would be modified. Venus, who is strongest in Pisces and weakest in Virgo, would have a comparable effect.

If, on the other hand, you were to find both pleasant planets or both horrid planets in the same house, naturally their effect on that section of your life would be intensified. Only one planet, Mercury, is an odd sort of chameleon. Both Indian astrologers and their Western counterparts agree that he is, understandably, mercurial, and will change according to whether he finds himself in the same house with a good or a bad planet. By himself he is good — best of all when he is alone in Virgo, least in Pisces.

About the sun, Eastern and Western astrologers disagree. Both agree that the sun controls power and wealth and has its greatest strength in Aries and its smallest in Libra. But in the West astrologers feel that it is the over-riding force in human life, and generally speaking, a good one. In India they feel that it is a powerful force for bad, but can, under very lucky circumstances, combined with beneficent forces be only powerful.

In India we feel that it is the moon (controlling intellect, temperament, the kind of misery or joy which arises from circumstances rather than interior emotional conditions) which is more powerful than the sun. Admittedly, the sun controls your heart, but your mind is more important. So they say.

Finally there are Rahu and Ketu. Alone they simply accentuate the sign in which they are found. Together they are rather unpredictable, sometimes good with a good arrangement of planets, sometimes mischievous given an unfortunate distribution. Indeed, there can be such an unnerving scattering of the heavenly signs on a horoscope that, in the old days, a mother seeing nothing but misery, death, and despair in view for her daughter in her marriage would marry her formally to a banana tree in the garden so that the troubles would be taken out on the tree, and when the time for a proper marriage came her daughter and son-in-law would have a better chance of happiness and success. A *mangali,* as such a woman is called in India, would then, perhaps, be able to evade the threatened disaster to her husband and resulting misery to herself.

However, now you have all the relevant factors for a simplified — yes, I do mean *simplified* — version of the outlines of your life and character. You can, in general terms, read your chart. Taking all these elements into account, you can, for example, pick on the most intricate house on my friend's chart, 10, to see what the general tenor of the stars would be on her profession, worldly recognition, honor, popularity, credit. You would keep in mind the basic structure of her character (Virgo). You would consider the effect of the basic characteristics of Gemini, which for her dominates her tenth house, remembering that, curiously enough, in her case, the masculine-feminine nature of Gemini might indeed serve as a clue to the kind of work she would do, especially in the field of social work or in her attitude at home as wife. You would then take into account the fact that the moon in its light quarters is beneficent, but not in its dark phases. (In her case it was in a dark phase.) This will give you an idea of her temperament, intellect, and all the rest of the aspects that the moon controls — if you keep in mind that the moon is next door to its most powerful house. Then you think about the effect of Mercury and its special attributes, and equally of Rahu and *its* special attributes. Finally — and this is the most complicated of all — you assess the interaction between all these powers, influences, attributes, and you have an overall picture of one section of her life.

There. You see? As my Southern astrologer said, there are no secrets. It's easy. But for greater detail, or even month-to-month information, take my advice, go to a professional astrologer. It's quicker.   SANTHA RAMA RAU

Book of Stars and Constellations. Persian, 1690. *N. Y. Public Library*

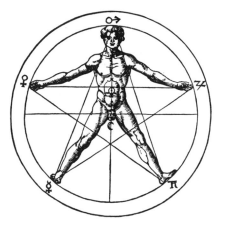

2. A BRIEF HISTORY OF ASTROLOGY
IN THE WEST

By the fifteenth century, assimilated influences from the Orient, Greece, and Rome had been combined, standardized, and refined to give astrology essentially the form it has today.

The impressive spectacle of the shifting, changing sky made a profound impression on early man, and prompted him to manufacture explanations for what he observed. Very often he was content to embellish and glorify the constellations, the rising and setting sun, and the waxing and waning moon with imaginative stories tailored to fit the folklore of his tribe. His link with the physical world was so immediate that satisfactory explanations were imperative. Archaeologists and anthropologists have found artifacts from prehistoric times decorated with symbols for the sun, moon, and stars.

It took centuries of empirical observations embroidered with fanciful tales to approach the orderly arrangement that the Babylonians fashioned into the science of astronomy-astrology. The reputation of the Babylonians and Assyrians (later referred to jointly as Chaldeans) for possessing magical powers was widespread. In fact the very name Chaldean became synonymous with magician. Among Greek writers, Strabo (died 24 A.D.) asserted that the Chaldeans were skilled in astronomy and the casting of horoscopes. Achilles Tatius (fourth century) reports the existence of a tradition wherein the Egyptians mapped the heavens and inscribed their knowledge on pillars.

25

Ceiling of Rameses VI tomb.
Thebes. *Photo: Eliot Elisofon*

The same tradition declared that the Chaldeans claimed the glory of this science, and attributed its foundation to their god Bel. Diodorus Siculus, a contemporary of Augustus, tells us that the Babylonian priests observed the positions of certain stars in order to cast horoscopes and that they interpreted dreams. The general evidence of serious writers leads us to believe that astrology formed part of the religious system of the Babylonians, and certainly it exercised considerable influence over the minds of the dwellers between the Tigris and Euphrates.

When Ashurbanipal, King of Assyria (669-626 B.C.) added to the royal library at Nineveh, his contributions of clay tablets included many documents which related exclusively to the astrology of the ancient Babylonians, who in turn had borrowed it with modifications from the Sumerian invaders of the country. Among these was a series called *The Day of Bel,* which was declared by the learned to have been written in the time of the great Sargon I, King of Agade (c. 3000 B.C.). With such ancient works as these to guide them, the profession of deducing omens reached such importance in the last Assyrian Empire that a system of making periodical reports came into being, and by these the King was informed of occurrences in the heavens and earth and was told what the future appeared to hold in store.

The astrology of the Chaldeans spread to Egypt, to Greece, and eventually to the Roman Empire. Accounts of the influences of the signs and planets were augmented, synthesized, and pre-

The astrologer.
Albumasar

Aristotle

served by astrologers, poets, physicians, and scientists who had a flair for writing. One of the earliest Roman works preserved for posterity is the *Astronomicon*, a lengthy poem composed about the first century A.D. by the poet Marcus Manilius. In the second century the great astronomer and mathematician Claudius Ptolemy wrote a work entitled *Tetrabiblios* or *Four Books on the Influence of the Stars;* and perhaps because of his authorship of the *Almagest*, which handed to posterity the Ptolemaic system of the universe, his text on astrology remained a leading authoritative work in the field for more than fifteen centuries.

In its long, involved history astrology has disappeared for hundreds of years at a time, only to be re-born like the phoenix from its ashes wherever learning and experimental science flourished. In about the tenth century in Europe, astrology began to make a comeback. It had survived in Arabic manuscripts, many of which were translations of Latin, Greek, and Hebrew originals. Translations of original works by Arabic authors began to appear in the libraries of learned men. The *Mathematic of Alhandreus*, supreme astrologer, was one such masterly work. In England Abelard of Bath, in a book entitled *Natural Questions*, discussed astrology with the zeal of a scientist and the cultural outlook of a widely traveled scholar. Abelard recognized the value of the learning and wisdom of the East, and its vigor when compared with the moribund culture of the West. He discussed problems of alchemy, mathematics, and animal behavior along with astrology. "The stars are imbued with life," he wrote. "They are superior animals whose fire is gentle and harmless and thus obedient to and in harmony with sense and reason." He also pointed out that nations are ruled by particular planets which influence their character and fate.

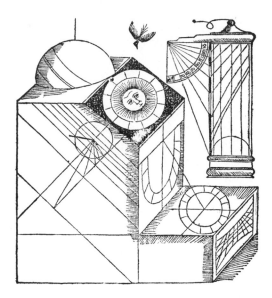

Horologiographia. Sebastian Munster, 1533

To the end of the twelfth century, learning flowed from the Arabic world and Spain to northern Europe. The demand for Latin translations of Arabic manuscripts dealing with mathematics, astronomy and astrology, and experimental sciences was created by scholars who found the extant Latin works inadequate for their purposes. This great awakening of the intellect, which was to culminate in the glorious concepts of the Renaissance, gave rise to hotly contested theories about everything under the sun. Some European writers went so far as to assert that astrology was modern and scientific and that religion was the rank residue of ancient superstitions. Their opponents called them heretics who were seduced and deluded by Satan into their infatuation with mathematics. More moderate points of view generally prevailed, however. Nature was allowed to follow set patterns, even though God ruled the world.

Astronomer. Engraving by Straduanus. *Bettmann Archive*

28

Florentine citizens. 15th century

Tower with astronomical devices. Jacques Perret

A great many seemingly extraneous factors must be taken into account if we are correctly to assess the importance of astrological thought in Europe during the Middle Ages and the Renaissance. Wars, changes of government, capricious royal edicts, plagues, and inexplicable natural phenomena all contributed to the uncertainty and forebodings of disaster that were common to the daily life of the times. Credence in portents, signs, and predictions has a rather rational basis, given the topsy-turvy succession that made up everyday life. Derek Brewer in his *Chaucer* (1953) states that his interest in astronomy and astrology (the two were indistinguishable in his day) was an important element in his thought. Chaucer's interest in the psychology of dreams and physics is shown in *The House of Fame,* and there are many references to the natural sciences and medicine in his *Canterbury Tales.* These subjects neither diverged from his poetry nor were hostile to it. On the contrary, they were in part the very material of his poetry, and they helped him to focus his view of the world, of human character, and of the course of good and ill in human life.

The desire for a total view, a *summa,* of earthly knowledge and experience is characteristic of the men of the high and late Middle Ages, whether they wrote in prose or verse. There are such encyclopedists as Vincent of Beauvais (died c. 1264) and the Englishman Alexander Neckam (1157-1217), the great theologians St. Albertus Magnus (c. 1206-1280) and St. Thomas Aquinas (c. 1225-1274); and, chief among the poets, Dante (1265-1321).

Nostradamus

Famous astrologers, including Tycho Brahe

During the early Middle Ages (about 1200) three distinct branches of astrology had been developed. One was judicial astrology, which ascertained the individual's destiny according to a horoscope cast for the moment of his birth. Another was horary astrology, which answered questions by means of a horoscope cast for the moment that the question was asked. And the third was natural or mundane astrology, in which events of national importance were forecast.

Dante knew of these three branches of Astrology and made references to them in both the *Purgatorio* and *Paradiso*. Chaucer, Milton, Spenser, and Shakespeare also made astrological allusions in their works. Chaucer actually cast horoscopes for some of the characters in his *Canterbury Tales,* such as Constance and the Wife of Bath. The latter had five husbands, and during the course of her tale she attributed her lustiness to her horoscope, which had Mars placed in Taurus. Chaucer also says that the Oxford scholar, Hende Nicholas, "hadde learned art, but al his fantasye/ was turned for to lerne astrologye."

A contemporary of Dante's, Johannes Campanus (died about 1297) a mathematician, and chaplain and physician to Pope Urban IV, is credited with inventing the system of the twelve houses of the horoscope. Regiomontanus or Johann Müller (1463-1476), a professor of astronomy at Vienna who printed books on trigonometry and some of the earliest ephemerides, translated the *Almagest* of Ptolemy.

The most renowned and controversial figure in the world of astrology was Nostradamus (Michel de Nostre-Dame). This greatest of all seers was born in St. Rémy in 1503 and served as astrologer and physician to three French kings. The quatrains of Nostradamus are still consulted with the hope of finding the key to his chronology. Many of his predictions came true in his lifetime, and astrologers claim that others have come to pass since, such as the rise of Oliver Cromwell, the

Culver

...tolemy, and Copernicus. Hevelius.

Dante

birth of Napoleon, and the exact date of the end of the Second World War. However, Nostradamus is reported to have said that he was afraid that mankind as a whole was not ready to hear the whole truth and that predictions of the future would have harmful effects. Consequently he wrote down his predictions in obscure verses that were impossible for the layman to interpret.

Another important astronomer-astrologer who lived in the sixteenth century was the Dane Tycho Brahe (1546-1601), who worked in Denmark under the patronage of King Frederick II. He designed instruments in metal and supervised the mechanical workmanship; he also studied the tables prepared by Copernicus and brought them into a more precise and correct form. He did much to advance the study of the motions of the planets, and traced that of Mars to such a point of exactitude that Johannes Kepler (1571-1630), who was then one of his assistants, based his discovery of the three laws of universal gravitation on this research. Kepler designed a telescope with two convex lenses and crosswires in the focus for use as a pointer to fix the positions of stars. In an address given at the University of Copenhagen he defended the practice of astrology, stating, "We cannot deny the influence of the stars without disbelieving in the wisdom of God. Man is made from the elements, and absorbs them as much as food or drink, from which it follows that man must also, like the elements, be subject to the influence of the planets.

Three laws established by Kepler were studied and incorporated into Newton's study of dynamics. These were: (1) That the planets describe ellipses with the sun at a focus of each ellipse. (2) That a line drawn from a planet to the sun sweeps over equal areas in equal times. (3) That the square of the periodic times are proportional to the cubes of the mean distances from the sun. These laws emphasize the quality of Kepler's mind, which was not untypical of those of other Europeans concerned with astrology in the fifteenth and sixteenth centuries.

31

William Lilly

Galileo Galilei

Galileo Galilei (1564-1642) a contemporary of Kepler, was another great man of the period. His work in terrestial dynamics (much of it conducted from the top of the leaning tower of Pisa) and experiments with the pendulum led to Huyghen's invention of the pendulum clock, which became a very valuable tool in the hands of astronomers. Galileo was also responsible for designing one of the first practical telescopes, and through its use he discovered sunspots, craters of the moon, Jupiter's moons, and the rings of Saturn. He kept making improved telescopes until he produced one with a magnification of thirty-two times. He himself made hundreds of these instruments and they became much in demand. He also wrote about astrology, and two of his books contain horoscopes prepared by him.

The Englishman William Lilly (1602-1681) is the most renowned of the seventeenth-century astrologers. He was not an astronomer but was able to read and assimilate the information from books on astronomy-astrology that had been translated from Latin into English. As a professional astrologer he wrote and published one of the earliest almanacs of prophecies. His most famous book, *Christian Astrology, modestly treated of in three volumes* is largely concerned with expounding astrological interrogations, and Lilly emphasizes questions concerning thefts and hidden property. He drew up a horoscope in order to catch a thief who had stolen money from one of his clients. He also made the following judgment on a horoscope which he cast for King Charles I: "Luna is with Antares, a violent fixed star which is said to denote violent death, and Mars, which is approaching Caput Algol, which is said to denote beheading, might intimate that." Two years later the King suffered precisely this fate. Some of Lilly's predictions got him into trouble. He had accurately predicted the great fire of London and after the event came about in 1666 a committee of inquiry into the causes of it was appointed by the House of Commons. Lilly, suspected

Origin of the Milky Way. Tintoretto.

of complicity, was summoned before the committee, but was acquitted. A typically indefatigable man of the Renaissance, Lilly also turned his attention to medicine, earned a license to practice it, and is believed to have used much of his astrological knowledge in the treatment of patients.

The popularization of astrology in the sixteenth and seventeenth centuries did little to advance its reputation. Penny almanacs and handbooks started to be produced in the first half of the sixteenth century. These kept the man in the street happy with garbled astrological nostrums pirated from the authoritative textbooks of Ptolemy and Albertus Magnus that had been translated into English. Astrology on this low level could hardly be taken seriously, and the whole subject came in for a considerable amount of criticism.

Johannes Kepler replied to critics of his day by pointing out that the ordinary uneducated man expected a series of sensational predictions, signs, and portents of marvels or catastrophes and was therefore pandered to by charlatans. The reasonable moderation of scholars adept at astrology bored those with untutored minds, and in many cases their explanations of the movements of the planets and their various influences were altogether foreign and incomprehensible to them. Noblemen, scholars, surgeons, and theologians continually engaged in debate with one another over the fine points of interpretations. Their disagreements, however, were not on the score of the validity of astrology but involved such questions as free will versus predestination, or whether or not the soul was free of the planetary influences while the body and mind remained subject to it.

The high status that astrology enjoyed among scholarly men during the Renaissance was due partly to the fact that all sciences had a place in the humanistic revival of learning. Science (in the abstract) was not worshiped as blindly as it is today. It was one of the many forms that knowledge or even wisdom could take. Theology and poetry, architecture and painting, politics and business all claimed the proper amount of attention from an educated man. Dilettantes were rare. Traditionally, astrology was a learned man's study, and it was necessary for the scholar to read Latin, Greek, and occasionally Hebrew or Arabic — languages that were also required for the

Goethe

Louis XIV visiting the Paris Observatory. Engraving: S. Le Clerc. *Bettmann Archive*

study of medicine, philosophy, theology and the law. In addition, a thorough grounding in mathematics was necessary for charting the planets' positions for any given moment. In short, astrology was not the plaything of the credulous, illiterate man who could be misled by quacks. It was a highly intellectual pursuit. Commentary on traditional astrological concepts and fresh insight into its problems was provided by renowned scholars in the course of their writings on physics or mathematics. Their treatises were often copied by hand and were circulated among friends for their opinions.

The charge that astrology is a lot of childish superstition has always been made by people without a true sense of poetry. Goethe, in a letter written to Schiller in 1798, says, "The superstition of astrology has its origin in our dim sense of some vast cosmic unity. Experience tells us that the heavenly bodies which are nearest us have a decisive influence on weather and plant life. We need only move higher, stage by stage, and who can say where this influence ceases? The astronomer observes that the heavenly bodies are subject to mutual disturbances; the philosopher is inclined, nay rather forced, to assume that action can take place even at the greatest distances; thus man, in his presentiment, needs only to go a stage further, and he will extend such influences to the moral life, to happiness and misfortune. Such fanciful ideas, and other of the same kind, I cannot even call superstition; they come naturally to us and are as tolerable and as questionable as any other faith."

A resurgence of interest in astrology appears to have occurred in the late nineteenth and early twentieth centuries. During this period several books revived the researches of earlier astronomers and also brought into focus the practice of casting a horoscope in the traditional way. There was a much closer contact with Asia, particularly with India, where astrology had been practiced and respected since ancient times. Combining all available knowledge on the subject from the East and the West, writers attempted to set down as simply as possible the character of the planets and their effect on persons born under their influence. Not only the month but the year, day and hour and place of birth made a difference in casting any individual's horoscope.

Particularly important are the writings of Alan Leo (1860-1917) and Isabelle Pagan, both of whom are represented in this book, and of Evangeline Adams (adviser to J. P. Morgan) because they have had much influence in our own century. Most modern books in English analyzing the zodiac and pointing to the characteristics of those born under each of the signs would appear to be directly or indirectly based or inspired on Alan Leo's and Isabelle Pagan's research.

The endorsement of noted thinkers in our own day has brought about an overwhelming interest in all the arts and sciences, and astrology has been no exception. That there has been a certain overpopularization of the subject, as in the sixteenth century, does not alter the fact that the basic truths that go back almost to the beginnings of mankind should be taken at their true worth.

Albert Einstein (1879-1953) said, "I believe that the cosmic religious sense is one of the strongest and noblest motives behind scientific research." And Dr. C. G. Jung (1875-1961) Freud's most notable successor, stated that Western civilization gains little and may be losing much by what he called "the contemptible treatment and defamation" of ancient arts which "defied a reasonable explanation and made too exclusive a claim on intuition. After two hundred years of intensive scientific progress we can risk testing them in the light of modern truths." And, in fact, in his *Interpretation of Nature and the Psyche*, Jung published an "astrological experiment," a statistical examination of the horoscopes of four hundred couples. Concentrating on the placement of the sun and moon in the horoscopes of husband and wife, he arrived at the following results: The most frequent combination was the husband's and wife's Moon in the same sign (conjunction). The next was the Sun in the husband's horoscope exactly opposite the Moon in the wife's horoscope (opposition). The third most frequent combination was the Sun in the husband's horoscope in the same sign as the Moon in the wife's horoscope (conjunction). Conjunction means that the Sun and Moon or two or more planets are within a few degrees of one another in one sign of the zodiac; opposition means that they are 180 degrees apart in the opposite sign of the zodiac. Lacking the refined techniques of modern statistical research, Greek and Roman astrologers commonly held that a man should marry a woman who had the moon in the same sign of the zodiac as his sun.

Jung recognized numerous parallels between psychology and astrology. He employed an astrologer as a member of his staff, and used the horoscopes drawn up for his patients as a preliminary orientation toward their basic character. People of Doctor Jung's caliber who read such works as the Tibetan Book of the Dead, investigate a Taoist religion named "The Golden Elixir of Life," and are acquainted with the *I Ching*, or *Book of Changes* are well qualified to deal with astrology, to place it in its proper context, to extract what is good and useful from it, to appreciate the systematization of folk psychology, and to gain an insight into human nature which has been incorporated into astrology's vast literature.

Astrology shares the poetry and grandeur of philosophy and many religions. Like any other attempt at erecting a valid structure, it could not exist in a vacuum. It shares a firmly entrenched position with architecture, painting, and music. The comparison with architecture is particularly apt. The Acropolis, hewed out of huge chunks of marble, is divine in conception, while most of our modern buildings are merely engineering feats, without spiritual, emotional or humanistic concepts. All of which suggests that we should agree with Jung that ancient concepts must be looked at again as if they were as elemental as the waxing and waning of the Moon and as the rise and fall of the tides. The cosmic sea, recognized by St. Thomas Aquinas, Jung, Einstein, and others, is the starting point for astrological observations.

Sigmund Freud

Albert Einstein

Photos: Wide World

Carl Gustav Jung

37

Orrery, invented and constructed in 1830

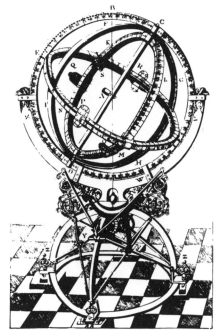

Bettmann Archive

Armillary sphere

3. THE PLANETS

Five planets were known by the Babylonians, who called them Nebo, Ishtar, Nergal, Marduk, and Ninib. These planets were renamed successively by the Egyptians, Greeks, and Romans, who chose the names of their own deities according to characters considered to bear the closest resemblance to the Chaldean Gods. Ideologically speaking the Greek and Roman interpretations were the closest, and today we continue to use the Roman names. Aphrodite was renamed Venus, Hermes was renamed Mercury, Ares became Mars, Zeus became Jupiter, and Cronus became Saturn. On March 13, 1781, a new planet (previously considered to be a fixed star) was discovered by Sir William Herschel. At first this planet was called Herschel, then Georgium Sidus, "the Georgian star," but as this name was disliked outside England it was named Uranus, after the Greek God of the skies. Another planet appears to have been discovered more or less simultaneously in 1846 by a French astronomer Urbain Jean Joseph Leverrier and the Englishman John Couch Adams. This planet was given the Etruscan name Neptune after a deity identified with Greek sea god Poseidon. Pluto was discovered in 1930 by Clyde Williams Tombaugh of the Percival Lowell Observatory in Arizona. Its name is a euphemism for the Greek deity of the underworld, otherwise known as Hades. It takes Pluto 284 years to pass through the twelve signs of the zodiac; thus his influence, perhaps fortunately, is relatively minor in individual horoscopes.

Mercury

Venus

Mars

The rulerships of the five planets are traditionally divided into masculine and feminine manifestations: e.g., Aries was ruled by the masculine side of Mars, Scorpio by its feminine side; Gemini by the masculine side of Mercury, Virgo by its feminine side; Libra by the masculine side of Venus, Taurus by its feminine; Sagittarius by the masculine side of Jupiter, Pisces by its feminine; Capricorn by the masculine side of Saturn, and Aquarius by its feminine. The Sun ruled Leo and the Moon ruled Cancer. There is a certain amount of disagreement among modern astrologers about the rulership assigned to the three new planets. Neptune has tentatively been given the rulership of Pisces, Uranus to Aquarius, and Pluto to Scorpio. Some astrologers consider them as co-rulers with the traditional planets assigned to these three signs of the zodiac.

Mercury was considered neutral but mischievous, since he could be influenced either for good or evil, depending upon his proximity respectively to Jupiter or Saturn. He was characterized as the messenger of the gods. Mercury is considered hermaphrodite, both masculine and feminine, although his masculine side is assigned to Gemini and his negative side to Virgo. His main attributes are derived from the Babylonian Nebo, or Nabo, the prophet or herald, patron of scholars, and god of astrology. His gem is an amethyst, the talisman a turquoise.

40

"Being well-dignified, Mercury represents a man of a subtle and political brain and intellect, an excellent disputation or logician, arguing with learning and discretion, and using much eloquence in his speech; sharp and witty, learning almost anything without a teacher; ambitious of being exquisite in every science . . . a man of unwearied fancy, . . . able by his own genius to produce wonders." (William Lilly.)

Venus has kept most of the characteristics of the Babylonian Ishtar. She is a feminine planet, like the moon. In Greek mythology she became Aphrodite, born from the foam of the sea. She rules the love nature, children, pleasure, luck, wealth, and art. Venus in her positive manifestations influences our ability to attract, to love, and to express our artistic talents. If she is badly placed in a horoscope she may negatively influence the emotional nature, producing weaklings prone to erotic, frivolous pastimes and rather pretentious displays of bad taste. If she is well placed, her influence functions at the highest level. Her gem is an emerald, the talisman a ruby.

"Venus makes singers and charming people, ardent lovers of flowers and elegance. . . . They have genteel manners . . . are given to games and various diversions, to laughter and joyous living,

Jupiter

Illustrations from Michael Maier's "Viatorium, hoc est de Montibus Planetarum septem, feu Metallorum." Rouen, 1651. *Courtesy Emil Offenbacher*

Saturn

Sun

Moon

rejoicing in the companionship of friends and in eating and drinking. They are benevolent, tender by nature, soft, and gentle-voiced." (Albohazen Haly.)

Mars, the fiery and flamboyant planet, was called Nergal in Babylonian times. His rapid progress and his red color both obviously qualified him for his role as god of war. To Mars was assigned the positive rulership of matters relating to courage and heroism, and, negatively, to matters having to do with destruction and wounds. The Egyptian conception of Mars lingered for some time in early Greek astrology. He was originally designated as Heracles, slayer of dragons and monsters, the benefactor of humanity. Later the ideas of courage and destruction were separated and destructiveness was assigned to the negative rulership of Mars. His gem is a ruby, the talisman a topaz.

"*Mars* is a planet . . . fiery and violent; he is a destroyer and a conqueror, delighting in slaughter and death, in quarrels, brawls, disputes, contests, and other contraventions; he is quickly moved to vehemence and devastation. . . . He is instrumental in stirring of seditions; he inspires wars and battles and rules over the ravaging and laying waste of lands, over pillage, plundering, ruin, and destruction." (Albohazen Haly.)

Jupiter, the Babylonian Marduk, one of the many early personifications of the powers of the sun, was transformed by the Greeks into Zeus. Marduk was the chief God in Babylonia, and so became the "Father Heaven" of the Greeks and Romans. According to Ptolemy, the influence of Jupiter is temperate, salutary, and activating. Firmicus Maternus goes even further in his praise of Jupiter, stating that if he alone illuminated the earth, men would be immortal. Jupiter is given dominion over religion, philosophy, science, and law. He is believed to have a beneficent influence on voyages and shipping. Positively, Jupiter is the ruler of Sagittarius, and of Pisces. His gem is a carnelian, the talisman a sapphire.

"He makes the native of great ability of mind, honorable . . . of fine reputation, just . . . gentle of disposition, quiet, unruffled, eschewing vain things; such a person . . . meditates and plans good actions. . . . He is diligent and well-doing, and knows how to guard, serve, and retain friends." (Albohazen Haly.)

Saturn was called Ninib and was referred to as the "steady one" (*Kaiawanu*) by the Babylonians. He was considered the highest in heaven of all the planets and was identified by the Greeks with their old deposed ruler of the gods, Kronos, who was represented as carrying a sickle-shaped sword. This image is still used today as old Father Time in New Year's celebrations. Because of an old popular etymology identifying Kronos with chronos (time), and because of the Greek myth of Kronos eating his children, Saturn becomes the personification of the alleged generative and destructive power of time. Saturnine traits are reticence and diplomacy, hard work, perseverance, and selfishness. His gem is a turquoise, the talisman a tourmaline.
"Saturn is evil, produces and fosters men of melancholic complexion. He signifies profound silence, mistrust and suspicion, moving men to complaints and mutterings." (Alchabitius.)

Jai Singh's observatory, Jaipur, built 1734

HOMO
FIGURA-
TUS,
ET
SYMBOLI
CUS.

Cor   Pectus   Brachia   Collum   Caput

Pudenda

Coxa   Crura   Tibia   Genua   Pedes

Omnia subiecisti sub pedib, Ejus. Psal.

O. Scarlatini, Augsburg, 1695

Horoscopion. Ingolstadt, 1533. Apianus

4. *THE TWELVE SIGNS OF THE ZODIAC*

According to the traditions of astrology, the first key to a character analysis of any individual lies in the position of the Sun in his birth sign. This shows his basic character, with emphasis placed on the spiritual qualities of his nature. If the Sun is well aspected, it represents man's highest aspirations, if badly aspected, it represents his less worthy aims.

People born between March 21 and April 20 (to take the first month of the zodiac calendar) have the Sun in Aries, and their tendencies are different from those of people born between April 21 and May 21, when the Sun is in Taurus, or between May 22 and June 21, when the Sun is in Gemini, and so on.

The first part of each analysis is based on the Sun in the sign. Typical characteristics of evolved and primitive types are given, and these can also be taken as representing the higher and lower sides of each sign. Naturally, the more educated and spiritually evolved a man is, the less his weaker nature shows.

While the Sun sign represents the first basic distinction, the rising sign is also a very important factor in astrological interpretation. The rising sign (the zodiacal sign rising at the east horizon at the time of birth) traditionally influences the physical body of a human being and either strengthens or weakens the tendencies of his Sun sign. Thus if an individual is born with the Sun and his

45

rising sign in Sagittarius, obviously he will be a more typical Sagittarian than if his rising sign was, for example, in Virgo. The reader is referred to a chart at the end of the book with the help of which his rising sign can be found. Should his rising sign be Aries, Taurus, Gemini, or any of the other zodiac signs, by reading the characteristics of that particular sign as well as of the Sun sign, he can arrive at a better understanding of his or any of his friends' individual character.

A third key is to be found in the position of the Moon at the time of birth. The moon, according to astrological tradition, primarily affects the subconscious mind, which in turn influences conscious thoughts, actions, and general character. Brief analyses based on the combination of the Sun and Moon signs are given at the end of each of the following signs. Readers will probably quickly detect which one applies to them, and to check whether they are right they can refer to the ephemerides on the last pages of the book.

The person who hesitates between two signs, in other words, one who is born at the very beginning or very end of a sign (generally referred to as being born on the cusp) must decide which sign has the stronger impact on his individual character. No other astrology rule may be applied in such cases.

After taking all this into account, it will be seen that only one out of many people is entirely typical of his Sun sign.

To arrive at a really definite analysis of any individual, the charting of an individual horoscope becomes necessary. How this is done is explained in Chapter 7. The casting of a horoscope from

The Influence of the Moon on Women's Minds. Franc MS. 17th century. *Bibliothèque Nationale, Paris.*

Astronomicum Caesareum. Ingolstadt, 1540. Petrus Apianus. *Metropolitan Museum of Art*

the ephemerides and tables of houses is an operation that can be mastered in an hour. However, the interpretation of the horoscope is a matter of art. Prepared analyses of the planets in each sign of the zodiac or each house may be used to arrive at a rough outline of what the horoscope represents. But this approximation is not the same as a synthesis, which an astrologer would arrive at in his professional report. It is in the synthesis that the astrologer's skill shows more clearly. The clichés applying to the place of Venus in the romantic life, Mars' role in activity or Mercury's influence in the intellectual sphere are never considered separately. They are only factors that have to be integrated and woven into an intricate structure of good and bad aspects, modifying one another until a well-rounded picture of the individual emerges.

In the half-title page introducing each zodiac sign, the sign is denoted as being Fixed, Cardinal, or Mutable. Fixed signs denote bulk, weight, mass, and stability; they give reserve, resistance, power, and rigidity. The fixed quality corresponds to intellectuality, moral stamina, and will. Cardinal signs denote activity — motion, expression, changeableness; they give alertness, restlessness, flexibility, and suppleness. The cardinal quality corresponds to the soul in its various conditions, animal, human, or spiritual, as a modifying influence operating in the world of form. Mutable signs denote harmony — vibration, rhythm, and symmetry; they give plasticity and adaptability, and some instability. The mutable quality corresponds to the body, the vehicle of the spirit and soul, or the plastic medium upon which the spirit exerts its power of transmutation.

Note: The pictures of personalities in the following pages are grouped by their Sun signs. No attempt has been made to associate any of them with the specific text appearing on the same page.

The following color illustrations are reproduced from the fifteenth-century illuminated prayer book, *Les Très Riches Heures du Duc de Berry,* begun about 1409 by Pol de Limbourg and his brothers, Jan and Hermann, and completed many years later by another famous painter, Jean Colombe. The original manuscript is now in the Musée Condé at Chantilly in France.

48

CALENDAR

January

February

March

April

May

June

November

December

July

August

September

October

March 21 through April 20

THE RAM

The sign of the
Warrior or Pioneer

A cardinal fiery sign
Energetic, impulsive, enthusiastic, positive, enterprising

Ruler: Mars

Gems: amethyst, diamond

Color: red
Metal: iron

Harmonious signs for business, marriage, or
companionship: Sagittarius, Leo

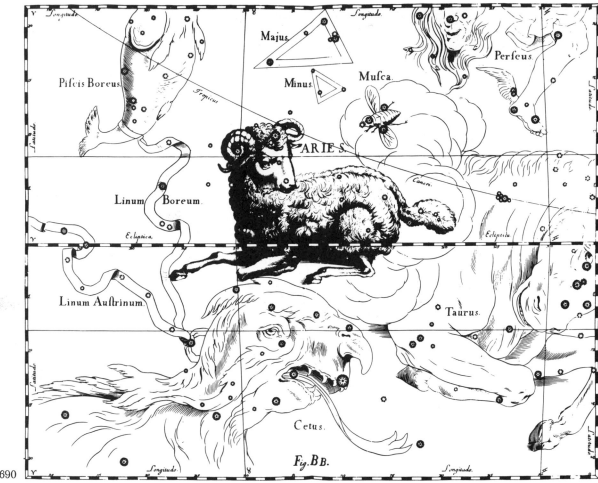

The Arietian Type

Evolved Type. The true Arietian, or Martian, is the captain, the leader, the pioneer among men, in sympathy with new thought, rapidly assimilating fresh ideas, always in the van of progress in whatever kind of work he may take up. He gets to close quarters in his battles, and fights best with his head — that is to say, in the field of thought. Enterprise and ardor are characteristic, and the channels into which these are directed will vary according to the condition and limitations of the individual. Most Arietians show a definite preference for work which gives some opportunity for personal leadership. They enjoy overcoming difficulties, and will go out of their way to challenge opposition. Hope and enthusiasm are with them wherever they go, and their happy knack of forgetting failure helps them through times of stress. Sometimes, but rarely, hampered by diffidence and shyness, and never by pessimism, they carry through their undertakings with confidence and dash and brilliance that disarm criticism.

The type is generally softened in women, but still displays its characteristic warmth and vitality. The female Arietian cannot abide half-hearted work or want of enthusiasm in those around her, and finds the cautious ultra-scrupulous person who weighs every word and deliberates over every decision a terrible trial, a feeling which she can generally make abundantly evident to the individual in question. She very often craves for more scope for her energies, and larger opportunities of swaying and leading her fellow creatures than can be

Thomas Jefferson: Sun in Aries. (Portrait by Rembrandt Peale.)

found in the ordinary routine of domestic duties, and is frequently to be found on committees and on deputations connected with social and political reforms.

Tranquillity and serenity are seldom appreciated at their true value by this type, and still more seldom achieved; but Arietians are delightfully refreshing to meet, for they are bright and lively in society, and a boon to all who desire help in arousing public interest in their social and charitable undertakings. Other and very different types of humanity may excel in planning details and in organization, but without efficient aid from the Arietians, the most desirable projects often make little headway, and the best-laid schemes fall to the ground.

Primitive Type. The primitive Martian type suffers from excess of the qualities associated with it. Courage, hope, and enthusiasm in enterprise become recklessness and heedlessness. These people must always be doing something, and if their energies are not carefully guided for them they rush headlong into activities which they are incapable of carrying to a successful issue. They fail in work requiring tact and patience and self-control, and their eager desire to see immediate results is often both a misery and a temptation to them. In order to bring about conditions or events on which they have set their hearts they will sweep aside every obstacle that confronts them, without scrutinizing closely the means they employ to get rid of it; and the results are useless friction, fierce opposition, and endless delay. After such a state of affairs has been brought about, our warrior waxes more militant than ever — fighting failure instead of accepting it, and blaming others for the miscarriage of his plans. Consequently he is the last person to think of the true remedy for the muddle he is in, which is generally a patient retracing of the steps taken. Abandoning the enterprise is a much more congenial method of extricating himself from an awkward position; and, this having been done, the restless energy pours itself forth into fresh channels, until brought up by further obstacles.

A constant source of trouble is the intense desire to "play lead" or to dominate others personally and to associate only with intellectual inferiors. At the same time this craving for personal leadership in action is not associated with the desire for positions of responsibility. In early youth the type is apt to make a very bad subordinate, and is happier when working at a distance from headquarters, where close supervision is impossible. One source of trouble is that he has as a rule very little power of reading character correctly; this tells especially in his blundering choice of a hero to worship. He is extremely self-willed, refusing to listen to reason, or to hear any criticism of the idol of the moment.

No type gives the impression of such perfectly straightforward sincerity; and yet none can begin to compete with it in sheer audacity in uttering and maintaining what it knows, or ought to know, to be untrue. These people can make themselves blind and deaf to whatever they please. Their position may be utterly untenable, but they stick to their guns, determined to drive their schemes forward with such earnestness and conviction that only those who have already caught them tripping can find any room for doubt. This trait is partly responsible for the loss of old and trusted friends. The tendency of the Arietian is to make very rapid progress in development, and so to grow away from his old friends, disconcerting and distressing them by sudden and unexpected changes in his convictions. It is practically impossible for him to regain, even temporarily, his former point of view. His custom is to throw the past behind him and go forward; and those who attempt to stop him are frequently swept out of the way with a contempt which arouses all their resentment.

Love and Friendship. Enthusiastic friendship fills a large place in the emotional life of Arietians, and the same impetuosity and ardor that are shown in this direction also characterize their love affairs. No type is warmer-hearted, or more frank and generous in showing affec-

58

Alessandro Temini, 17th-century engraving. *N. Y. Public Library*

ODORATO	MARZO	ARIETE
Godo di quest'odor soaue, e grato.	Porto à i viuenti la stagion nouella	Oh se di vil Montone in Destrier forte,
Questo appaga il desir del senso mio;	Al gelo, et alle Brine io dò comiato;	Cangiar potessi a mio piacer la spoglia
Seguir questo piacer ogn'hor uoglio,	Fò zeffiro spirar con dolce fiato,	Dell'Auriga celeste all'alta soglia.
Nè nò per altro mai cangiar mio stato.	E la selua apparir vestita, e bella.	Vorrei il carro condurre, all'aure, e l'vie.

tion; but these tendencies are apt to lead to trouble, even among the highly developed, and the sorrows that follow rash engagements and imprudent marriages are among the forms of discipline they are called upon to face. The Arietian frequently mates with a husband or wife who can hold his or her own, and may succeed in making of matrimony a more or less merry duel; for as a rule people of this sign are blessed and assisted by a sense of fun and a real gift of enjoying a situation; but there is apt to be a good deal of sparring, and of wasted energy in consequence. Occasionally, however, the warrior contrives to settle down with some gentle and adaptable mate who admires his energy while finding it impossible to emulate it, and who makes up for the Martian's slap-dash way of going at his work, by patiently following after him, and filling in details that he has overlooked in his haste.

If falling in love is for him a dangerously headlong performance, falling out of love is more dangerously headlong still, for loyalty and tenacity are not among the virtues of this sign, and the desire for change of surroundings and companionship is difficult to master. Separation or divorce are resorted to in circumstances which would not be found unendurable by those born under the more adaptable and forbearing signs.

In Drama and Fiction. The Arietian type is a favorite one in fiction, and supplies the hero of many a dashing exploit and hairbreadth escape; for the fact that Arietians lead their followers *personally*, taking the lion's share of any danger involved, and never shirking or sparing themselves, makes them peculiarly fitted to arouse popular sympathy. Shakespeare has drawn a splendid example in Harry Hotspur. Hotspur's tendency to hyperbolic eloquence, criticized by some as inappropriate to a soldier and a man of action, is quite characteristic of the type, and the glowing declaration:
"By Heaven, methinks it were an easy leap,
To pluck bright honour from the pale-faced
     moon;
Or dive into the bottom of the deep,
Where fathom-line could never touch the
     ground,
And pluck up drowned honour by the locks"
could have been uttered only by a son of Mars at white heat. Portraits of more primitive Arietians are also to be found in light literature — headstrong rebels, bumptious bullies, and demagogues.

Mural by Francesco del Cossa, 15th century. Palazzo Schifanoia. *Photo: Anderson*

Religion. We may look for possible Arietians among popular leaders and great orators of all ages. Among them, two stand out with special clearness — Mohammed, the enthusiastic and well-beloved prophet of the desert; and Moses, the leader and lawgiver of Israel. The scriptural assertion — surely a mistranslation! — that the latter was a "meek" man may give us pause; but analysis of his life and character leaves little room for doubt, and the four magnificent orations ascribed to him in the book of Deuteronomy show the martial characteristics so strongly that the astrologer should find little difficulty in accepting the idea that the scribe was actually "inspired" to give them accurately.

We find equally good examples in the Koran, especially in the more rhetorical passages such as the opening paragraphs of Chapters 79, 81, and 82; and the Prophet's reply to his relatives when they tried to dissuade him from his message would, taken by itself, be enough to proclaim the son of Mars: "Though you set the sun against me on my right hand, and the moon upon my left, I will *never* give it up!"

Physical Characteristics and Health. The Arietian type is active, energetic, and muscular. The movements are quick and impulsive; the whole personality is intensely alive. As regards physical health and energy, this is a magnificent type, but its very excess of vitality is a danger. The headstrong tendency to carry an enterprise through in wholly adverse circumstances or at an unsuitable time is naturally responsible for frequent disappointment, which results in irritation, anger, and impatience. The remedy for this type is self-control — the cultivation of patience, tranquillity, gentleness, forethought, and humility. Faith in others, whether superiors or equals, may also be recommended; for during illness the Arietian's fond delusion that no one can really do anything properly but himself runs away with him, and no amount of mistakes and blunders on his own part will cure him of it.

Moses. Michelangelo.
Bettmann Archive

BORN UNDER THE SIGN OF ARIES

Ilka Chase

Marlon Brando

Clare Boothe Luce

Culver

Michael Caine

Julie Christie

Charlie Chaplin

Ann Zane Shanks

Henry James

Culver

SUN IN ARIES

The primary characteristics of the Sun in this sign are force and energy, and the fundamental basis of the character will consist of an ambitious, aspiring, and enthusiastic nature. During the month that the Sun remains in this sign, the twelve lunar positions will either considerably modify this primary influence or accentuate it and increase its manifestation. But without the Moon to focus the rays of the Sun and to collect the influences that are constantly being distributed, the individual character would be always flying off at a tangent. In studying each of these combinations, however, it is important to remember that the solar force is the primary and energizing influence, and the lunar center always secondary.

Sun and Moon in Aries

This position of Sun and Moon gives rise to great activity of thought and quickness of perception, with inclinations to excitability. Those born under this combination have an intense desire to be at the head of things, to be intellectual pioneers. They have an abundance of energy and vitality, and are masterful, independent, and self-reliant. The personality is forceful and original. Positions of authority and responsibility will seem to fall naturally to the native's lot. In some cases he will be militant, domineering, intolerant of opposition or contradiction, hard and unyielding. The combination increases self-esteem and independence. Troubles follow impulsive actions and rash conduct. There is a tendency to live too much in the mind and some danger of becoming too self-centered or conceited.

Sun in Aries and Moon in Taurus

The Sun is exalted in Aries, and the Moon in Taurus, a combination which strengthens both positive and negative elements and produces a strong character. With the force of the Sun in Aries behind the physical nature, the ideal and practical are well blended. There are the will and energy to originate and the steadiness and practical ability to execute. The native can both plan and perform, preach and practice, direct others and do the work himself. He is likely to occupy some position of responsibility. The intellect and intuition are both marked, but there is usually a tendency to be self-willed and dogmatic. His affections are warm; he makes friends readily and is faithful to them. This is a good position for financial success, for positions of trust and authority.

Photo: N.B.C.

Arturo Toscanini: Sun in Aries

Vincent Van Gogh: Sun in Aries. (Self-portrait)

Sun in Aries and Moon in Gemini

While this combination gives considerable mental activity and manual dexterity, there are apt to be restlessness and over-exertion. The nature is changeable, loving variety, and there is a lack of determination and tenacity of purpose. This combination produces artistic tendencies, and makes those under its influence clever writers. However, the dualistic tendencies of Gemini cause much of the qualities of Aries to be wasted, so that there is frequently less done than is talked about. The native is witty, lively in mind and speech, prone to exaggeration and of great mental ingenuity. In a bad horoscope, there is a tendency to deceit or dishonesty.

Sun in Aries and Moon in Cancer

This is an exceedingly sensitive combination, giving a considerable amount of ambition and love of fame. The Moon, here placed in the executive sign Cancer, will add the power of achievement to the idealism of Aries, increasing intuition, imagination, and memory. There

Starry Night. Van Gogh.
Museum of Modern Art

are two somewhat contradictory sides to the character — one enterprising, active, and domineering, the other sensitive and domestic. The sensitiveness of this position causes those born under it to feel surrounding conditions keenly, and to suffer from them occasionally. When not too approbative they are able to reason and arrive at correct conclusions. The combination gives caution, acquisitiveness, and the ability to design and plan.

Sun in Aries and Moon in Leo

This combination gives remarkable intuition, a warm heart, the power of clear thinking, and a certain amount of originality of thought and action. This position favors all matters connected with music and the drama. The personality is strong, positive, forceful, and, when aroused, displays energy, enterprise, ambition, and self-reliance. The native is good-humored and candid, having some fondness for show and ceremony. He generally possesses a good opinion of himself, and likes the good opinion of others, even their flattery.

Sun in Aries and Moon in Virgo

This combination stimulates the critical and discriminative tendency of the Moon in Virgo. It emphasizes the practical nature and brings out scientific characteristics. The solar position considerably improves the lunar characteristics and makes the mind more logical and accurate in its judgments. It gives considerable ability in literary pursuits, but also awakens the exacting tendencies of Virgo. It intensifies the love of study, and gives considerable musical ability. Often there is greater ability than there is opportunity to use profitably.

Sun in Aries and Moon in Libra

We have now reached the opposition of the Sun and Moon; therefore all that is contained in the Aries nature may find its expression in the equilibrium and balance of Libra. It causes a keenly sensitive nature, receptive to music and fine arts. It makes those born under it observant, alert, sociable, companionable, amorous, disliking to live or work alone. Mental abilities are adapted to outward use in the world. These people are good counselers and advisers and they enjoy recognition.

Sun in Aries and Moon in Scorpio

The martial element is strongly marked, disposing the nature to be hard, dogmatic, positive, and jealous. People born with this combination are sometimes proud and conventional, matter-of-fact and materialistic; but they can be very destructive when it suits their ends.

Pierpont Morgan Library

Albumasar, Jean, Duc de Berry MS., 1403

Sun in Aries and Moon in Sagittarius

This combination gives a very quick, sympathetic nature, but there is a tendency to go to extremes. It strengthens the sincerity and straightforwardness of the personality, gives impulsiveness and a tendency to chatter. The native is changeable, irresolute, given to enthusiasms that do not last, though he has plenty of energy and determination while in the mood. He is generous and humanitarian. This combination produces good teachers; it is also good for traveling and exploration.

Aries. Book of Stars and Constellations. Persian, 1630

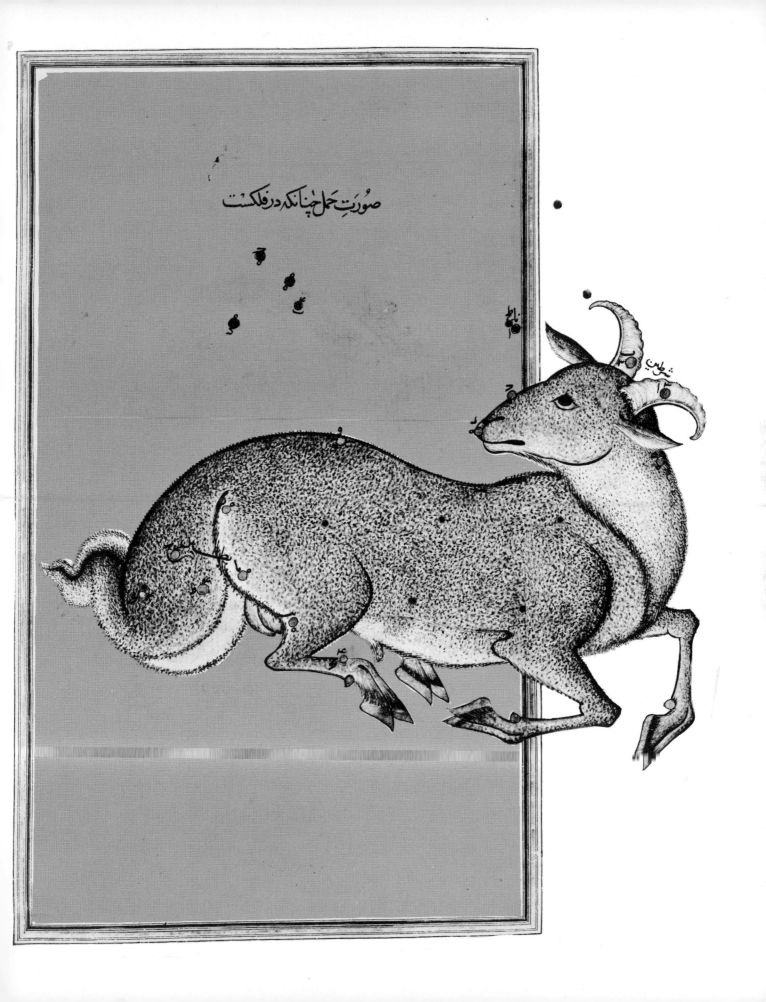
صورت حمل چنانکه در فلکست

Harry Houdini: Sun in Aries

Sun in Aries and Moon in Capricorn

The naturally saturnine qualities of the Moon in Capricorn are accentuated. The personality is exacting, and inclined to fluctuating moods. This is a sensitive combination; cleverness is much appreciated, and the brain is very receptive. It is a good polarity for business, and for all pursuits depending upon energy and force of character. People born with this combination are masterful and ambitious, sometimes worldly and materialistic. They are suited to a public career, although their tact and diplomacy are often over-ridden by impulse, self-assertiveness, and love of flattery. Those under the influence of this combination tend to aim for leadership, and to domineer rather than rule over others. They love wealth for the power it gives. In a bad horoscope a hard, selfish, ill-tempered, gloomy nature is found.

Sun in Aries and Moon in Aquarius

This combination brings out all the pleasing characteristics of the Moon in Aquarius, giving an original, positive, and combative mind. The personality is at times eccentric, and in speech sometimes hasty, erratic, brusque, or without consideration for others. It intensifies the artistic faculties, and gives some ability in literary matters, with a bright, clear mind, well able to express itself. Imagination, intuition, and sensitiveness are much increased, and there is a love of educational and scientific work. It increases the feeling of independence, but gives the ability to deal with others successfully. The native lives largely in the mind, and influences others through the mind. He is witty and can be very sarcastic. Determination and enterprise are combined, the Aries nature being steadied and its influence made reliable.

Sun in Aries and Moon in Pisces

This combination is not altogether harmonious, the Sun in Aries being too strong for the lunar position. This produces a discontented, restless, and often worrying nature. However it

Mars. Mediaeval Housebook, Castle Wolfegg

FAMOUS PEOPLE BORN WITH THE SUN IN ARIES

Leonardo da Vinci:	April 15, 1452
Joseph Haydn:	March 31, 1732
Thomas Jefferson:	April 13, 1743
Washington Irving:	April 3, 1783
J. P. Morgan:	April 17, 1837
Henry James:	April 15, 1843
Vincent van Gogh:	March 30, 1853
Arturo Toscanini:	March 25, 1867
Harry Houdini:	April 6, 1874
Charlie Chaplin:	April 16, 1889
Clare Boothe Luce:	April 10, 1903
John Gielgud:	April 14, 1904
Tennessee Williams:	March 26, 1914
Alec Guinness:	April 2, 1914
Simone Signoret:	March 25, 1921
Peter Ustinov:	April 16, 1921
Marlon Brando:	April 3, 1924
Michael Caine:	March 14, 1933
Jean-Paul Belmondo:	April 9, 1933
Julie Christie:	April 14, 1941

considerably tones down the impulsiveness of Aries, and when the two are working harmoniously it increases kindliness and gives a love of the profound and mysterious. Sorrow causes those born under it to think more deeply than those under most of the Aries combinations. There is a danger, in a bad horoscope, of dishonesty. Otherwise, the personality is charitable and sympathetic. This position gives success in public institutions, and confers some authority of a quiet and unobstrusive kind.

Peter Ustinov: Sun in Aries

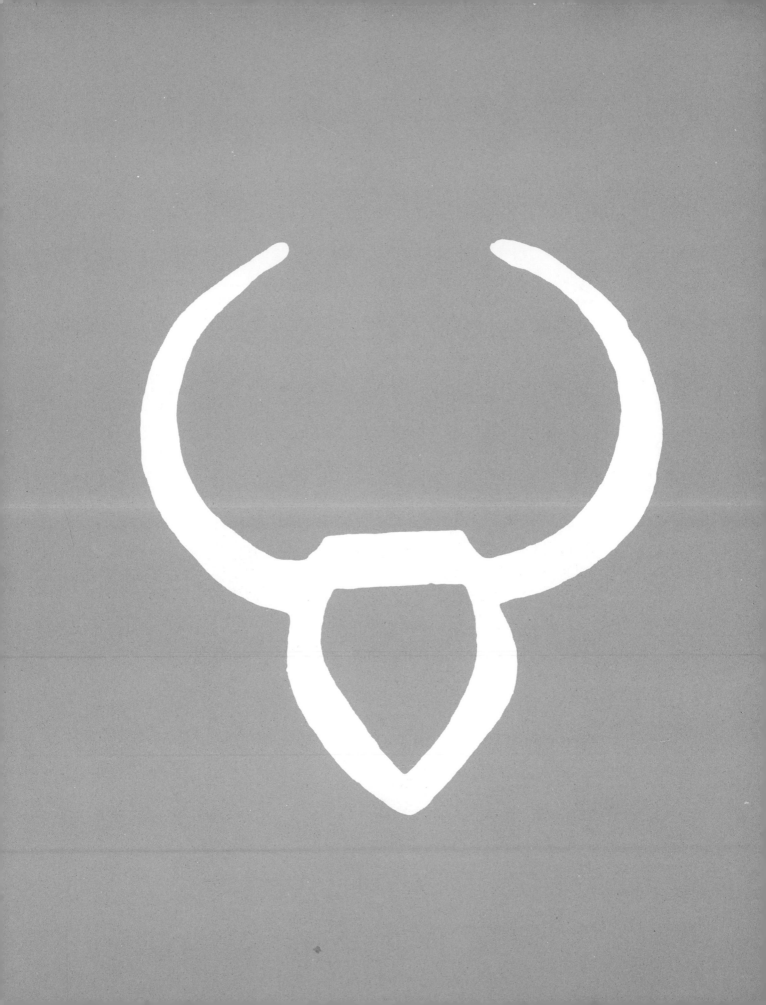

April 21 through May 21

THE BULL

The sign of the
Builder or Producer

A fixed earthy sign
Stubborn, steadfast, systematic, persevering, kind-hearted, often musical

Ruler: Venus

Gems: moss-agate, emerald

Colors: blue and pink
Metal: copper

Harmonious signs for business, marriage, or
companionship: Capricorn, Virgo, Cancer

Triumpho di Fortuna. Fanti.   *Pierpont Morgan Library*

The Taurean Type

Evolved Type. The chief characteristic of the highly developed Taurean is his stability of character and of purpose. His is the steadfast mind, unshaken in adversity, and his the power of quiet persistence in the face of difficulties. He has found his true position with regard to the universe, and that position is the center. Identified with the very heart of things, he refuses to be hustled or frightened or pushed into any false position, and generally excels in work requiring a sense of true proportion and a just appreciation of relative values. He understands the importance of system, method, and order, enjoys routine and regularity, and often shows constructive ability, especially in matters concerning the foundations and beginnings of enterprise.

He works best when spurred by necessity or when inspired by the love of others, especially of his wife and family. In hard circumstances his patience and perseverance are marvelous. He generally has a horror of debt, and shows care and prudence in the administration of affairs. Acting as mainstay or prop in material ways is peculiarly congenial to him, and consequently the type makes ideal trustees and guardians — people who will make large sacrifices of time and energy, rather than fail those who have confided in them.

Their commercial integrity also fits them for many kinds of public office. People of this type suit subordinate positions, junior partnerships, and so forth, generally preferring to have boundaries and limits set by someone in supreme authority. Obedience comes easy to them,

72

Ulysses S. Grant: Sun in Taurus. *Photo: Matthew Brady*

Harry S. Truman: Sun in Taurus

Della tramutatione metallica. Nazari, 1599

but if nagged they make a stand, and their occasional outbursts of wrath are sufficiently vehement to cause considerable consternation to those who have aroused them. Besides excelling in the building up of commercial or other undertakings, Taureans are very successful in agricultural pursuits.

The quick recognition of relative and essential values which shows in people of this sign gives them almost invariably the delightful gift of humor. Their feet never lose touch with the solid ground, and they generally know not only where they stand themselves, but where other people stand also, so that the claims of the charlatan and exaggerations of more excitable individuals merely amuse them. Their laughter has, however, no touch of malice, and the true Taurean enjoys a joke against himself as wholeheartedly as any. It is consequently difficult to ruffle him, and his kindly tolerance and warmth of heart are calculated to make him a favorite among friends, many of whom find his leisurely ways and tranquil presence very soothing.

Honoré de Balzac: Sun in Taurus (Portrait by Gerard Seguin, Musée de Tours.) *Bettmann Archive.*

Primitive Type. The primitive Taurean naturally prefers to keep his good things to himself, and often by seeking to save his life loses it; for excess of vitality stored up, instead of overflowing for the benefit of others, is a danger to him. He is self-centered and quite incapable of seeing anyone's point of view but his own. His steadfast nature and splendid persistence show as a mulish obstinacy and a pig-headed determination to hold his own. Tranquility and restfulness are represented by laziness and sloth, and the inherent loyalty characteristic of the developed type, as well as its strength and solidity of character, are recognizable only in foolish dislike of change, and a dogged disinclination to strenuous exertion of any kind. The primitive Taurean is absurdly over-cautious and exasperatingly deliberate. His filial devotion to his Mother Earth and gratitude for her gifts are often perverted to a gross materialism accompanied by much self-indulgence. He is never aggressive in battle, and avoids it if possible, but when pushed to the wall, or persistently goaded, will sometimes astonish his opponent by an outburst of fury, quickly succeeded by a resumption of stolidity. The sense of humor is conspicuous, and although his joke may take some time in the making, it is usually a genuine achievement, even if it is distinguished rather for its breadth than for its depth.

Love and Friendship. The Taurean shows himself exceptionally capable of faithful and enduring friendship and affection. His loyalty lives on in spite of neglect or rebuff. In both sexes there is a tendency to fall in love early and keep it up late, and the devotion of people of this type is almost invariably offered to living realities, not to ideal or abstract heroes and heroines. At the primitive stage the nature is somewhat over-amorous and sensual, and even when well developed there is enough of the *earthy* or physical element about the affection to make the Taurean friend or lover crave strongly for the physical presence of the be-

Alessandro Temini, 17th-century engraving

VDITO
'Da questa Melodia soaue e cara,
Sente l'alma portarmi in Paradiso:
E da tanto piacer resta conquiso
Il mio cor, per dolcezza così rara.

APRILE
Verdeggiante ogni pianta, et ogni prato,
'D'erbette, e fiori si riueste il colle;
Mentre io men rido lasciuetta, e molle,
A bagnar di rugiada, il suolo amato

TAVRO
Di me l'alto Motor, il gran Tonante
Pigliò sembianza, e forma: e sopra il dorso
Portò la bella Europa, e in uan soccorso
Chiedeua la meschina, in Mar sonante.

loved. Any pretext that will give an opportunity for communication is seized and held onto with dogged persistence. Trouble and inconvenience and even absurdity are of no account, if a chance arises to deliver a note or gift. The on-looker may deride, the adored one may grow restive and even cross, but the steady pursuit goes on till it ends either in victory or defeat.

If a rival triumphs, a certain amount of philosophy comes to the rescue, and the very lovable humility of the type asserts itself. The disappointment is accepted without bitterness or resentment, for Taureans are rarely handicapped by pride and self-conceit though frequently by shyness and self-consciousness. If the pursuit is successful, the marriage goes forward, and the union is generally satisfactory; for a sense of proportion prevents a Taurean husband or wife from exacting too much.

Marriage with a primitive Taurean is, how-

ever, somewhat of a trial, and trouble may arise on account of his or her laziness and self-indulgence. The women make splendid mothers and welcome their offspring with great delight, never wearing them out by fussy attentions, constant supervision, and correction. In the primitive type physical well-being and comfort are apt to be given a very high place, and when a life of comparative idleness and luxury is possible, conditions are not too closely scanned. A mercenary marriage sometimes suggests itself to the type as a comfortable solution to many difficulties.

Religion. The religious tendency of the Taurean is occasionally conspicuous by its absence; but even in the most materialistic of the sign, there is always an inclination to hold settled convictions, one way or another, rather than to be harassed by difficulties and doubts. He generally knows what he believes, and disbelieves, and has no objection to stating it. The Taurean inclines to accept the teachings of his early youth; he is averse to change, though tolerant of development.

Literary Style. The Taurean habit of mind is contemplative. He is apt to take his time about telling a story, and to dwell at considerable length on points which interest him or strike him as important, especially if they have anything to do with the foundations of the plot or the essential qualities of the characters. His sense of proportion, however, keeps this ruminating tendency in check; and when critically examined these meditative passages are generally found to be integral parts of the whole. His attention to solidity of structure makes for permanence and durability, and Taurean literary work stands the wear and tear of time better than most, because it gets down to bedrock, and is very little affected by passing fashions.

He has the builder's instinct for what is essential, and never troubles about decoration till he has his proportions fixed and his walls fair and square before him. Consequently the ornament introduced is well chosen, emphasizing

76

all that is good and permanent in the structure, and thereby adding greatly to the effect of the whole. If there is any carelessness it is in the matter of finish, but even then his roughness and lack of polish are due rather to the material handled than to want of judgment in the builder.

To the true-born Taurean nothing is common or unclean. Anything that concerns the ordinary daily life of working, suffering, slowly evolving humanity seems to him legitimate and suitable as a subject for literary treatment. The physical plane is his chosen field of operations, and he takes it as he finds it. Even when dealing with the loftiest topics he prefers to shows the higher qualities dramatically, as they work visibly in human experience. Consequently the parable or allegory at its best and pithiest may be looked for from writers with a strong Taurean strain in them. One of the finest examples in this line is the short meditation in which Shakespeare's melancholy Jaques tells the forest exiles in *As You Like It,*

> "All the world's a stage,
> And all the men and women merely players."

Shakespeare's actual birthday is unknown, but we do know that the Sun was in Taurus when he was born, and can see for ourselves how strongly he answered to this influence.

In Real Life and in Fiction. In fiction, lovable examples of the Taurean abound. Kent in *King Lear* is one of them; and among Shakespeare's women there is Helena, the amorous heroine of *All's Well That Ends Well,* who along with

Mohammed. Albumasar, 13th-century MS. *Bibliothèque Nationale, Paris*

Falstaff. Derby Porcelain, 18th century.
Museum of Fine Arts, Boston

Venus. Mediaeval Housebook, Castle Wolfegg

joke of considerable breadth, and delighting the easily tickled by his grotesque clowning and facial play. Surely Falstaff had some flavor of the same influence about him, although no one sign could possibly account for all of him!

Physical Characteristics and Health. The Taurean is said to be well proportioned, usually on a generous scale. The voice is musical. Dangers to his health are ignorance, inertia, and self-indulgence, to which may be added, in the case of primitive Taureans, sensuality, gluttony, and drunkenness. The natural vitality, always abundant, should be given out freely and generously for the pleasure or benefit of others; otherwise it consumes itself, and morbid conditions rapidly develop. Death in these circumstances is usually sudden. Of games in early years the favorite will probably be football, and the finest and most congenial exercise singing.

many attractive qualities shows some of that deliberate disregard of convention which makes one of the dangers of this sign wherever the passions are concerned.

The burlesque Taurean is fat, thick-necked, gross, and overfed-looking, and often has a great love of low comedy, heartily relishing a

79

They are nevertheless remarkably strong characters, fearless, persistent, hopeful, and can easily attain success in the financial world.

Sun in Taurus and Moon in Gemini

The restlessness of Gemini is considerably steadied here by the Taurus quality. There is less diffusion, and more initiative force. Those under this combination are inclined to be somewhat selfish and assertive, but the intellectual tendencies of the Moon in Gemini give them a command of language and ability to write. While somewhat unenterprising, the native has a love of the beautiful in nature and art and good intellectual abilities.

SUN IN TAURUS

The Sun in Taurus makes the individual character behind each lunar expression more firm, plodding, enduring, and determined; but there will be a tendency to move more slowly and act more cautiously, quietly, and practically than when the Sun is in Aries.

Sun in Taurus and Moon in Aries

This combination gives a strong personality with a tendency to be impulsive, headstrong, and dogmatic. There are considerable amounts of persistence and exactitude. When those born under this combination make up their minds to carry out any purpose in life, they nearly always succeed; but they expect others to conform to their requirements. They are enterprising, independent, and fitted for positions of responsibility. Success in life comes through their energy, the desire to excel, and their ability to organize.

Gehinnom

Sun in Taurus and Moon in Cancer

The sensitiveness of Cancer is somewhat accentuated, so that the emotions are easily upset. This combination increases timidity and reserve; it also produces economy. Imagination is keen; there is some tendency to go to extremes, especially when influenced by others, and the desire for sensation is increased. On the whole it is a fortunate combination, offering rewards through property and inheritance.

Sun and Moon in Taurus

This combination is the most solid and practical of influences. Those born with it are determined and not easily thwarted. At the same time, they are friendly, companionable, cheerful and may be musical or artistic; they possess a great amount of self-control, but are sometimes too self-contained, reserved, and often secretive.

Sun in Taurus and Moon in Leo

The emotional and sensational nature is much increased with this combination. There is a tendency to exaggerate, to go to extremes, also to be easily influenced in matters connected with speculation and sensational pleasures. Affections may be easily drawn into unfortunate channels, and the native often expresses keen likes and dislikes. He has a good constitution, sound health, is self-confident and fond of show; may be popular or cut something of a figure socially. Care will be necessary to avoid over-indulgence. The nature is ardent, at times passionate: there is some poetic ability, the imagination being vivid.

Sun in Taurus and Moon in Virgo

Critical faculties are accentuated by the practical Taurean nature behind the personality. In all business pursuits people with this combination are precise, persistent, and pronounced in their judgments. They have abilities in several different directions, can manage more than one type of business, and are eminently adaptable. While sometimes lacking in enterprise, they can quickly apply and develop the suggestions of others. Virgo being the ruler of the business world, the personality here has the best facilities for expression. The moral nature is firm. Behind much apparent pliability there is a fixed determination which brings success.

Sun in Taurus and Moon in Libra

This combination usually causes the personality to arrive at faulty decisions, often the result of another's influence. It produces a certain amount of determination, usually of a stubborn nature. Those born under this influence are apt to be guided by feelings rather than reason. They have ability in music or art. Outwardly they seem to be observant and intellectual, but at heart are emotional and sensuous. The personality is generally affable, refined, and polished, but there is likely to be some jealousy and vindictiveness toward opponents.

Culver

Wide World

Yehudi Menuhin

BORN UNDER THE SIGN OF TAURUS

Salvador Dali

Audrey Hepburn

Wide World

Bertrand Russell

Jerome Ducrot

Culver

Barbra Streisand

Albert Finney

European

Vladimir Nabokov

Culver

Sun in Taurus and Moon in Scorpio

This position gives a certain amount of vanity and self-esteem. Feelings are strong, yet there is reserve, a good deal of secretiveness, and a tendency to be conservative, except when opposed or angered. Jealousy, pride, and appetites need curbing. Success in life comes through determination and self-reliance.

Achaemenian capital. 4th century B.C. *Louvre*

Sun in Taurus and Moon in Sagittarius

The determination behind the Sagittarius personality will incline those born under this influence to go to extremes in all things. It gives a tendency to impulsive action and hasty speech. There is, however, an interest in science, and a tendency toward philosophy and religion. The native is generous, charitable, and sympathetic, but his aspirations are usually higher than his inherent abilities, so that promises usually outrun performance. He is hopeful, optimistic, and of great vitality, but he wastes energy in fits of overwork, undertaking more than he can accomplish.

Sun in Taurus and Moon in Capricorn

This is a very practical combination characterized by economy and caution, with an aptitude for making carefully thought-out plans and schemes, which are generally carried to a successful issue. The whole character is independent and determined. Ambitions are high, but chiefly concerned with conventional ideals. Those born under this influence are well able to build up a fortune; they are especially adapted for a public life and have great ability to organize and carry out ambitious plans.

Sun in Taurus and Moon in Aquarius

This too is a practical combination. Thoroughness and prudence are combined with honesty of purpose, sincerity, and refinement. Those born under this combination are well able to concentrate their thoughts, and are industrious, persevering, and successful, yet tend to be reserved and somewhat self-centered. It is suitable for holding public offices or appointments, for working through companies, associations, factories, or large bodies of people, and tolerably good for acquiring money and possessions.

Sun in Taurus and Moon in Pisces

Those born under this combination are hospitable, receptive to the wants and requirements of others, kind, and pliable, and have plenty of friends and acquaintances. They are fortunate socially, but rather less so in business or public life. The disposition inclines toward good living, peace, and harmony. Prosperity increases later in life.

Margot Fonteyn: Sun in Taurus

Queen Elizabeth II: Sun in Taurus

FAMOUS PEOPLE BORN WITH
THE SUN IN TAURUS

Niccolò Machiavelli:	May 3, 1469
Oliver Cromwell:	April 25, 1599
Catherine the Great:	May 2, 1729
Honoré Balzac:	May 20, 1799
Ulysses S. Grant:	April 27, 1822
Johannes Brahms:	May 7, 1833
Sigmund Freud:	May 6, 1856
Bertrand Russell:	May 18, 1872
Harry Truman:	May 8, 1884
Vladimir Nabokov:	April 23, 1899
Fred Astaire:	May 10, 1899
Bing Crosby	May 2, 1904
Salvador Dali:	May 11, 1904
Daphne du Maurier:	May 13, 1907
Yehudi Menuhin:	April 22, 1916
Ella Fitzgerald:	April 25, 1918
Margot Fonteyn:	May 18, 1919
Sugar Ray Robinson:	May 3, 1921
Queen Elizabeth II:	April 21, 1926
Audrey Hepburn:	May 4, 1929
Willie Mays:	May 6, 1931
Albert Finney:	May 9, 1936
Barbra Streisand:	April 24, 1942

May 22 to June 21

THE TWINS

The sign of the
Artist or Inventor

A mutable airy sign
Restless, versatile, clever, exuberant, expressive

Ruler: Mercury

Gems: beryl, aquamarine

Color: yellow
Metal: quicksilver

Harmonious signs for business, marriage, or
companionship: Aquarius, Libra

Hevelius, 1690

The Geminian Type

Evolved Type. The chief characteristic of this type is exuberance or overplus of intellectual energy, which must find expression and usually does so in a variety of ways. This craving for diversity and impatience with repetition or sameness leads, in the case of fully developed Geminians, or Mercurians, to brilliant results, alike in experimental science, literature, and art. They really strike the true keynote of their being, joy, only when in the act of expressing some essential part of themselves; and having attained such expression they are rarely content to rest upon their oars. Theirs is a charming type, whose true function it is to make life more interesting and beautiful for themselves and others; to stimulate, refresh, and revive their fellow men by force of exhortation and example. A keen desire for intellectual satisfaction is the driving force of this sign, and when their religious sense is awakened they sometimes undergo much suffering, for they *must* understand and reason upon the faith that is in them, and if their surroundings are unsuitable, and the teaching offered them uncongenial, doubts and difficulties arise which must be overcome by hard wrestling before peace is attained. The Geminian's craving for perfect expression and desire to influence those around him makes it impossible for him to suffer in silence and alone; he must make friends and relatives face the same problems, and if they cannot understand and sympathize, the intellectual suffering of the Geminian increases to such an extent that it brings a martyrdom of

Mercury. From an old German engraving

misery, the very intensity of which brings relief through increased endeavor toward the attainment of some logical result. Any kind of sympathetic appreciation is welcome at such times, but intellectual approbation is particularly prized.

The exaltation accompanying achievement is frequently followed by a keen and critical examination. If the verdict is unsatisfactory the Geminian will probably abandon that particular line of endeavor and start off on another tack, but will likely resume the abandoned task as

be selected, and, if that is impossible, a hobby should be encouraged which will give the necessary relief and become to some extent a secondary profession. These people generally enjoy their work and often hold strong convictions as to the duty of taking a bright view of life, the way they throw themselves heart and soul into an occupation is a source of great refreshment and inspiration to those who work with them. In marriage they look for intellectual sympathy and companionship, ignoring differences of age and condition if they can find the

suddenly as he dropped it, and carry it through brilliantly to a successful issue. These quick changes, especially noticeable in childhood and early youth, are often a source of perplexity and dismay to the parents, but the developed Geminian knows his own business best; he should be left free to follow his apparently erratic course and never be tied too closely to drudgery or routine of any kind. A profession which allows variety of occupation should invariably

response, appreciation, and support for which they crave.

Religion. The type of religion most congenial to the Geminian is best understood by a study of the writings of St. Paul. His epistles are excellent examples of the Geminian style, and in them we find much that is characteristic, for example, many sudden digressions, interpolations, and changes of subject, often making the

Alessandro Temini, 17th-century engraving

TATTO	MAGGIO	GEMINI

Tal' hor finto è il mirar, finta è la bocca,	Di Giacinti, Amaranti, gigli, e Rose,	In un sol parto doi gemelli amati
Che finta fà sentir uocé mendace;	Son' io la Madre: e de gl'amanti amica.	Siam nati per bontà della Natura;
E finto è il gusto, et è l'odor fallace;	Non può contro di me stagion nemica,	E tra il Toro, et il grancio per ventura
Ma finto non e già, quelche si tocca.	Portar ne i giorni miei l'hore noiose.	Eterni sù nel ciel siam collocati.

train of thought hard to follow; a curiously impulsive insistence in following out any separate thread of reasoning, and a frequent abandonment of the argument before it is sufficiently clear to carry conviction to the reader—though to the writer the logical sequence is apparently complete; a strong tendency to self-analysis and introspection and a constant recurrence of the first personal pronoun; an intense interest in his own intellectual development, and an eager desire that others should understand his particular difficulties, trials, and temptations, and rejoice with him in his victories. The particular point of view held at the moment is always considered the right and only one, not merely for himself but for others. Outward forms and ceremonies are to him of little importance compared with the holding of sound dogma concerning life and religion.

Primitive Type. The thievish propensities of the Mercurian are much in evidence. The primitive Geminian will take from anyone, not merely accepting but exacting, as his due, sympathy, attention, consideration, admiration, time, energy, and pecuniary assistance — in fact, anything and everything that will feed his egotism or further his physical and intellectual development. He writes "I" with a particularly large capital, and is apt to feel that nothing which does not intimately concern his own happiness, well-being, and comfort is of any importance whatever. Sickness, suffering, sorrow, and loss are tragedies indeed when they touch him, and as such to be proclaimed aloud, reiterated, and lamented until everyone is convinced of their existence and magnitude. When they only affect others they are merely a nuisance and a discomfort, representing the negative and unimportant part of life, dull and depressing subjects, not to be dwelt upon any longer than is absolutely necessary. The craving for joy and variety which, later on, will act as a spur, at this period takes the form of an effervescent restlessness and perpetual dissatisfaction. A constant demand for entertainment, novelty, and excitement results in a tendency to shirk uncongenial

92

duties. Routine work of any kind is particularly resented, and until he understands intellectually the advantage of regular and punctual attention to minor details in housekeeping, office work, etc., the Geminian doomed to such labor feels like a bird in a cage. The root of all such unhappiness and rebellion is generally the secret conviction that he or she, however heedless and incompetent, is meant for better things, and is consequently thrown away on drudgery of any kind.

There is always a strong desire to be in the very center of things; and if these people find themselves in any way inferior to those around them, and are compelled to take a back seat, they feel sore and ill-used — and show it. They are bad listeners, and often resent the suggestions of others, however practical and sensible

Albumasar, Jean, Duc de Berry MS., 1403.
Pierpont Morgan Library

they may be; shying away from any plan proposed, and frequently substituting some crazy scheme of their own. Geminians are also prone to rapid and complete changes in point of view, and are generally incapable of realizing either that they have changed or that it is possible and even right for other people to hold different convictions and opinions from themselves. They are deplorably lacking in persistence and tenacity, and often strikingly deficient in memory, which defects make it difficult for them to realize the value of old associations, to put themselves in the place of others, and to acknowledge and discharge debts of gratitude.

Nevertheless they are generally wonderfully business-like and exact when there is any question of what is owing to them, for even when quite comfortably off, they always feel hampered by poverty. Their desire to spend and to acquire is always in excess of their means, and though they may have occasional fits of lavish generosity, such outbreaks are often made an excuse for subsequent meannesses or demands. Many of them manage to combine a sensitive disposition with selfishness, verging not exactly on *deliberate* cruelty but on a type of cruelty which is born of an innate desire to abolish sorrow in whatever form it may be met with, and get away from it into the sunshine again. Thus the sick are either neglected altogether, or tormented by ill-judged ministrations and inopportune admonitions. Sometimes futile attempts are made to goad them into cheerfulness by ineffectual argument or by such insistent exhortation as leaves them utterly exhausted and more in need of help and consolation than ever. In love affairs they keep a cool head and a keen lookout for their own advantage, are rarely carried away by passion, and can generally steer clear of complications that will hamper their career or tie them down to an uncongenial life. The question they ask themselves about marriage is, almost invariably, "What will this give me?" and rarely "How much can I give?"

Physical Characteristics. The Gemini type is generally associated with a slender figure, agility of movement, and small features. The eyes are often gray or hazel, bright but not very large; complexion is pale as a rule, even when quite healthy, but inclined to flush or darken, and very easily tanned. The feminine edition is particularly fascinating, and the more artistic and sensitive among the men have the same charm. The type is most easily recognized by its alert, eager bearing, sympathetic manner (verging on the gushing), and quick unexpected movements. The sandals of Mercury are winged, and though probably the symbol was chosen chiefly as representing speech — the winged words which are set free through the working of the intellect — it is peculiarly appropriate in other ways too. The movements, both physical and mental, are unexpected. There is a tendency to advance in short, quick flights; to alight again as suddenly, and apparently on impulse, to survey the surroundings with eager curiosity and interest, and, when the point of view has nothing fresh to offer, to dart off again — generally in some unforseen direction. Sometimes they seem to take a half-mischievous delight in their own power of disconcerting and astonishing other people by their methods of procedure. This is specially true of the feminine or artistic type; the masculine edition suggests the hawk rather than the song bird. The flights are longer and more sustained, and generally mean business. There is less loquacity and more watchfulness, less of the characteristic "temperament" and a keener intellect.

North America is said to be very largely under the influence of this sign, and among the brilliant financiers of its great cities, and also among their highly sensitive, adaptable, and charming women excellent examples of the two classes described above are to be found. More primitive Geminians may also be recognized — unscrupulous but clever men, to whom sudden and shifty financial moves are as the breath of life; and high-strung, restless women who exhaust their energies in a chase after excitement and variety, and then make the resultant nervous prostration an excuse for every kind of self-indulgence.

Burlesque editions of the Geminian are to be

seen in the caricatures of Brother Jonathan at his cutest, in the "Artful Dodger" of Charles Dickens, and, generally speaking, among the whole confraternity of nimble-fingered gentry whose ability in their profession shows intellect, and whose motto may be written, "All that's thine is mine; but what is mine is my own."

The Geminians' *nervous* type of energy will carry them through almost anything they want to do, but fails them as soon as work becomes irksome, uncongenial, or dull. The chief danger that threatens the finer type of Geminian is physical exhaustion due to the strain of artistic production. In the less evolved, vanity and egoism are the origin of the trouble, and the subject becomes excessively exacting to those around him, imagining that no one really understands or appreciates him, and giving way to tearfulness, wayward temper, childish rebellion, hysteria and other manifestations of overstrung nerves. Geminians are more or less children as regards health, and those forms of treatment generally applied to children suit them best. Fresh air and sunshine, regular hours, a light diet and above all *plenty of sleep* are recommended.

In an ancient list of creatures said to be ruled by this sign, are found, amusingly, the house sparrow and — the common flea. Geminians are masters of light skirmishing and are hardly ever really beaten. They understand instinctively the advantages of a sudden change of front, of unexpectedness of attack, and of rapidity of retreat. Watch the sparrow and see the Geminian method of warfare. All is peace and harmony, when suddenly one of them fluffs out his feathers and goes for some astonished rival with all his might, gives him a disconcerting peck, and promptly retires to safety. The Geminian child may be seen following the same tactics. In the schoolroom, he is generally the center of joyous activity and merry play. He likes everything to go on happily and brightly, but he prefers to strike the keynote in the harmony himself. If his will is crossed, and the others take a negative attitude when he makes a suggestion, he may stand it the first time, and even oftener, but sooner or later he rebels and flies out suddenly, to the consternation and discomfort of the whole group, especially as he or she usually ends by a burst of weeping which ensures an easy victory next time. A reputation for "tantrums" can be used as a very efficient piece of armor.

IL BAGATTEL.

Radio Times Hulton

John F. Kennedy: Sun in Gemini

Bob Hope: Sun in Gemini

Hyginus, 15-century Italian
MS. *N. Y. Public Library*

Queen Victoria: Sun in Gemini

SUN IN GEMINI

The Sun in Gemini as the motive force behind the lunar expression gives a dualistic and restless tendency, the desires always running on intellectual lines. The individual character will be dual in expression. Will power is strong, and there is some pride or love of pedigree.

Sun in Gemini and Moon in Aries

In intellectual matters this is a powerful combination. The nature is ambitious, positive, and somewhat lacking in sympathy. There is a liability to live too much in the head, also a tendency to become erratic and too self-willed. The nature is lacking in calmness, steadiness, self-control, and perseverance. Natives are combative, disobedient, witty, sharp-tongued. They often have talents in art, and are likely to travel.

Sun in Gemini and Moon in Taurus

This combination indicates a considerable amount of wilfulness, activity, restlessness, and a tendency to measure all things from an intellectual standpoint. There is a certain amount of self-esteem and independence, and the feelings are not so active in this polarity as in the other combinations. Judgment is impartial. With suitable planetary positions popularity may be enjoyed, while there is ability amounting to genius in some intellectual direction. The Moon expresses the Sun very clearly in this combination, giving artistic tendencies, refinement, and literary ability.

Sun and Moon in Gemini

This combination indicates considerable wilfulness, activity, restlessness, self-esteem and independence. There is a tendency to measure all things from an intellectual standpoint. Feelings are not so active. There is much dexterity with the hands. With suitable planetary positions pop-

Deauville. Raoul Dufy. The painter was born with the Sun in Gemini

ularity may be enjoyed, and ability amounting to genius in some intellectual direction. Temperament is docile and judgment impartial. The Moon expresses the Sun very clearly in this combination, giving artistic tendencies, refinement, and literary ability.

Sun in Gemini and Moon in Cancer

This combination inclines toward economy and thrift in the home and in all matters concerned with the welfare of others. There is likely to be a great deal of traveling; also much restlessness and a longing for sympathy from others. Imagination and artistic talents are well developed. The receptive nature is very easily affected and upset by surrounding conditions, but good memory, and a well-stored and comprehensive mind, intuitional, versatile, and agreeable, brings success in all matters relating to public affairs.

Sun in Gemini and Moon in Leo

In this combination the personality suffers somewhat, as there is not sufficient firmness in the background to support the Leo inclinations. There is likely to be too much impulse and abundant sympathy, affections being keen but easily moved. The native fluctuates; is at times self-confident and hopeful, works well and achieves much; but often feels he has greater powers than he can express outwardly. There is some love of display, the imagination is active, and there is poetical and dramatic ability.

Sun in Gemini and Moon in Virgo

This is a good combination, the Mercurial elements coming out forcibly and inclining the mind to be studious, critical, and analytical. It often gives a love for chemistry. With regard to the mind, however, it is a very sensitive combination and there is apt to be some mistrustfulness and a melancholic tendency. Persons born under this combination may obtain great benefit through serving others. They can be impartial and judicial, seeing both sides of a question, yet

Culver

are apt to be changeable, undecided, and lacking in perseverance, so that they do not always get credit for all the abilities they possess. This position gives a strong will.

Sun in Gemini and Moon in Libra

This combination increases the intuitions and bestows much refinement with a sympathetic nature. It produces foresight, sharpens the perceptive faculties, inclines the native to study, and gives a great amount of imitativeness and ability for writing. The faculty of comparison is well developed. There should be success in artistic pursuits, and a cheerful, sociable, humane nature. The native lives sympathetically with family and relatives, and may marry a relative.

97

Photo: Bignou Gallery

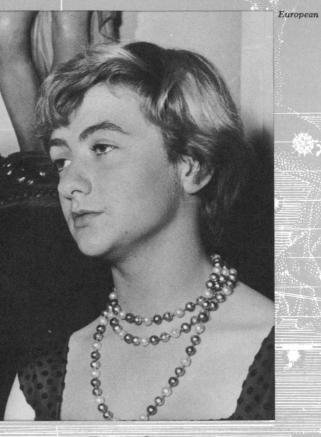

Françoise Sagan

BORN UNDER THE SIGN OF GEMINI

Bob Dylan

Duchess of Windsor

Marilyn Monroe

Duke of Edinburgh

Ian Fleming

Laurence Olivier

Gemini. Book of Stars and Constellations. Persian, 1630

Sun in Gemini and Moon in Scorpio

This combination accentuates the critical faculties which tend to become hard and severe. There is much determination, argumentiveness, assertiveness, over-sensitiveness, jealousy and self-esteem. There is also sarcasm, liveliness, and wit, with some practical business ability and power of management; but the usual cheerful self-confidence sometimes gives way to irritable, and quarrelsome moods.

Sun in Gemini and Moon in Sagittarius

These two signs produce activity and restlessness, resulting in lack of continuity and nervousness. There is an instinctive love of traveling, with considerable mental capacity, both intellectual and intuitive. Under favorable conditions the native is humane, generous, and benevolent, with an inclination to philosophy or religion; he is genial, companionable, and of quick and good judgment. There is apt to be a considerable waste of mental energy, much enthusiasm, and exceptional force of character.

Sun in Gemini and Moon in Capricorn

This is a good business combination, as it gives Saturnine steadiness to the Mercurial tendency. The individuality is quick, the personality often slow; there may therefore be a considerable lack of harmony, but by labor, patience, and perseverance a great deal of good work may be done by the personal character in building up the individuality. There is good memory, with mental abilities of the solid kind (not showy), but the native is too serious, and despondent at times. This combination gives a love of science, some tact and diplomacy, and often much ingenuity.

Sun in Gemini and Moon in Aquarius

This is a good combination of the airy signs, producing a great deal of mental and physical activity. Those born under it are good character readers and good students of metaphysics. They can make the most of a good education, are able to make acquaintances easily, but tend to be reserved and somewhat independent. At times they are erratic, but always inventive and original.

Sun in Gemini and Moon in Pisces

This combination while intensifying a desire for knowledge also causes restlessness and irritability. There are frequently dissatisfaction and a yearning for the unattainable. Under favorable planetary positions, however, the native is charitable, benevolent, social, sympathetic, and has common sense and good judgment. There is some likelihood of traveling, and some ability for medicine or nursing. The combination produces great receptivity, and suggests success in uncommon pursuits.

FAMOUS PEOPLE BORN WITH THE SUN IN GEMINI

Ralph Waldo Emerson:	May 25, 1803
Queen Victoria:	May 24, 1819
Walt Whitman:	May 31, 1819
Mary Cassatt:	May 22, 1845
Frank Lloyd Wright:	June 8, 1869
Igor Stravinsky:	June 5, 1882
Cole Porter:	June 9, 1893
Duchess of Windsor:	June 19, 1896
Bob Hope:	May 29, 1903
Beatrice Lillie:	May 29, 1903
Jean-Paul Sartre:	June 21, 1905
Laurence Olivier:	May 22, 1907
Ian Fleming:	May 28, 1908
Rosalind Russell:	June 4, 1911
John F. Kennedy:	May 29, 1917
Duke of Edinburgh:	June 10, 1921
Marilyn Monroe:	June 1, 1926
Françoise Sagan:	June 21, 1935
Bob Dylan:	May 24, 1941

June 22 to July 22

THE CRAB

The sign of the
Prophet or Teacher

A cardinal watery sign
Tenacious, patient, sensitive, sympathetic, motherly,
changeable, easily influenced

Ruler: the Moon

Gems: moss-agate, emerald

Color: violet
Metal: silver

Harmonious signs for business, marriage, or
companionship: Pisces, Scorpio, Taurus

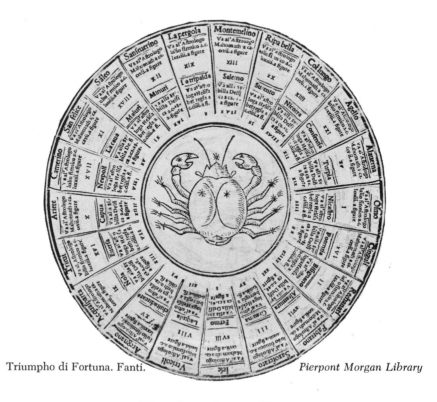

Triumpho di Fortuna. Fanti.   *Pierpont Morgan Library*

The Cancerian Type

Adaptability with tenacity — in one word, *patience* — is the essential force of this sign and of its ruler. The Moon waxes and wanes, shines in full radiance or suffers eclipse, but in all its varying stages is ever constant in its inconstancy. Cancer, the crab, when once he has seized an object, and means to have it, will rather lose his claw than let go, and having lost it, will grow another to take hold again.

Evolved Type. The highly evolved Cancerian is the master of many moods. The whole gamut of emotion lies open to him; he can feel, and make others feel, joy, sorrow, compassion, horror, and despair as no other type can, seizing the imagination and holding it by the power of his imagery and the intensity of his own feel-

ings. The past and future are as real to him as the present. His memory is retentive, and the history of his own nation, family, or class is immensely important in his eyes. He is the teacher *par excellence,* and cares little for smoothness of outline or grace of form so long as he can drive his lesson home. His style is picturesque, vivid, often dramatic; and he continues to deliver and redeliver his message, changing and adapting its form while preserving its essence, until he succeeds in arousing the attention of his audience and kindling its enthusiasm. Public speakers of all kinds are found under the influence of this sign, as also editors and literary men who have a strong personal hold over their readers, and actors and dramatists in whom imagination is a predominant feature. These people

104

Diana. From an old German engraving

love to come into touch with the public, to claim its interest and stimulate its imagination; and if large audiences are unattainable and a public career impossible, the natural bent will find scope and outlet in the schoolroom or among friends and relatives.

Affections are strong and the maternal element particularly marked. No lapse of time or separation by distance ever seems materially to lessen love or friendship or weaken family ties. The son is as near to the heart and as present to the mind of the Cancerian parents as he was in his infancy, so that the sense of separation hardly exists, and long voyages are permitted or undertaken by this type with a composure and pleasure which many less deeply devoted to home cannot begin to understand. Early memories of childhood and old ties of friendship are a treasure for Cancerians, who will correspond for years with people to whom they were attracted in their teens, have never met since, and are not likely to meet again.

John Quincy Adams: Sun in Cancer.
(Portrait by John Singleton Copley)

The striking success of this type in the field of teaching is partly due to this tenacity of recollection, and to the vivid pictures of childhood and youth. His memory frequently carries him back to babyhood, faithfully recording striking experiences of the third and fourth years and sometimes even the emotions experienced at eighteen or twenty months in connection with certain clearly recorded scenes. This fact, together with the sensational tendency of the sign, makes early training and education extremely important.

Injudicious or unsympathetic discipline may cause him suffering quite out of proportion to his faults and shortcomings. Injustice rankles long, and even when the victim is sufficiently large-minded to understand and forgive it, his retentive memory makes it impossible for him to forget. It is not always easy to hit on the right discipline for this type. Severity is useless, coercion almost impossible; force may ensure outward obedience for a time, but it always engenders fierce resentment, and sooner or later the inborn tenacity reasserts itself, and the Cancerian goes on his own way at the first opportu-

XVIII

LA·LUNE

Tarot card.
Bettmann Archive

nity. Nevertheless, the nature is loving, loyal, and sympathetic. Tales of chivalry and heroism are excellent for the active and ever-growing imagination, which craves constant nourishment, and which, if starved, is apt to become morbid, leading to untruthfulness, both willful and unconscious.

Drawing by Jean Cocteau

Kirsten Flagstad: Sun in Cancer

Love and Friendship. This type is very romantic and imaginative where the affections are concerned, though often too shy or proud to betray the fact; for ridicule is torture to the Cancerian. In consequence, the story of his love affairs is frequently a tragic sequence of misunderstandings and heartaches. The patience and tenacity of the sign show in this as in all other matters, and a misplaced affection, even if apparently conquered for a time, will recur

Jean Cocteau: Sun in Cancer

and reassert itself in spite of everything that reason and common sense and worldly wisdom may say against it. When such a love as this — strong and lasting — is based on real sympathy and understanding, and is triumphant in the end, the happiness attained is as intense as the previous suffering was severe; for where feeling is concerned this type knows no half-measures, and its love, which has much of the maternal element in it, is characterized by a yearning to give, while asking for little in return.

Primitive Type. Primitive Cancerians are the slaves, instead of the masters, of their moods. They are prey to sentimentalism, sensationalism, and exaggerated emotion of every kind — mere aggravating bundles of contradictions and inconsistencies. At the early stages this is often a very unhappy sign. A sense of latent power, as yet unexpressed and inexpressible, gives the undeveloped an absurd idea of their own importance and of the deference and consideration due to them from others. Moods of exalted self-sufficiency are followed by others of exaggerated shyness and humility. Fierce pride and independence alternate with helplessness and loneliness. There is as wide a difference between the two conditions as there is between the crab in his normal state, i.e., encased in his natural

armor of plated bone, all knobs and joints and elbows and claws — ever ready for defense, if not for aggression — and the same creature at its period of growth, when it slips off its old shell and becomes scarcely recognizable — a thin-skinned, helpless, semi-transparent object, lying hidden in the crevices of the rock and trembling at the approach of every foe. In like manner, Cancerians will sometimes shun their fellow creatures for weeks, giving way to morbid feelings of self-consciousness, shyness and depression; after which they will emerge again and make some desperate effort to challenge the attention of their fellow men and regain their own self-respect.

We find a tendency to dramatic methods, a craving for emotional experience which leads them at times to heights of folly. A schoolgirl of this type found a morbid pleasure in giving her classmates the impression that she had gone mad; and a bright boy of sixteen presented himself at school with his head elaborately bandaged, and posed for a whole blissful day as the hero of a dangerous accident, reveling in the sympathy and interest of teachers and boys, recounting and elaborating with gusto the exact circumstances connected with his wholly imaginary injury. Of the same breed was Tom Sawyer, and it is not surprising to find that the horoscope of Tom Sawyer's biographer, Mark Twain, shows us Jupiter, the planet representing the mental activity, in this imaginative sign of Cancer.

Physical Characteristics. The bony structure is generally the most striking feature of the Cancerian. The limbs, and especially the arms, are long in proportion to the body; the shoulders are broad, the hands and feet large, the skull of a generous size with an overhanging brow, high cheekbones, and a pronounced lower jaw, sometimes with irregular or rather prominent teeth. The nose in the plainer specimens is often insignificant, even in the handsomer varieties it has an inclination to turn up. The mouth is wide and expressive, with a generous smile and great possibilities both of sweetness and of grimness.

Diana. Houdon. *Frick Collection*

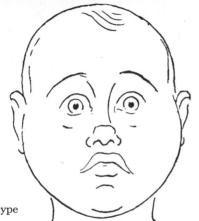

Lunar type

The eyes are often short-sighted, deep-set, and wide apart. The eyebrows are distinctly marked, sometimes almost meeting with a decided downward curve, just over the bridge of the nose.

In the case of women the structural characteristics are naturally softened to a less bony build, and many of them have considerable grace of movement. The best-looking among them more than make up in expression for any want of regularity in feature, and many successful actresses suggest the type, notably those who excel in intensity and in imaginative power.

Religion. The religious tendency inspired by this sign is best understood by studying the writings of the prophets of all times and nations. One of the most striking examples is to be found in Jeremiah, whose lamentations and other writings, full of wonderful imagery and of deep feeling, show strongly and unmistakably the influence of Cancer. The Cancerian clings to his convictions and assumes the defensive at a moment's notice if the faintest breath of criticism is breathed upon his beliefs, customs, country, or family. His outlook is apt to be pessimistic and he is too often tempted to force a change of mood by taking refuge in alcohol. But all this moodiness, crustiness, and angularity is only on the outside, and beneath the hard shell beats a heart full of warmth, tender whenever it has to deal with sickness or suffering, with the impotence of infancy or the helplessness of old age. His religion is simplicity itself as far as rites and ceremonies are concerned.

Health. The emotional nature is generally too strong for the physical, and when they have been upset by bad news, or are anxious about some loved one, there is a strong tendency to exaggerate the symptoms and to become a prey to serious apprehensions of a complete breakdown. These terrors are increased if such a collapse would mean financial difficulties for the family; and as worry is one of the most fruitful causes of illness, grave symptoms may actually develop, brought about entirely by ill-controlled feelings and morbid imagination. Touchiness, bitterness, resentment, and hurt pride are serious factors to be dealt with in trying to keep the body healthy. Gloomy forebodings begin to hold sway, and the efforts of much-tried relatives to cheer the sufferer are often treated as heartlessness and want of sympathy. In fact, the Cancerian enjoys a good old revel in awful possibilities.

Among recreations for Cancerians, gardening should be given a large place. The characteristic tenderness of the sign comes out strongly in the care lavished on seedlings and in the delight taken in their growth; and those born with the Sun in this sign are sometimes extremely successful in their horticultural efforts. This is not reputed a long-lived type. Of those who do survive to old age, many are hampered by recurrent attacks of various commonplace and unromantic afflictions — generally preventable — which interfere with their usefulness and their serenity, especially if they are men.

BORN UNDER THE SIGN OF CANCER

Nelson Rockefeller

Gina Lollobrigida

Ringo Starr

Culver

Richard Rodgers and Oscar Hammerstein II

Bob Golby

Gertrude Lawrence

Duke of Windsor

SUN IN CANCER

Tenacity, attachment, and clinging desire for objects are very marked. This position makes the individual character sensitive, impressionable and highly emotional, often lacking in self-reliance, and with a yearning for sensation. There is power to sense the general conditions of others.

Sun in Cancer and Moon in Aries

This combination produces a great deal of activity and persistence. There is a liability to become headstrong and go to extremes, also a love of fame and a desire to be at the head of things. The native is independent and dislikes control. He is rebellious, often discontented, and will usually change his occupation more than once. The parents will affect the life considerably and he may not get on with them. The strong impulse in the personal character can bring many sorrows.

Sun in Cancer and Moon in Taurus

At its best this polarity gives a share of energy, perseverance, and practical ability. There is a fair amount of independence and resolution. The native inclines to run in a groove for a time, but changes come, perhaps suddenly, and a different groove is lived in. There are some morbid tendencies, and self-control must be practiced before success can be obtained. The nature is imaginative, impressionable, sympathetic, and

very easily affected by others. There is a certain amount of good fortune, and some success is achieved in business or with houses or land.

Sun in Cancer and Moon in Gemini

This combination produces a personality susceptible to education, and makes the brain versatile and exceedingly sensitive. The nature is somewhat irresolute, liable to change, and wanting in patient perseverance. There is a love of knowledge and a great deal of activity and energy, especially in literary matters and travel. Artistic tendencies may be displayed.

Henry VIII: Sun in Cancer
After Hans Holbein's painting. *Bettmann Archive*

Sun and Moon in Cancer

Fancy and imagination are strong, and there is a liability to go to extremes. This combination gives independence, with conservatism or a clinging to ancient customs and habits; yet there is also much changeableness. Inertia will produce laziness, but, when other planetary influences allow, the tenacity and motive power will be great. There is a good parental influence in early life, with possible inheritance from parents. The native is acquisitive and careful in money matters; and there is some good fortune through property, houses, or land.

Sun in Cancer and Moon in Leo

This combination produces very keen and sensitive feelings. It awakens the animal side of the nature, and there is a liability to go to extremes, causing restlessness, especially where love is concerned. There is appreciation of the drama, and sometimes a craving for ardent feelings and sensation. Affections are strong, and the nature romantic. On the whole the combination is good for health and worldly success.

Sun in Cancer and Moon in Virgo

The Moon in Virgo contributes to a sensitive and passive nature, with a certain amount of discrimination in all matters where the feelings and emotions are concerned. There is a good business polarity, either as manager or employee. There are adaptability and agreeableness, but a tendency to worry, especially about business matters.

ISIDIS
Magnæ Deorum Matris
APVLEIANA DESCRIPTIO.

Livre d'Astrologie.
Georgius Zothorus

La Lune

Sun in Cancer and Moon in Libra

This combination gives balance to the sensitive, emotional nature of Cancer and increases the perception and affections, particularly in matters connected with home life. It also gives ability for writing, and a love of fame and recognition. The native is emotional or sensational, and displays some ability for music or art, loving beautiful and harmonious sights, colors, and sounds. He is observant and very conscious of what goes on. There are many changes in his life — very likely a change of occupation, and certainly changes of residence. He may leave his parents while young.

Sun in Cancer and Moon in Scorpio

This combination enables the personality to have a solidifying effect upon the sensitive nature of Cancer, making it harder (and sometimes selfish); there is apt to be pride and vindictiveness, especially in matters connected with the feelings. It gives a love of display and attracts the opposite sex. There is early death of, or separation from, a parent. In some cases the native follows closely on parental lines, both in character and occupation; in others a great change occurs, and an entirely new environment and occupation is taken up.

Sun in Cancer and Moon in Sagittarius

In this combination the personality is too active for the individuality; it stimulates the emotional nature, giving much activity coupled with restlessness and a constant yearning for the unattainable. The native has a changeable yet companionable and kind nature, and is generally a quick worker. He is fond of traveling and of exploring new scenes, thoughts, and ideas.

Sun in Cancer and Moon in Capricorn

This makes the individual character more practical and ambitious, with an aptitude for business. The native is acquisitive, desirous of wealth, and is likely to accumulate money or property. The parents' heredity and family influences play an important part; sometimes he wishes to be independent of them but finds it impossible. There is an inability to express internal feelings. Many obstacles will come, but ambitions will be keen and there will be a love of fame and a desire to lead others.

Sun in Cancer and Moon in Aquarius

This combination gives ability in matters connected with associations, and some success in public life. It favors material rather than spirit-

John D. Rockefeller: Sun in Cancer.
(Portrait by John Singer Sargent)

ual objectives, yet gives general artistic ability. The native is tactful, careful, and diplomatic. He is rather reserved, quiet, and self-contained, and has some inclination for mystical pursuits; he is more sociable and companionable within than he appears to be on the surface. One of the parents dies early.

Sun in Cancer and Moon in Pisces

This is a harmonious combination of watery signs, awakening the emotional nature and making the mind receptive. There is much fancy, and a desire to obtain knowledge. Psychic faculties may be developed, and there will be an interior knowledge of the public mind and its requirements. The native is domesticated, good-natured and sociable, showing to more advantage in the family circle than in public life. He is changeable, fond of sensation and novelty. The position tends to success.

FAMOUS PEOPLE BORN WITH
THE SUN IN CANCER

Henry VIII:	June 28, 1491
Rembrandt:	July 15, 1606
Jean Jacques Rousseau:	June 28, 1712
John Quincy Adams:	July 11, 1767
Henry David Thoreau:	July 12, 1817
John D. Rockefeller:	July 8, 1839
Calvin Coolidge:	July 4, 1872
Helen Keller:	June 27, 1880
Marc Chagall:	July 7, 1887
Jean Cocteau:	July 5, 1889
Pearl S. Buck	June 26, 1892
Duke of Windsor:	June 23, 1894
Kirsten Flagstad:	July 12, 1895
Oscar Hammerstein II:	July 12, 1895
Ernest Hemingway:	July 21, 1899
Louis Armstrong:	July 4, 1900
Nathalie Sarraute:	July 18, 1900
Gertrude Lawrence:	July 4, 1901
Richard Rodgers:	June 28, 1902
Nelson Rockefeller:	July 8, 1908
Jean Anouilh:	June 23, 1910
Marshall McLuhan:	July 21, 1911
Saul Bellow:	July 10, 1915
Andrew Wyeth:	July 12, 1917
Ingmar Bergman:	July 14, 1918
John Glenn:	July 18, 1921
Gina Lollobrigida:	July 4, 1928
Ringo Starr:	July 7, 1940

July 23 to August 23

THE LION

The sign of the
King or President

A fixed fiery sign
Proud, generous, trusting, energetic, domineering, authoritative

Ruler: the Sun

Gems: ruby, diamond

Color: orange
Metal: gold

Harmonious signs for business, marriage, or
companionship: Sagittarius, Aries

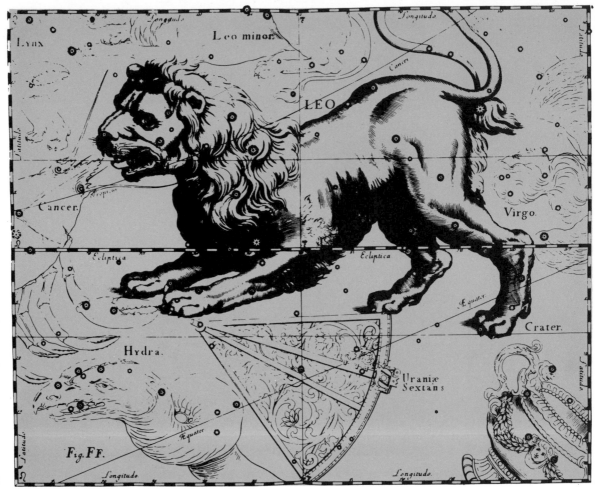

Hevelius, 1690

The Leonian Type

Evolved Type. It is said that no one can stand before the Apollo Belvedere without instinctively straightening his shoulders and drawing himself up to his full stature. The fully developed Leonian has something of the same effect upon his fellow men. His faith and trust in humanity, his serene conviction that those who are working for him will do their best, and that even those who fail him will be better in the future, all combine to awaken a generous response in the hearts of others. He gives to those around him fresh courage, and sets them striving to fulfill his expectations.

He is the ideal head of any large enterprise, institution, or undertaking. Many-sided himself, he understands and appreciates the qualities of all the other types, and never wastes his energy by asking from anyone what it is not in his or her power to give. Therefore he is particularly successful in organizing activities and distributing duties, giving to the specialists facilities and opportunties for exercising their various faculties. Commands, to be effective, must be easily understood, and therefore his style is simple and straightforward. Approval is definite and unmistakable, and displeasure is intimated without hesitation or circumlocution.

He holds the past in reverence, as the parent of the present, and looks forward to the future as its child. He encourages both science and art by his personal interest and patronage, and takes measures for the well-being of the sick and poverty-stricken. He practices self-denial and shows constant consideration for others by

118

Apollo. From an old German engraving

his punctuality, method, and forethought; and though his own life is simple he can show regal hospitality, shining as host, and delighting to give of his best to the guest and stranger. It is characteristic of the Leonian type of hospitality that it is always the welcome that really crowns it with success, and never either the richness of the feast nor the splendor of the entertainment. In fact, both may leave something to be desired, especially in humble homes, for the mastery of detail is difficult for this type; but the harmony of the gathering will be undisturbed and each guest will be made to feel that he has in some way contributed to the general enjoyment.

Love and Friendship. The emotions of this type tend to be over-generous and too wide-spread, and the characteristic faith in human nature frequently results in misplaced affections and unwise friendships. Heartaches, broken en-

Apollo Belvedere. *Vatican*

gagements, and unhappy marriages are frequent; but on the other hand the inborn magnanimity and power of forgiveness are such that in many cases the sufferer can adjust himself or herself to apparently impossible conditions, avert a tragedy, and bring success out of failure by a sheer act of faith.

Religion. The type of religious expression natural to the Leonian is the hymn of praise. The temples of Apollo were specially designed for ceremonial — "all beautiful, without and within"; and the worshipers who met to do him honor in ancient Greece and Rome passed in triumph through his courts and out along the highways, crowned with garlands and chanting his praises. The psalms of David, in the original, probably form the most perfect examples of Leonian style in existence, and even in translation have served as models to many of our greatest writers. Among their special characteristics we may note the constant recurrence of the words "majesty" and "glory," and their marvelous clearness and lucidity — a clearness attained partly by simplicity of phrasing and partly by careful repetition of important passages.

Lateran Museum, Rome

George IV: Sun in Leo.
(Portrait by Lawrence.)

Sun. Lithograph: Andre Masson

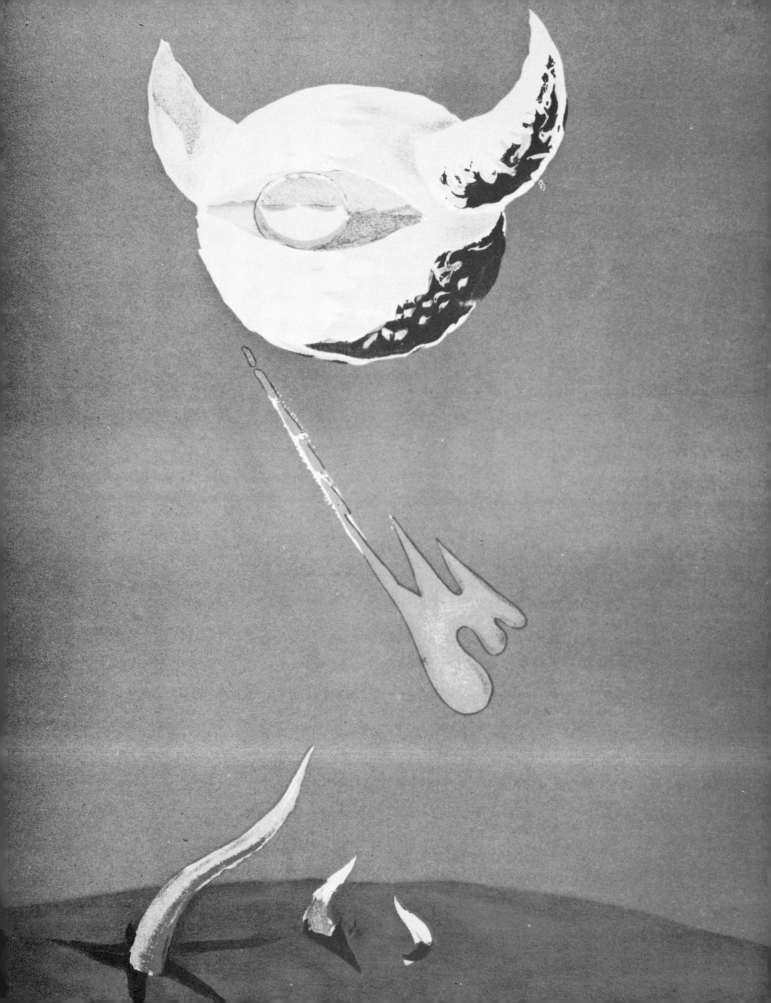

Curiously enough, moods of deep despondency are characteristic of many Leonians. The forethoughtful outlook naturally suggests forebodings; and the lack of ability to deal with difficulties in detail leads, at times, to a state of dejection that seems at first sight to be incompatible with the normal bearing of the sign. This condition is generally associated with inefficient heart action, but it is also due partly to an entire absence of resentment, rancor, and bitterness. These feelings are vicious and objectionable in themselves, but they are active; and by encouraging a fight, they keep their victims from being crushed by sorrow, as the Leonian is too apt to be. He simply waits with resignation till faith, which never altogether fails him, can gather strength enough to lift him out of his despondency.

Primitive Type. Primitive Leonians are generally afflicted with an unquenchable thirst for personal glory, and ambition for positions of responsibility and authority, which they are incapable of filling with success. Many, especially those of the commanding or masculine type, contrive to give themselves the illusion of kingship by assuming airs of self-importance and lording it over their inferiors and juniors. The gentler or more feminine type seeks, above all things, a comfortable throne — a well-cushioned one, at that — and asserts her queenship by betraying a marvelous skill in delegating disagreeable duties, a total incapacity for serving either herself or anyone else, together with a wondrous power of swallowing flattery. The lion seen through a diminishing glass is very much like the domestic cat — an animal attached to its

home and, as far as in it lies, to those who are willing to stroke it the right way; but it is never much inclined to put itself out for anybody.

A talent for deputing work is first cousin to the habit of shirking it; and the state of muddle found in some Leonian kingdoms is due to the fact that the monarch has claimed the throne too soon, and is inclined either to fidget in it or to snooze. At this early stage the tolerant attitude is apt to suggest that nothing matters very much; and the comprehensive intellect tries to cover so large a field of activity that it loses the ability to estimate relative values, and for lack of a clear focus cannot distinguish mountains from molehills.

The vice of kings is favoritism; Leonians are apt to select those who can make themselves useful, or who flatter them by showing a certain amount of dependence on their favor. Their love affairs develop along the same lines, and are apt to be numerous and unfortunate. They very often marry beneath them — possibly from a desire to make sure of at least one "subject" — and not infrequently find that their judgment has been at fault, and that the submissive and devoted fiancée shows a tendency, after marriage, to usurp the throne.

Physical Characteristics. This sign is most easily recognized by its commanding presence, stateliness of bearing, and deliberation in speech and movement. It is not easy to pass over a Leonian in a crowd, and even when he is small he generally makes his presence felt. The body is symmetrical, the limbs well proportioned, the step firm yet light, the stride longer than average. Many of them excel in dancing. The features are marked, and in some cases rather heavy — either "Roman" or somewhat feline in type — and generally show decided character. Astrological tradition declares that Italy, especially its capital, and also a large part of France are much under the influence of Leo; and certainly the dignity of the typical Roman, and the importance of his native city as an organizing center, accord well with such a theory. The feminine edition of the Leonian has less solidity

The Queen turned crimson with fury, and, after glaring at her for a moment like a wild beast, began screaming "Off with her head! Off with——"

Alice and the Red Queen.
From *Through the Looking Glass*

of build and more grace, and even when short in stature she can play the queen in society and reign over her own circle in fitting style.

In Fiction. A couple of quaint caricatures of this type are to be found in *Through the Looking-Glass*, where, in the Red and White Queens, Lewis Carroll has given excellent sketches of the fussy Leonian and her more helpless sister. The Red Queen is a stickler for etiquette and always knows exactly what other people ought to do; is always ready with advice, order, and reprimand, disdains circumlocution, and is inclined to flat contradiction in conversation. The White Queen is gentle and helpless, is afflicted with dark forebodings — as when she is about to prick her finger — and is so absolutely without resource that she can only bewail her fate and await it, while after the accident she depends entirely upon Alice to adjust her shawl and fasten her brooch.

Literary Style. Alexandre Dumas *père* was born with both the Sun and rising sign in Leo, so is doubly Leonian, and shows the influence strongly, both in his choice of a field for his literary activity and in his method of treatment. Like Sir Walter Scott — also born with the Sun in Leo — he was extraordinarily prolific in the production of historical romances of considerable length, dealing largely with the fortunes of royal and princely personages, or with questions of chivalry, of honor and of glory. Both told their tales in a straightforward style, and both neglected the useful art of pruning.

Health. In the matter of health Leo rarely does things by halves, and is generally either exceptionally strong — radiating vitality around him — or always on the sick list. The dangers to health are discordant and inharmonious surroundings, and the sorrow that springs from misplaced or unrequited affection, wounded vanity or lack of praise.

123

SUN IN LEO

The Sun in Leo gives a good moral nature. It makes the individuality sincere and ardent in all matters of affection; firm, self-reliant, magnanimous, sometimes austere, and determined. Many experiences will be in connection with love affairs.

Sun in Leo and Moon in Aries

There is a love of philosophy, and a tendency towards religious thought. Determination and love of leadership are marked. The combination gives a persistent, dominant, enthusiastic, and energetic nature, along with combativeness, but there is a necessity for restraint where feeling is concerned. It gives success in life, for the native is independent and can make his own way. He is self-reliant, firm, positive, yet generous and good-humored. He will form his own opinions and not be led by others.

Sun in Leo and Moon in Taurus

This combination gives a determined nature with an inclination to put heart into physical things. It strengthens business intuitions, making the native a good banker or stockbroker. The character is strong, firm, at times obstinate. The native is likely to be popular and to become a public figure. He is sociable, companionable, good natured, agreeable and is fond of pleasure, sensation, and emotion.

124

Sun in Leo and Moon in Gemini

This gives energy to the personal nature, with much determination behind it. It inclines the native toward music, drama, and the arts, and gives him ability for writing and poetry. The hands are ever ready to express the heart. The combination makes gifted, enthusiastic, and lovable people whose abilities may amount to genius. The mind is broad, comprehensive, and fertile. There is a good family influence in early life, and many acquaintances and friends.

Colonel T. E. Lawrence: Sun in Leo

Sun in Leo and Moon in Cancer

This causes great sensitiveness, and often sorrow in love affairs, and gives a tendency to go to extremes. It is a good combination for the mind, the brain being receptive to influences from the heart. It stimulates the emotions and makes the feelings keen and sensitive. The sexual nature is strong. The native is sociable, affectionate, loving companionship and the family circle. He is fond of children, of pleasure and sensation, and of living in fine surroundings. The combination gives financial success, especially when associated with other members of the family.

Sun and Moon in Leo

This combination gives an independent nature. Those born under it are often rather self-centered and proud, yet can be kind-hearted and generous. They are capable of holding their own under great difficulties, but are apt to take extreme measures. There is often reserve, yet a strong desire for affection, and usually some fondness for show in position or appearance. The combination gives much intuition, vitality, energy, and resourcefulness. The native has plenty of friends, by whom he may benefit. He is a person of some note in his sphere, will rise in life, or will make the acquaintance of those in superior positions.

Sun in Leo and Moon in Virgo

The Moon is in the first sign from the Sun. This gives resourcefulness and good business instincts. The native has high ideals, yet has a tendency to be critical, restless and anxious. There is ability for music, literature, or any subject where the ideal and practical are blended. It is a combination that achieves success, yet is sometimes lacking in enterprise. These people may succeed better through others than when working on their own account. They are apt to think their work somewhat beneath them, and that they are fitted for better positions than they occupy. At best they are good practical workers, can accomplish much, and they fraternize readily with others.

From The Psalm Book of Charles Knowles

Herbert Hoover: Sun in Leo

Alfred Hitchcock: Sun in Leo

BORN UNDER THE SIGN OF LEO

Wide World

Jacqueline Kennedy

Dorothy Parker

George Bernard Shaw

Culver

Wide World

Princess Margaret

Henry Ford

Wide World

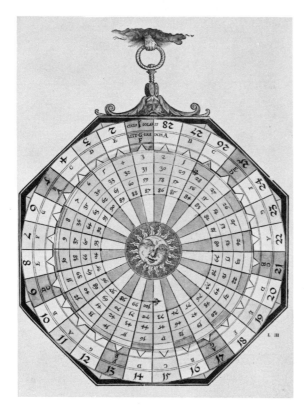

Leo nature quite hidden under this hard exterior. The native is much attracted by the senses which may take a high or low form, passional, emotional, or mental, according to the general condition of the horoscope. In love affairs he often goes to excess. He has an ardent, fixed nature, and inclines to be worldly.

Sun in Leo and Moon in Sagittarius

The Moon is in the fifth sign from the Sun, and therefore in perfect harmony with it. It produces restlessness, yet this is a hopeful and successful combination. The native has a benevolent and good-hearted disposition, but sometimes lacks caution and self-restraint. He has active sympathies, intuitive foresight, and is good at

Leo. Book of Stars and Constellations. Persian, 1630

Astronomicum Caesareum. Ingolstadt, 1540. Petrus Apianus

Sun in Leo and Moon in Libra

This harmonious and successful polarity strengthens the affections, gives compassion and a desire to do public good. There is a love of poetry, music, and art, and the native may have considerable ability in one of these. His mind is strong and active, he associates readily with other people, is friendly, companionable and dislikes loneliness.

Sun in Leo and Moon in Scorpio

This combination gives some austerity, there is an inclination to be rather hard, proud, and arrogant, with much love of show. Persons born under this influence often have their internal

128

philanthropic work and sports. There is much hope and joy in the nature, and a great love of pleasure.

Sun in Leo and Moon in Capricorn

This combination tends to harden the inner nature. The personality is inclined to be rather selfish and worldly, but the heart is always pulling away from externals. This combination gives a love of power and leadership, an ability to organize and govern, and is good for either a business or political career. The ambitions are keen and determined, and the native is likely to occupy a prominent or responsible position in his sphere. Generally speaking, it is good for length of life and for money or property.

Sun in Leo and Moon in Aquarius

This combination, equivalent to the Moon's being in opposition to the Sun, gives intuition and ability to judge human nature quickly, together with some very marked occult tendencies, refinement, much determination and will-power. The native is independent, good-natured, sociable, but with some exterior reserve.

Sun in Leo and Moon in Pisces

In this combination there is often discontent and dissatisfaction. The native is inclined to be dreamy and passive. Nevertheless, with a good horoscope, he will be kind and generous, and will benefit from these qualities in others.

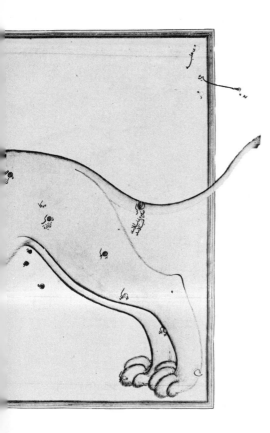

FAMOUS PEOPLE BORN WITH THE SUN IN LEO

Napoleon:	August 15, 1769
Sir Walter Scott:	August 15, 1771
Alexandre Dumas:	July 24, 1802
George Bernard Shaw:	July 26, 1856
Henry Ford:	July 30, 1863
Orville Wright:	August 19, 1871
Herbert Hoover:	August 10, 1874
C. G. Jung:	July 26, 1875
T. E. Lawrence:	August 15, 1888
Mae West:	August 17, 1892
Dorothy Parker:	August 22, 1893
Aldous Huxley:	July 26, 1894
Henry Moore:	July 30, 1898
Alfred Hitchcock:	August 13, 1899
Ogden Nash:	August 19, 1902
Dag Hammarskjöld:	July 29, 1905
Julia Child:	August 15, 1912
Fidel Castro:	August 13, 1927
Jacqueline Kennedy:	July 28, 1929
Princess Margaret:	August 21, 1930
Princess Anne:	August 15, 1950

August 24 to September 23

THE VIRGIN

The sign of the
Craftsman or Critic

A mutable earthy sign
Exact, methodical, industrious, discriminating, intelligent, chaste

Ruler: Mercury

Gems: pink jasper, hyacinth

Color: gray or navy blue
Metal: quicksilver

Harmonious signs for business, marriage, or
companionship: Capricorn, Taurus

Triumpho di Fortuna. Fanti.   *Pierpont Morgan Library*

The Virginian Type

Evolved Type. The chief characteristic of the fully developed Virginian is his marvelous power of discrimination. He tests everything in the furnace of his criticism, separates, sifts, classifies, and arranges his materials and his men, recognizing at a glance the potential value of each, and organizing the work entrusted to him to make the very best practical use of everyone and everything. Hand and brain generally work together, especially in all matters in which accuracy and method are important. His clear head and thrifty ways make him an excellent manager.

An ideal staff of officials for any company, club, or association would include a Leonian as president, a Cancerian and a Scorpionian as vice-presidents, a Taurean as treasurer, and a Virginian as secretary. The last-named generally does the hardest work and gets small thanks for it. If he fails in his duties, the society he serves will probably go to pieces, but few realize that, and he is generally too much occupied by practical details to care greatly whether they do or not. His business is to carry on the activities of the concern with strict attention to the rules of a constitution which is framed and directed by others, and when he has done all that is his duty to do, the vote of thanks, by his own directions, goes to the chair. In this matter the Virginian is wise as usual. It is not his province to command, and when he attempts to issue orders in his own person, or to assume airs of authority, he very frequently gives offense; but people will readily work with him and accept services

Alessandro Temini, 17th-century engraving

LVSSVRIA	AGOSTO	VERGINE
Dalla crapula, e l'otio io nacqui al mondo,	All'apparir del mio cocente raggio,	La pudicitia mia (che mia dir lice)
Et hor uiuo trà lussi, e trà bagordi;	Arde ogni pianta et ogni fior languisce;	Mi trasse colassù nell' alti giri;
Né mai quietan per me, li sensi ingordi	Si secca ogni fontana, e inaredisce,	Per fuggir della Terra i rei mastiri;
Fin che non traggon l'huom giu nel profondo.	E il fiume nega al Mar l'antico homaggio.	Vergine in Ciel mene uolai felice.

8

judgment in their adaptation and ornamentation. When well off they generally dress with care and taste — never showily or ostentatiously, and sometimes even with a certain puritanical sobriety, but always suitably. They are keenly intellectual, and somewhat critical both of themselves and of others. Even at its brightest this type tends to be a grave one, for it has few illusions, but when wedded to one of the gentler and more loving signs, nothing can exceed its charm. The pointed speech then becomes extremely witty, and the clear eyes are always wide open to whatever is lovely and of good report. If there is any virtue, life's keen critic will point it out, and if there is any praise he will utter it; and though his native penetration

Virgo. Astrological Treatises of Albumasar, 14th-century Flemish MS. *Pierpont Morgan Library*

from him; for he is splendidly capable, and very quick to see how a thing should be done, though disinclined to trouble his head about why. Virgo, like Taurus, is one of the earthy or "service" signs.

However, the Virginian is not always doomed to work without reward or appreciation. Untiring industry, practical ability, clear vision, and critical acumen bring him to the front sooner or later — though it is often later, for this type generally seems to start handicapped in some way. Success has been achieved notably in the lines of criticism and literature, also in art. These people work best alone in studio, study, or workshop — have small patience with underlings, assistants, and apprentices, and no patience at all with the critics unless their comments show exceptional discrimination and are helpful.

Women born under this sign are often skilled in some form of handcraft, finding a use for the most unlikely materials and showing great

134

Elizabeth I. Sun in Virgo
Unknown artist

refuses to leave him in ignorance of the short-comings of humanity, his healthiness of mind will prevent his dwelling upon them or indulging in morbid analysis of anything objectionable or unclean.

Certain astrologers have declared that this is a selfish sign, but the type of selfishness that demands and exacts assistance and attentions from others is the very last accusation that could be brought against Virginians, many of whom dedicate their lives to working, often for inadequate pay, and always finding far more satisfaction in helping others than in working for their own benefit. They give freely and ungrudgingly of their time and strength and ability up to the very measure of their natural forces, and sometimes beyond them; but nevertheless there is a limit to their generosity, and when demands are excessive and unreasonable they know how to say no, and to stick to it. They are rarely lavish in their affections, never prodigal of praise, and usually prudent in the expenditure of their income. An accompaniment of this love of giving active service is an intense dislike of accepting it, and a horror of dependence in old age, which naturally leads to the care of their resources, and makes many of them live simply and frugally; but when ample wealth is at their disposal, and they have no need to worry about the future, they spend wisely and well, generally receiving full value for their money.

Love and Friendship. The Virginian heart, like the steel of Vulcan, is true metal, and not easily melted; but when once it finds itself in love's furnace it glows with a pure white heat, and takes a long time to cool. His love affairs are few, and when, as often happens, they are unfortunate, he takes refuge in his one panacea of hard work, and is apt to shrink from the society of his fellow men. Neither sex seems to care much for children, though both make very careful and conscientious parents. When highly developed they accept celibacy easily, caring little for posterity so long as they can serve their own day and generation. They have the instinct of chastity and turn with repulsion from litera-

Mercury. 14th-century engraving, Florentine school

ture dealing with sex problems, especially if there is anything morbid or unwholesome in the treatment of the subject. Students may smile, remembering that among men born with Virgo strongly accentuated are several notable examples whose lives have been far from ideal in the matter of purity. In accounting for such exceptions, the horoscope must as always be examined in detail, special note being taken of the position of Venus. If it is in a susceptible or fickle sign, the Virgo influence will be to some extent counteracted. Environment must also be considered. Thus, in the case of Charles II, the planet of love, found in Taurus — the most amorous sign — will account for his responding more easily to Venus than to the sterner call of Vulcan.

Aglauros Turned into Stone by Mercury. J. W. Baur, 17th-century engraving

Religion. Astrological tradition associates this sign with the holy hermits. Saints of this type were generally believed to have played their part in the world before leaving it, and were frequently reputed to have suffered much through the affections. Elderly Virginians will generally own that the descriptions of these pure and peaceful lives — the cave for shelter, the stream for the bath, the simple diet — appeal to them strongly.

Literary Style. Literary men born under this sign (or with this sign rising) excel in the mastery of detail and are exceedingly industrious and prolific, adapting their genius to the demands and necessities of their day. Dickens, who gave the hour of his birth to an American inquirer as seven-fifty a.m., and so must have been born when Virgo was rising, is as typically Virgo as he is Aquarius — the sign under which he was born (February 7, 1812). He never spared himself and published in rapid succession a large number of novels, in most of which the side characters and detailed descriptions are of much more importance to the reader than the heroes and heroines or the main outlines of the plot. His gallery of clear and definite portraits is extraordinary. In *Bleak House* alone there are over eighty distinct characters — all people capable of interesting the reader in their personalities and concerns; and, although his work in

life was that of a writer of light fiction, and he used his wit to keep his audiences thoroughly entertained, his real aims and ideals were utilitarian. His great ambition was to better the physical condition of the poor, and to interest the men and women of his generation in such questions as workmen's dwellings, prison reform and relief. In spite of his great kindliness and charming personality, his attitude of mind was always intensely critical, and his portraits of his fellow creatures far from flattering. In fact, when he attempts to idealize, as in the case of such a character as Little Nell, he fails to produce a convincing portrait, and his most lovable characters are full of weaknesses and intensely human. Among significant facts, for the astrological student, are to be noted his failure to find happiness in marriage, and his resentment of criticism.

The average Virginian, instead of mastering detail, allows detail to master him, and if he takes up literature is more likely to succeed as a critic of other men's work than in any field demanding creative power. His style, though concise and clear, is somewhat formal. He will draw up an index or a catalogue, compile a dictionary, or lend a hand in the production of an encyclopedia. Hard work never daunts him, and to express himself with neatness and precision is a real joy; but apart from citicism his pen seldom runs freely, and his letters are usually the driest of the dry.

Louis XIV: Sun in Virgo. (Sculpture by Bernini.)
National Gallery of Art, Washington

Primitive Type. It has been said that the critics are those who have failed, and of these critics the most captious and impossible to please are the undeveloped Virginians. The advanced type, bringing its clear vision and fine discrimination to bear upon the work entrusted to it, sees at a glance all the practical possibilities and opportunities for usefulness involved. The primitive type only sees the impossibilities and the flaws; and it finds them, by preference, in work done or schemes drawn up by others. The developed Virginian never asks for praise; the primitive Virginian never gives it. The former will conquer adverse circumstances, and make his very handicaps contribute to his success. The latter quarrels with every condition imposed upon him, resents his limitations, and blames circumstances for his failures. His ambition to achieve something practical and his inability to do so are apt to result in impatience, nervous irritability, and ill-humor. If hampered by ill-health or in any way restricted in his activities, he takes it cantankerously, meeting all the kindly remonstrances of his friends with a snap and a growl.

He has very little laziness about him, and if he is under wise guidance will be rigidly faithful to orders; but these must be clear and precise, and the reversal of one of them, especially if sudden and unexpected, will upset the Virginian's temper completely, and make him, for the time being, a very disagreeable companion. His horizon is bounded by the circle of his own duties, and by concentrating his attention solely on details he loses sight of the larger outlines and consequently cannot adapt himself to changes which spring from causes beyond his ken. He is apt to make mountains out of mole-hills and is the kind of man who is capable of surveying some masterpieces of art in stony silence and who, before turning away, will point out some trifling error in the darkest corner of the background or some tiny flaw in the construction of the frame. In fact, at his worst, he exercises a most depressing effect upon his fellow creatures.

Virginians who find themselves prone to such habits of thought and speech should cultivate

Paris. The city is considered to be under the influence of Virgo. *Photo: Suschitzky*

138

the appreciative faculties and force themselves to enter kindly and sympathetically into family and social life; otherwise they will develop into machines, spending their days in a dreary round of drudgery, and allowing love and friendship to slip away. Marriage, if resorted to in time, is a remedy, but it is surprising how "old-maidish" these people — men and women alike — can be. The male Virginian allows business to absorb him to such an extent that all outward signs and tokens of his affection tend to disappear; and his wife, becoming convinced of his indifference, looks for sympathy and companionship, and, if at all vain or weak, is tempted to accept the admiration and attentions of others. Women of this type can become so absorbed in house-cleaning that they scarcely lay aside their dusters to give their wearied husbands a kindly welcome home. Consequently they, too, pave the way for rivals.

Physical Characteristics. The Virgo type is associated with a somewhat wiry build, generally strong and muscular, capable of enduring long hours of steady work and much physical fatigue. The expression is always intelligent and sometimes keenly critical. The type at its best is exceedingly handsome. The beauty depends on regularity of feature and fineness of form, and lacks plastic grace, unless one of the softer, more loving elements in the horoscope — Libra, Venus, Pisces, etc. — is strongly emphasized, in which case there is great personal charm, ready repartee, and a sparkling wit. Even at its gentlest this type is always critically alive to the faults and failings of those around it — dearest friends included. Though France is ruled by Leo, the city of Paris is said to be specially under the influence of Virgo. The Parisian is generally handsome, tastefully and suitably dressed, has few illusions and no cherished beliefs; is skeptical, practical, makes an excellent craftsman, and is often exceedingly witty. Leonian tolerance is associated with the life of the gay city; but it is often asserted that the foreign elements of the population are responsible for its reputation, and not the native-born Parisians,

who are usually hard-working, frugal, and temperate. The irritable bachelor uncle of the comic papers is a burlesque of this type, and another is the angular spinster with her sharp speech, dislike of children, and weakness for cats — which animals are traditionally said to be ruled by Virgo.

Photo: Nickolas Muray

D. H. Lawrence: Sun in Virgo

Health. Virgo is an extraordinarily healthy sign and more capable than any other of incessant and unremitting labor. In fact, the chief dangers to health are overwork and absorption in purely practical matters, leading to a certain skeptical and unsympathetic attitude of mind. There is seldom any serious illness. Virginians are inclined to be fastidious and fussy about their food, and especially about its purity and the manner in which it is prepared and served.

SUN IN VIRGO

This gives an innately practical nature, with a highly discriminative individuality. It connects the personality with maternal and family affairs, the home instincts being strongly marked.

Sun in Virgo and Moon in Aries

This combination gives keen mental abilities, and tends to fit those born under it to take the lead in business affairs. The personality is mirthful, witty, active, sharp, impulsive, and quick to foresee, while the solid nature of the solar influence behind it enables the whole combination to work harmoniously. The native is good at debate, argument, and controversy, but is apt to be independent and hence a little difficult to get on with. He tends to be unyielding, and sometimes exaggerates his own importance or abilities.

Sun in Virgo and Moon in Taurus

This combination brings out all the intuitive faculties. It strengthens the scientific or practical ability, gives keen perception, poetic instinct, and some reserve and secretiveness. There will be a tendency to be overcautious. The native is fortunate in business and money matters and is practical, methodical, and persevering. He is a capable employee, or as an executive gets on well with those in his employ. He appears more obstinate than he really is at heart; for though

140

he is not easily influenced by others he often has doubts in his own mind, though he may not admit this.

Sun in Virgo and Moon in Gemini

This combination quickens the intellect and speech. There is general ability, but often loss of opportunity arising from irresolution. The native is fitted for some scientific or professional career, in which intellect is more important than practical business ability. He would do well as reporter, editor, or in any literary capacity, in educational pursuits, or as secretary or agent. He is much concerned with relatives. He displays some reserve and also some lack of enterprise, but has good critical and judicial ability. He will change his occupation, or follow two at once. Friendship and hospitality are marked features in this combination.

William Howard Taft: Sun in Virgo

Mercury with Jupiter, Juno, and Apollo. Vincenzo Pacetti. *Villa Borghese, Rome*

Sun in Virgo and Moon in Cancer

This combination is somewhat over-sensitive. It produces an economical, persevering, and industrious nature, with strong leanings to everything pertaining to family affairs. There is some tendency toward conservatism or sectarianism. There is adaptability and agreeableness, with subtlety of mind and quick appreciation of the motives of other people. If Mercury is prominent, the combination gives a smooth and persuasive tongue and fluent speech. There is more in the native than appears on the surface. Though sometimes reserved he makes acquaintances easily.

Sun in Virgo and Moon in Leo

This combination softens the critical side of the Virgo nature, and stimulates the Leo side. The native is proud of his own accomplishments, and exhibits some love of show and ceremony and a liking for fine clothes. If an author, he displays grandeur of style. There is a keen love of beauty in nature and art, with poetic feeling and a generous, warm-hearted, humanitarian disposition. There will be many love episodes.

Sun and Moon in Virgo

This quickens the whole of the Virgo nature, giving great love of everything of a maternal character, or where relatives and home life are concerned. This combination increases discrimination, independence, self-reliance, and foresight; but there is a tendency to be too self-contained and somewhat self-centered. Although refined and polished, there is also a tendency to be too methodical and precise; but it is a fairly good business polarity, inclining to accuracy in the most minute details. The native is a hard worker, frugal and persevering.

Sun in Virgo and Moon in Libra

This combination gives independence of thought, together with talent for philosophic or scientific writing. It quickens the perceptive faculties of Libra, and gives great ability in all matters where fine judgment and perception

141

Lyndon B. Johnson

Ann Zane Shan

Wide World

Peter Sellers

Greta Garbo

BORN UNDER THE SIGN OF VIRGO

European

Culver

Lauren Bacall

Sophia Loren

Leonard Bernstein

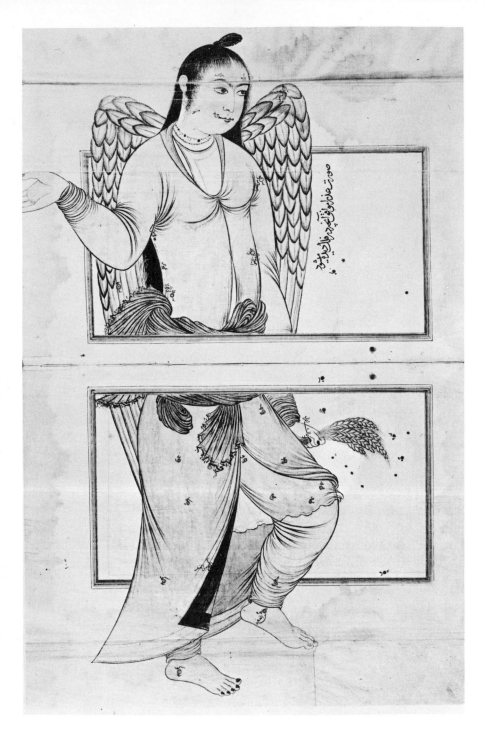

Virgo. Book of Stars and
Constellations. Persian, 1630

are required. It strengthens the intuition, imagination, and ambition, and gives a very clear
mentality. The native, however, is not sufficiently patient, and is liable to change and
fluctuate in opinion. If well educated, he will
have a wide range of reading and be well up
in many subjects. There is some inclination toward travel, and much artistic ability.

Sun in Virgo and Moon in Scorpio

This is a rather selfish combination, inclining
the native to be hard and somewhat careless
of other people's feelings, except members of
his own family or those who minister to his
personal comfort. The sympathies are slight,
jealousy is easily aroused, and there is a ten-

dency to be unforgiving and severe. Criticism and judgment are keenly developed, and this combination is good for all matters connected with industry. The Scorpio persistence of character and self-reliance strengthen the Virgo nature in this respect. This is a fortunate combination for nursing or doctoring.

Sun in Virgo and Moon in Sagittarius

The Moon in Sagittarius tends to make the personality incline toward philosophy. There is a strong desire to teach others. Those born under this combination are suited for occupations connected with religion, learning, science or travel. There is a tendency to be impulsive and to make hasty judgments. Dual tendencies are often found in this sign, such as religious instincts and commercial enterprise, philosophy and love of power. Nevertheless, it is a successful combination, especially where acquisition of wealth is concerned, though the native is rather lacking in persistency.

Sun in Virgo and Moon in Capricorn

This is the most practical of all combinations. While there is much independence, and a tendency to lean toward materialistic and selfish lines of thought, there is splendid ability and a desire to accumulate wealth in either the professional or business world. This combination produces shrewdness and a calculating mind. It is good for government occupations, or those connected with public authorities, all official appointments, managerships, and also for stockbrokers. The mind is serious and somewhat gloomy at times, but determined, and the memory is often very retentive.

Sun in Virgo and Moon in Aquarius

This combination intensifies the intuitive faculties and quickens impressions. It often acts along practical lines and gives ability for business pursuits, especially in trading with large companies. The discriminative faculties are well developed, and there is much ability to judge human nature. The native has an original mind, is ingenious and inventive. He has opinions to which he adheres, and is not easily persuaded differently. He is fond of the company of a few, is fortunate in his friends and acquaintances but is apt to be despondent at times. He is unconventional, yet is sometimes lacking in enterprise and self-assertion.

Sun in Virgo and Moon in Pisces

This combination makes the personality restless with a great love of change and novelty. There is apt to be much dissatisfaction, some irritability, and lack of self-reliance. The native makes a good employee; he is a good worker, very correct in details, although lazy at times. He is sympathetic and charitable, and receives sympathy and charity from others. With a bad horoscope the native is liable not to be straightforward, or suffers from this in others. He often follows obscure occupations. A hospitable nature is always displayed.

FAMOUS PEOPLE BORN WITH THE SUN IN VIRGO

Savonarola:	September 21, 1452
Queen Elizabeth I:	September 7, 1533
Cardinal Richelieu:	September 9, 1585
Goethe:	August 28, 1749
Lafayette:	September 6, 1757
William Howard Taft:	September 15, 1857
Maurice Chevalier:	September 12, 1888
John Gunther:	August 30, 1901
Greta Garbo:	September 18, 1905
Lyndon B. Johnson:	August 27, 1908
Ingrid Bergman:	August 29, 1917
Leonard Bernstein:	August 25, 1918
Lauren Bacall:	September 16, 1924
Peter Sellers:	September 8, 1925
Sophia Loren:	September 20, 1934

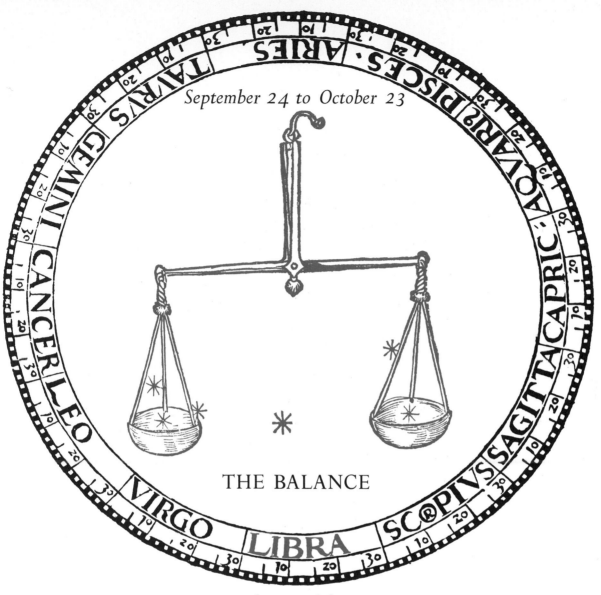

September 24 to October 23

THE BALANCE

The sign of the
Statesman or Manager

A cardinal airy sign
Alert, just, artistic, painstaking, honorable,
well balanced, affectionate, sympathetic

Ruler: Venus

Gems: diamond, opal

Color: indigo blue
Metal: copper

Harmonious signs for business, marriage, or
companionship: Aquarius, Gemini

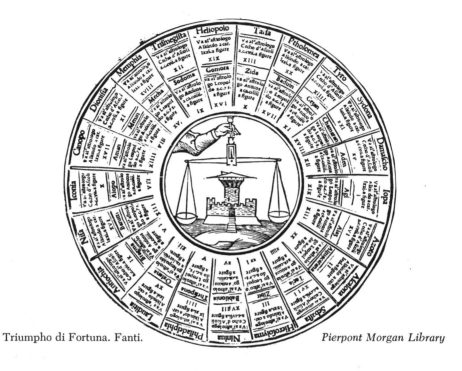

Triumpho di Fortuna. Fanti.   *Pierpont Morgan Library*

The Libran Type

Evolved Type. The Libran's strength lies in his power of concentration, his intensity of application, and his capacity for sustained effort. He works in splendid spurts, followed by periods of complete relaxation, during which he usually declines to use any of his faculties whatever unless urgently required to do so. He feels perfectly satisfied lounging in an armchair and smoking a cigarette; and when he has rested long enough, and no longer, he rises and goes at his task again with the same indomitable energy as before. That is the normal, healthy, average man, and if he is succeeding in life he is generally in one way or another a specialist.

A woman who has accepted the profession of wife and mother dares not allow herself to specialize in anything. If she has a hobby dear to her heart, she must renounce it — at any rate until her children are old enough to look after themselves. She must be alert and alive and resourceful and ready for every emergency all day long; turning herself quickly and adroitly from one thing to another. She must exercise endless tact and diplomacy, keep her temper, never show impatience or irritation, and welcome her husband at the end of the day with a bright smile and loving word. After the children have gone to bed, she is expected to be his sympathetic and responsive companion. It is the kind of life that would kill a man or drive him crazy in six months; but the weaker sex will keep it up bravely for twelve or fifteen years without a break, and keep sane. The power that gives her most assistance in her task is the

148

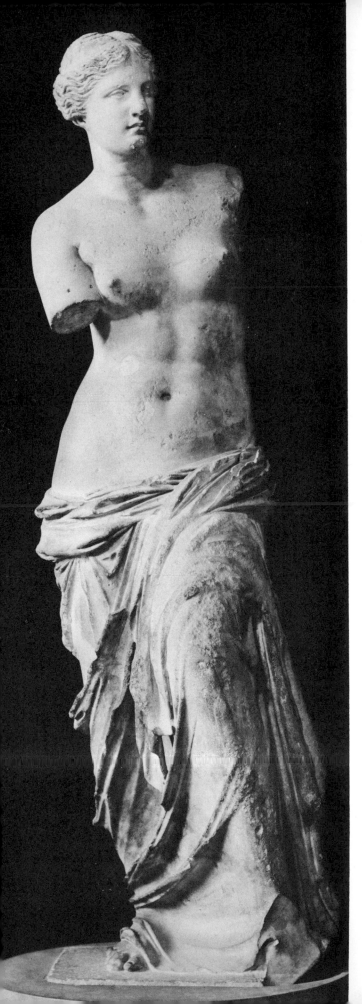

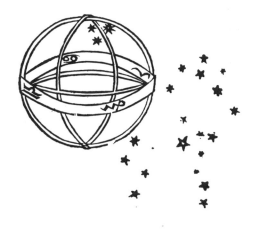

Venus de Milo. *Louvre*

Venus. Florentine engraving, 15th century

power associated with Libra and the planet Venus. Loving and beloved, the natives can fill their days with what are called the little things of life, that is to say with constant petty items of self-sacrifice of the kind that no one notices — and they can do it cheerfully.

Librans are as many-sided as Leonians, and sometimes share their difficulty in choosing a profession, often making a false start, and then changing; but they do not have the Leonian tendency to depute their duties to others, however competent. In most cases their desire for perfection makes them exceedingly painstaking and patient, and particularly careful about detail; so that they rarely have to undo anything they have done; there is rarely anything meretricious, showy, or slapdash in their methods; they are immensely popular with both men and women, for, owing to their gentle manners, courtesy, and genuine appreciation of what is admirable in others, they have very few enemies. They are scrupulously honorable in money matters, and do well in spheres in which ready tact, social charm, or all-round ability tell.

The innate strength of this type consists in a certain sane, wholesome, and well-balanced element that runs through their whole nature. These people hate injustice and unfairness and everything ill-proportioned and ugly in life, and also dislike exaggeration and all feelings that are morbid, depressing, hysterical, or strained. Their normal and natural form of expression is art and music in all its forms. Vocal music especially is a rest and refreshment to them — their relaxation when they are wearied, their remedy when they are sick or sad.

Religion. The keynote to the religious life of the Libran is harmony. There must be no harsh notes, no discordant element in his worship. The wrangling of the theologians, the petty persecutions of one sect by another, the bickerings and jealousies and narrownesses too often associated with religious observances have turned many people of this type away in disgust; for if they cannot find beauty and concord they will content themselves with striving after

Harris & Ewin

Eleanor Roosevelt: Sun in Libra

beauty of life, and leave rites and ceremonies alone. They tend to live a good deal in the present, letting the past bury its dead, and are seldom inclined to worry over the slowness of their progress or their probable fate in the future.

When a man is known to be dying, the Libran has no thought of reminding him of past misdeeds, failures, and mistakes. The important thing is to cheer him up and make him realize how much progress he has made, and how much he — and his friends through him — have to be thankful for. The church especially seems to attract this type into its ministry. In such a post the Libran will give every satisfaction. His eloquence will be gently persuasive, his homilies carefully considered and neatly rounded, sometimes perhaps tending to truism, platitude, and mild pedantry, but free from all startling eccentricities.

150

Love and Friendship. To the typical Libran, love affairs are naturally among the most important events in life, and even in old age the subject never loses its interest. The well-developed Libran chooses his mate early, marries as soon as he can afford to do so, and makes an excellent husband, tender, affectionate, and very easy to live with. The only danger he runs is that of a too youthful engagement, for love-making comes easy to him, and is generally crowned with success. He may consequently be tempted to propose to the first pretty girl who

to hurt anyone's feelings, so finds it almost impossible to say a decided no, and sometimes needs to have it pointed out that too much hesitation on that point is only prolonging the agony, and is consequently a very mistaken form of kindness. She makes the ideal wife, her whole being revolving round her husband, whom she sometimes idolizes to such an extent that the children come in a bad second; for this sign, though intensely conjugal, is not particularly maternal. When children arrive, nature asserts itself, and they are tenderly cared for;

United Features Syndicate

Charlie Brown: Sun in Libra

Dwight D. Eisenhower: Sun in Libra

smiles at him, and live to regret it; but his innate refinement and somewhat fastidious taste will probably save him.

His sister Libran runs the same dangers, and shares the same protections. She is generally immensely popular with the opposite sex, because of her gentle uncritical attitude and frank admiration for the manly qualities. She hates

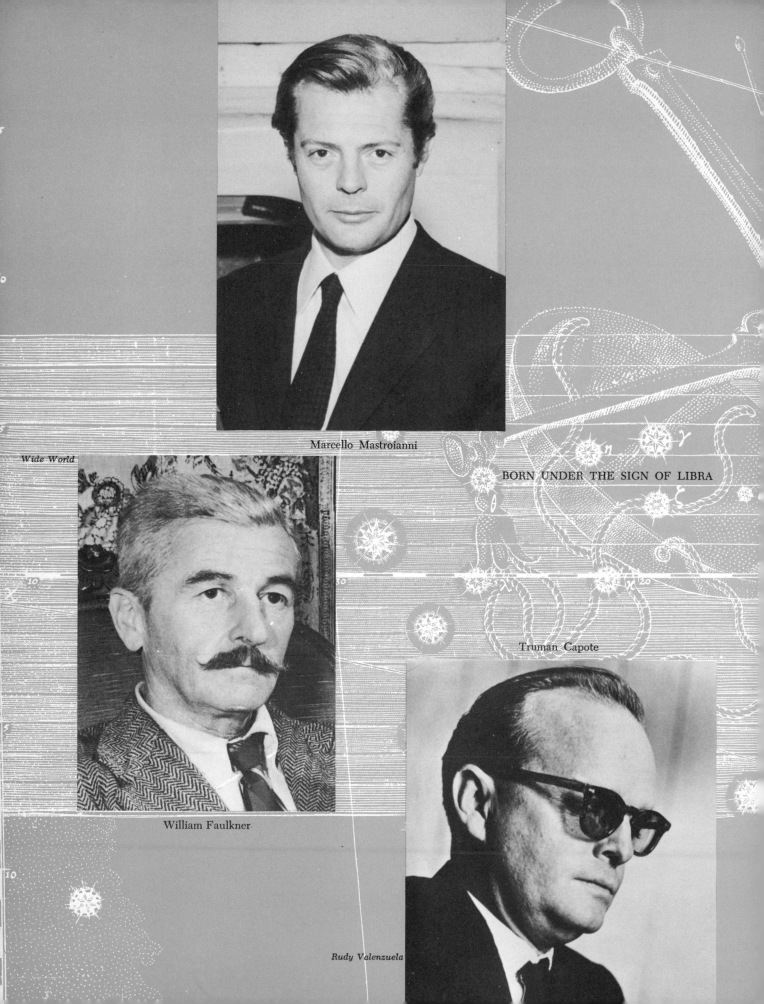

Marcello Mastroianni

BORN UNDER THE SIGN OF LIBRA

Truman Capote

William Faulkner

Rudy Valenzuela

Deborah Kerr

Julie Andrews

John Lennon

Venus

but the husband distinctly plays lead. The impulse that makes a woman seek her mate, turning from all thoughts of pride and self-sufficiency and craving for the qualities which she can only find fully developed in the opposite sex, is a

beautiful impulse, complete in itself, grounded on true humility, and requiring no excuse or justification whatever.

Primitive Type. People with Venus against them in their horoscope are handicapped instead of helped in their career by their all-round tendencies, and primitive Librans suffer in this way to such an extent that their parents and guardians are sometimes in despair over their start in life. Their partiality for equal development is apt to make dabblers of them, and they take up one thing after another, to throw it aside in favor of something else. The rudimentary desire for perfection has also its drawbacks, making them potter and trifle over their work, wasting time in weighing straws and splitting hairs; and they are apt to become confused and bewildered if they are asked to make a decision or hurry up. Sometimes they will prevaricate and temporize, and hedge in the most annoying way when a straightforward and energetic policy is called for. Tact and diplomacy run to seed are uncommonly like insincerity and moral cowardice.

This tendency to trifle is naturally carried throughout, and is specially noticeable in the sphere of the affections. The natural impulse to seek the mate develops early, and is translated by these people into a tendency to regard every second member of the opposite sex they come across as the not impossible he, or she. They never break their hearts about anyone, for their memories are short; but there are frequent sprains and bruises, and a great deal of wasted energy. The gentleness of the men is apt to make them soft and weak with women, and if they remain long unmarried, or are absent from home for any lengthy period, they may drift into the unmanly position of playing tame cat to the first energetic and unscrupulous woman who is willing to take trouble enough to annex them.

For women under this sign the peril is naturally graver, for, though the power to appreciate what is good and beautiful in others is a great gift, absence of the critical faculty is often a handicap. To be easily pleased and to please as easily; to be born attractive, and with a craving for everything that is fair and lovely in life and a dislike of all that is ugly and sordid and mean; to be gentle, yielding, good-tempered, and incapable of saying no; to live habitually in the present and for the present, caring little for past ties and less for the possibilities hidden in the future — these can, in certain circumstances, be dangers indeed. Their very guilelessness and innocence are the Libran's worst enemies.

Physical Characteristics and Health. An old writer describes those born under Venus as "having a love dimple in the chin, a lovely mouth, cherry lips, and a right merrie countenance." The whole personality projects an atmosphere of kindliness and contentment. The type appears well-nourished and is inclined to plumpness, dimples, curves, and rounded contours generally, though not to excessive fat. They have often a sweet voice, a bright ringing laugh, and are intensely appreciative of fun in others. In fact, they are so charming that it is difficult to suggest a caricature of the type. Browning's poem, "A Fair Woman," touches delicately upon Libran weaknesses, and Shakespeare's picture of Cressida — so sweet and lovable and responsive, so hopelessly incapable of lasting love and loyalty — is a graver and more bitter description of the type.

Librans have a natural instinct for health and sanity, and by keeping the balance true generally manage to avoid serious breakdowns of any kind. But if circumstances push them too far in the direction of concentrated specialization, or if they give way to excessive emotion, and especially if their sense of justice and fair play is outraged in any way, the constitution will suffer. When below par in any way, Librans will find their best remedy in rest, careful diet, and development of the appreciative faculties connected with all that is best and most beautiful in music, poetry, or art — especially in music.

Brigitte Bardot: Sun in Libra

SUN IN LIBRA

This produces a harmonious individuality, with a tendency to act through perception more than through reflection. There is a keen love of justice and great power of comparison. There is also sensitiveness, with ambitions on intellectual lines.

Sun in Libra and Moon in Aries

Reason and perception are well blended in

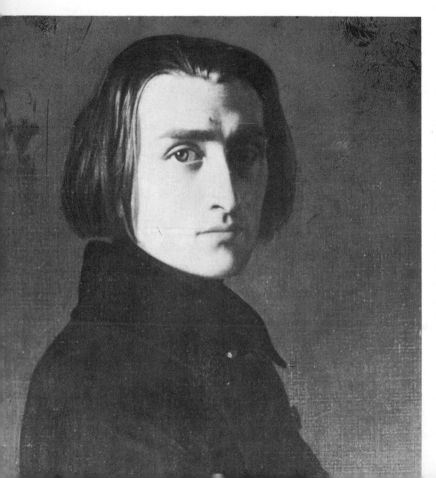

this combination, and there should be a great amount of refinement, and mental ability. The personality is active, the individuality quiet. The will power is fairly strong, making the native active, independent, and at times aggressive on the surface. At heart he is quiet, harmonious, and affectionate. He is fond of change, quick to appreciate new ideas, possibly impatient at times, and lacking in perseverance. An inharmonious marriage is probable, few being able to respond to the ideals of this combination. There is much power and influence over others. This combination is good for all who love athletics.

Sun in Libra and Moon in Taurus

The Venus nature is well harmonized in this sign. Perseverance, endurance, patience, and caution are manifested. There is inventive ability, but the personality is apt to be somewhat too receptive to physical surroundings and conditions. The combination suggests gain through partnerships or marriage, and is usually fortunate for money, friends, and popularity. There may be aptitude for music or acting. Practical ability is shown in the domestic sphere, together with the ability to remain happily married.

Sun in Libra and Moon in Gemini

This harmonious combination gives refinement, artistic taste, and some oratorical ability. It also gives a great love of knowledge and intensifies intellectual aspirations. The natives easily adapt to different occupations, conditions, or careers in life, their nature varying with the influence of the ascendant or rising sign. If the latter tends to domesticity, there will be much affection, emotion, and faithfulness; if to study or intellectual pursuits, there will be ability in this direction. The native lives harmoniously with the family, is observant, versatile, and has many interests. Some indecision may be displayed, and a want of stability, but this may easily be overcome. Thought and feeling are well combined, and this gives great influence over others, especially through speech.

Franz Liszt: Sun in Libra. (Portrait by Henry Lehmann.)
Bettmann Archive

Sun in Libra and Moon in Cancer

This combination intensifies sensitiveness and the emotional nature; it inclines to anxiety, especally in home affairs. It also produces changeableness, but with a desire for progress. To some extent this is a contradictory combination, for there is a sympathetic domesticated disposition, yet at the same time a good deal of ability for a public life. The outer nature will be quite different from the inner; and this polarity varies a great deal with the strongest planet. Attraction to family and relatives is marked.

Culver

Sarah Bernhardt: Sun in Libra

Sun in Libra and Moon in Leo

This combination brings the character and personality into harmony. It gives a strong inclination toward spiritual things, and sometimes makes the nature rather too idealistic. The feelings and impulses are strong; there is an intense love of beauty, and great enthusiasm in pursuit of an ideal. The native is popular, has many friends, and is hopeful, sociable, and generous.

The love nature is intense and sincere. It is difficult for such a person to remain single, so that he or she is apt to marry too much in haste. There is poetic and musical ability, and either the artistic or moral nature will have many opportunities for development.

Sun in Libra and Moon in Virgo

This combination gives a critical personality. It tends to lead the mind into practical matters, giving intuition in business affairs. It is a refined combination and produces an attractive personality. There is good general mental ability with, in some cases, special aptitude in some one direction (determined by the ascendant, or the strongest planet). The native is companionable, but sometimes lacking in determination or strength of will.

The Concert. Israhel W. Mackenem, 15th-century print

Sun and Moon in Libra

Although this combination gives a clear perception, there is apt to be too much reliance upon others, and an inability to move forward spontaneously. The character is affable, courteous, obliging, and well-disposed. There are foresight and mental sensitiveness, coupled with humanitarian views and a desire to do good. These are, however, often spoiled by a self-centering inclination that makes ideals hard to achieve. The fate of the native will be influenced largely by other people, through marriage, partnership, or general association. At its best, this polarity may produce a harmonious mind, hopeful, and practical along its own lines. Such people are popular and contented, artistic or musical, with an ardent love of beauty.

Sun in Libra and Moon in Scorpio

Love of approbation and an ambitious nature are characteristic under this combination. The native is fully aware of his own abilities and is inclined to be aggressive. Outwardly he may be positive, matter-of-fact, worldly, hard, and sometimes a little coarse, but when intimately known he will seem much more genial and yielding. When the personality has the greater power, energy, industry, and ambition are displayed. With favorable planetary positions the native may be very practical and make a good executive.

Sun in Libra and Moon in Sagittarius

This is a good combination, although the personality is inclined at times to be rather reckless and careless, over-active and excitable. It intensifies the activity of the brain and increases the rapidity of speech. This combination gives ability for public speaking, and brings success in other pursuits. The native has a fruitful, imaginative, well-stored mind, and his abilities in connection with religion or law are specially marked. Social and benevolent, of good disposition, he will be a universal favorite.

Sun in Libra and Moon in Capricorn

This influence usually produces some musical ability, and inclines the native to neatness and orderliness of mind. It gives some amount of caution, prudence, worldly wisdom, and sometimes selfishness. This latter shows mainly in the lower type of character, in a higher type it appears as self-control. The emotions and impulses are disciplined and well regulated. The combination is favorable for popularity and public recognition. Ambitions will be achieved, and there will be considerable prominence in some sphere, but there is danger of reversal. There is likely to be some misfortune or disharmony connected with the parents.

Sun in Libra and Moon in Aquarius

This harmonious combination gives splendid foresight, especially in matters connected with humanitarian principles, large businesses, and associations; also the ability to judge human nature. The disposition is kind, gentle, and humane; sometimes too unresisting, though never where principles are at stake. The mind is original and inventive, and the memory is usually good. The nature is reserved and controlled, yet sociable and friendly.

Sun in Libra and Moon in Pisces

There is a great deal of restlessness in this combination, together with some industry and perseverance. There is apt to be a tendency to dream rather than to be practical. When the mind is busily occupied, the nature is improved.

The disposition is sociable and affectionate, charitable and humanitarian; but it will be lacking in strength unless this is supplied by the ascendant or other planets in the horoscope.

FAMOUS PEOPLE BORN WITH THE SUN IN LIBRA

Franz Liszt:	October 22, 1811
Nietzsche:	October 15, 1844
Sarah Bernhardt:	October 22, 1845
Eleanor Roosevelt:	October 11, 1884
T. S. Eliot:	September 26, 1888
Dwight D. Eisenhower:	October 14, 1890
William Faulkner:	September 25, 1897
George Gershwin:	September 26, 1898
Helen Hayes:	October 10, 1900
Graham Greene:	October 2, 1904
Michelangelo Antonioni:	September 29, 1912
Deborah Kerr:	September 30, 1921
Marcello Mastroianni:	September 28, 1924
Truman Capote:	September 30, 1924
Mickey Mantle:	October 20, 1931
Brigitte Bardot:	September 28, 1935
Julie Andrews:	October 1, 1935
John Lennon:	October 9, 1940
Charlie Brown:	October 1

Mickey Mantle: Sun in Libra

October 24 to November 22

THE SCORPION

The sign of the
Governor or Inspector

A fixed watery sign
Energetic, independent, passionate, determined, with strong likes and dislikes

Ruler: Mars

Gems: topaz, malachite

Color: deep red
Metal: steel

Harmonious signs for business, marriage, or
companionship: Cancer, Pisces

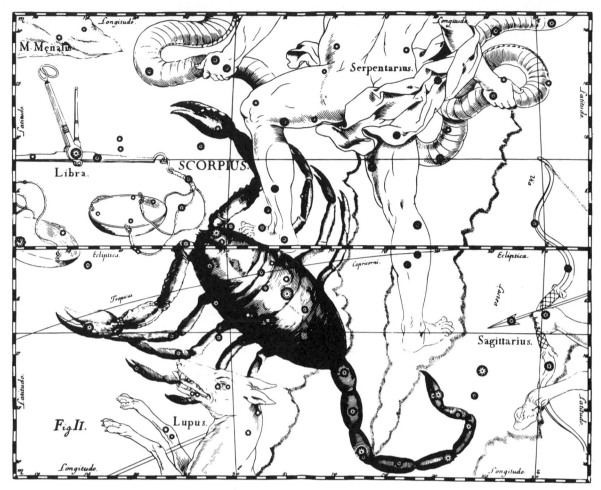

Hevelius, 1690

The Scorpionian Type

Evolved Type. The kingdom of Scorpio is a kingdom of power. His highest achievement is the manifestation of that power in the most gigantic of tasks — absolute self-mastery. The destruction of egotism, the domination of desire, the abolition of everything that can retard his moral, mental, and physical regeneration; the attainment of complete control over the will, intellect, passions, emotions, bodily activities, and psychic faculties — these are, or ought to be, his ambitions, and very frequently, in spite of false starts, failures, and shortcomings, he makes considerable progress on the way to realizing them. Further, he not only desires rapid progress for himself, but craves it also for others, and gives freely of his own magnificent vitality

to hasten their development. It is this characteristic that draws so many of this sign into the medical profession, and makes astrologers refer to it as pre-eminently the physician's sign.

When the ideal doctor — who may stand very well for the ideal Scorpionian — enters the sickroom, the first impression he gives is that of power, a quiet, resolute strength and a capacity and determination to overcome suffering, disease, and death. Such a man can impress his will on the most fractious and rebellious of patients.

Scorpionians are generally more or less psychic, but often fail to realize it. They make such exceptionally good use of their sense perceptions that they attribute their achievements in rapid diagnosis and other kinds of detective

Alessandro Temini, 17th-century engraving

GOLA   OTTOBRE   SCORPIONE

Vn Vitio ch'à principio, ha fine ancora;	Anch'io d'Ambrosie, e Nettari, e di creta,	Biforcate hò le mani, adunche, e nere
Sol io mai non finisco, e mai mi stanco:	D'Alicante, di Lachrime e claretti;	Et hò la parte estrema assai pungente:
Mi conformo à ogni etade, e mai nõ manco,	Di Chianti, Albani, Asprini, e Grechi, eletti,	Si guardi ogn'un dal mio rabbioso dente,
D'eccitar appetiti, ardenti ogn'hora.	Abbondo sempre rubiconda, e lieta.	Che uccide, ò auuelena, ò impiaga, ò fere.

Bettmann

Marie Antoinette: Sun in Scorpio

work entirely to quickness and accuracy of observation, in which they know that they excel over the majority of men. As a rule, too, their psychism is of a healthy and normal type, and allows its possessors to sense their finer impressions intuitively and without effort, rarely disturbing them by disconcerting and incomprehensible glimpses into the unseen world. Doctors who feel inclined to disclaim such powers should ask themselves candidly how often they have diagnosed a difficult case correctly before definite and recognizable symptoms have appeared, or how often they have had premonitions of a sudden summons to cases which, as far as outward knowledge went, seemed independent of their aid; or even been impelled to go to them just in the very nick of time.

Besides striving to conquer death and disease, Scorpionians find intense satisfaction in dominating the forces of nature — for the benefit of mankind. They excel as practical engineers, and long before they have learned to show patience and forbearance, will display these qualities to an admirable extent when called upon to deal with a refractory piece of machinery. Though rarely quite original in their work, they are clever in utilizing other people's ideas of a more daringly inventive turn, apparently finding stimulus and inspiration in the very difficulties that had checkmated their predecessors. Anything that calls for strenuous effort, heroic endurance, and the breaking down of opposition and obstacles is congenial to them. Their analytical methods and power of criticism stand them in good stead in many walks of life, and some do brilliantly at the bar, usually making their way to the front by their success in dealing with criminal cases.

The intense virility of this type naturally makes it somewhat difficult for women born under it to accept the limitations and restrictions imposed by their sex, and most of them regret that they were not born men. The female native has an intense and very natural scorn for the type of woman who shirks matrimony and motherhood, and if cut off from these possibilities herself is often at a loss as to how to employ her energies, for her desire to dominate cannot be altogether held in check.

The power of concentrating on whatever work is taken up makes Scorpionian women the best housekeepers and cooks of all. Every corner in their domain is kept spotless. Dinners are served to the minute, piping hot, and nothing is ever presented burned, or underdone, or otherwise spoiled by careless cookery. Their spring cleaning is their annual holiday. The harder the task, the more these people seem to rise to it.

Love and Friendship. In love and friendship Scorpionians tend to be intense and distinctly exclusive, and are prone to sudden and strong antipathies and likings. They despise gush and sentimentality, dislike demonstration of all kinds, and often find much difficulty in expressing their inner thoughts and feelings even when they desire to do so — which is rarely, for they are taciturn and laconic by nature, and exceedingly reserved. When deeply moved, however, their feelings find utterance, and they are then apt to say more than the occasion might warrant;

The **Universe Book Club** *is proud to offer*

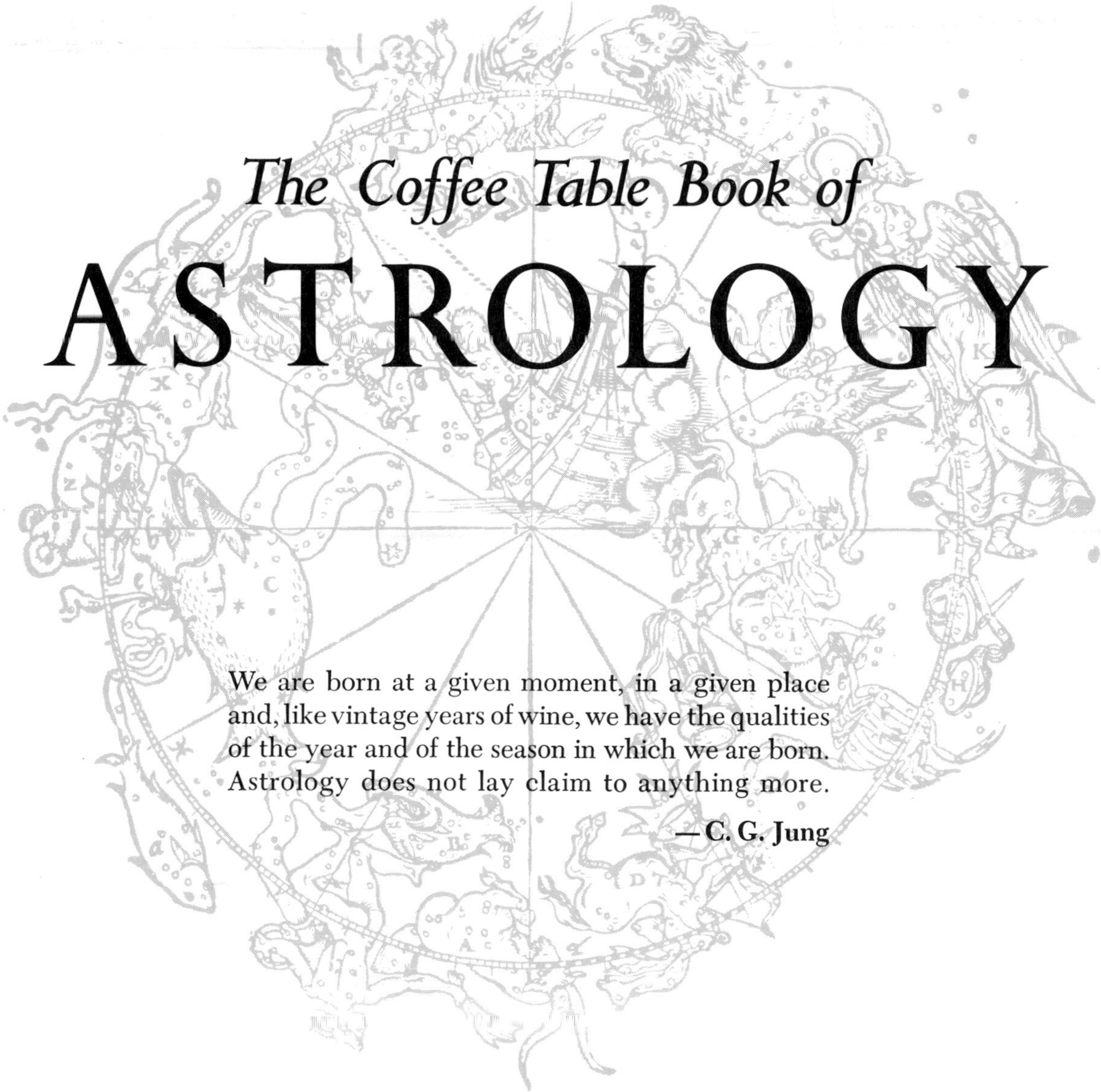

The Coffee Table Book of

ASTROLOGY

We are born at a given moment, in a given place
and, like vintage years of wine, we have the qualities
of the year and of the season in which we are born.
Astrology does not lay claim to anything more.

—C. G. Jung

*A unique, beautifully illustrated collector's volume which
presents some of the most famous and lucid writings on the
absorbing, far-reaching subject of astrology*

March 21 through April 20
THE RAM

April 21 through May 21
THE BULL

May 22 to June 21
THE TWINS

June 22 to July 22
THE CRAB

A LUXURI
fascinati

CLARK GABLE— Sun in Aquarius

BOB DYLAN—Sun in Gemini

ELIZABETH TAYLOR—Sun in Pisces

JULIE ANDREWS—Sun in Libra

LEONARD BERNSTEIN—Sun in Virgo

JOHN F. KENNEDY—Su

HUMPHREY BOGART—Sun in Capricorn

MICHAEL CAINE—Sun in Aries

"The horoscopes show on
fully responsible for his
of overcoming his weak.

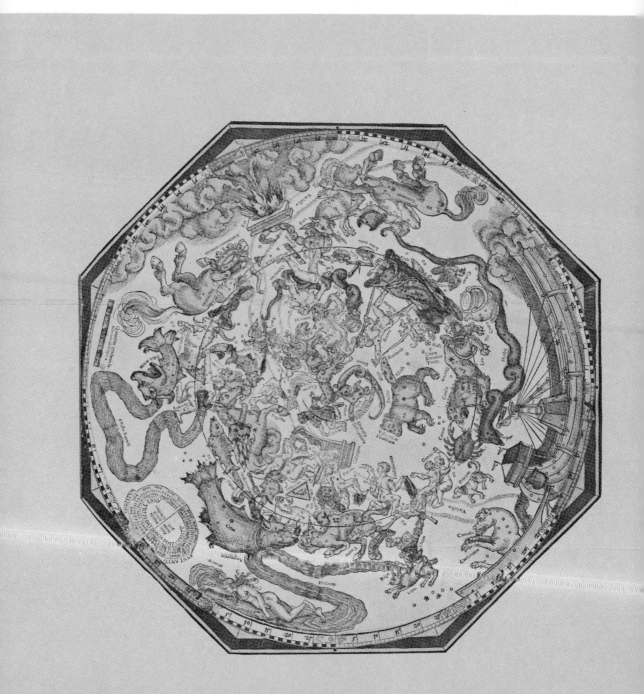

THE ARCHER
November 23 to December 21

THE GOAT
December 22 to January 20

THE WATER-BEARER
January 21 to February 19

THE FISH
February 20 to March 20

...UME MEASURES A FULL
8¼″ by 10½″

Publisher's Edition $8.95

**MEMBERS'
EDITION $4.95**

...he color illustration shown here full-size is from
...e 15th-century illuminated prayer book, *Les Trés
...iches Heures du Duc de Berry*, now in the Musée
...ondé at Chantilly in France. It is an example of
...ne fine and rare artwork reproduced in *The Coffee
...able Book of Astrology.*

uman tendencies, which means that man is

s and through self-knowledge is capable

ses and achieving his highest aims."

WHEN things seem beyond your control, do you wonder how much the fault lies not in "ourselves" but "in our stars"? How do you explain away those painful periods when nothing but catastrophe strikes your financial or romantic life? Or those eerie days when a series of long-lost friends reappears out of the blue? When two children are born and raised under the same roof, why is one the teacher's favorite and the other a dunce?

Is it merely coincidence that ballet dancers Nijinsky and Nureyev are both Piscarians...that Richard Burton and Elizabeth Taylor have harmonious signs for marriage (he Scorpio, she Pisces), that many of the most seductive actresses of the last few decades were born under the sign of Virgo (Greta Garbo, Ingrid Bergman, Lauren Bacall, Sophia Loren), that a positively unnatural number of writers are Librans and that Aquarians practically monopolize scientific conventions?

For 5,000 years astrology has given answers to the vexing existential questions that plague men. It has been used, abused, exploited by charlatans, condemned as nonsense, hailed as a science, accepted as a religion. In the present century noted men such as Einstein, Spengler and the Nobel Prize Winner Dr. Carl Gustave Jung have admitted that there is a great deal to it as a science.

Yet, whether or not *you* are a firm believer, "The Coffee Table Book of Astrology" offers you hours of enjoyment. The superb illustrations, many of which have been carefully reproduced from museum collections, alone are worth several times the price of this magnificent volume. And the selected texts will continually lead to startling observations—some are likely to give even the most skeptical among us serious pause for thought. After all, you could be delving into the mystery of the stars...finding out what you are and what you *could* be.

Publisher's Edition $8.95 • **MEMBERS' EDITION $4.95**

THE LION — July 23 to August 23
THE VIRGIN — August 24 to September 23
THE BALANCE — September 24 to October 23
THE SCORPION — October 24 to November 22

IOUS BOOK

ng to read, to own, to share!

TODAY, when the science of astrology has become so popularly accepted—and books dealing with this science are being published by the hundreds—it is surprising how difficult it is to find an astrology book addressed to the intelligent reader with relevant, handsome illustrations *and* excellent text. This month's selection, *The Coffee Table Book of Astrology,* is that one-of-a-kind volume…and the Universe Book Club is truly proud to be able to offer it to you.

For this book is not only one of the largest, most attractive astrology books ever published, it is also a lucidly written, documented work covering a wide scope rarely achieved until now. Here is offered the classic writings of Isabelle Pagan which form the basis for the twelve zodiac signs and brilliant analyses of the basic character and personality traits —*both good and bad*—for each sign…and Alan Leo's sober research for further qualifications according to the position of the moon at the hour of one's birth. With these famous, respected writers you can delve into the mystery of the stars and seek out what makes you what you are and could be. You may also learn to account for the exaggerated reasoning of your admirers, decipher the odd characteristics of your enemies, and, at least in some degree, find answers to the otherwise inexplicable course of human events.

Among the many features of this collector's work are Santha Rama Rau's intriguing "Written in the Stars"; the notations of Shakespeare's artistic use of astrology by Johnstone Parr; Zoltan Mason's learned essay on astrology in relation to religion; and excellent instructions by Norah Wydenbruck on how to cast a horoscope…plus hundreds of drawings and paintings related to astrology, valuable up-to-date charts and tables, and the birth dates of great persons who were born under each sign. (Discover what traits you have in common with them!)

in Gemini

for the Scorpion has a sting to its tail. Sometimes, though more or less tongue-tied, they have their pens well under control, and write delightful letters — terse, pungent, and abounding in detail and humor.

Scorpionians — especially the women — are not easily mated, and are apt to prove exacting and

Marie Curie: Sun in Scorpio

quite difficult to live with. Strong and efficient themselves, it is almost impossible for them to make full allowance for the shortcomings of others, or to understand why natures, dispositions, temperaments, and ideals should differ so widely. Geminians are especially trying to their nerves. They mate best among themselves, or with Cancerians, who resemble them in intensity and excel them in sympathy and imagination; for in spite of their passionate tendencies Scorpionians can be unrelentingly stern, especially where principle is involved. They are in little danger of wrecking their lives through rash

engagements or hasty and ill-considered marriages; and though their personal magnetism may attract many, especially those of weak or vacillating character, they will probably find no difficulty in administering a rebuff which, in such cases, may be the truest kindness. They very often recognize the future husband or wife at first sight and seldom waver in the matter, though they rarely confide their hopes or intentions to friends or relatives until everything is practically arranged.

Religion. The great masters and founders of religion have been healers, and in early times the offices of priest and physician were one. It is often an eminently devout impulse that carries the Scorpionian into the medical profession. He is seldom an irreligious man, though his uncompromising tendency may make him shock orthodoxy by claiming to be considered so. Further, though he often abandons his childhood faith, he rarely gets quite out of touch with ideas impressed upon him by the teachers and thinkers he reverenced most during the period of his early manhood, and in later years will surprise the younger generation by the extraordinary rigidity of his beliefs. His chief demand upon dogma is that there should be no sickly sentimentality about it. He prefers it to be bracing and virile in quality.

Dr. Jonas Salk: Sun in Scorpio

Literary Style and Religion. The list of Scorpionians who have distinguished themselves in literature is long, and their "hallmark" is strength and virility of style. One of their characteristics is courage in tackling difficult subjects.

Goethe, Milton, and Victor Hugo (born respectively with the Sun in Virgo, Sagittarius, and Pisces) are three of the intellectual giants born with Scorpio rising. Martin Luther, a great "destroyer and regenerator," was strongly under Scorpio's influence, his horoscope showing it

Kalendar. Johann Stöffler, 1518

strikingly emphasized by the Sun, Mars, Jupiter, Mercury, and Saturn — all in the ninth house, suggesting religion. Goethe has recorded his exact hour — noon — on the authority of his father; so we know that the 17th degree of Scorpio was rising. Milton was born "between six and seven in the morning." Our choice here consequently lies between Scorpio and Sagittarius, and although his biographer thinks that the "half an hour after six" mentioned by our contemporary is "probably correct," the astrologer is impelled to place the event some minutes earlier; for no gleam of true Sagittarian sunshine brightens Milton's personality. The prevailing tone, the characteristic mood and disposition of Milton's mind, even in early youth, consisted, we are told, in a deep and habitual seriousness. His striking qualities were austerity, self-command, and a stoic scorn of temptation. In his earliest poems he chose death for his theme, and he took little part in the amusements of his

166

college companions. The treatment of his chosen theme, *Paradise Lost*, is in the true Scorpionian vein. He gives to Lucifer — the real hero of the poem — a regal dignity and a tragic beauty, and his oft-quoted exclamation, "Better to reign in Hell than serve in Heaven," is echoed by many a son of this sign.

Martin Luther, in his efforts to reform the Church, swept away the doctrine of purgatory — leaving the trembling soul to chose between the immediate bliss of heaven or the horrors of hell; and implying that the vast majority would be doomed to the latter. Goethe takes his hero through sin and suffering to regions of the blessed, and in his case also it is the earlier passages of his poem that are most eagerly and frequently read. Mephistopheles is a more living and quite as famous a creation as Faust himself, and one of the poet's best-known utterances is of the very essence of Scorpionian philosophy, *"Entbehren sollst du; sollst entbehren"* — a line in which the poet tells us that in this world we must do without — and endure.

Martin Luther: Sun in Scorpio.
(After the painting by Holbein.)

stronger than other men's; his courage never fails him, and his will is iron. If he fails to find his way to self-mastery, he may make havoc of his life, developing into the reckless gambler, the insatiable drinker. Apart from the type of Scorpionian sketched above, we find many who are undeniably on the straight road, and yet have a heavier burden of aggressive and unlovable faults to struggle against. It is practically impossible for them to take the second place graciously and contentedly, and their vigilant

It always requires some effort to turn from the pleasant duty of dwelling on the fine qualities of a sign to the ungracious labor of cataloging its weaknesses and defects. All the signs in turn, and often several at once, bring their various forces to bear upon us, so that no one can really congratulate himself on being free from the special failings attributed to any particular one. Whatever we possess in the way of self-control and moral backbone — of ability to stand on our own feet and exercise our own will — we owe to the power of Scorpio manifesting in us.

Primitive Type. This type never wavers or wobbles, and whatsoever the Scorpionian's hand finds to do is done with energy and might. Therefore, when he is bad he is thoroughly bad. Experiences which arouse in other types feelings of mild discontent or half-formed dislike, awaken in his breast anger and resentment, fierce rebellion, jealousy, and hate. His passions are

outlook makes them abnormally and disagreeably quick in detecting the backslidings of their fellow creatures. To discover that others are weaker, more forgetful, or more self-indulgent than themselves feeds their self-esteem, and they hail the exposure of failure or lapse with evi-

167

Pablo Picasso

Grace Kelly

Katharine Hepburn

Photos: Wide World

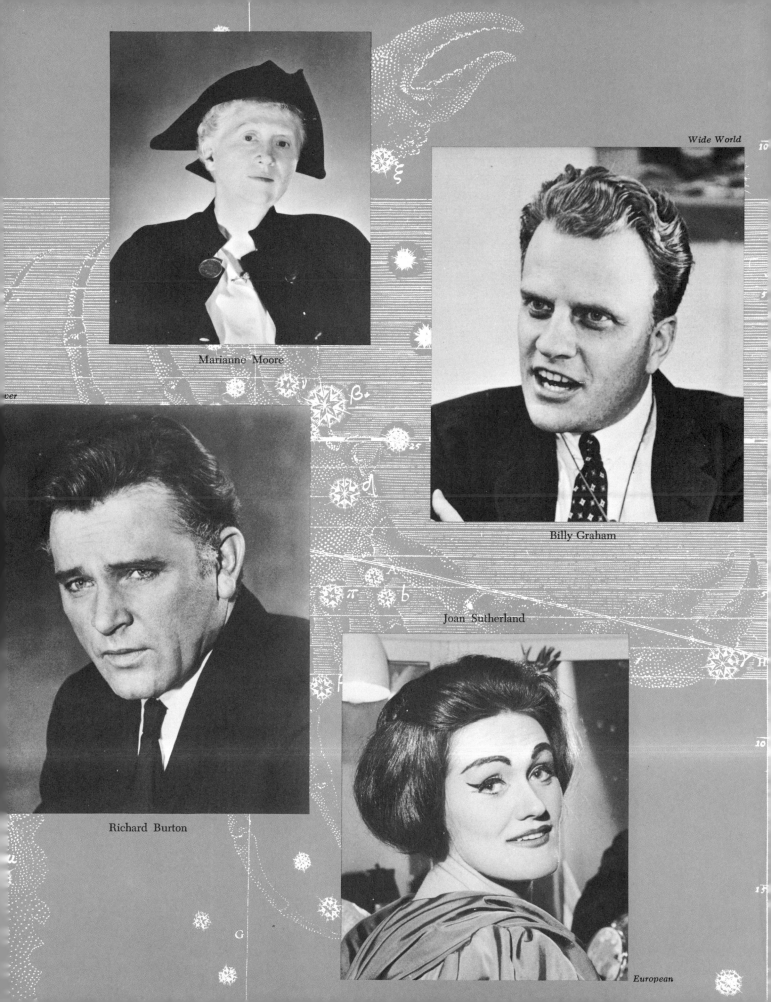

Marianne Moore

Billy Graham

Richard Burton

Joan Sutherland

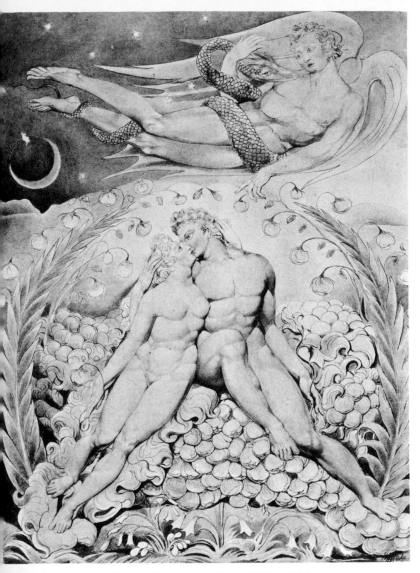

Satan with Adam and Eve. William Blake

born under this sign to adjust themselves to the conditions and limitations imposed on them by their sex, especially in ill-educated communities. They carry out their allotted tasks carefully enough, working, scrubbing, scouring, and setting in order with fierce energy, and are often held up to admiration by outsiders as model wives and mothers — a verdict which they themselves heartily endorse. One of the peculiar traits

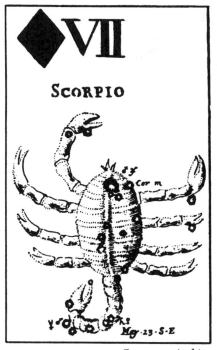

Tarot card

dent satisfaction that is annoying to witness, and galling to the victim of the moment. A tendency to enjoy seeing their friends and intimates waste their time and energy leads Scorpionian humor to express itself in practical jokes.

Even Scorpionians of the primitive type are often attracted to the medical profession, though their motives for entering it are rather mixed, and frequently include a morbid desire to know the worst that can be known of frail and diseased humanity. Drugs, especially poisons, have a curious fascination for them, and they are always in favor of drastic treatment.

It is difficult for primitive female specimens

that adds much to the difficulty of home life under a Scorpionian's sway is that she — or he — dislikes to acknowledge any inferiority by asking questions, and, is, nevertheless, deeply hurt if left in ignorance of any trivial facts known to the other members of the household.

Physical Characteristics. This type is said to have a powerful, muscular, and somewhat thickset frame with dark eyes and strong and rather heavy features. Scorpionians are generally proud of their command of feature and immobility of expression. They rarely give themselves away by flushing, wincing, or starting, however deeply their emotions may be stirred. Their aim is to read everybody else like an open book and remain inscrutable themselves, and their characteristic reserve and psychic intuition make such an ambition easy of attainment.

Health. The ideal Scorpionian has a magnificent physique and phenomenal powers of endurance, and in consequence is frequently tempted to defy the laws of health, indulging in prolonged spurts of excessive work and taking pride in the fact that he can go on without rest, food, or sleep. But when he is ill the Scorpionian is thoroughly ill. A rest cure is the Scorpionian's best remedy, giving the magnificent power of recuperation always associated with this sign a chance to assert itself. But he loves heroic remedies and is seldom content to let well enough alone. In many cases, he is difficult to nurse, because he knows — or thinks he knows — just exactly what the nurse ought to do; and has no hesitation about allowing her to feel that she has failed in her duty.

Mars

Mars and Venus United by Love. Veronese. *Metropolitan Museum of Art*

SUN IN SCORPIO

The Sun in Scorpio gives a firm, determined, and reserved individuality, with an inclination to be dignified, proud, secretive, and full of desire. The individuality may be either well disposed or selfish, according to degree of progress. Scorpio is a sign of strength, independence, and industry.

Sun in Scorpio and Moon in Aries

This combination gives stubbornness, positiveness, impulsiveness, and sometimes extremes of anger and jealousy. It makes a dogmatic, self-assertive character full of keen likes and dislikes. The passions are often strong. The native has courage, resolution, resourcefulness, and independence, and is sure to make his mark in life in some way. He will probably be known for his strength of character and will. In most cases he will be practical and desirous of bringing all theories to the test of action. The feelings and the intellect may be well developed. The worst defect is a lack of calmness or humility.

Sun in Scorpio and Moon in Taurus

The lunar tendencies here will reduce some of the positiveness of the Scorpio nature. This combination makes good medical men with a remarkable intuition regarding disease. It also suggests success in business, the nature being firm and determined. In this and other directions he will have a fixed course of life, and will persevere in following it out. He will be un-

changing and conservative in most habits and customs, both good and bad. His domestic and social side is well developed; and if planetary positions accord, he will develop artistic, musical, or other cultural interests. He is cheerful, generally good-natured, and fairly fortunate except when "cross-aspects" occur.

Sun in Scorpio and Moon in Gemini

As a rule, the personality is inclined to extremes and is easily drawn into reckless habits. People born under this combination are clever and shrewd. They make good writers and literary critics. They have invention, wit, pungent sarcasm, and a capacity for sustained intellectual effort. And they could subsist by literature, traveling, clerical or scientific work, or by superintending others in one of these directions.

Sun in Scorpio and Moon in Cancer

This is a harmonious combination, but those under it are easily led by others into acts of folly. Early marriage is recommended, for the powers of attachment are strong, and the life may be influenced for good. The native has a rather hard and practical nature in things that necessitate his going out into the world and mixing with men, but a kinder and softer side in social matters or family life. If planetary positions harmonize, he will have considerable business ability; will earn or inherit money or property, and manage it economically.

Drawing. Picasso

Sun in Scorpio and Moon in Leo

This combination inclines the mind to romance, and love affairs of an intensely passionate and emotional nature are apt to result. It gives pride, some arrogance, much love of power, coupled with ardor, imagination, emotion, energy, and ambition. There is some love of grandeur and ostentation, and considerable dramatic feeling. The nature is strong and commanding, firm and self-directed, even when most emotional. It is well able to influence others, and to control, direct, and organize.

Sun in Scorpio and Moon in Virgo

This is the most critical of the twelve lunar positions. Those born under it are proud, passionate, and liable to sarcasm and bitter speech. They are apt to criticize themselves severely and to be dissatisfied with their own achievements when these fall short of perfection. They make friends among those in humbler positions, and are greatly affected through the death of some particular friend or a subordinate. It is a good combination for a writer, doctor, chemist, or scientist. Females make good nurses.

Sun in Scorpio and Moon in Libra

This combination gives a tendency to "second sight." There is some inclination toward the mystical, and a love for all that is psychic, romantic, and wonderful, under certain planetary influences there will be no occult ability, but business foresight instead. Under affliction this position can cause an inharmonious marriage or in some cases death of the marriage partner. There is a charitable and benevolent disposition, but under bad aspects the native may suffer from enmity, treachery, and deceit. He has a good and well-meaning nature but sometimes takes the wrong path in life. He is likely to have many friends and will gain by marriage or partnership.

Sun and Moon in Scorpio

This combination gives much independence and self-reliance. Those born under it are inclined to be materialistic. They have the ability to govern others, but there is always a tendency to override, domineer, and master. They are proud and somewhat reserved, yet have a tendency to inquisitiveness. These characteristics vary greatly according to the planetary positions and aspects. If Mars and Saturn are strongest, the native is capable, practical, and unyielding. If Jupiter or Venus are strongest, he will have a lively imagination, active emotions, and warm feelings. He generally has much energy and activity, a capable executive nature, and in some cases a firm, decided character with an iron will.

Sun in Scorpio and Moon in Sagittarius

This combination produces an impulsive and aggressive nature with a tendency to indiscreet and explosive speech. Natives have an innate

conservatism combined with progressive ideas. They are busy, practical workers, enthusiastic and ardent for any cause that interests them. Their vitality sometimes leads them to overdo it mentally or physically, and there is terrible anger on occasion. They follow occupations connected with religion, make good soldiers or sailors, or have ability for law or medicine — these tendencies depending upon planetary positions to bring them into prominence.

Sun in Scorpio and Moon in Capricorn

This intensifies the pride of Scorpio, and gives strong inclinations toward self-indulgence. At the same time there is a great amount of patience, perseverance, and endurance. The combination is apt to give a rather hard nature, with self-will and fixedness of opinion and habit. Natives are somewhat aggressive, alternating at times between extremes of rashness and caution, liberality and thrift. Supported by suitable planetary positions, they may have business and executive ability, financial acuteness, and prudence in investments or in buying and selling. Ambition is combined with determination, and very high attainments are possible.

Nehru: Sun in Scorpio

Sun in Scorpio and Moon in Aquarius

This combination gives an ability for government jobs and a tendency to mix in large concerns. There is a love of external appearances, wealth and grandeur, but also some love of the occult. It produces liveliness, acuteness, inventiveness, and originality, which, under affliction, may become irritability, nervous worry, or aggressiveness. The native is sometimes opinionated and dogmatic, lacking pliability and adaptability. He may do things in his own way or not at all, is apt to have keen likes and dislikes, and makes a faithful friend or an unchanging enemy. He has natural dramatic power and is much attached to home life. He has much strength of will and mental concentration. Death may be comparatively sudden.

Sun in Scorpio and Moon in Pisces

This combination gives a restless and anxious nature. The mind is somewhat mathematically inclined, but there is a tendency toward deception and duplicity. If other planets permit, the native is affectionate, warm-hearted, sympathetic, charitable, benevolent. Under affliction he is apt to be unlucky and constantly thwarted. There is usually more promise than performance. He may benefit by children and friends. This position tends to mysticism and religion. It increases offspring. There are ambition and difficulty in rising to his proper sphere.

Theodore Roosevelt: Sun in Scorpio

FAMOUS PEOPLE BORN WITH THE SUN IN SCORPIO

Martin Luther:	November 10, 1483
Benvenuto Cellini:	November 1, 1500
Marie Antoinette:	November 2, 1755
Fyodor Dostoevski:	October 30, 1821
Auguste Rodin:	November 12, 1840
King Edward VII:	November 9, 1841
Theodore Roosevelt:	October 27, 1858
Marie Curie:	November 7, 1867
Pablo Picasso:	October 25, 1881
Marianne Moore:	November 15, 1887
Jewaharlal Nehru:	November 14, 1889
Charles de Gaulle:	November 22, 1890
André Malraux:	November 3, 1901
Katharine Hepburn:	November 9, 1909
Dylan Thomas:	October 27, 1914
Jonas Salk:	October 28, 1914
Indira Gandhi:	November 19, 1917
Billy Graham:	November 7, 1918
Richard Burton:	November 10, 1925
Joan Sutherland:	November 7, 1929
Grace Kelly:	November 12, 1929
Mike Nichols:	November 6, 1931
Charles, Prince of Wales:	November 14, 1948

175

November 23 to December 21

THE ARCHER

The sign of the
Sage or Counselor

A mutable fiery sign
Candid, impulsive, restless, impatient, generous,
insatiably curious, nature-loving, sport-loving

Ruler: Jupiter

Gems: carbuncle, turquoise

Color: light blue
Metal: tin

Harmonious signs for business, marriage, or
companionship: Aries, Leo, Sagittarius

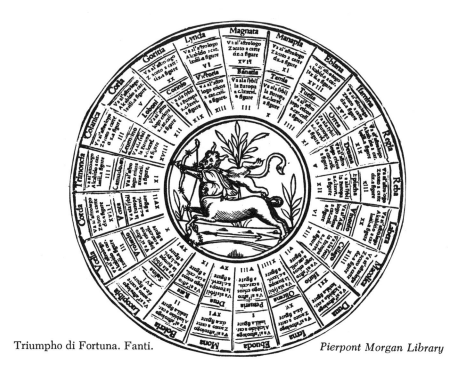

Triumpho di Fortuna. Fanti.　　　　　　　*Pierpont Morgan Library*

The Sagittarian Type

Evolved Type. The chief characteristic of the fully developed Sagittarian is his extraordinary power of mental activity. He brings his reason to bear upon every phenomenon that comes under his observation, and finds his most congenial occupation in getting to the bottom of things in general, facing the facts of life, and reducing its problems to their simplest terms. His curiosity is insatiable; his mental energy never flags. He interests himself intensely — and often succeeds in interesting others — in the relation of cause to effect and effect to cause. He comes readily into touch with his fellow men, takes an eager interest in their welfare, especially in their education. He is sometimes a very successful teacher of the Socratic type, teaching his students to observe and reason and think for

themselves. He is consequently better adapted for training older pupils than beginners. The Sagittarian's skill in dialectic makes him a formidable antagonist, and foolish objections and suggestions meet with small mercy from him. The Archer aims well, showing an intuitive knowledge of the weak places in the armor of his adversary, and seldom missing the mark. This tendency naturally makes the legal profession, and especially the bar, a suitable field of activity; but literature and journalism and the teaching of philosophy or religion are the most congenial occupations of all. The study of medicine is more rarely taken up, but some Sagittarian doctors are brilliant brain specialists.

Sagittarians are almost all keen sportsmen of one kind or another — excellent shots, enthusias-

178

Alessandro Temini, 17th-century engraving

INVIDIA   NOVEMBRE   SAGITARIO

Cætera iure mei cedunt Elementa trophæis,   *Cede a raggione ogni Elemento altero*
Cum tot ego Pisces, et Mónstra natantia pascam.   *A me cede Pesci e Mostri accolgo in seno*
Per me post casus varios Mercator auarus.   *D'auido Cor dopo 'l soffrir non meno*
Diuilijs fruitur varijs, quas India miltit.   *Dell Indico tesor sozio il pensiero*
                                 Allesandro Temini fecit a S. Saluator in Venetia.

tic fishermen, golfers, hockey players, etc. They show a special predilection for outdoor work, such as geological research and difficult explorations, and the training and exercise of horses and of dogs — the animals which respond most quickly to their owners. This type revels in the open air, and cannot endure the stale atmosphere of stuffy rooms. They have an immense sympathy for those doomed to a life of confinement in workshop, factory, or mine, and are often keen social reformers.

Horologiographia. Sebastian Munster, 1533.

If these interests are taken up by Sagittarians, they will spare no pains to collect the necessary information, and show much practical common sense in suggesting remedies; for their theories are drawn up not in the study from books alone, but from actual contact with humanity. They are willing to fraternize with all sorts and conditions of men, and to learn from anyone whatever he has to teach. At the same time they are much too clear-headed to be carried away either by anarchist doctrines or by socialism of the

180

sentimental type; for in spite of their tendency to regard mankind as one great family, they realize that in the matter of understanding, at any rate, we are not all "free and equal."

The man who looks with friendly eyes on humanity, and comes very easily into touch with his fellow creatures at large, naturally feels less need of family life than do those whose geniality is not always available, and who are less quick to understand the position, mental attitude, and essential characteristics of the men and women they meet. Sagittarians are often extraordinarily detached from their kindred. If they happen to find their immediate relations congenial, well and good — they add them to the list of their friends, and treat them as such; if not, they point out their faults and foibles with unfailing frankness, and will publicly discuss and comment upon them with a freedom that makes more reserved types gasp. The native treats parental authority as a subject for inquiry and investigation. He is ready to submit if parental wisdom can be demonstrated to him, but he tests that wisdom in ways peculiar to himself, and woe to the father or mother who fails to pass his tests.

Wide World

Martin van Buren: Sun in Sagittarius

he has loved before, or explains clearly and logically exactly why he has been led to take this step, and what makes him think it may prove advantageous to him in the long run, may possibly find favor with a woman who has learned by bitter experience just how little the typical lover's sigh may prove worth; but he will make small speed in winning the average romantic young girl. What leads the Sagittarian lover into blunders of this kind is a misunder-

The best way to deal with the young Jupiterian is to meet him fair and square on his own ground — the mental plane; to answer his questions honestly and without prevarication; to administer discipline reasonably and logically, and, above all, to admit ignorance and even error where they exist. The influence of this sign produces the kind of child who, when he has driven his seniors to the last stage of despair by his questions, and has been told that he must on no account dare to say "Why?" for the next half-hour, looks up with redoubled interest and eagerly demands, "Why not?" The delightfully wide-awake youngster can develop first into an *enfant terrible* and later into a tiresome tease, and among those strongly under Sagittarian influence we find those whose outspoken comments spare nothing and nobody, and who take — and show — positive delight in the discovery that they can compel some unfortunate individual to give himself or herself away by losing self-control.

Love and Friendship. The same frankness and outspoken sincerity which characterizes the many friendships of this type are also to be found in connection with its love affairs. But in that field of activity there is generally more chance of breeziness' blowing up the clouds than of its dispelling them. The man who prefaces his proposal by an honest admission that

Jupiter. Mediaeval House-book, Castle Wolfegg

standing of his own type. He ought to choose his wife on the mental plane, (putting mental response and mutual understanding first), though without ignoring the usual questions of temperament and character. Instead, he is very apt to choose by logic alone, and to argue himself into a condition in which he is ready to decide for or against the momentous step without fully comprehending what he is doing.

A girl may be everything that can be *reasonably* demanded — healthy, handsome, capable,

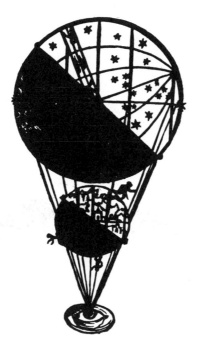

popular — without being gifted with a single quality of heart or mind that will make a suitable mate for him; and yet in a great many cases the youthful Sagittarian will go light-heartedly forward, beginning as a rule with a so-called friendship which is merely a thinly disguised flirtation, and too often ending in a precipitate engagement which he finds it impossible to fulfill; for this is the type of man that absolutely refuses to go to the altar with a lie on his lips, and tie himself to what he feels to be impossi-

182

ble conditions. In consequence, broken engagements, with all the accompanying pain and humiliation and loss of self-respect, are not uncommon. The more fortunate escape with a refusal, which serves the same purpose of pulling them up and making them think; either experience, taken the right way, may be a blessing in disguise. However, primitive specimens are apt to take such blows badly, and develop a touch of cynicism, for they have little or no idealism to help them along, and romance too often dies early in consequence.

"Once bitten, twice shy," and our sportsman develops a self-protective prudence and caution to a rather unlovely extent — shuns the *ingénue* and hovers around the married women, or seeks the society of his seniors, who are capable of giving his somewhat precocious mind the companionship which it craves, and who are less likely to be misled. Not infrequently a friendship formed in this way ends in matrimonial felicity, but there is a danger that this inclination to dominate the emotions and be guided by common sense may produce a tendency to evade matrimony altogether, and the Sagittarian may end a bachelor, an experience always to be regretted in his case, for his nature demands emo-

Masquerade. Peter Brueghel

tional exercise to complete it. If, on the other hand, he succeeds in finding a woman who really understands, loves, and trusts him, his whole nature expands, he reaches his highest possibilities, and makes an enthusiastic and very devoted husband, proud of his wife and of all her achievements, grateful for her affection, and very quick to make allowance for shortcomings.

He mates best with his own wide-awake type, or with women of Aries, whose energies he likes to dominate and direct. But the other fiery sign, Leo, is also capable of yielding him a suitable partner, and its characteristic qualities of faith, tolerance, and magnanimity are sometimes extremely necessary. Sagittarians demand freedom in their choice of companions — of both sexes — as in all other fields; and a wife of narrow sympathies, who fancies that she can have her Sagittarian husband "all to herself" by shutting him off from exchange of ideas with anyone else, will have a poor time of it. He may shrug his shoulders and submit to her whims, for he is eminently practical in conduct, and always inclined to make the best of any situation his own blunders have brought him into; but his thunderbolts of sarcasm will be hurled with increasing frequency, and the marriage, though outwardly

decorous, will be no true union, but merely an ill-assorted partnership on the physical plane.

The women of this type run the same dangers as the men, and their bright frank ways with the opposite sex are very often misconstrued — friendship being mistaken for love and love for friendship by a mystified mankind, which looks for, and very often prefers, uncertainty and evasiveness in a woman. When a tragedy of misunderstanding has occurred, pride generally comes to the rescue, and the heartache is carried off with a laugh and a brave front, or possibly by such a divertingly burlesque account of the whole affair that listeners are left with an impression that it was all a joke from beginning to end — an impression they are usually quite ready to spread by announcing that "she never really cared for him at all." After such an experience the Sagittarian cultivates self-control, and finds great difficulty in letting herself go beyond the safe limits of a pleasant friendship with just a spice of flirtation to flavor it, so may easily acquire a reputation as a coquette, unable to take either herself or anybody else seriously. This state of affairs frequently leads to spinsterhood, but there is no fear of her degenerating into the sour or embittered type of old maid.

Metropolitan Museum of Art

183

Primitive Type. Primitive Sagittarian tendencies naturally take a more accentuated and less desirable form. Matrimony is frankly decried by both sexes as an intolerable burden, a tie and a bore. The men safeguard their personal liberty by cultivating a blunt and boorish discourtesy with women who are their equals, and permit themselves to relax into easy-going familiarity only with those whom no one can expect them to marry. The women often allow their breezy unconventionality to degenerate into free-and-easy ways with men, and, especially if they have an inclination for sport, imitating the tricks and manners of their male comrades in gait and speech.

Both sexes at this stage tend to become inherently selfish and inconsiderate, in spite of a certain rough kindliness of manner; because this type lives in the present and is consequently apt to lack loyalty and sympathy — qualities which demand memory of the past for their development. They rarely allow their emotions to carry them away, and are seldom inclined to be vicious. They are careless of reputation, both for themselves and others, to an extent that argues a real want of consideration, and, as far as the men are concerned, a total lack of chivalry. This last failing is due to the fact that, although they usually hold strong views — based on the dictates of reason — on the essential difference between the sexes, and are even inclined to dogmatize on the subject, they are generally able to see that a woman may be different from a man without being his inferior; and when that point is reached, a crude logic sometimes suggests that since she is his equal she can surely fend for herself and fight for her own hand. Women who do so successfully very often win Sagittarian respect, while the more appealing and helpless and emotional types merely irritate and annoy.

Ancient astrologers tell us that the faults of this type are "such as are easily pardoned," and this is just as well; for they certainly tend to come to the surface, and are very easily seen. There is, in fact, a curiously childlike transparency about these people — probably due to the

Shepherd's Kalendar. John Wright, 1631

absence of complex emotions, such as jealousy or vindictiveness — which makes them easy to understand, and ensures speedy detection if they attempt to go off their own straightforward line and dabble in deceit. Sagittarian theft is invariably exposed, and the comparatively harmless fibs in which many of this type indulge when convenient are rarely believed, even for five minutes. They cannot lie or cheat successfully; and will do wisely, even from the low standpoint of immediate self-interest, never to make the attempt.

Religion. In religious matters the Sagittarian is very often something of a skeptic, because his activity of mind compels him to examine the faith he is born in; and if the teaching provided by environment seems illogical and un-

184

satisfactory, he cannot help seeing and pointing out its fallacies and shortcomings. At this juncture, however, his practical common sense frequently comes to his aid, reminding him that no system of theology devised by the mind of man is likely to represent accurately and adequately the whole truth about the nature of Deity, and that some sort of working hypothesis is nevertheless necessary. Selecting and accepting certain premises as foregone conclusions, he may succeed in silencing his own doubts, and in arguing both himself and others into a fairly orthodox position.

Literary Expression. The Sagittarian's love of argument, and enjoyment of active encounters with antagonistic thought, lead him to make free use of dialogue form when he turns to literary expression. There is also a tendency to discursive and tangential talk and the needless introduction of extraneous matter — possibly very entertaining, for the Sagittarian never lacks humor, but too unexpected to be harmonious or artistic.

In history and literature the first name that presents itself is the sage of sages, Socrates. Everything recorded of him proclaims the Sagit-

tarian; his conversational method of learning and teaching; his mental activity, his utter lack of pose and readiness to consort with all sorts and conditions of men; his warfare against ignorance and self-satisfaction; his uncompromising attitude and defiance of public opinion; the geniality which endeared him to his friends, and made him always a welcome guests at other men's tables; the quaint homeliness of his similes and illustrations, condemned as inelegant and uncouth by the fastidious scholars of the day; his indifference to family life, and startling theories about marriage; and his own blunder in selecting a mate.

This great philosopher called upon logic instead of love to send him a wife; and, cold and pitiless, it responded by giving him Xantippe. No doubt, when he chose her she was everything that reason could approve, but in all the intangible essential ways that really count the marriage was a hopeless misfit. Who can measure the scorn with which the high-spirited and probably ambitious woman must have looked down upon the ugly, undignified little husband who spent his idle days in what must have seemed to her profitless and unremunerative chatter among men with whom she had no

Death of Socrates. J. L. David. *Metropolitan Museum of Art*

ideas in common, and women for whom she had no respect? She cleaned his house for him all the same; but when she had finished — unless tradition belie her — she emptied her slop pail over his head.

Shelley, born with the Sun in Leo but with Sagittarius rising, gives a notable example of how this "benign" influence may handicap a man if its tendencies are carried to extremes. Shelley was so utterly devoid of family feeling that he used to entertain and horrify his school fellows by cursing his own father; and so incapable was he of understanding what the average man means by the marriage tie, that he invited the wife he had forsaken to join him on a tour with the girl with whom he had eloped. A very strong Leo accentuation smoothed out the Sagittarian "kinks" in many of his verses, but there are plenty of obscure and irregular passages in them, and his attitude of flat rebellion against the existing order of things, and of skepticism in matters of dogma and doctrine, are extremely characteristic.

Physical Characteristics. Sagittarius generally has a well-shaped head, breadth of forehead, a frank and open countenance, quick movements, and an inclination to vigorous gesture — expressive, but sometimes far from graceful. The eyes are generally bright and observant, and often twinkle or dance with fun. The ideal Jupiterian model is the marble of Jove in the Vatican; and the type at its plainest is seen in the bust of Socrates. Shelley was of the snub-nosed variety. Many of this type are short, broad-shouldered, and rather thick set, growing fat in old age; but others are tall, athletic, and somewhat commanding in stature and bearing. They are generally restless, absolutely unable to sit still or remain in the same posture for five minutes together, and their disregard of convention, bright self-confidence, and readiness to come to the front on every occasion make them conspicuous wherever they are.

The country traditionally associated with the influence of Sagittarius is Spain; and Spaniards certainly have much of the Sagittarian pride and

Bettmann Archive

Mary Queen of Scots: Sun in Sagittarius
(Portrait by Clouet.)

independence, as well as something of its buoyancy. They are often keen mountaineers, good shots, and excellent horsemen, and though it is curious to find the bullfight preferred as a national pastime by a people under so genial a sign, sport is never really merciful, and the Archer is always inclined to enjoy a successful hit, on all the planes.

In Drama and Fiction. This type occurs frequently in literature. Shakespeare gives us two delightful characters — Benedick, who will "still be talking" though "nobody marks" him; and Rosalind, whose candid admission, "When I think, I must speak," betrays the same tendency. The former's diatribes against marriage are particularly characteristic, and his list of the virtues and graces he personally intends to exact in a wife has been echoed, time and again, by other Sagittarians, most of whom, however, have had to content themselves with somewhat less of a paragon when the time came. The characteristically Sagittarian touches about Rosalind are her buoyancy and playfulness, the frankness with which she owns her love for Orlando to her cousin and confidant, and the willful way-wardness which makes her disguise it from him and play indifference until the last possible moment. Petruchio, in *The Taming of the Shrew*, is a more primitive and much less lovable speci-

Jupiter. Drawing by Lorenzo Bernini

men. Bottom, the weaver, and Sancho Panza were also born under the sign. Caricatures of the type have been presented by Aristophanes in his comedy *The Clouds*, in which Socrates and his school are depicted as engaged in serious argument over the measurements of the hindleg of a flea and its power of leaping and

Rudyard Kipling in his delightful description of the *Elephant's Child* in the *"Just So" Stories*.

Sagittarius at the zenith often gives something of the same bright optimism and childlike confidence in others, and the Moon in Sagittarius also confers popularity as a rule. The Sun in the sign seems rather to increase the longing for wisdom and understanding, and its effect may be seen in the later writings of Thomas Carlyle and in the music of Beethoven.

Health. Almost the only dangers that threaten the health of the typical Sagittarian arise from his over-activity of mind and body. He has too many schemes and projects on hand to attend to all of them satisfactorily: and there is, in consequence, a continuous depletion of the life forces through unnecessary scattering of energy. Rapidity of movement, reckless riding, and other rough forms of exercise, such as mountaineering, are responsible for a larger percentage of sprains and fractures than falls to any other type. If the Sagittarian survives his allowance of accidents he will probably live on to a good old age, retaining his faculties to the last.

Ludwig van Beethoven: Sun in Sagittarius

(Portrait by Stieler.) *National Library, Vienna*

serve of Taurus lessens the impulsiveness of Sagittarius and gives more stability. The native is nearly always reliable. He possesses warm affections, geniality, sympathy, and imagination. He has some qualifications for artistic, musical or allied pursuits. He is faithful, conscientious and honorable. It is a fortunate combination for worldly success, the foresight of Sagittarius being used for practical ends.

SUN IN SAGITTARIUS

The Sun in Sagittarius inclines the individual toward science, philosophy, and religion. It gives much activity, a restless spirit, but a frank, honest, sincere, and liberty-loving nature. In undeveloped egos there will be a rebellious and dominative spirit, but in the advanced there is a love of law and order.

Sun in Sagittarius and Moon in Aries

This combination intensifies activity. There will be great desire to excel, and sometimes to overreach, others. The personality is strong and tends to override restraint. Impulse, energy, and activity predominate, and may be expressed through almost any channel, according to the strongest planet in the horoscope. The native will usually be generous, ardent, enthusiastic, willful, and sometimes rebellious, espousing causes or movements zealously, and defending his friends as himself. In a good horoscope he can accomplish much by pioneering, bringing about reforms, originating and improving. Under cross aspects he may be lacking in restraint and calmness, too militant and aggressive, even destructive. He is likely to travel, to change his residence and occupation.

Sun in Sagittarius and Moon in Taurus

This is a sympathetic combination. While the solar position expands the sympathies, the re-

188

Sun in Sagittarius and Moon in Gemini

This combination quickens the activities of Sagittarius. There is a liability to become hasty in speech, overexcited, and too active. There is a great love of education. The combination inclines to a nervous condition. There is considerable journalistic ability. Judgment and memory should be good. The nature is active, often a little abrupt and liable to change and irresolution. The native benefits through relatives, and may marry one.

Sun in Sagittarius and Moon in Cancer

In this combination of fire and water, many mistakes are apt to be made through the impulsive and imaginative characteristics of Cancer. It gives intuition but inclines somewhat toward sensation, increasing the imagination and the emotional and affectional nature. Appreciation of nature and art is intense, and with suitable planetary positions the native may show considerable ability for painting, music, or allied pursuits; also religious tendencies of an imaginative kind. This position tends to voyages, and is somewhat favorable for money and property.

Mark Twain: Sun in Sagittarius

Culver

Sun in Sagittarius and Moon in Leo

This splendid combination awakens either the passional or spiritual side of the nature. It tends to make the mind proud, but quick and alert, with the ability to sense other minds. This is the most affectional combination, the heart being very active. Love can go out to many, and there is apt to be some confusion in this respect. There is adaptability for religion, philosophy, politics, and some ability for the drama, either as author or interpreter. There is also a love of grand surroundings. With suitable planetary positions, the native may accomplish much in life and perhaps make a great figure. In itself this combination sometimes produces a more imaginative than practical nature.

Sun in Sagittarius and Moon in Virgo

This gives excellent discriminative powers; there are intuition, refinement, power of language, and a love of harmony. The mind is active and tends to make the personality bright and clear in thought and speech, though very critical. There is good intellectual ability, suitable for literature, law, the ministry, and a variety of pursuits in which educational endowments can be utilized. The native may occupy some public appointment. This combination tends toward a domesticated nature; under affliction, however, the subject may show irritability or despondency. This position generally shows common sense, sober judgment, and quiet dignity.

189

Paul Klee

BORN UNDER THE SIGN OF SAGITTARIUS

Wide World

Julie Harris

European

Mary Martin

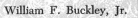

William F. Buckley, Jr.

Truman Moore

Frank Sinatra

Maria Callas

Sun in Sagittarius and Moon in Libra

In this combination the personal characteristics tend to equalize and modify the impulse of Sagittarius. It awakens the ambitions, and gives a fairly strong personality, with quick and accurate perception, added to great powers of comparison. There is also likely to be some artistic or musical ability. This combination gives popularity, and attracts friends and acquaintances of fairly good social standing who will be congenial to the native and may benefit him, and among whom he may marry. It gives imagination and good nature, sincerity and hopefulness, unless afflicted, and is a generally harmonious polarity.

Wide Worl

Sun in Sagittarius and Moon in Scorpio

Here the Martial-Jupiterian influence predominates. There are apt to be sarcasm in speech, pride, considerable temper, contentiousness, and impetuosity. The combination gives perseverance and persistence, with plenty of energy and a strong desire for independence. It is good for health and bestows both endurance and working power. Marked muscular strength is probable, with some tendency to fleshiness. There is a fair amount of practical executive ability. The native will be free and generous, and if aspects are favorable will earn or inherit wealth.

Sun and Moon in Sagittarius

This combination gives independence and a great love of freedom, inducing a tendency to become rebellious. At the same time certain inclinations toward conservatism are present. It quickens the mental and physical powers. Sagittarius is well expressed by this combination, the love of travel, science, philosophy, and religion being strongly marked. There is sometimes much generosity, with strong social and benevolent feelings, and a fairly harmonious nature. The duality of Sagittarius will probably show strongly, causing occasional indecision of mind as well as changes in occupation or mode of life.

Sun in Sagittarius and Moon in Capricorn

Here personal characteristics steady the individuality, which on its side awakens the personal nature into greater activity, giving keen ambition in the direction of higher thought. There is decided musical ability, or at least great love for music. Though there is some liability to changeableness, the mind is industrious and practical, though somewhat sensual. There are good executive ability and sound common sense. The native is suited for a variety of pursuits, and has some ability for successful financial speculation. This combination tends to orderliness and method.

Pope John XXIII: Sun in Sagittarius

Sagittarius. Book of Stars and
Constellations. Persian, 1630

Sun in Sagittarius and Moon in Aquarius

This quickens the intuitions, and enlarges the views. It gives ability to deal with the public, but there is a liability to overexertion. It increases the qualities of imagination, and gives some attraction to the occult side of life. It will tend toward higher education, religion, philosophy, metaphysics, or any form of original thought or scientific investigation. It is also a good combination for commercial life, or any calling where the personality comes prominently before others.

Sun in Sagittarius and Moon in Pisces

This combination gives restlessness and an inclination to worry. There is a religious tendency, and an inclination to be charitable, sympathetic, and benevolent; but this is weakened by a lack of initiative. Work is best carried out when under the direction of others. This polarity is good for family life, for happy relations between parents and children. It tends somewhat to traveling, and is moderately good for property and possessions.

FAMOUS PEOPLE BORN WITH THE SUN IN SAGITTARIUS

Mary, Queen of Scots:	December 7, 1542
John Milton:	December 9, 1608
Spinoza:	November 24, 1632
William Blake:	November 28, 1757
Beethoven:	December 17, 1770
Mark Twain:	November 30, 1835
Toulouse-Lautrec:	November 24, 1864
Winston Churchill:	November 30, 1874
Paul Klee:	December 18, 1879
Pope John XXIII:	November 25, 1881
James Thurber:	December 8, 1894
Virgil Thomson:	November 25, 1896
Noel Coward:	December 16, 1899
Margaret Mead:	December 16, 1901
Alicia Markova:	December 1, 1910
Mary Martin:	December 1, 1914
Frank Sinatra:	December 12, 1915
Maria Callas:	December 4, 1923
William F. Buckley, Jr.:	November 24, 1925
Julie Harris:	December 2, 1925
Sammy Davis, Jr.:	December 8, 1925

193

December 22 to January 20

THE GOAT

The sign of the
Priest, Ambassador, or Scientist

A cardinal earthy sign
Ambitious, persevering, diplomatic, reserved

Ruler: Saturn

Gems: white onyx, moonstone

Color: green
Metal: lead

Harmonious signs for business, marriage, or
companionship: Taurus, Virgo, Libra

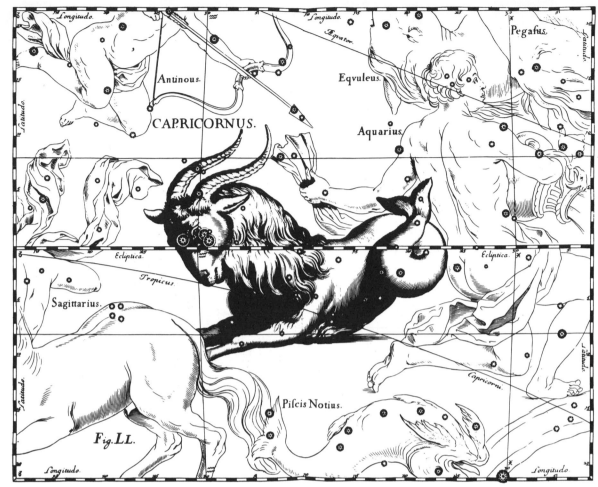

Hevelius, 1690

The Capricornian Type

Evolved Type. The typical Capricornian takes life earnestly and is generally an enthusiastic upholder of tradition and authority. When fully developed he has a fine historic sense which gives him a keen interest in the events of the past, and a profound understanding of the problems of the present. He frequently treads the path of scholarship, does well at the university, very often shines in diplomacy or in some kind of work which involves acting as an intermediary between those whose interests or theories clash, and generally enjoys life. Social legislation may claim a large share of his attention, and he usually has the welfare of the community strongly at heart.

This is not an easy type to analyze, and it is consequently difficult to sum up its character-

istics briefly; but two main elements are always found in connection with its highest manifestation in humanity, namely noble ambition, and an extraordinary power of adaptability to environment. The first of these qualities results in abnormal industry, and the second makes the type peculiarly fitted to take part in activities associated with city life, and with the guidance or government of large communities. Where civilized human beings congregate, it is necessary that the will of the majority should prevail if life is to run smoothly, and Capricornians not only acknowledge but proclaim that fact. They can accept conventions and traditional customs more easily than any other type, partly because historical values appeal to them, and partly because they possess an instinctive understanding

Alessandro Temini, 17th-century engraving

ACCIDIA

Ne superbo ne Auar, Son per usanza;
Mi assale il terzo nel fiorito Maggio:
N. Inuidia, ó gola, ó Ira há il mio lignaggio,
Ma sol carco d'Accidia, ed ignoranza.

DECEBRE

Finisco con miei giorni, il Mese, e l'Anno,
Nell'horida stagion fredda, e gelata:
Poco da Febo uengo riscaldata,
Pur uiuo lieta e non mi cal d'affanno

CAPRICORNO

Se di caprino latte (ha il ciel la uia)
Spremuto dalle poppe hisute, e nere,
D'una parente mia: sia ben douere,
Che anch'io goda lassù la parte mia.

of average humanity — its possibilities, its trials, and its shortcomings, and are therefore ready to admit the necessity of some kind of restraint. The native usually has a strong sense of the desirability of fixed standards of conduct, in social as well as in political and municipal life, and, accepting these readily himself, is inclined to insist upon their acceptance by others; but at the same time such insistence is of the diplomatic and persuasive order, for his ambition is not of the type that sweeps obstacles out of the way regardless of the interests or feelings of his fellow men.

The symbol of the sign — the Goat ascending the mountain — is a very appropriate one; for it is always depicted as *steadily following the upward path.* Every experienced climber knows that the beaten track is the safest road for those who desire to travel far, and that the attractive short cut is generally a delusion. Capricorn scarcely gives the latter a glance; his reverence and admiration for those who have preceded him, and have already attained the heights on

Woodrow Wilson: Sun in Capricorn

Henri Matisse: Sun in Capricorn

which his own soul is set, is tremendous. At times he may pause for a breathing space and look backward, remembering with gratitude the resting places and the guidance given in the earlier part of his journey, but he speedily resumes the climbing, and continues till the goal is reached; after which his ambition simply becomes more inclusive, and, embracing the careers of others, finds more and more scope as the years of the long full life go on.

Those who feel critical of such methods of attainment and are inclined to reserve their appreciation for work that is daring, experimental, and original, should remember that experiment may be carried too far. The tendency of some people to use the words "traditional" and "conventional" as terms of abuse is unjustifiable. If a conventional method happens to be a good one, it is folly to reject it; and to abolish all tradition and start afresh in any department of human activity — in building, engineering and in all technical handicrafts, as well as in poetry, music, philosophy, art, and religion — would involve a colossal waste of time and energy.

The crest of the wave rather than its first advance is the place for Capricornians, and none are quicker to feel the heartbeat of their own generation and to respond to it. Their enthusiasm is slow to awaken, but it is of the kind that grows and gathers force through coming into touch with the enthusiasm of the masses of their fellow men, and they frequently throw themselves into the task of guiding a popular movement — which has passed through its initial difficulties — to a successful issue, winning great praise and much esteem by their ability, especially in particular crises which require the exercise of tact and *finesse*.

Primitive Type. There is naturally another side to the picture; for until the complete and well-balanced development of the whole nature has been attained, ambition is often a source of worry rather than of happiness. It is a splendid spur or goad to activity, but to onlookers it is often recognizable only in the form of gloomy discontent with present circumstances. That other source of Capricornian strength, adaptability, has its other side. To be all things to all men *may* be a splendid achievement, for constant courtesy and consideration for others means constant self-control; but if the nature is ignoble such pliancy may take undesirable forms. There is a danger in this "earthy" type, with its keen realization of the use and value of experiences on the physical plane, that worldly success may be given a disproportionately large place, and the methods by which wealth and position can be attained will not be very closely scanned. Typical Capricornian employments, as has already been remarked, are those associated with mediatorial work; and a perfectly legitimate and useful form of the work is that of the middleman or broker; but what a man does is always less important than why and how he does it. The go-between who will do any kind of errand, however base, if it can be made to pay, is, in fact, a kind of "ambassador" in his own way. The Capricornian has none of the innate cruelty of the Scorpionian, but his ambition to make his way in the world makes

him unscrupulous in his use of the tool, and although he does not rejoice that others are weaker than himself he acquiesces in the fact and uses it.

It is in the regulation of their relations with their fellow creatures that the majority of Capricornians find most satisfaction. They have an intense desire to influence others — to manage them, mother them, direct, protect, persuade, convert, wheedle, attract, or meddle with them in one way or another. This tendency is of course apt to prove somewhat irritating to their

Goats. Berger's Kalendar, 1496

friends and relatives at times, especially when they are quite young; but as they advance in years and grow in wisdom, they learn to control it, and are naturally listened to with more deference and respect when they do speak. In fact, the longer they live, the better they are able to exercise their particular gifts. They like to remember and observe dates and anniversaries, and to make much of special occasions of social reunion, for they are excellent hosts and hostesses, and generally popular in that capacity, besides making charming guests. In later

Love and Friendship. This tendency to give importance to externals affects their friendships to some extent, for it makes them inclined to cultivate people of superior social position — to pay undue attention to those who are "in the running." In short, one of the vices of this type is snobbery, which appears and reappears in many strange guises, long after its victim fancies it has been overcome. At his worst the snob grovels before rank and wealth and scorns poverty and obscurity; but when he has got over that weakness, and has carried his social ambitions into literary, artistic, or political — or even religious — circles, his snobbery remains snobbery still, so long as he worships popular success and turns his back upon failure.

The Capricornian's interest in love affairs — his own and those of other people — is so characteristic of the type that it ought to have a chapter to itself. The consciousness of sex difference is very strong, and at the primitive stage it is almost impossible for these people to be easy and natural and altogether free from excitement in the presence of any member of the opposite sex. Their constant desire to breathe forth some sort of a challenge provokes many

life they are generally looked up to as authorities on matters of dress and deportment, and often consulted on questions of precedence or social procedure. It is in fact a real affliction for these people to have to appear anywhere in unbecoming or unsuitable garments, and they rarely grudge the time and trouble given to preparation for great occasions, inclining to the magnificent in their own attire, if their means will allow, and doing marvels in the way of making a brave show even at a considerable sacrifice of personal comfort.

Franco-Flemish tapestry, 15th century. *Metropolitan Museum of Art*

encounters of wit — not always of the most desirable type, for it is full of innuendo. Most people of this sign are, in early youth, and sometimes much later, incorrigible flirts. In the men the protective tendency — passing sometimes into patronage — is accentuated; and in the women there is usually a distinct craving for protection, which results in a manner that is often charmingly appealing and confiding.

Roughly speaking, ambition is the preponderating quality in the masculine type, while adaptability is so markedly present in the feminine variety that it sometimes fairly runs to seed, depriving its owner of the power of concentration or specialization altogether. If that is the

case, however, it will generally be found that ambition is not really absent, but merely vicarious, and that the woman who at first sight seems only bent upon making herself agreeable all round is in reality on the road to distinct social success, and that when once her own welcome is assured she will leave no stone unturned for the advancement of husband, brother, parent, or child. Especially is she in her element if she can forward a promising love affair, likely to result in what she terms a "suitable" marriage. She is a loving parent, and her policy is more in the direction of weeding out and giving to pleasing eligibles a fair field and a judicious amount of favor, than of actually forcing matters against the victim's will. Having disposed of her own sons and daughters successfully, she is generally more than ready to turn her attention to the children of her friends and relatives; for love and marriage have usually played so very important a role in her own life that she simply cannot understand that interest and interference, however kindly meant, may prove unwelcome to those who are naturally sensitive and reserved. The patching up of broken friendships and starting of new ones, the removal of misunderstandings and the smoothing out of troublesome tangles in family life are all congenial occupations. In the primitive type such a tendency naturally manifests in an irresistible inclination to have a finger in every pie.

Literary Style. The literary style of the Capricornian, like everything else about him, has two aspects. It is stately, sonorous, ornate, rolling on into long periods and imposing paragraphs; sometimes rhythmic, always weighty and impressive, frequently veiling rather than revealing its meaning by its wealth of heaped-up metaphor or over-elaboration of phrase; or else it is pithy and sententious, taking shape most readily in the maxim and the popular saying, and sometimes degenerating into the trite, the commonplace, and even the vulgar.

Religion. The religious life of the advanced Capricornian is the strongest and most important element in his nature, for ambition when it comes to its height is transmuted into aspiration. The handing on of tradition, the reverent rendering of ritual, and the dutiful observance of all kinds of ceremonial are thoroughly congenial to him. This practical adviser and disciplinarian, who is at the same time a man of the world, is well able to direct others, speaking as one who has received authority and never losing sight of the fact that to whom much is given from him shall much be required — a saying which he accepts very literally as applying to possessions as well as to the greater gifts of wisdom, love, and power. His religious teaching and ministrations are generally adapted to the needs of average humanity, and he is consequently apt to find himself rather at a loss when brought face to face with exceptions and minorities, his general solution being a dictum that they ought to ease the situation by conforming

202

Edgar Allan Poe: Sun in Capricorn.
(Painting by Cummings.)

to custom, however uncongenial or difficult it may be for them to do so.

The Jewish people and also the Hindu are said traditionally to be ruled by Capricorn. Rhythmic methods of counting prayers and invocations, such as the Hindu and Roman Catholic use of the rosary, or the turning of the prayer wheel by the worshiper in Tibet, are always suggestive of the influence of Saturn and are, of course, to be found all over the world, among Christians as well as among people of other faiths.

In Real Life. A strikingly typical son of Capricorn may be studied in the person of William Ewart Gladstone, born with the Sun and Mercury rising in that sign; and those who wish to understand its peculiarities should read the pages of his biography with care. His style in writing is of the ornate and elaborate Capricornian type, abounding in Latin constructions and very scholarly in diction. He was amazingly fluent of tongue, so much so that both in con-

in worldly channels, brought about his downfall in the end. The oft-quoted passage beginning

"Had I but served my God with half the zeal I served my king"

strikingly illustrates the change from lower ideals to higher. A less dignified Capricornian is Polonius in *Hamlet*; and also, at a lower social level, the garrulous and kindly old nurse in *Romeo and Juliet*.

Capricornians are said to attain their best period between the ages of fifty-six and seventy, a much longer and older prime than is enjoyed by any other type. Many of them live to well over eighty, some remaining hale and hearty. The chief danger to health is thwarted ambition, inducing discontent and gloom. Later in life, if prosperity is overdue and still tarries, and the limited outlook and cramping conditions show no signs of giving way, gloom and despondency may turn to melancholia. A change of air is beneficial and even essential in some cases, but it should not be a change to solitude. Capricornians always patronize the fashionable spa in preference to the moorland and mountain, and no type is more keenly interested in the exchange of facts or surmises concerning the various celebrities and nobodies who haunt such favored resorts. The best and most comfortable hotel that their means will allow is chosen on such occasions, and the skill of the chef is often considered an important point; for the Capricornian palate is sensitive, and its owner not infrequently gives considerable time and attention to its cultivation.

versation and in public oratory he was apt, as his contemporary Disraeli remarked, to be carried away "by the exuberance of his own verbosity." He was interested in ceremonial observances, conformed easily to social customs and conventions and observed the etiquette of his generation strictly.

Physical Characteristics. Capricornians are even more difficult to describe and classify physically than they are mentally and emotionally. Some of the old books insist much on the serious aspect of the Capricornian, his tendency to despondency, leaden looks, swarthy complexion, and sleek lank black hair. As a rule they are exceedingly lively and talkative.

In Drama and Fiction. Some of the statelier priests and politicians of Elizabethan drama suggest this Capricornian type — notably Cardinal Wolsey, with his splendor and his pride and the soaring ambition which, by running entirely

203

Cary Grant

BORN UNDER THE SIGN OF CAPRICORN

Carl Sandburg

Humphrey Bogart

Martin Luther King

Rebecca West

Marlene Dietrich

SUN IN CAPRICORN

This gives a very ambitious individuality, possessing much independence, strength of character, a keen love of justice, and a desire to attain to the highest position possible. Self-reliance and determination are expressed through this sign, which considerably strengthens the various personalities attached to it.

Sun in Capricorn and Moon in Aries

This combination gives ambition, a keen desire to be at the head of everything, determination, extreme independence and self-assertion. It gives an intense love of music. The native is of a capable executive nature, has strong will and much force of character. He can work hard and accomplish much, is suited for the army, for engineering or mining, for large business undertakings, or for public life. If the influence of Mercury is strong in the horoscope he will be suitable for literary pursuits or for philosophical or scientific occupations. His intellect is keenly critical, but not destructively so. If badly aspected, there may be some harshness, irritability, and an undisciplined nature, causing family and public conflicts.

Sun in Capricorn and Moon in Taurus

This gives a very persistent mind, much firmness and self-control, a desire to elevate and improve others. It is the most practical of this set of combinations, giving the native the ability to acquire wealth and do good with it. With favorable aspects, it is fortunate for possessions, legacies, worldly prosperity, and social and family life. It gives a strong but harmonious nature, with good feelings, patience, and faithfulness.

Sun in Capricorn and Moon in Gemini

The steadiness of Capricorn behind the activity of Gemini causes those born under this combination to be studious, yet inclined to give expression to all thoughts, especially those of a higher nature. This combination is good for occupations connected with intellectual work or travel. It produces consuls, ambassadors, literary men, accountants, scientists, public speakers, and professors. It gives an orderly, methodical, ingenious and sometimes profound mind, coupled with a good memory.

Bettmann Archive

206

Sir Isaac Newton: Sun in Capricorn

Capricorn. Plate from the synagogue of Dura

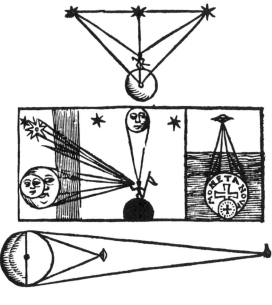

Louvre

Sun in Capricorn and Moon in Cancer

This combination increases the sensitiveness of Cancer, and gives an inclination toward economy, thrift, and prudence, but also a certain amount of selfishness. There is much tenacity, yet a love of change, and a desire for high attainments. With good aspects, there will be gain through parents or marriage. This polarity is good also for home life, possessions, honor, and reputation. The native will often occupy some public position, more or less notable according to the sphere of his birth, or he will hold some official post. In a good horoscope, success comes toward middle age.

Sun in Capricorn and Moon in Leo

Personal tendencies are toward affection in this combination. There is some love of ostentation and display, and ideals are high regarding artistic, social, or political interests. At its best, this polarity gives a dignified, self-reliant nature, ambitious of power and distinction, firm, strong-willed, and with much force of character. The native is honorable and kindly; he may have some dramatic power and an ability for occupations connected with public life and amusements. He is fitted for a prominent position, is ambitious of social distinction; he has some capacity for financial speculation and large business enterprises, and will probably succeed through them. There will usually be gain by legacy or marriage.

Sun in Capricorn and Moon in Virgo

In this polarity, the critical and analytical tendencies of Virgo are softened by the meditative and contemplative Capricorn nature. The native has an orderly and methodical mind and is logical, analytical, and clear-headed. Basically he is a little lacking in enterprise, but this may be supplied by the planetary positions. He is good in positions held under authority, or in those pertaining to medicine, law, or science. He has good business ability, and sometimes a literary one, but is usually at his best when associated with someone else, or in the employ of others.

Sun in Capricorn and Moon in Libra

The well-balanced brain of Libra and the thoughtfulness of Capricorn will give splendid intuition and foresight. It gives a love of popu-

Shepherd's Kalendar, 1631

larity and the desire for fame; it is favorable for partnership, marriage, and friendship. In a good horoscope it benefits parental and family life, and will produce a dignified, humane, well-balanced, methodical, and law-abiding nature of good disposition.

Sun in Capricorn and Moon in Scorpio

This combination gives positiveness and determination, strength of will, masterfulness, with some hardness and selfishness. The native is apt to be self-centered, difficult to influence, and materialistic. This feeling of independence is strong. In a good horoscope, he is able to control others, plan, organize, exert tact and diplomacy, and exhibit useful qualities as a leader in business, politics, or home life.

Sun in Capricorn and Moon in Sagittarius

The practical nature of Capricorn will steady the impulsiveness of Sagittarius and improve the executive ability. It is a good combination for explorers and also for the church, as it gives much religious ambition. There is decided business and financial ability, but the outcome depends greatly on aspects. If these are good, there will be gain through investments, speculative or otherwise, through travel, commerce, or occupations connected with the church or law.

Sun and Moon in Capricorn

This combination gives a thoughtful character, but with some inclination to despondency. There is apt to be too much independence at times. The feelings are not expansive, and there is a tendency to retire inwardly and live a life of loneliness. The native has good business ability; he is acquisitive, somewhat self-centered, reserved, steady, quiet, tactful, persistent, plodding, and thorough in his methods. Strong aspects from Mars or Jupiter will give more energy and ambition. If Mercury is strong in his horoscope he will possess more intellectual power.

208

James Watt: Sun in Capricorn. (After J. E. Lander's painting)

Sun in Capricorn and Moon in Aquarius

Splendid organizing ability, with success in large undertakings, is given in this combination. It quickens the perceptions, gives considerable intuition and the ability to read character accurately. Progress is made through careful forethought and steady persistence. Much depends on the aspects, however. With Uranus or Mercury prominent, the native will have an original and inventive mind, and a stronger instinct to marry, and with support from Venus or Jupiter there is likely to be geniality and popularity. Money may be gained through governmental or other official positions. There is usually good business ability, with success in financial operations and investments.

Sun in Capricorn and Moon in Pisces

This polarity tends to produce a quiet, undemonstrative, easy-going nature, moderately sociable and home-loving, sometimes rather retiring and self-distrustful. The native possesses better abilities than most people suppose, but lacks the energy or opportunity to use them to advantage. Some are careful and frugal, anxious about the future, but others are rather careless

Mountain Goat Falling. Persian MS., 13th century

Benjamin Franklin: Sun in Capricorn

or indifferent. They are charitable according to their means, and sympathetic, or, if circumstances necessitate it, they may benefit by the charity of others. They are suited for occupations connected with liquids, hospitals, charitable movements, and institutions. If the "ascendant" is a mercurial sign, they may make good writers, speakers, or preachers. They possess considerable tact, and do not show their whole nature on the surface by any means.

FAMOUS PEOPLE BORN WITH THE SUN IN CAPRICORN

Joan of Arc:	January 6, 1412
Isaac Newton:	December 25, 1642
Benjamin Franklin:	January 17, 1706
Alexander Hamilton:	January 11, 1757
Edgar Allan Poe:	January 19, 1809
Paul Cézanne:	January 19, 1839
Woodrow Wilson:	December 28, 1856
Henri Matisse:	December 31, 1869
Albert Schweitzer:	January 14, 1875
Pablo Casals:	December 29, 1876
Carl Sandburg:	January 6, 1878
Rebecca West:	December 25, 1892
Mao Tse-tung:	December 26, 1893
Humphrey Bogart:	December 25, 1899
Cary Grant:	January 18, 1904
Marlene Dietrich:	December 27, 1904
Simone de Beauvoir:	January 9, 1908
Galina Ulanova:	January 10, 1910
Richard Nixon:	January 9, 1913
Martin Luther King:	January 15, 1929
Thomas P. F. Hoving:	January 15, 1931

211

Saturn. Mediaeval Housebook, Castle Wolfegg.
Metropolitan Museum of Art

January 21 to February 19

THE WATER-BEARER

The sign of the
Truth-seeker or Scientist

A fixed airy sign
Honest, probing, broad-minded, amiable, humane, popular

Ruler: Uranus

Gems: sapphire, opal

Color: electric blue
Metal: uranium

Harmonious signs for business, marriage, or
companionship: Libra, Gemini, Aries

The Aquarian Type

Evolved Type. The chief characteristic of the typical Aquarian is his extraordinary breadth of vision. He is unbiased and open-minded, without prejudice or superstition of any kind. Tradition and authority leave him untouched. When he finds himself face to face with them, he regards them with tranquility and serenity, and possibly with a certain friendliness and interest; but no amount of natural courtesy toward them will make him refrain from turning on them the searchlight of the truth-seeker. His ways are neither militant nor aggressive. He can wait; and the longer he waits, the more clearly he realizes the difficulty of attaining certainty about anything that is worth knowing and the folly of condemning too hastily the theories of other truth seekers who are just as likely to be in the right as he is. This results in an entire lack of pose, and perfect freedom from vanity and self-conceit as far as knowledge is concerned.

He is willing to learn from anyone, for the only thing of which he is sure is that he does not know very much. If after patient inquiry and deep probing he realizes that he has made a discovery or exposed a fallacy, he is generally eager to pass the information on to others as quickly as possible, even if in so doing he has to recant views he has formerly advocated, and abandon some of his favorite theories. He is, in fact, the finest possible type of scientist, the student of laws, the truth-seeker, patient, dispassionate, and untiring, whose method is to take a comprehensive view of his subject, form his own hypothesis, and then marshal his facts, trying and testing his theories until they are proof against assault. "What is the *truth* of the matter?" is his one concern, and the pet question of the prosaic craftsman — who so often advances a bogus claim to a scientific attitude of mind — "What is the *use* of it?" rarely enters into his calculations at all.

Abraham Lincoln: Sun in Aquarius
(Painting by George P. A. Healy.)

Franklin D. Roosevelt: Sun in Aquarius

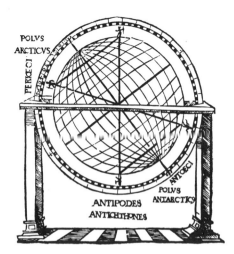

Primitive Type. The faults of the primitive Aquarian may be summed up in the one word "inefficiency," for breadth of vision seems to bewilder rather than to assist those who possess it, and a wide outlook is often accompanied by such deplorably short sight — figuratively speaking — that practical details are lost in a general haziness. However conscious these people may be of an overpowering number of things they ought to be doing, they have great difficulty in deciding just where and when to begin. They are consequently inclined to fritter away a good deal of time and energy, often missing their best opportunities by wavering over trifling decisions, and showing a lamentable lack of practical common sense in adapting available means to the end in view.

They have very little power of concentration, and though generally amiable and well-meaning

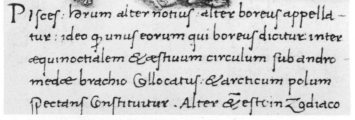

are apt to blunder into difficulties through lack of imagination and tact. Their memory is sometimes deficient — or possibly only rather slow. Important details are forgotten till it is too late to consider them, and their work is too often attacked in a hesitating and apparently heedless kind of way.

Another accusation frequently brought up against them is that of moral and physical cowardice; and there certainly is a peace-at-any-price tendency about most of them. They may possibly be induced to fight for what they feel to be important truths, or in defense of those weaker than themselves; but anyone skilled in strategy can get the better of them, at any rate for the moment, for they are easily betrayed into allowing their attention to wander to abstract questions of right and wrong when they ought to be holding themselves in readiness and concentrating their energies on points of possible attack or defense. Most of them, especially the women, are apt to feel flurried and bewildered when they have blundered into a battle. They have no resource beyond some cherished conviction, hitting out clumsily and blindly, goaded to the effort chiefly by the desire to get the trouble over as quickly as possible. In the confusion of the moment, point after point may possibly be yielded, but when the atmosphere is clear, again, the chances are that our Aquarian will be found just exactly where he or she was before. If the outlook is really a wide one, it cannot be narrowed to please those who do not share it. This fact, taken in conjunction with the typical truth-seeker's attitude of mind toward tradition, results in disconcerting departures from precedent. The laws they hold in honor are not necessarily those most revered by the particular communities, and Aquarians are apt to go their own way, ignoring convention and authority, and so meet with a good deal of hostility and criticism.

Many students have been puzzled by the fact that this inclination to defy public opinion is much stronger in people born with Uranus

Hyginus, 15th-century Italian MS.
N.Y. Public Library

Saturn

rising than in those born with Aquarius rising, and find it difficult to accept Uranus as the ruler of Aquarius in consequence. Aquarians, generally speaking, are too tranquil in temperament, too gentle and kindly in disposition, to outrage the feelings of their families and friends by startling eccentricities of conduct; but the planet Uranus rising in any of the more energetic and enterprising signs and especially in any of the cardinal signs, with their tendency to come before the public in one capacity or another, may easily lead to what seems to others amazing and unaccountable decisions and extremely peculiar behavior, especially if associated with an ill-disciplined nature. In the case of those who have sufficient balance and self-control to avoid foolish extremes, Uranus rising is often associated with a dash of genius; but to have it rising where the nature is ill-balanced and the judgment faulty suggests a stormy career indeed, especially if it is in Aries or Gemini.

Love and Friendship. This eleventh sign of the zodiac is naturally associated with the eleventh house in the horoscope, which, according to tradition, tells us something of the special relationship of any man to humanity as a whole. It speaks of his friends and of the experiences that come to him through friendship, and also suggests the favor or disfavor of the general public. The Water-bearer is represented as pouring forth liberally the water — the emotion — which he carries; and the affections of the true-born Aquarian are certainly far-reaching and widespread. His attitude to the whole world is kindly and humane. People of this type will take any amount of trouble to increase the comfort and well-being of those around them, and find great satisfaction in devising simple pleasures for others. Charities, and societies for the amelioration of social conditions among the poor, often find in them willing contributors.

The Aquarian has a way of looking at life's problems from the outside rather than from the center. Instead of trusting others, he studies them, scrutinizing their words and actions and if possible even their thoughts, earnestly, patiently, and carefully; and as humanity, conscious of its own shortcomings, is not particularly keen on being vivisected, it is apt to grow restive during the process. It also craves for personal and particular appreciation and attention, and the acquaintances of the Aquarian often find it somewhat of a shock to realize that the very kindliness and interest which tickled their vanity and delighted their egotism when they first met him are equally at the disposal of later comers. If they are of a jealous and exacting disposition, friendship with him will prove impossible; but in rejecting it they show little judgment, for the friendship of the Aquarian is founded on an understanding and personal esteem which go right down to the foundations of character, and his tranquil affection is crystalline in its purity and sincerity, and well worth having.

The above characteristics sometimes result in a certain isolation and loneliness so far as intimate affections are concerned, and the trouble is accentuated by a real incapacity for settling down to anything like a steady friendship, or definitely and distinctly entering upon terms of affection and intimacy for more than a very brief space of time. Where memory is not a strong point, loyalty to individuals cannot be expected to flourish, and if imagination is lacking and the thirst for knowledge great, the chances are that the individual will spend a good deal of time "putting his foot in his mouth" with his fellow men, however amiable and well-meaning he may be. As a matter of fact, we find Aquarians constantly getting into hot water through asking tactless and point-blank questions about the feelings and actions and opinions of others. They seem to lack intuition, and cannot rest content until they have reached the heart of the mystery. They often seem puzzled and a little disappointed to find that the hidden treasure didn't really amount to much after all, and are apt to add insult to injury by naïvely expressing their opinion to that effect.

Aquarians are slow to wed, although they generally do so in the end. They frequently make friendship the foundation of love, and choose a partner who is not merely a mate but a "chum" as well, and consequently capable of sharing in some at least of the many interests which go to make up the Aquarian's mental life. They are naturally well equipped for matrimony, possessing the priceless treasure of a wide and unprejudiced outlook, which can make allowances for difference of heredity, environment, training, and education. The kindliness and humanity of the sign also favor marriage, for the typical Aquarian is inclined by nature to exact little and to give much, is incapable of petty tyranny and puerile jealously, and carries a certain tender consideration into all the more intimate relations of the conjugal state.

Their dilatoriness is the more to be regretted; but it springs quite naturally from the characteristics of the type. Both men and women find it extraordinarily difficult to let themselves go, and cling to the delusion of a safe and pleasant friendship long after that has become an impossibility for the prospective partner. Even after the goal of matrimony is actually in sight, they shrink from any approach to definite love-making, hesitating and vacillating and evading to an extent that is really unfair and unkind. In favorable circumstances the first ardor of youth may possibly carry an occasional Aquarian into an early engagement, but, if so, it will probably be years before any further step is taken. The very kindliness and consideration of this sign prevent an Aquarian lover from urging his betrothed to face circumstances that he deems too hard for her, and she shrinks from becoming a burden to the man she loves. Courage and faith and hope are shoved into the background while fear and doubt and delay win the victory all along the line. The chances are that some rival with a little more fire will cut the Aquarian out; in which case, after heaving a few sentimental sighs, he will probably relapse into friendliness again, repeating the experience from time to time as the years go on, without even beginning to understand just how and where he blunders.

"Faint heart never won fair lady," and the woman who is called upon to choose between a man who, whatever his faults may be, can and does play the convincing lover with energy, and one who is apparently not very sure whether he wants to marry at all, is not very likely to place her happiness in the hands of the doubter. Nothing is more fatal to romance than the discovery that the supposed admirer is a cold-blooded examiner in disguise, who is testing and trying, weighing and deliberating, as he has probably done in the case of other "possibilities" already. So the years may slip by till middle age is past. The fortieth birthday or the happy wedding of the last bachelor friend suddenly awakens our sentimentalist to the fact that he is preparing for himself a childless and lonely old age, and having done his part as dutiful son

Kalendar. Johann Stöffler, 1518, *N.Y. Public Library*

KL Januarius ¶ Capricornº

			Solis motus		Lune motus medius.			Lune Centrum.			Lune argumentū medium		
			G	m̄	S	G	m̄	S	G	m̄	S	G	m̄
1	A		Circumcisio domini	20	21	0	13	11	0	24	23	0	13	4
2	b	4 Nõ	Octaua Stephani	21	22	0	26	21	1	18	46	0	26	8
3	c	3 Nõ	Octaua Ioannis	22	23	1	9	32	2	13	9	1	9	12
4	d	2 Non	Octaua Innocentum	23	25	1	22	42	3	7	32	1	22	16
5	e	None.		24	36	2	5	53	4	1	54	2	5	19
6	f	8 Idus	Epiphania domini	25	27	2	19	3	4	26	17	2	18	23
7	g	7 Idus	¶ Clauis lxx.	26	28	3	2	14	5	20	40	3	1	27
8	A	6 Idus	Erhardi Epiſcopi	27	29	3	15	25	6	15	3	3	14	31
9	b	5 Idus		28	31	3	28	35	7	9	26	3	27	35
10	c	4 Idus	Pauli primi eremitę	29	32	4	11	46	8	3	49	4	10	39
11	d	3 Idus	¶ Aquarius	0	33	4	24	56	8	28	12	4	23	43
12	e	2 Idus		1	34	5	8	7	9	22	35	5	6	47
13	f	Idus	Octaua epiphanię Hilary epī	2	36	5	21	18	10	16	58	5	19	51
14	g	19 Kaſ	Februarij Foelicis in pincis	3	37	6	4	28	11	11	20	6	2	55
15	A	18 Kaſ		4	38	6	17	39	0	5	43	6	15	58
16	b	17 Kaſ	Marcelli papę	5	39	7	0	49	1	0	6	6	29	2
17	c	16 Kaſ	Antonij monachi	6	40	7	14	0	1	24	29	7	12	6
18	d	15 Kaſ	Priſcę virginis	7	41	7	27	10	2	18	52	7	25	10
19	e	14 Kaſ		8	42	8	10	21	3	13	15	8	8	14
20	f	13 Kaſ	Fabiani et Sebaſtiani martiꝝ	9	43	8	23	32	4	7	38	8	21	18
21	g	12 Kaſ	Agnetis virginis	10	44	9	6	42	5	2	1	9	4	22
22	A	11 Kaſ	Vincentij martiris	11	45	9	19	53	5	26	24	9	17	26
23	b	10 Kaſ		12	46	10	3	3	6	20	46	10	0	30
24	c	9 Kaſ	Timothei apoſtoli	13	47	10	16	14	7	15	9	10	13	34
25	d	8 Kaſ	Pauli conuerſio	14	48	10	29	25	8	9	32	10	26	37
26	e	7 Kaſ		15	48	11	12	35	9	3	55	11	9	41
27	f	6 Kaſ	Ioannis Chryſoſtomi	16	49	11	25	46	9	28	18	11	22	45
28	g	5 Kaſ	¶ Clauis xl.	17	50	0	8	56	10	22	41	0	5	49
29	A	4 Kaſ	Valerij epiſcopi	18	50	0	22	7	11	17	4	0	18	53
30	b	3 Kaſ		19	51	1	5	18	0	11	27	1	1	57
31	c	2 Kaſ		19	51	1	18	43	1	5	50	1	15	1

¶ Carnes torreo Ianus en trementes
Et lętus comedo: bibóꝗ ad ignem

Dies 31 Anni.

B ij

Charles Lindbergh

Clark Gable

Jeanne Moreau

Tallulah Bankhead

BORN UNDER THE SIGN OF AQUARIUS

European

Culver

Colette

Mia Farrow

Babe Ruth

Adlai Stevenson

ide World

he then sets about doing his wooing in earnest.

In spite of his own exemplary conduct as husband and father, the Aquarian type is rarely rigidly orthodox on the subject of the marriage law. Faithful and loyal to his promises himself — at any rate *after* the tie has been definitely formed — he is ultra-tolerant in his estimation of those who are not.

Literary Style. Among writers who have the Sun in this sign and who answer strongly to the influence of Uranus are Francis Bacon and Charles Darwin, both renowned as having altered and enlarged the outlook of their brother scientists to a remarkable extent. Both had the Sun—indicating success—in Aquarius, and probably Darwin had it at the Zenith, for his life suggests Cancer as ascendant.

John Ruskin, whose birth hour has been recorded, shows the Sun rising in Aquarius, and Uranus close to the zenith. That Ruskin abandoned verse as he grew older is probably no loss to literature, especially as he gave us in its place some of the most beautiful passages of

Triumpho di Fortuna. Fanti
Pierpont Morgan Library

descriptive English prose that have ever yet been penned. The opening chapters of *The Stones of Venice* may be cited as examples of his style at its finest, but to the end of his literary career he shows all the most striking of the Aquarian characteristics — simplicity, sincerity, the attitude of the truth-seeker and the habits of the student, and an intense interest in sociology and the real welfare of humanity as a whole.

Religion. The religious tendency of the Aquarian is to a thoughtful and reverent agnosticism, founded on the recognition of the fact that the finite human mind cannot hope to grasp the infinite. If he takes any interest in forms and ceremonies, it is to examine and compare them, and he treats the traditional teachings of the great founders of religion in the same way, accepting no other man's verdict, but probing and inquiring into the matter for himself. The jottings and journals of Marcus Aurelius, the great philosopher, Emperor of Rome, suggest the

Charles Dickens: Sun in Aquarius

Aquarian mind at its noblest and best. This grand old pagan viewed life steadily and viewed it whole, in spite of his moods of agnosticism, in which he realized that the greatest of all facts — those that seemed to him most essential — were not, and could not be, logically proved, and that there was possibly much human error mixed with the dearest and most sacred of his own convictions.

Physical Characteristics. The influence of this sign often shows physically in remarkable nobility of feature, and especially of profile. It is emphatically the sign of the man. The dispassionate and platonic tendency of the type in its emotional life finds a curious echo in the physical vehicle, for the men not infrequently show some feminine trait, and the women some characteristic that is censured in them as masculine. Sometimes a man otherwise well proportioned will have a breadth of hip almost as great as his breadth of shoulder, suggesting that his manly form has somehow been built upon a feminine skeleton. (Astrologers observe with interest that doctors are now describing people who in structure or measurement show characteristics of both sexes, as "Uranians." The type is increasingly common, as humanity is at present responding freely to the influence of Aquarius.) And narrow hips and a masculine habit of movement and posture have been noted in exceptionally fine and essentially womanly specimens of this type. As a rule these people are tall and fair, with blue or grey eyes, deep-set and wide apart; and many of them have the student's trick of the slightly drooping head, suggesting that the thoughts revolving in the busy brain have actual weight. Their voices are gentle, and somewhat monotonous, and they seldom laugh; but many of them have a peculiarly winning and delightful smile which derives a special charm from its unexpectedness.

Their movements are generally as leisurely as their thoughts, but in spite of their serene and tranquil ways they can be exceedingly outspoken and even severe at times — especially if what has roused them is some manifestation of

John Barrymore: Sun in Aquarius

slyness, hypocrisy, and double-dealing. Nothing will shake their conviction that the truth ought to be trusted, and those who tell it so ingeniously as to give a false impression to their hearers without actually uttering a falsehood themselves arouse Aquarian indignation as strongly as those who pervert it or keep it back.

Health. Aquarius is said by the older astrologers to "rule the blood," and the only characteristic symptom of Aquarian ill-health is a sluggish circulation, manifested in cold hands and feet. Friendship and sunny fresh air are the best remedies.

223

SUN IN AQUARIUS

The Sun in Aquarius gives a refined individuality with a love of everything humanitarian. These people are faithful, sincere, just, with very broad sympathies and a desire to embrace the whole of humanity.

Sun in Aquarius and Moon in Aries

This combination gives a firm character, quiet, and not very expressive, but with perceptive ability. Natives are good judges of human character. They are persevering, but liable at times to go to extremes. They have determination and persistence of purpose and cannot endure being controlled or thwarted. They will go to unreasonable lengths to have their own way, and are fond of imposing their will upon others, leading or controlling. And yet they are not always fortunate when the whole responsibility for any affair is theirs. If they learn to submit to association with others, if not as subordinates, then as partners or companions, they will usually obtain the best results.

Sun in Aquarius and Moon in Taurus

This polarity makes an excellent character reader. He inclines to the practical, and is faithful, sincere, firm, just, and reliable. Once having found a congenial channel to work in, these people do not easily forsake it, for change of any kind is foreign to their nature. Whatever their mode of life may be, they tend to continue faithfully and ploddingly in it, and vary or alter their course only under extreme necessity. In business or profession they usually accumulate honors, money, or possessions, whichever they may have set their minds upon, although these may not come until middle or old age. The influence is good for friends, acquaintances, and social and public relations generally.

Sun in Aquarius and Moon in Gemini

This combination intensifies the intellectual qualities, giving a studious mind, well adapted for literary pursuits. Also displayed are considerable industry, neatness, and attention to details. These people may be fitted for almost any occupation calling for acuteness and originality of mind, or mental resource. They usually succeed as speakers, preachers, writers, or teachers. They are sometimes a little retiring, liking reserve and seclusion, but this may easily be counteracted if Jupiter or Venus is prominent, as it does not arise from an unsociable nature. They are kind and good-hearted, and have many acquaintances if few intimate friends.

Sun in Aquarius and Moon in Cancer

This combination intensifies the economical, tenacious, and sensitive tendencies of Cancer, and gives great intuition. If the horoscope is fairly harmonious, these people have a strong attraction to home life, marriage, friendship, social and domestic matters. If aspects are adverse, their greatest misfortunes will come through these channels. They have good mental abilities, but are usually more emotional than intellectual.

Sun in Aquarius and Moon in Leo

This polarity intensifies the love nature, and there is an inclination to worship those who are loved. The nature will tend toward either the intellect or the feelings, according to the balance of influences in the horoscope. There are an active intellect and a lively imagination, which may help to achieve great things. There is also a sense of dignity and pride, coupled with a liking for society, a love of approbation, a desire for distinction, honor, and for "cutting a figure" or taking the lead. Leo adds warmth, ardor, and imagination to the Aquarius nature.

Sun in Aquarius and Moon in Virgo

This combination intensifies neatness, precision, carefulness, and awakens the critical faculties. It gives prudence, practicality, and business ability, and there is usually a love of science and intellectual pursuits in general. There may be some lack of demonstrativeness, activity, or hopefulness. Such a person prospers best in association with another who would supply the initiative or enterprise.

Sun in Aquarius and Moon in Libra

This combination gives splendid powers of judgment, remarkable perception, a very intuitive mind, and much foresight. It awakens the spiritual side of the nature, and gives balance and equilibrium. Success in marriage is indicated. There are considerable imagination, love of the beautiful, and a keen appreciation of music and the other arts, all of which will be active if Venus is strong. It conduces to sociability, popularity, partnership, and friendship.

Sun in Aquarius and Moon in Scorpio

Scorpio inclines the nature to be somewhat worldly and selfish, with ability to play upon the nature of others. People born under this combination are apt to be positive, self-reliant, sometimes self-assertive, proud, and not easily influenced. Sometimes they are irritable, abrupt, or aggressive. Less desirable characteristics may easily be toned down if "benefics" are prominent; then the nature becomes extremely useful in the world. Such people are practical, businesslike, firm, and hard-working, suited for positions of prominence or responsibility, and likely to gain money, property, power, and dignity.

Vanessa Redgrave: Sun in Aquarius

Sun in Aquarius and Moon in Sagittarius

This combination makes the personality rather too quick for the slow, steady individuality; but it adds concentration to the impulsive nature of Sagittarius. Speech is apt to be impulsive and abrupt. These people have considerable literary ability, imagination, and love of beauty, which tend to increase the number of acquaintances and friends. There is fitness for a career in connection with religion, philosophy, law, acting, or one of the fine arts.

Sun in Aquarius and Moon in Capricorn

This combination makes the personality shrewd, tactful, and eager to attain great heights, which are often reached through favoritism and the help of friends. There is much solidity of thought and ability for political matters. Ideas are broad and the mind subtle. The native has a somewhat serious, grave, thoughtful nature, with a good deal of firmness, patience, and perseverance. There are ambition, tact, a power to face difficult or adverse circumstances unmoved, an ability to control other people, a good memory, and suitability for positions of responsibility. The favor of the public, of acquaintances, and of superiors is likely to be gained.

Sun and Moon in Aquarius

This combination gives a great deal of discretion, discrimination, and careful thought. It intensifies the clearness and brightness of the Aquarian intellect. It is not an altogether fortunate combination in a worldly sense, but it makes the mind positive, self-reliant, original, fairly active, humane, well-disposed, and well-balanced. With good aspects the native is likely to be very popular, and to have many acquaintances and a pleasant home life. Marriage is extremely probable.

Sun in Aquarius and Moon in Pisces

This combination gives perseverance and

Aquarius. Book of Stars and Constellations. Persian, 1630

carefulness, awakening the studious side of the Pisces nature, but much depends upon planetary influences and the aspects to Sun and Moon. Imagination, love of beauty, musical or artistic ability, refinement, sentiment, charitable

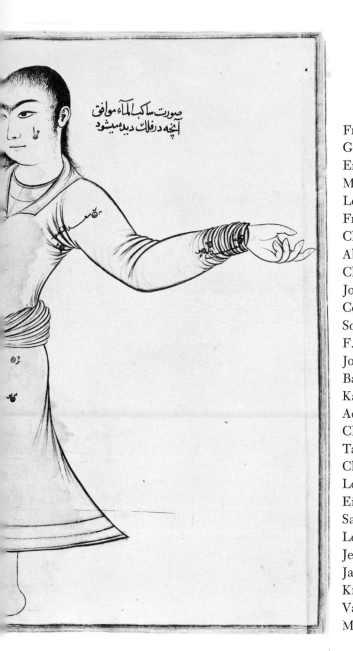

صورت ساكب الماء موافق
آنچه در فلك ديده ميشود

FAMOUS PEOPLE BORN WITH
THE SUN IN AQUARIUS

Francis Bacon:	January 22, 1561
Galileo:	February 15, 1564
Emanuel Swedenborg:	January 29, 1688
Mozart:	January 27, 1756
Lord Byron:	January 22, 1788
Franz Schubert:	January 31, 1797
Charles Darwin:	February 12, 1809
Abraham Lincoln:	February 12, 1809
Charles Dickens:	February 7, 1812
John Ruskin:	February 8, 1819
Colette:	January 28, 1873
Somerset Maugham:	January 25, 1874
F. D. Roosevelt:	January 30, 1882
John Barrymore:	February 15, 1882
Babe Ruth:	February 6, 1895
Katharine Cornell:	February 16, 1898
Adlai Stevenson:	February 5, 1900
Clark Gable:	February 1, 1901
Tallulah Bankhead:	January 31, 1902
Charles Lindbergh:	February 4, 1902
Louis Nizer:	February 6, 1902
Eileen Farrell:	February 13, 1920
Santha Rama Rau:	January 24, 1923
Leontyne Price:	February 10, 1927
Jeanne Moreau:	January 23, 1928
James Dean:	February 8, 1931
Kim Novak:	February 13, 1933
Vanessa Redgrave:	January 30, 1937
Mia Farrow:	February 9, 1945

feeling, and sympathy are often unconventional. Unless positive tendencies are given by the ascendant or planetary positions, the nature is unassuming, a little retiring, agreeable and sociable, more suited for some relatively quiet and unambitious occupation than for one involving publicity, responsibility, or conflict. The native benefits by friends and patrons.

February 20 to March 20

THE FISH

The sign of the
Poet or Interpreter

A mutable watery sign
Gentle, kind, retiring, sensitive, unlucky
often melancholy

Ruler: Neptune

Gems: chrysolite, moonstone

Color: sea-green
Metal: tin

Harmonious signs for business, marriage, or
companionship: Cancer, Scorpio, Virgo

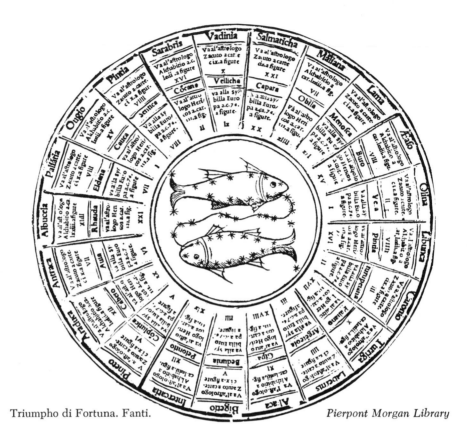

Triumpho di Fortuna. Fanti.   *Pierpont Morgan Library*

The Piscarian Type

Evolved Type. The strength of the typical Piscarian lies in his ideals and aspirations rather than in his actions. He usually has little worldly ambition, cares nothing for rank or power, seldom succeeds in making money, and rarely accumulates it. He is indifferent about restrictions and limitations, so long as the inner self is left free to feel, dream, and grow according to its own nature. Many people born under this sign are attracted to the cloister or shrink from society and from any competition, rivalry, and strife. Many others go to sea, or spend available recreation time on a yacht or fishing boat, preferring the silent world of waters. With the vast ocean below and the star-spangled sky above, they rest content, calm and fearless; for

solitude and solitary musing are frequently the luxuries most prized by the type, especially if their lives are in uncongenial surroundings.

And yet it is difficult to say that any particular profession is impossible or unsuitable for a Piscarian. Individual commercial enterprise is least likely to be a success; however, if the business signs — Taurus and Virgo — are accentuated in his horoscope, the quick intuition and plastic mind given by Pisces may favor such undertakings. But as a rule the Sun, Moon, Neptune, or any striking group of planets in Pisces must be taken as inimical to worldly prosperity, because these positions indicate that the native will never make it his first consideration.

230

Alessandro Temini, 17th-century engraving

GVSTO   FEBRARO   PESCE

Io gusto ogni piacer, lieta, e contenta,   La stagion dedicata à i Bacchanali   Nell'onde christalline il patrie ostello,

Nè mi turba il pensier l'affanno, e il duolo: È da me posseduta in feste, e in gioco: Hebbi dal factor dell'vniverso:

All'eterno goder spiegato ho il uolo,   Passo l'hore felice: e nulla, ò poco   Et hora nelle sfere alte conuerso,

E il martir, e il dolor, mai me tormenta   Mi trauaglian la mente gl'altrui mali.   Per far corona al sol lucente, e bello.

George Washington: Sun in Pisces
(Portrait by Joseph Wright.)

Curiously enough, the yearning for unity and the sense of completion carries many Pisceans onto the stage. This may to some extent prove trying and uncongenial, but the actual work of interpretation always gives these people intense delight. Receptivity of mind makes them accept the thought of the poet or playwright as naturally as if it were their own, and, once possessed or inspired, they revel in calling up the necessary emotions. These, in their turn, dominate the action, and so transform, for the time being, the whole personality. Further, the sensitiveness peculiar to the type gives Piscarians a very special pleasure in feeling they are in touch with their audience; for that is to them a foretaste of the enlarged consciousness for which they yearn.

In proportion to their delight in such achievements, however, is the measure of their de-

spondency after failure; in some cases fits of unreasoning apprehension beforehand, and all the horrors of stage fright, are recurrent. Analyses of the horoscopes of successful actors and actresses show an amazing preponderance of this particular influence; there are few, if any, of the first rank without at least one planet in the sign. Ellen Terry had a quadruple accentuation, consisting of Neptune, the Sun, Saturn, and Mercury!

Apart from theatrical life, the true-born Piscarian generally learns sooner or later that all the world *is* a stage, and whether he plays lead or simply walks on he realizes more fully than is possible for other men that his life is only part of a stupendous whole, and that the setting of the scene is transistory, elusive, and of little importance compared with the rendering of the piece. This is why many Piscarians are peculiarly fitted to enter the church, the army, and the navy, or to take employment in institutions such

Ellen Terry: Sun in Pisces

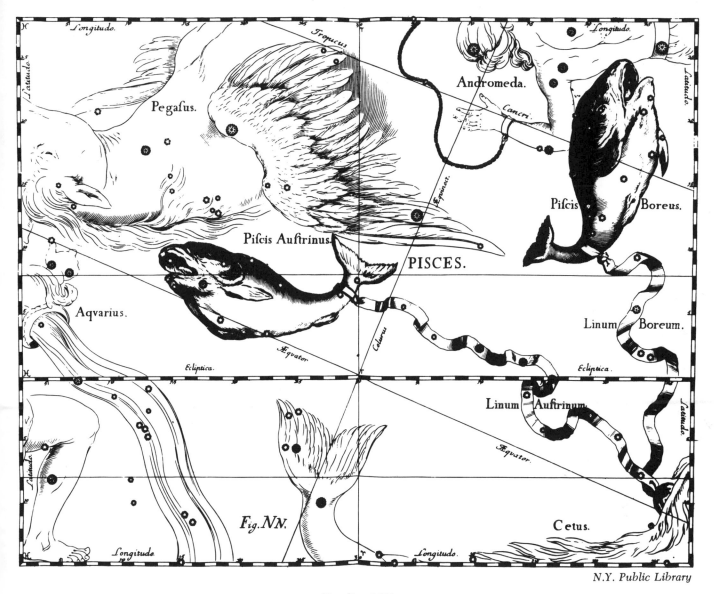

Hevelius, 1690

as hospitals, universities, colleges, or in any other service which emphasizes the fact that the whole is greater than any of its parts, or teaches a man to regard himself as a mere unit, whose duty it is to put self and self-seeking aside. Government service is suited to this type; because the salaries, though small, are steady and regular. Life is often simplified for Piscarians by the fact that they accept celibacy easily, and many, especially women, lead cheerful and busy lives, content to sink their own individuality and fill up the odd corners of family life.

233

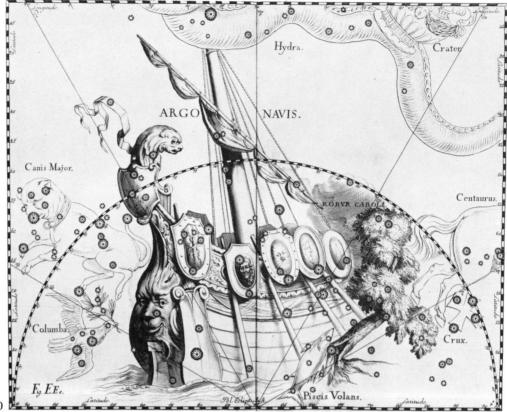

Primitive Type. The primitive Piscarian is almost invariably an anxiety to his friends. Lacking the spur of worldly ambition and even, sometimes, the desire to be self-supporting and independent, he drifts aimlessly through life, waiting vaguely for the prompter and incapable of using his discrimination when the cue comes. He will accept any suggestion that fits the emotional need of the moment, and, as a variety of emotional experiences is the true path of his evolution, that condition is constantly changing. Like a rudderless boat he drifts on a sea of sensations, caught by every passing current, driven by every wind that blows. The wistful yearnings for completion which make the real compelling force of the sign are translated into cravings for comforts, emotional excitement and, too often, for stimulants.

Even the fitness for celibacy and monastic life has its dark side in the earlier stages, merely manifested as a peculiar inability to understand the sanctity of marriage or to appreciate the qualities of faithfulness and loyalty. When highly developed, these people are pure yet very loving; but at the primitive level they are prone to strange adorations and antipathies which they do not attempt to control — reveling in the emotional exercise of a devotion that is positively abject, or shrinking with repulsion from an apparently harmless and innocent person. They are always more or less psychic and intuitional. Unless training leads this type in the direction of greater balance and self-restraint, nervous irritability, varied by sudden explosions of temper will become habitual.

Piscarians at this level also lack a sense of proprietorship, and cannot see why they should not be allowed to help themselves from the superfluity of others. Commercial integrity and a conscientious discharge of debts are altogether beyond them; and, though if they have money they are always quite willing to part with it, they can never understand why someone else who has the cash at hand should not meet their obligations for them.

Physical Characteristics. The stature is generally rather insignificant; the skin is soft the hair fine and silky, the eyes light, and the complexion pallid. The best-looking among them have better proportions, clear complexions, and dimples instead of wrinkles. All disadvantages are generally atoned for by the plasticity of feature, mobility of expression, and extraordinary grace

of movement and gesture. Even their somewhat deficient coloring seems to change and brighten as they forget themselves and their shyness in congenial society. A touch of the Neptune influence often adds great charm to childhood, and even in old age a certain childlike grace is sometimes retained, making the personality extremely lovable.

Piscarians are common in literature, but rarely play leading parts. An exception is Hamlet, the precise interpretation of whose character has been the subject of much debate. He is psychic, emotional, impressionable, prone to moods of loneliness and despondency, liable to sudden outbursts of severity which contrast strangely with his habitual gentleness. He is deeply religious, yet unrestrained in his flights of daring speculation, and so utterly devoid of ambition that he declares that he could be bounded in a nutshell, and yet count himself king of infinite space. Students who wish to have a clear conception of the tendencies of the Piscarian type should read and re-read Hamlet's utterances, remembering, however, that in his character, if authorities on Shakespeare are correct, we have inextricably mixed up a youth of twenty and a man of thirty. Many consider it practically certain that in the original draft of the play Shakespeare gave poignancy and pathos to the plot by making the unfortunate Prince a student at college, (as certain of the lines seem to show) and that his age was afterward advanced ten years (with some of the more philosophic speeches added) because Burbage was too fat and heavily built an actor to play so youthful a part effectively. The play, by judicious omission, can still be taken either way, but at whatever age the character is read, the influence of Neptune sways it.

Health. People strongly dominated by the vibrations of Neptune rarely fear death. They are frequently somewhat frail, but if the nature is finely balanced and activities are wisely guided, they will probably enjoy excellent bodily health.

Hamlet. Watercolor by Delacroix

Literary Style. The literary style of the Piscarian is hard to define and practically impossible to parody, for it is so plastic that it tends to vary with the mood of the moment. It abounds in delicate shades of expression and is characterized by appropriate and illuminating turns of phrase. It is subtly suggestive, graceful, natural, and never commonplace. The works of Piscarians retain their hold upon the reading public because they deal with underlying realities, even while apparently discussing the ordinary events of everyday life.

At his supreme moments the Piscarian's realization of the essential unity of all things is so overwhelming, that he finds utterance in marvelously pregnant phrases, full of vitality and essential truth.

Chopin: Sun in Pisces. (Painting by Delacroix.)

When Jupiter, the planet of the mind, is placed in Pisces, and Neptune is in any powerful position, then we may expect to find a very high level of achievement from people born under these configurations. Most astrologers are agreed in thinking that Pisces was in a descendant position when Shakespeare was born, in which case his horoscope works out with Neptune in Gemini at the very Zenith, thus making the Piscarian influence a dominant one, and accounting for his marvelous intuition and inspiration, as well as for the perfect ease and naturalness of his expression.

In the New Testament, certain passages from St. John are revealing. The most mystic — and consequently the most Piscarian — of his chapters, "I am the vine, ye are the branches," is a clear, concise, and illuminating statement of the essential unity of the human and the divine. And the passage beginning "Let not your hearts be troubled" is also exquisitely perfect from the literary point of view. Other saints and mystics of the early Christian Church suggest the domination of Neptune in their life and works. This is especially true of St. Francis of Assisi, whose famous hymn proclaims his love for his brother the Sun and his sister the Moon. The life of St. Francis is one long record of ceaseless devotion and self-sacrifice, and the descriptions of his physical characteristics and constitution point clearly to the influence of Pisces. His stature was insignificant, his health fragile, and he had what his devoted disciples envied as "the gift of tears." He was utterly indifferent to the ties of home and kindred and regarded all men equally as his brethren.

Around the Fish. Paul Klee

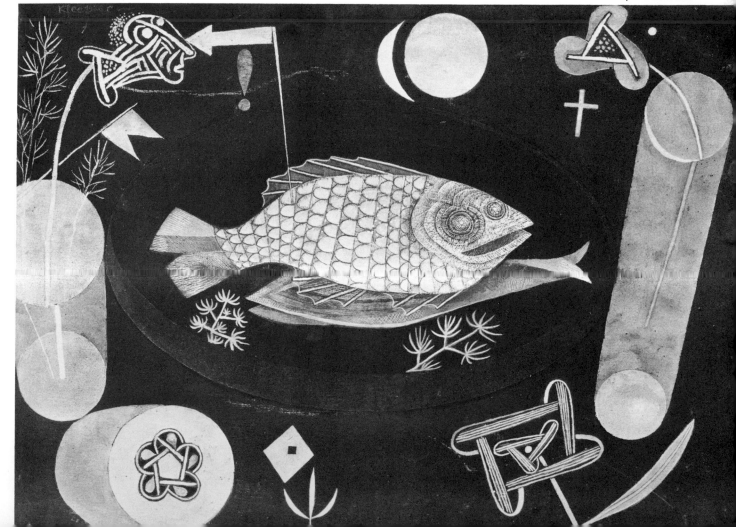

Vaslav Nijinsky

Rudolf Nureyev

Harry Belafonte

BORN UNDER THE SIGN OF PISCES

Ann Zane Shanks

Svetlana Stalin Alliluyeva

Wide World

The Earl of Snowdon
(Antony Armstrong-Jones)

John Springer

Enrico Caruso

Elizabeth Taylor

SUN IN PISCES

The Sun in Pisces tends to make the individual nature emotional and receptive, meditative and imitative. This is not the strongest of the twelve signs, but it gives a very deep internal nature. Developed are extremely altruistic characters, filled with an inexhaustible love for all created beings.

Sun in Pisces and Moon in Aries

This combination adds force and energy to the Pisces sign, and gives more self-reliance and considerable willfulness. There is positiveness, energy and activity. The native is busy and brisk, interested in details, full of ideas, words, enthusiasms, and is a copious worker. There are likely to be hopefulness, ardor, and active fancy. New causes or pursuits are taken up eagerly, though sometimes with too much haste, so they are dropped again. There is sometimes too much change and novelty and too little persistence and self-control. Though generous and kind-hearted, the native may be difficult to get on with, and may sometimes be his own worst enemy.

Sun in Pisces and Moon in Taurus

The firmness of Taurus strengthens the vacillation of Pisces, and makes a kind, quiet, sociable, and pleasant nature. The native is attracted to home and friends; he is somewhat fortunate in money matters; he displays carefulness, some economy, and a tendency to slow and patient accumulation. There is some business ability as well as musical or artistic ability. There will be little ambition, and quieter or relatively subordinate positions are more fortunate. This polarity tends toward steadiness and conscientiousness.

Sun in Pisces and Moon in Gemini

This combination produces indecision and an inclination to restless activity and worry. The native is easily affected by the moods of others, and is rather fanciful. This polarity makes the mind active, yet there is likely to be irresolution, or at least lack of continuity or fixity of purpose. There is sometimes diffidence or reserve, lack of enterprise, initiative, or ambition, yet, the native learns readily and sometimes shows decided precocity. A love of teaching or preaching is often associated with this influence, and nearly always a love of traveling. In some cases there are changes of occupation or unnecessary changes of residence, or two occupations are followed or two residences kept.

Fish. The Psalm Book of Charles Knowles

Sun in Pisces and Moon in Cancer

This intensifies the imaginative and sensitive nature of Cancer, and increases the receptivity and economy. The emotional aspect is keen but not lacking in reflection, and the whole nature is harmonious, sensitive, imaginative, and hospi-

240

Delne fecit

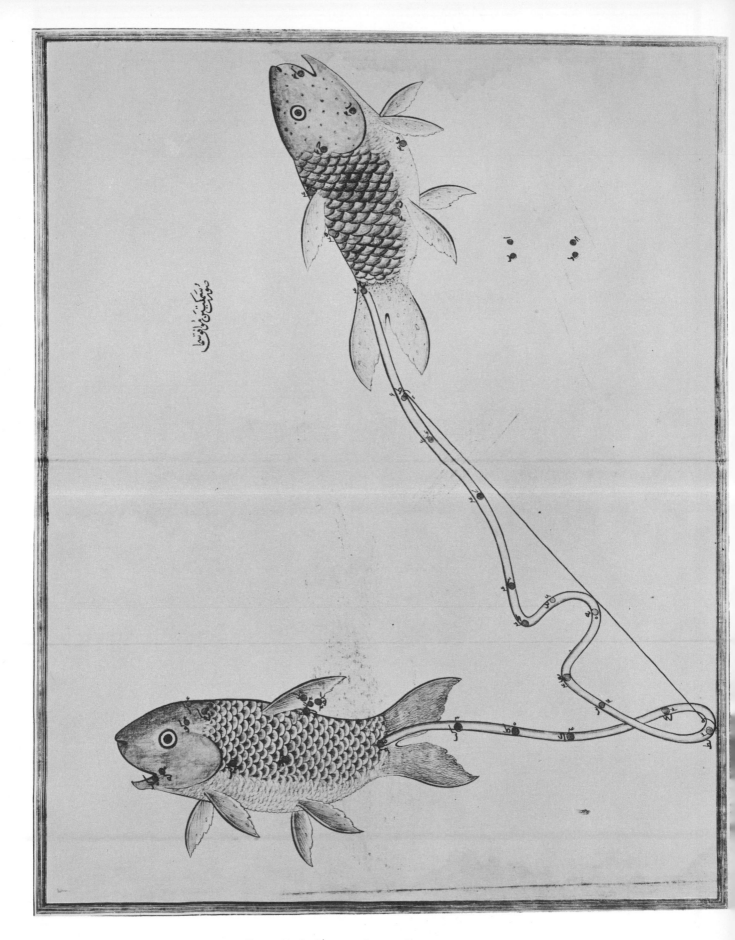

Pisces. Book of Stars and Constellations. Persian, 1630

table. Feelings, emotions, love of home and family, sympathy, kindness, and companionship are marked. There is usually a strong attraction to the mother, a resemblance to her, and also benefit through her or her side of the family. Music, painting, poetry, religious and charitable influences will be congenial; and either directly or indirectly the native will benefit through hospitals and charitable organizations. There is a tendency to economy and carefulness especially in small matters.

Sun in Pisces and Moon in Leo

This combination produces a continual yearning for the unattainable. It inclines toward the romantic, weird, and mysterious. It often places those under its influence in positions they cannot maintain, making them erratic and liable to varying moods. Under favorable planetary aspects they will have considerable ability as writers. There are generous disposition, much warmth of heart, sympathy, and charitable feelings, also some love of outward show, much social ambition, a sense of dignity and personal worth, a considerable regard for appearances, and a love of fine surroundings, whether in furniture, clothes, house, locality, or scenery. There is apt to be more promise than performance. In some cases there may be lack of practical ability and worldly knowledge; in others too free a rein is given to sensations, feelings, and passions. The influence is good generally for home, family, and children.

River God. Pisanello.
Pierpont Morgan Library

Sun in Pisces and Moon in Virgo

Pisces is considerably improved by this combination. The intuition is active, and the critical nature of Virgo gives much inspiration. The native is a good worker in a variety of directions, and possesses good all-around abilities. He may be suited for literary, legal, or medical pursuits, or well adapted for business. In some cases there will be a receptive, self-distrustful disposition, showing reserve, diffidence, and coldness; but a positive and quietly affectionate nature can easily be called out. Prudence, steadiness, and common sense are well to the fore, and much may be done in a quiet way. These people are likely to be esteemed, but are rarely fortunate in a worldly sense.

Sun in Pisces and Moon in Libra

This inclines the native to inspirational and spiritual things. In a fortunate horoscope there will be a benevolent, sympathetic, kindly nature. Those born under this combination are usually popular, they easily make friends, and are hopeful, cheerful, sociable, and well disposed. They have much imagination, frequently some special artistic faculty, and a great appreciation of music and religion. They are inclined to associate with others, whether as friends, partners, or companions, and have no liking for a lonely or isolated life.

Sun in Pisces and Moon in Scorpio

A good deal of energy works out through these two watery signs and the combination produces practical and executive business ability. Sailors, fishermen, wine or spirit merchants, sometimes chemists, and people connected with hospitals are found under this polarity. The native will sometimes find himself in a calling that does not wholly accord with his real nature, and yet will be quite unable to change it; and the same often happens with adopted habits and customs, from which he cannot free himself. He is often misjudged by the world, and may seem

too positive, hard, conventional, or unyielding; for the real inner nature is much more kindly and sympathetic than it seems outwardly. The character will vary a good deal, from generosity to selfishness, from a hard-working self-sacrificing disposition to self-indulgence or sloth, and from active kindly emotions to jealousy, morbidity, and vindictiveness.

Drawing. Renoir. (The painter was born with the Sun in Pisces.) *Louvre*

Sun in Pisces and Moon in Sagittarius

Although this is a somewhat excitable and irritable combination, with impulsiveness and a propensity for chatter, there is much sympathy in the nature, and strong feelings of charity and religious sentiment. In a good horoscope this polarity gives warmth, activity, and expansiveness, which may tend in some philanthropic or humanitarian direction in philosophy, in social and family life, or in the world of art. In any of these directions the native may attract considerable notice. He will be a busy worker and accomplish much, while fully appreciating ease, comfort, luxury, and the "good things" of life generally. There is some ability for public speaking or a public career. There is a love of change, some likelihood of a change of occupation, and many changes of residence, coupled with a general love of travel, especially by sea. Two pursuits or occupations may be carried on simultaneously. The intellect is acute and penetrating, seeing both sides of a question. There are great possibilities in this polarity if suitably supported by the rest of the horoscope. Otherwise the well-intentioned internal nature will fritter its energies away in a multitude of useless projects.

Sun in Pisces and Moon in Capricorn

The Capricorn nature contributes a practical influence here. There will be prudence, economy, forethought, and ability in planning, organizing, and in the handling of property and investments. The native has more inclination for public than private life, but the possibilities vary according to circumstances. There are usually quietness, sobriety, and self-control. In some cases there will be lack of initiative, and a tendency to despondency; in others, the personality will appear hard, reserved, and lacking in candor.

Sun in Pisces and Moon in Aquarius

This combination gives a quiet and retiring disposition. The native makes friends easily, has many acquaintances, and is likely to be popular. He is often better suited to some public pursuit rather than a purely domestic one. He has considerable power of imagination and a fascination for the mysterious or weird, and is often inclined toward musical or other artistic tastes. He has sound judgment and a good memory. Local or national public interests are likely to attract his sympathies and enthusiasm.

Sun and Moon in Pisces

This combination gives a hospitable nature, but there is a tendency to be over-anxious and restless. The imagination is active, but sometimes rather morbid. The native is usually sympathetic, imaginative, good-natured, easy-going, romantic, and affectionate. There is some inclination to religion, and the native may be associated with charitable or similar institutions. Psychic experiences rather easily manifest themselves, and the same may be said of the imaginative faculty through music, painting, or literature. There is some love of traveling, of change, and novelty: this tendency may also show as vacillation, irresolution, lack of promptness and decision, unless harmonious aspects or rising planets strengthen the character. When Jupiter and Venus are strong in the horoscope, the native will have a hopeful, buoyant, sociable, and thoroughly good-natured disposition.

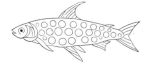

FAMOUS PEOPLE BORN WITH THE SUN IN PISCES

Michelangelo:	March 6, 1475
Handel:	February 23, 1685
George Washington:	February 22, 1732
Victor Hugo:	February 26, 1802
Chopin:	February 22, 1810
Auguste Renoir:	February 25, 1841
Ellen Terry:	February 27, 1847
Enrico Caruso:	February 25, 1873
Albert Einstein:	March 14, 1879
Vaslav Nijinsky:	February 28, 1890
W. H. Auden:	February 21, 1907
Rex Harrison:	March 5, 1908
Zero Mostel:	February 28, 1915
Svetlana Stalin Alliluyeva:	February 28, 1926
Harry Belafonte:	March 1, 1927
Edward Albee:	March 12, 1928
Earl of Snowdon (Antony Armstrong-Jones):	March 7, 1930
Elizabeth Taylor:	February 27, 1932
Rudolf Nureyev:	March 17, 1938

Dies diei eructat verbum

nocti indicat scientiam

Numerus Mensura Pondus

Videbo Cælos tuos, opera digitor tuor.

Non Inclinabitur in sæculum sæculi

Ponderibus librata suis

Erigor dum Corrigor

Cl. Ptolem.

SPIRITUAL ASTROLOGY

Modern man's knowledge of astrology is clouded by the many superstitious beliefs and misuses that have continuously been made in the name of this science. On the highest level, astrology provides a key to the understanding of the spiritual relationship between man and the universe.

The kind of abuse to which astrology has been put is exemplified in the unscrupulous type of person who is prepared to make one or another kind of unscientific and therefore inaccurate prediction purely for the sake of material gains. There are other people, eager for power, who have tried to realize their ambitions by studying the horoscopes of people they wish to exploit. Astrology is not alone in suffering from such dishonesty; parallel cases are to be found in medicine, in psychology, and in most other professions and sciences, and no profession can be blamed for the wrong kind of people who try to associate themselves with it.

A classic example of both the use and misuse of astrology is to be found in the figure of Hitler, who employed several astrologers to advise him on the timing of his offensives. The British intelligence services were aware of this and in turn summoned an astrologer to help them find out what Hitler's moves were likely to be. The good or bad use of astrology always depends on the goal.

Another instance of misuse of astrology is the case of an ailing patient who refused food and care because his horoscope indicated that he was to die. In absurdity this parallels the story of the

247

Atlas of Constellations. Schiller, 1627.

quack astrologer who starved himself to try to make sure that his death would coincide with the date he had calculated he would die.

Astrology can be put to the right use in such matters as the choice of a suitable profession or business, in the study of one's own character, and in personal and business relationships. As a result the serious student must inevitably gain a better understanding of human nature and of the weaknesses and particular struggles of others. Astrology deals with the past and the present. And on the basis of cause and effect the future is also delineated. J. P. Morgan employed an astrologer to guide him in many of his financial moves. Dr. Jung found it invaluable in the preliminary study of a new patient's character, and many other noted men, from early popes, princes, and kings to the present-day efficient businessman, have recognized its usefulness. It is not unlikely that the science will one day be offered for study at a college level so that the educated man can profit by it as he once was able to do in the universities of Paris and other European cities in the great days of the Renaissance.

Besides its everyday applications, astrology operates on a higher plane. This facet of it, dating from the earliest known civilizations, is referred to as spiritual or esoteric astrology. Man has always sought to understand why the universe was created and to define his position in it and his relationship to it.

According to astrological precepts the different parts of the body are ruled by each of the twelve signs of the zodiac. Aries governs the head; Taurus the throat; Gemini the shoulders, arms, hands, and lungs; Cancer the breast and stomach; Leo the heart and back; Virgo the intestines; Libra the kidneys; Scorpio the private organs; Sagittarius the hips, thighs, and liver; Capricorn the knees; Aquarius the calves and ankles; and Pisces the feet.

Even minor physical characteristics such as the lines of the forehead, those in the palms of the hands, and moles on the face and body, have a certain significance that has been interpreted. For instance, on the forehead, straight lines denote good fortune, winding lines denote struggle, distorted lines denote variety, mischief, and deceit, Many lines signify a changeable personality. Simple and straight lines denote a good and honest nature and long life. Broken lines are of the na-

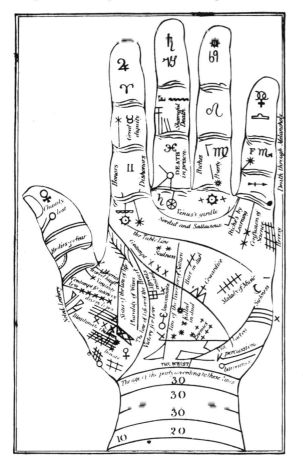

Astrological signs related to the palm

Relationship between the zodiacal signs and the human body

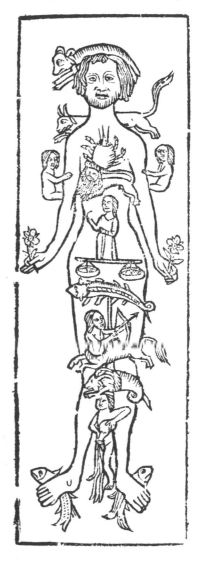

ture of Saturn and Mars and therefore indicate a hot temper. Two or three lines at the root of the nose and cut in the middle are signs of lasciviousness. Many books have been written on these special characteristics, although the modern astrologer usually neglects them as being too fatalistic. Judgments based on the form of the head have also become obsolete. Aristotle mentions that a square forehead denotes magnanimity. A forehead pointed at the temples of the head, with

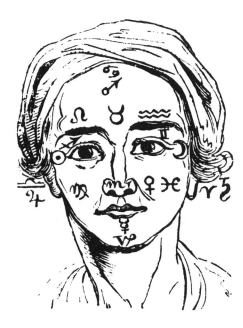

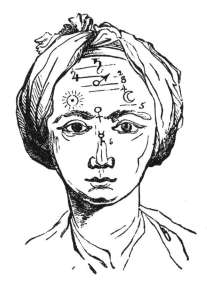

The forehead .... ♂ Mars.
The right eye .... ☉ Sol.
The left eye .... ☽ The Moon.
The right ear...................... ♃ Jupiter.
The left ear .... ♄ Saturn.
The nose .... ♀ Venus.
The mouth .... ☿ Mercury.

♐ Sagittary .... The right eye.
♑ Capricorn........ The chin which is nadir.
♒ Aquarius ········ The left eye brow.
♓ Pisces .... The left cheek.
♈ Aries............ The left ear.
♉ Taurus ·········· The middle of the forehead.
♊ Gemini ·········· The left eye.
♋ Cancer .... In the forehead the zenith.
♌ Leo .... The right eye-brow.
♍ Virgo .... The right cheek.
♎ Libra .... The right ear.
♏ Scorpio............. The nose.

Horoscope represented
as celestial writing

Celestial Hebrew alphabet

ק ך ̃ך ̃ך ̃ך ̃ך ̃ך ̃ך ̃ך ̃ך
ך ̃ך ̃ך ̃ך ̃ך ̃ך ̃ך ̃ך ̃ך ̃ך

250

Horoscope of the world

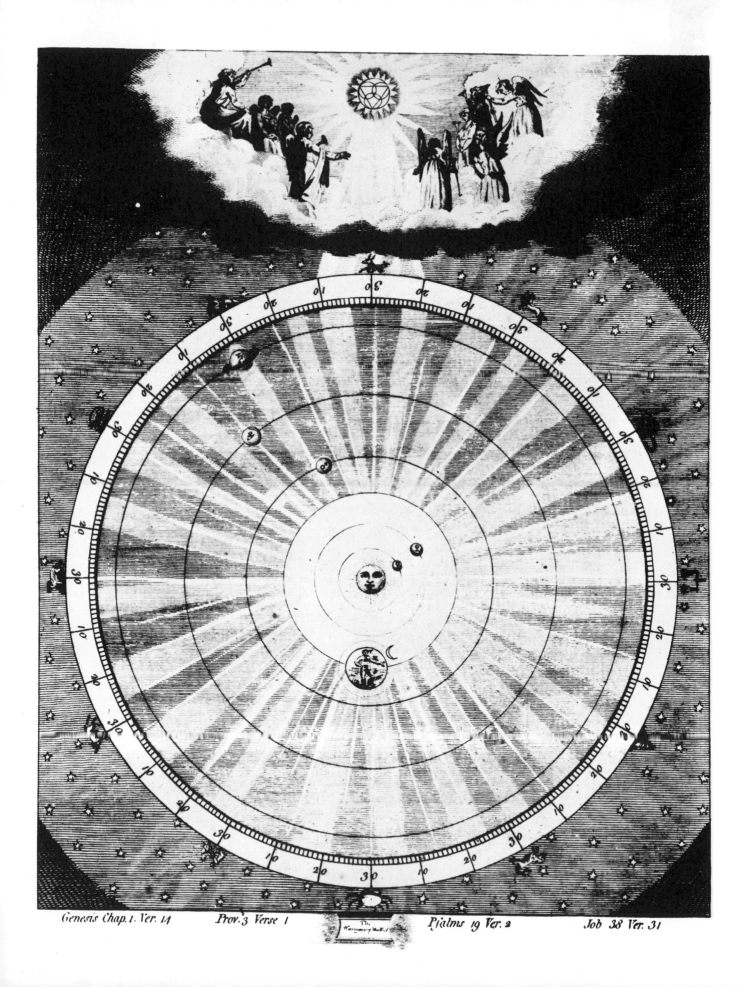

Genesis Chap. 1. Ver. 14   Prov. 3 Verse 1   Pfalms 19 Ver. 2   Job 38 Ver. 31

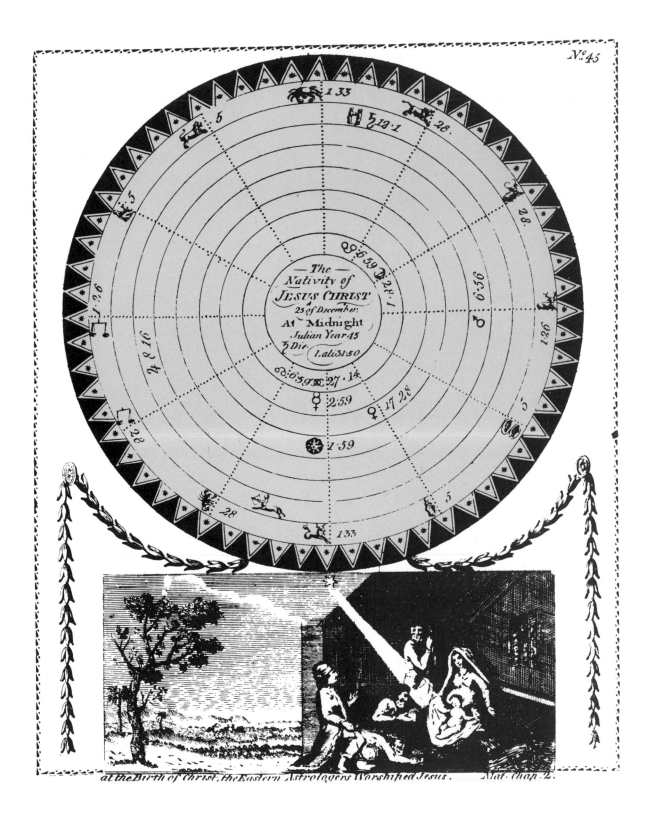

at the Birth of Christ, the Eastern Astrologers Worshiped Jesus.   *Mat. Chap. 2.*

bones showing as if almost uncovered by flesh, denotes vanity, inconstancy, and irresolution in business. The broad forehead denotes gluttonous tendencies, and so on.

Most cosmogonies are in accord with astrology. The constellations and planets represent divine signs, and the horoscope is the sacred writing which the esoteric astrologer endeavors to decipher. Many mythologies and religions have seen their gods and saints embodied in the constellations.

In spiritual astrology the zodiacal sign which rises in the east, called the Ascendant or rising sign of the birth chart, is recognized as the key sign of the zodiac in which the soul wished to reincarnate itself.

Fortunate rising signs according to traditions, are those ruled by Jupiter or Venus — Sagittarius, Pisces, Taurus, Libra, and Cancer, in which sign Jupiter is exalted. About every two hours the rising zodiacal sign changes. Aries is followed by Taurus, Taurus by Gemini, and so on through to the last of the twelve signs, which is Pisces. Thus, for a horoscope it is not merely the birth date which is important, but the hour at which a person is born.

Overzealous followers of astrology try to make their important decisions or actions coincide with the hour at which a fortunate sign is rising; however, in esoteric astrology it is maintained that every sign in the sky has fortunate as well as unhappy characteristics. This makes any nervous speculation entirely unnecessary.

Firmicus Maternus, the Roman astrologer, calculated the birth chart of the world in great detail. He explained that this knowledge was given to Aesculapius by Mercury. The Sun was in the fifteenth part or degree of Leo, the Moon in the fifteenth degree of Cancer, Saturn in the fifteenth degree of Capricorn, Jupiter in the fifteenth degree of Libra, Mercury in the fifteenth degree of Virgo, and the Ascendant in the fifteenth degree of Cancer.

That many different horoscopes have been calculated for the birth of Christ is also well known and has been commented on at length by Dr. Jung in his book *Aion* (Volume 4 in the Bollingen Series). The same effort has been made for the birth of each country, and it is always said that if a person's birth chart is in harmony with the chart of his country, he will achieve honor and receive recognition from his countrymen.

The most important part of the astrologer's study is the spiritual side of human nature, and a person's goals are viewed in the light of the relationship in his horoscope between the Sun sign, the Moon sign, and the rising sign at birth. Man's nature is threefold: the Sun represents his relationship to the divine spirit, the Moon relates to his soul, and the Ascendant sign to his physical body. The question has been asked, must man believe that everything is foredestined and that he cannot escape fate? Has he free will and is it possible for his nature to change? Hindu astrology cannot endorse free will, since it is based on the theory of reincarnation. The Hindu maintains that man must continue to reincarnate on earth until he has paid for mistakes he made in previous lives. Western astrology does not accept this fatalistic attitude. It is true that in the Ecclesiastes it is written: "To everything there is a season and a time to every purpose under the Heaven. A time to be born and a time to die." But already in the early Middle Ages the following teaching is found in an astrological treatise by Abraham Ibn Ezra: "The beginning of wisdom is the fear of the Lord; that is the starting point, for when a man refrains from following his eyes and his heart in their tendency to satiate his concupiscence, then knowledge comes to rest within him; furthermore, the fear of the Lord protects him from the decrees of the heavenly bodies and from their sway as long as he lives."

America Independance 4. July 10 H 10 m P.M 1776

Union Federal

Revolution of America

American astrology has always been connected with spiritual aims based on the Bible. It is written: "And there shall be signs in the Sun and in the Moon and in the Stars. . . ." We accept free will and reject a fatalistic attitude. The horoscopes show only human tendencies, which means that man is fully responsible for his acts and through self-knowledge is capable of overcoming his weaknesses and achieving his highest aims.

ZOLTAN MASON

A Table of the Fortunate Days of the Week,

To Persons who have the Moon in any of the Twelve Signs.

FROM ALCABITIUS, A FAMOUS ASTROLOGER.

The Moon in ♈ at Birth. Their fortunate day is *Tuesday.*	The Moon in ♉ at Birth. Their fortunate day is *Friday.*
The Moon in ♊ at Birth. Their fortunate day is *Wednesday.*	The Moon in ♋ at Birth. Their fortunate day is *Monday.*
The Moon in ♌ at Birth. Their fortunate day is *Sunday.*	The Moon in ♍ at Birth. Their fortunate day is *Friday.*
The Moon in ♎ at Birth. Their fortunate day is *Saturday.*	The Moon in ♏ at Birth. Their fortunate day is *Tuesday.*
The Moon in ♐ at Birth. Their fortunate day is *Thursday.*	The Moon in ♑ at Birth. Their fortunate day is *Monday.*
The Moon in ♒ at Birth. Their fortunate day is *Wednesday.*	The Moon in ♓ at Birth. Their fortunate day is *Saturday.*

255

Mr. WILLIAM
SHAKESPEARES
COMEDIES,
HISTORIES, &
TRAGEDIES.

Published according to the True Originall Copies.

Martin Droeshout sculpsit London.

LONDON
Printed by Isaac Iaggard, and Ed. Blount. 1623.

5. SHAKESPEARE'S ARTISTIC USE
OF ASTROLOGY

Although Shakespeare's collected plays include more than a hundred separate astrological allusions, the ideas found in the majority of such references are little more than mere commonplaces. In his use of astrology we have another illustration of how a master artist works, of how the true creative genius may be master of no field of knowledge and yet possess a sixth sense and a sponge-like capacity for absorbing essentials of knowledge in any field. Although his plays as a whole teem with allusions to the influence of the stars, it is not apparent that Shakespeare knew the technicalities of astrology any more than did his fellow dramatists — indeed, if as much.

But that human beings are but helpless puppets of the stars is stated definitely and continually from *Titus Andronicus* to *The Winter's Tale*. The dukes of Bedford and Exeter affirm that the stars "consented unto Henry's death" and "plotted" his "overthrow." The dauphin Charles comments that Mars' shining upon the French caused them to be victorious in battle against the English. The "star-cross'd" Romeo believes the apothecary's poison is the only thing that will "shake the yoke of inauspicious stars" from his "world-wearied flesh." Antony attributes his first defeat to the fact that the stars have forsaken him; the moon's eclipse, he says, portends his ultimate fall; and Octavius Caesar laments that his stars and those of Antony made the two generals "unreconcilable." Pericles attributes the loss of all his fortunes to the "ire" of "angry stars." Prospero's powers and fortunes, he says, depend upon "a most auspicious star." Hermione attributes her unjust treatment and imprisonment to the fact that "some ill planet reigns." Others throughout the plays advocate the same belief.

Often Shakespeare's characters maintain that one's fate and disposition depend upon the stars at one's birth and their relationship with other stars at that time. Julia tells Lucetta that Proteus is not a deceitful lover because "truer stars did govern Proteus' birth." Richard III informs Elizabeth that the princes were murdered because "at their birth good stars were opposite." Throughout Shakespeare's plays we find that a character's immediate actions and undertakings might be favored or hindered by the stars: planets might strike felling blows at man, be responsible for various disasters (especially plagues), and bode much ill-fortune if they wandered from their "spheres." These are the tenets of astrology, incidentally, that Shakespeare used most.

Several of Shakespeare's characters are governed by particular stars, and Shakespeare is always consistent in assigning the planet which would endow the appropriate qualities. Posthumus was born under the benevolent planet Jupiter, and consequently has a favorable destiny at the end of the play. Monsieur Parolles would be born under Mars because he would be known as a soldier. Elizabeth, who weeps throughout *Richard III* is indeed "governed by the *watery* moon." The astrologers assigned *weeping,* however, to Saturn rather than to Luna. Possibly the moon's influence on the tides precipitated Shakespeare's remark here. Conrade, who was born under Saturn, and Aaron, whose desires Saturn governs, are both fitting exponents of that planet's generally malign influence. Edmund was evilly "compounded under the Dragon's Tail" and the malignant stars of Ursa Major. Autolycus, born under Mercury, the planet of rogues, vagabonds, thieves, and liars, is (as Autolycus says) a "snatcher-up of unconsidered trifles" who skips over the laws of morality at his pleasure. John of Gaunt speaks of England (astrologically?) as "this seat of Mars." All astrologers were agreed that England is ruled by Aries, whose lord is the planet Mars. Cf. Claudius Ptolemy, *Quadripartitum,* Bk. II, ch. iii: "Britain, Galatia, Germany, and Barsnia have a greater share of familiarity with Aries and Mars." Cleopatra, in her final moment of stability, refuses to be governed by the "fleeting" and varying moon. Being born "in a merry hour" and under a star that "danced" is exactly suitable for the mirthful and mischievous Beatrice; and Benedick was, as he says, certainly *not* born under a "rhyming planet" if the best he can do is to rhyme "lady" and "baby."

The signs of the zodiac are mentioned in six of Shakespeare's plays. Only in *Twelfth Night,* however, does the reference connote any astrological significance, and even there the allusion is a ludicrous one made by the two boisterous knights of Olivia's household. The two buffoons, Sir Andrew Aguecheek and Sir Toby Belch, know little astrology. Sir Andrew thinks that the sign Taurus rules the sides and heart of the human body, and is corrected by Sir Toby who contends that it rules the legs and thighs. Both knights, as might be expected, are wrong. Taurus governed the neck and throat, and the most ignorant Elizabethan theater-goer probably knew it. Such humor is wasted on modern audiences.

Shakespeare's characters frequently express the idea that various celestial phenomena forebode disastrous events to come upon a group of people or upon some particularly important personage. The common harbingers of these unfortunate events were comets, meteors, and eclipses. Bedford informs his companions that comets import "changes of times and states." Charles of France sees in the flaming brand or signal torch "a comet of revenge" and "a prophet to the fall of all our foes." Calpurnia reminds Julius Caesar that not only comets but "The heavens themselves blaze forth the death of princes." Often the wonder and amazement that comets cause among the populace are remarked upon. The Welshmen in *Richard II* leave their ranks and disperse when the "meteors fright the fixed stars from heaven," because the Welshmen fully believe that such a phenomenon portends "the death and fall" of the king. The Papal legate Pandulph contends that any exhalation in the sky will be looked upon as "meteors, prodigies, and signs" portending the downfall of King John. Prince Hal remarks to Bardolph that the meteors and exhalations portend merely "hot livers and cold purses," but Worcester, who deserted King Henry's forces, is likened to an "exhal'd meteor" and looked upon as "a prodigy of fear" and "a portent of broached mischief to the unborn times."

Shakespeare's characters — like Elizabethans in general — were not always fully certain just how far astral influences extended. The general opinion among them seems to have been that the stars are not omnipotent, but that they strongly incline the soul one way or another and that few men can resist their power. That a person could fight the malignancy of the stars is uniquely illustrated by Bedford when he assumes that King Henry's ghost can "combat with adverse planets in the heavens" and "scourge the revolting stars." Helena understands astrology's limitations when she exclaims:

> "Our remedies oft in ourselves do lie,
> Which we ascribe to heaven. The fated sky
> Gives us free scope, only doth backward pull
> Our slow designs when we ourselves are dull."

With reservations Warwick would agree, for he says, "Few men rightly temper with the stars." Cassius, however, discredits astrology sternly when he reminds Brutus that the blame for being an "underling" lies not in one's stars but in oneself. A condemnation of astrological beliefs is also in Hotspur's mind when he argues rather convincingly with Glendower against the probability of influences of meteors and other celestial phenomena. Cardinal Pandulph's remarks are unquestionably sarcastic when he comments that the common people will call any "natural exhalation in the sky" a meteor, a prodigy, and a sign. And Edmund bluntly characterizes astrology as "the excellent foppery of the world."

Although few of these references indicate any special knowledge, or necessitate here a gloss, we are not quite justified in concluding that Shakespeare possessed only a meager knowledge of astrology. It is true that he cast no horoscopes for any of his characters, as did Chaucer for Constance and the Wife of Bath, and his passages give no indication that he was familiar with the *hyleg*, the *alcocoden*, or the *algebuthar*. But his allusions give evidence enough that he possessed a common or general knowledge of the majority of astrology's tenets — a knowledge of the manner in which the stars were reputed to govern life below. His *dramatis personae* speak of stars, planets, comets, meteors, eclipses, planetary aspects, predominance, conjunction, opposition, retrogradation, and all sorts of astro-meteorology. They know that the Dragon's Tail exerts an evil influence, that Mercury governs lying and thievery, that Luna rules vagabonds and idle fellows, that Saturn is malignant and Jupiter benevolent, that the signs of the zodiac rule the limbs and organs of the body, that planets influence cities and nations, that each trigon or triplicity pertains to one of the four elements, that stars rule immediately as well as at birth, that one with a strong constitution might avert the influence of his stars, and so on. Although they do not go into details regarding the technical workings of the science, his characters on the whole seem to possess a general knowledge of stellar influence on human destiny.

Shakespeare's astrological references are ubiquitous, occurring in his poems, comedies, histories, and tragedies. Sometimes the passages indicate that the stars are agents in the plot and action; oftentimes they are mere rhetorical flourishes, embellishments, metaphors. Sometimes they are spoken jestingly by the humorists of the plays; often they are stated quite seriously by the principals. Some of the passages are intended to illustrate character or personal characteristics. A few of them ridicule a belief in astral influence. None connects astrology with medical practice, although it is clear that Shakespeare was aware of the belief that planets and signs of the zodiac influence mental and physical health. No astrologers or almanack-makers appear as characters in his plays. He never uses the words "astrologer" or "astrology." In *Cymbeline* astrologers are called "astronomers"; in *Venus and Adonis* they are called "star-gazers"; in *Sonnet 107* they are called "augers"; and in *King Lear* "sectary astronomical."

Few allusions are made to the practice of astrologers, the passages almost always referring to the potency of the heavenly bodies themselves. There are just as many astrological references — of various kinds — in the later plays as there are in the early ones.

The use of astrology that looms largest in Shakespeare's dramas is the free utilization of astral philosophy in the creation of some especially artistic and beautiful lines. Innumerable astrological passages in the plays are so composed as to make them particularly striking and dramatically effective. In such lines as the following we see the master artist taking common astral tenets and — apparently not caring whether the resultant astrology is "scientifically" correct or not — remolding his raw materials into something effective and artistic:

PROSPERO: I find my zenith doth depend upon
A most auspicious star, whose influence
If now I court not, but omit, my fortune
Will ever after droop.
(*The Tempest*, i.ii.181–184)

RICHARD: Three glorious suns, each one a perfect sun;
Not separated with the racking clouds,
But sever'd in a pale, clear-shining sky.
See, see! they join, embrace, and seem to kiss,
As if they vow'd some league inviolable:
Now they are but one lamp, one light, one sun.
In this the heaven figures some event.
(*III King Henry VI*, ii.i.26–32)

FALSTAFF: . . . we that take purses go by the moon and the seven stars, and not by Phoebus, he, that wand'ring knight so fair. . . . let men say we be men of good government, being governed as the sea is, by our noble and chaste mistress the moon, under whose countenance we steal.
(*I King Henry IV*, i.ii)

ROMEO: . . . my mind misgives,
Some consequence yet hanging in the stars
Shall bitterly begin his fearful date
With this night's revels and expire the term
Of a despised life closed in my breast
By some vile forfeit of untimely death.
(*Romeo and Juliet*, i.iv.106–111)

OTHELLO: It is the very error of the moon:
She comes more nearer earth than she was wont,
And makes men mad.
(*Othello*, v.ii.109–111)

ULYSSES: The heavens themselves, the planets, and this centre,
Observe degree, priority, and place,
Insisture, course, proportion, season, form,
Office, and custom, in all line of order:
And therefore is the glorious planet Sol
In noble eminence enthroned and spher'd
Amidst the other; whose medicinable eye
Corrects the ill aspects of planets evil,
And posts, like the commandment of a king,
Sans check to good and bad: but when the planets,
In evil mixture, to disorder wander,
What plagues and what portents! what mutiny!
What raging of the sea! shaking of earth!
Commotion in the winds! frights, changes, horrors,
Divert and crack, rend and deracinate
The unity and married calm of states
Quite from their fixture!
(*Troilus and Cressida*, i.iii.85–102)

CASSIUS: The fault, dear Brutus, is not in our stars,
But in ourselves, that we are underlings.
(*Julius Caesar*, i.ii.140–141)

CALPURNIA: When beggars die, there are no comets seen,
The heavens themselves blaze forth the death of princes.
(*Julius Caesar*, ii.ii.30–31)

HELENA: Monsieur Parolles, you were born under a
charitable star.
PAROLLES: Under Mars, I.
HELENA: I especially think under Mars.

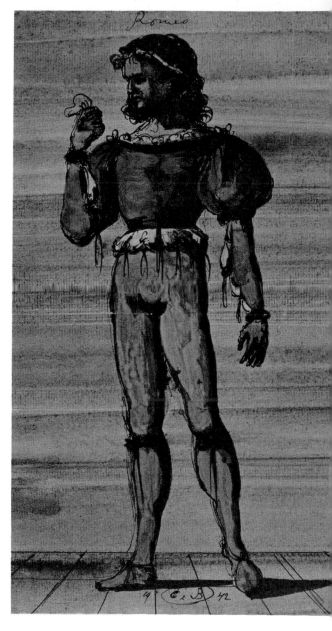

Romeo. Sketch by Eugene Berman

261

PAROLLES:	Why under Mars?
HELENA:	The wars have kept you so under, that you must needs be born under Mars.
PAROLLES:	When he was predominant.
HELENA:	When he was retrograde, I think rather.
PAROLLES:	Why think you so?
HELENA:	You go so much backward when you fight. . . .
PAROLLES:	I am so full of businesses, I cannot answer thee acutely.

(*All's Well That Ends Well*, i.i.206–220)

There are few places in Elizabethan or Jacobean drama where words are used more effectively than in these passages. Although they show a minimum knowledge of astrological technicalities, they doubtless exhibit the most *artistic* use of astrology in the Elizabethan and Jacobean drama.

The purpose in this essay is, of course, to discover Shakespeare's use of astrology — not to ascertain his attitude toward it as a valid or invalid science. Since Shakespeare speaks only through his characters, who oftentimes contradict one another, it is virtually impossible to determine with any certainty what attitude the dramatist entertained. To assume that he believed as did the loyal and good Earl of Kent, the estimable Helena, or the heroic Pericles would be dangerous; to assume that he put his own thought into the mouths of Edmund, Cassius, and the impetuous Hotspur would be equally unwarranted. But inasmuch as in the four-hundred-odd lines of astrological allusion Shakespeare presented character after character sanctioning astral influence and allows only four characters — two villains, the Papal legate, and a "hothead" — to deride it, it seems hardly likely that he seriously mistrusted the science himself. At any rate, the numerous astrological passages scattered throughout his dramatic works indicate that he was at least considerably interested in astrology and that he used the science abundantly in the creation of some of the most striking passages in his plays.

That Shakespeare incorporated astrology in his plays because it would have an appeal to the audience there cannot be much doubt. That he employed it merely for this reason does not explain why there are many astrological passages in the Sonnets. Any theory that Shakespeare used bits of astrological lore as grist for his mill, as trappings for his plays, has definite limitations. Elizabethans possessed a thorough-going belief that the stars and planets, comets and eclipses, exercised at least a limited influence on human beings and mundane affairs; and it was not merely the ignorant who accepted these beliefs. Shakespeare was merely holding an artistically reflecting mirror up to life.

JOHNSTONE PARR

6. GAME OF THE SPHERES

Here, on the next two pages, is a fascinating game that appears to have originated in France. The engraving was made for Monsieur Pierre Seguier, Chevalier, Chancellor of France and Duke of Villemor, by E. Vouillemont in 1661, at Paris.

Briefly, the rules of the game are as follows:

Two to six people may participate (four is the conventional number).

You may play with one or two dice, and chips or counters. Each player contributes an agreed amount of chips to the kitty.

The dice are thrown by each player. The player with the highest score places one chip or counter on sphere 4, (*Region de Feu:* Fire). Each of the others places his chip or counter in descending order on spheres 3, 2, and 1. During this game each player throws the dice in turn, moving forward (by the throws on the dice), toward sphere 70 (*Ciel Empirée:* Home of the Gods). However, players must throw the correct number to end exactly on sphere 70; otherwise they must keep retreating by the amount shown on the dice over and above the correct number, until they finally make it.

Various advantageous and disadvantageous spheres are encountered which cause the player who lands on them to move forward or backward or remain there for a number of turns.

Players landing on the following spheres must observe the rules:

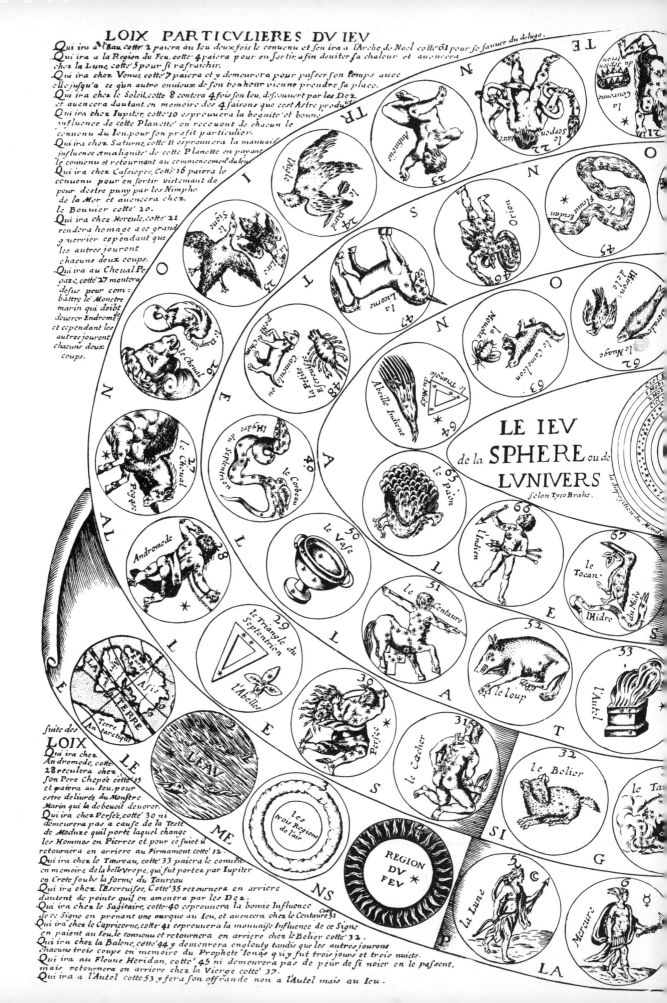

LOIX PARTICVLIERES DV IEV

Qui ira a l'Eau, cotte 2 paiera au Ieu deux fois et sen ira a l'Arche de Noel cotte 61 pour se sauuer du deluge.

Qui ira a la Region du Feu, cotte 4 paiera pour en sortir, afin deuiter sa chaleur et auencera chez la Lune, cotte 5 pour se rafraichir.

Qui ira chez Venus, cotte 7 paiera et y demeurera pour passer son temps auec elle jusqu'a ce qu'un autre envieux de son bonheur vienne prendre sa place.

Qui ira chez le Soleil, cotte 8 contera 4 fois son Ieu, descouuert par les Dez et auencera dautant, en memoire des 4 saisons que cest Astre produit.

Qui ira chez Iupiter, cotte 10 esprouuera la begnité et bonne influence de cette Planette en receuant de chacun le cenuenu du Ieu, pour son profit particulier.

Qui ira chez Saturne, cotte 11 esprouuera la mauuaise influence et malignité de cette Planette en payant le cenuenu et retournant au commencement du Ieu.

Qui ira chez Cassiopee, Cotté 16 paiera le cenuenu pour en sortir virtement de peur destre puny par les Nimphe de la Mer et auencera chez le Bouuier cotté 20.

Qui ira chez Hercule, cotté 21 rendera homage a ce grand guerrier cependant que les autres joueront chacuns deux coups.

Qui ira au Cheual Pegaze, cotté 27 montera dessus pour combattre le Monstre marin qui doibt deuorer Androméde et cependant les autres joueront chacuns deux coups.

LE IEV de la SPHERE ou de LVNIVERS
selon Tyco Brahe.

suite des

LOIX

Qui ira chez Andromede, cotte 28 reculera chez son Pere Chepée cotté 15 et paiera au Ieu, pour estre deliurée du Monstre Marin qui la debuoit deuorer.

Qui ira chez Persée, cotté 30 ni demeurera pas a cause de la Teste de Meduze quil porte laquel change les Hommes en Pierres et pour ce suiet il retournera en arriere au Firmament cotté 12.

Qui ira chez le Taureau, cotté 33 paiera le cenuenu en memoire de la belle Vrope, qui fut portez par Iupiter en Crete soubz la forme du Taureau.

Qui ira chez l'Escreuisse, Cotté 35 retournera en arriere dautent de points quil en amena par les Dez.

Qui ira chez le Sagitaire, cotté 40 esprouuera la bonne Influence de ce Signe en prenant une marque au Ieu, et auencera chez le Centaure cotté 51.

Qui ira chez le Capricorne, cotté 41 esprouuera la mauuaise Influence de ce Signe en paient au Ieu, le cenuenu et retournera en arriere chez le Belier cotté 32.

Qui ira chez la Balene, cotté 44 y demeurera englouty tandis que les autres jouront chacune trois coups en memoire du Prophete Ionas qui y fut trois jours et trois nuicts.

Qui ira au Fleuue Heridan, cotté 45 ni demeurera pas de peur de se noier en le passent, mais retournera en arriere chez la Vierge cotté 37.

Qui ira a l'Autel cotté 53 y fera son offrande non a l'Autel mais au Ieu.

explication du present IEV

CE IEV contient toutes les parties de l'uniuers, les 4 Elemens, les 7 Planettes, les Figures, ou Constellations Septentrionales, les 12 Signes du Zodiaque, les vieilles et nouuelles Estoilles Meridionales, et les trois derniers Cieux superieurs, On comence ce IEV a la Terre, le premier Element, et l'on finit au Ciel Empireé le plus hault de tous les Cieux, ou l'on Gaigne la Partie et tout ce qui sera sur ledict IEV.

Ordre du IEV. On y peut jouer auec deux Dez communs, deux, trois quatre, cinq, et six personnes, Chacun une fois et a son rang, selon quil se trouuaira place. le IEV d'un chacun sera marqué de pieces differentes et auec'd'autant de points quil en sera decouuers par les Dez.

On comiendra de ce que l'on doict mettre au IEV d'un Double, d'un sol, d'un Teston, d'une Pistole si l'on veut, que l'on mettra dans le milieu du IEV pour le profit de celuy qui Gagnera la partie.

Que s'il amene plus de points qu'il ne faut pour ariuer iustement audict Ciel Empireé il retournera en arriere d'autant de point qu'il en aura de surplus.

Tous les payements seront de la valeur du IEV et celuy qui sera rencontré d'un autre, luy paiera le contenu et s'en ira prendre sa place en luy cedant la sienne

A Paris Chez A. de Fer, dans l'Isle du Palais a la sphere Royale 1671. auec priu du Roy

Le Bouuier — 20

19 — La Teste ou Cheuelure de Berenice

NO — 18 — La Grande Ours

17 — le Charetier au

16 — Cassiopée

VE — les Poissons — 43

le Vaisseau — 42

la Colombe — 60

le Coq Dinde — 61

15 — le Chanceau au

VA — 41 — le Capricorne

DI — 40 — le Sagitaire

1 — Cephée

EL — 14 — le Dragon

T — 13 — la Petite Ourse

le Grand Chien — 58

39 — le Scorpion

ME — 38 — la Balance

la Lieure — 37

O — 12

N — S

A Tres Haut et Tres Puissant seigneur Messire Pierre Sequier Cheualier, Chancelier de France, Duc de Villemor

Par son tres Humble et tres Obeissant seruiteur E. Vouillemont 1661

69 — CIEL CHRISTALLIN

57

36 le Phenix

55 — le Poisson la Grue

36 — le Lyon

37 — la Vierge

35 — l'Escreuisse

le Dard du Midi

34 — les Gemeaux

le Soleil — Mars — 10 — Iupiter — 11 — Saturne

suite des LOIX

Qui ira au Coq, Dinde pour en manger iusqu'a ce qu'un autre voulant en auoir sa part vienne prendre sa place

Qui ira a la Colombe, de Noel cotté 60 retournera au commencement du Ieu, pour sauoir s'y les Eaux du deluge sont retirées de dessus la Terre.

Qui ira au Triangle, du Midy cotté 64 aura ce priuilege que s'il amene trois points au premier coup qu'il iouera gagnera la partie entiere sans estre obligé de faire le reste.

Qui ira au premier Mobille cotté 68 ne pouuant suiure son mouuement si rapide reculera chez le Paon cotté 65

Qui ira au Ciel Empireé cotté 70 gagnera la partie et tout ce qui se trouuera sur le Ieu.

Le tout Graué et mis au Iour par Estienne Vouillemont Graueur Ordinaire du Roy pour les Cartes Geographiques, Plans de Villes, et autres Tailles doûces demeurant A Paris en L'Isle du palais au coin de la Rue du Harlet A la Fontaine de Iouuence auec priuilege de sa Majesté pour Vingt Ans 1661

Ceux qui desireront auoir vne plus profonde connoissance de tous ces signes, ou Figure Celeste, ils liront, Sacro Bosco Clauius, ou Boulanger.

Sphere 2 (*L'eau:* Water). Pay two chips or counters to the kitty and move to Noah's Ark (61) to escape the deluge.

Sphere 4 (*Region du Feu:* Region of Fire). Pay a chip to the kitty to escape the heat, and advance to sphere 5 to be refreshed by the moon.

Sphere 7 (Venus). Pay a chip to the kitty for a pleasant visit with Venus until another player, envious of your good luck, arrives to take your place.

Sphere 8 (*Le Soleil:* The Sun). Advance four times the score of the dice in accordance with the four seasons the sun produces.

Sphere 10 (Jupiter). You benefit from Jupiter's benign influence. Take a chip from the kitty.

Sphere 11 (Saturn). Pay a chip to the kitty and return to sphere 1.

Sphere 16 (Cassiopeia). Pay a chip to the kitty to escape the punishment of the sea-nymph, and advance to sphere 20, taking refuge with the herdsman.

Sphere 21. You pay homage to Hercules by skipping two turns.

Sphere 27 (*Le Cheval Pegase:* Pegasus). You have mounted Pegasus and must battle against the sea monster who is about to devour Andromede. Skip two turns.

Sphere 28 (Andromede). Return to sphere 15 and pay a chip to the kitty in order to be delivered from the sea monster.

Sphere 30 (Perseus). You cannot stay here; otherwise a glance from Medusa, whose head Perseus carries, will turn you into stone. Retreat to sphere 12.

Sphere 33 (*Le Taureau:* Taurus). Pay a chip to the kitty in memory of the beautiful Europa who was carried off by Jupiter in the guise of a bull.

Sphere 35 (*L'Escrevisse:* Crab). Turn back (instead of forward) by the number of places shown by the throw of the dice.

Sphere 40 (*Le Sagitaire:* Sagittarius). The good influence of this sign gives you a chip from the kitty and you advance to sphere 57.

Sphere 41 (*Le Capricorne:* Capricorn). Pay a chip to the kitty and move back to sphere 32.

Sphere 44 (*Le Balene:* Whale). You are swallowed up and must remain in the whale until the other players have each taken three turns.

Sphere 45 (*Le Fleuve Eridan:* River Heridan). You will drown if you try to cross the river. Go back to Virgo (sphere 37).

Sphere 53. Pay a chip to the kitty.

Sphere 59 (*Le Coq Dinde:* Turkey). Pay a chip to the kitty for your pleasant dinner and remain here until someone else lands to take your place.

Sphere 60 (*La Colombe:* Dove of Noah). Go all the way back to sphere 1 to find out whether or not the flood waters have receded.

Sphere 64 (*Le Triangle du Midy:* Triangle of Noon). You are privileged to an extra turn, or if the dice show three on your original throw, you win the game and pocket the entire contents of the kitty.

Sphere 68 (*Le Mobille:* The Armillary Sphere). The movement is too rapid. Return to sphere 65.

Sphere 70 (*Ciel Empirée:* Home of the Gods). Whoever reaches here first wins the game and is entitled to everything left in the kitty.

7. HOW TO MAKE A HOROSCOPE

A horoscope shows in symbolic form the positions of the signs of the zodiac and of the sun, moon, and the planets as seen from a particular place at a particular moment of time. Such a figure of the heavens, when erected for the moment a child is born, is known as the natal map or nativity, and the child as the native. Maps are drawn in two forms, the circular and the square. We shall consider only the circular form, the square form having now practically gone out of use, though this of course is only a different way of tabulating the same astronomical observations.

To understand a horoscope you must first of all understand two things: (1) what the map represents, and (2) what the symbols marked on it stand for. But this is not all; when you have learned how to read a map, you have still to learn how to interpret it. The mundane houses, usually known as "the houses," are the basis of every map, so I will start with these.

THE HOUSES

The blank form on which the map is erected is illustrated on the following page. You will see that it consists of six straight lines intersecting at a common point at equal angular distances, one

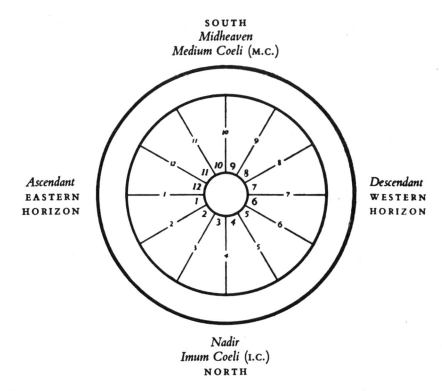

SOUTH
Midheaven
Medium Coeli (M.C.)

Ascendant
EASTERN
HORIZON

Descendant
WESTERN
HORIZON

Nadir
Imum Coeli (I.C.)
NORTH

The houses and cusps. The figures against the inmost circle denote the houses, and the figures on the radii mark their cusps. The 1st, 4th, 7th, and 10th houses are "angular," the 2nd, 5th, 8th, and 11th are "succedent," the 3rd, 6th, 9th, and 12th are "cadent." Angular houses are of the greatest strength and importance, succedent houses are next important, and cadent houses are weakest

of the lines being horizontal, another vertical, and the remainder oblique, the whole forming, as it were, a wheel with twelve spokes spaced at distances of 30°. These spokes are known as cusps, and each cusp is the beginning of one house or the end of another, making twelve houses in all. The two cusps lying horizontally (which form a straight line) represent the horizon, and the center of the circle the horoscoper or observer. Of the two vertical cusps, the upper points to the midheaven (*medium coeli*, or M.C.), the point above the observer where the sun culminates at noon, while the lower cusp points to the nadir (*imum coeli*, or I.C.), the point immediately below the observer and the midheaven. (The midheaven is not necessarily the zenith, though it may be in the tropics; technically, it is the point where the sun transits over the meridian.) The cusps above the horizon form the six houses over the earth; and the cusps beneath the horizon, the six houses under the earth. Of the two horizontal cusps, that on the left hand points to the east, or the ascendant, where the sun rises; and that on the right hand to the west, or descendant, where the sun sets. This is because the horoscoper is looking south toward the equator. (This arrangement is of course the exact opposite to that found in the ordinary geographical map.) Similarly, the nadir is regarded as being north, and the midheaven as south.

The 1st house is that below the eastern horizon, and the remaining eleven follow round the circle counter-clockwise. The cusp on the eastern horizon, i.e., the ascendant, or rising sign, is the cusp of the 1st house, the cusp of the descendant is that of the 7th house, the vertical cusps are those of the 4th and 10th houses, and the intermediate cusps are those of the 2nd and 3rd, 5th and 6th, 8th and 9th, and 11th and 12th, as you will see from the map. In this way the oblique cusps subdivide the quarters of the heavens (i.e., two quarters above the earth, and two below) each into three parts. The order of the houses is invariable, but their position on the map varies with regard to that of the observer. Maps for the northern hemisphere are erected just as we have described, but those erected for the southern hemisphere have the ascendant on the right and the descendant on the left, and the order of the houses runs clockwise.

The cusps of the houses are surrounded by two concentric circles, the inner of which is that whose radii are formed by the cusps. As I have already stated, the houses are the basis of the map, and on this are marked the positions of the signs of the zodiac with regard to the cusps, and the position within the houses of the two luminaries (sun and moon) and the seven planets; and the positions of all these are those apparent to an observer standing on the earth at the place of birth and at the moment of birth and looking toward the equator.

ZODIACAL SIGNS AND PLANETARY SYMBOLS

Having learned the positions and sequence of the houses and the meanings of the terms ascendant and midheaven, you must next learn the meanings of the symbols inserted on the map. These symbols represent the signs of the zodiac and the planets. For purposes of convenience I shall regard the Sun and Moon as planets, though technically speaking they are "luminaries." The signs of the planets and their names are as follows:

Sun	☉	Venus	♀	Saturn	♄
Moon	☽	Mars	♂	Uranus	♅
Mercury	☿	Jupiter	♃	Neptune	♆

The twelve signs of the zodiac and their names are as follows:

Aries, the Ram	♈	Leo, the Lion	♌	Sagittarius, the Archer	♐
Taurus, the Bull	♉	Virgo, the Virgin	♍	Capricornus, the Goat	♑
Gemini, the Twins	♊	Libra, the Balance	♎	Aquarius, the Water-bearer	♒
Cancer, the Crab	♋	Scorpio, the Scorpion	♏	Pisces, the Fish	♓

You must memorize the significance of these symbols at the outset, for they all appear on every map and you cannot begin to understand it without knowing them. The signs of the zodiac are marked between the concentric circles and mostly against, though sometimes between, the cusps of the houses and adjoining them is placed the number of degrees of the sign rising in arabic figures. Sometimes more than one sign occupies a house; when this is so, the sign which does not rise over either of the cusps is written midway between, and such a sign is called "intercepted."

The symbols representing the planets are marked, on the other hand, within the houses and their exact position within the sign is marked, as with the signs on the cusps, in degrees in numerals. If a planet is placed in a house occupied by more than one sign, and the sign in which it actually falls is ambiguous, the sign occupied is added after the figures giving its position, thus, ♀ 23° 16′ ♓; should the planet be "retrograde" (I shall explain this shortly), the sign ℞ is

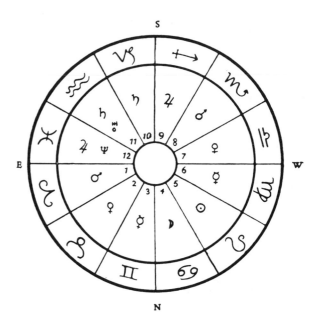

The signs of the zodiac and their rulers. The zodiac is a circle, so the signs fall into opposing pairs. Each zodiacal sign corresponds with a specific mundane house (as Aries with the 1st house, and so on) and exercises its influence, no matter what sign is then actually occupying the house. Further, each sign is ruled by a specific planet, or planets

added, thus, ♀ 23° 16′ ♓ ℞ . Now although each sign extends for 30° of the zodiac and each house extends for 30° on the map, you must remember that the degrees following the signs and the planets are not measured in the degrees of the houses. The positions of the signs and planets are calculated according to degrees in the signs of the zodiac, and how this is done and what the zodiac is I shall now explain.

The zodiac is the arc through the heavens apparent to an earth observer through which the sun and the planets travel and through the middle of which runs the ecliptic, that is to say, the path of the Sun. The paths of the planets, therefore, are all approximately in the same plane as that of the path of the Sun; their places of rising and setting lie, just as does that of the Sun, in the zodiac. For this reason we measure their positions in degrees along the ecliptic. For purposes of convenience we do not use the circular measure of 360°, but divide the circle of the zodiac into twelve signs of 30°, which are known by the names of twelve nearby constellations of stars whose positions remain constant. Each sign of the ecliptic is subdivided into three decanates, a decanate consisting of 10°. Thus we speak of the sign being in Gemini 15° rather than as being in longitude 75°, that is to say, not geographical but celestial longitude. Each planet moves through the signs at its own speed, the Moon moving quickest and Neptune slowest. The Sun, for example, occupies each sign for one-twelfth of the year; it is in Aries and Libra at the equinoxes, and in Cancer and Capricorn at the solstices, midsummer and midwinter. On the horoscope, the planets move as a rule counter-clockwise, though for short periods they go back on their path, and when they do this the movement is called "retrogradation," and is symbolized by ℞ . They do not of course actually go backward for a time and then return on their path; they only appear to do so to an earth observer. The directions in which planets move concern us mostly when we are comparing natal and progressed maps, or calculating transits; what we are principally concerned with is their position at any given moment relative to the signs which they happen to occupy. But their relation to each other, and to the ascendant and midheaven, as seen by the observer is important. Any such relationship is known as an aspect. Planets are said to be in "conjunction" when within about 12°, in opposition when they are six signs apart (180°), in "trine" when four signs apart (120°), in "square" when three signs apart (90°), and in "sextile" when two signs apart (60°). These are the principal aspects. When calculating aspects, always disregard the cusps of the houses and measure through the signs; the houses have nothing to do with aspects at all. But, as I have already stated, a planet can be in aspect with the ascendant or the midheaven.

While the position of the planets in the signs varies regularly according to time of year, the position of the signs themselves with regard to the cusps of the houses changes once every twenty-four hours, and each sign appears to rise, culminate, and set during this period. The signs appear to do so owing to the diurnal rotation of the earth on its own axis. But the signs do not necessarily rise, culminate, and set at equal intervals of time. Owing to the obliquity of the ecliptic to the celestial equator (which is a projection along the plane of the earth's equator to cut the circle of the ecliptic) the signs usually rise at unequal intervals, thus giving rise to the so-called "intercepted signs"; and actually all the signs only rise at exact two-hour intervals on the equator. Accordingly, on the horoscope the signs move clockwise, against the sequence of the houses. Also, remember we do not mark the degrees of the constellations of the zodiac but the degrees of the twelve signs of the ecliptic; for owing to the phenomenon known as "precession" the constellation Aries is no longer in the sign Aries, but is now in the sign Pisces, will shortly move into the sign Aquarius, and will move through the remaining signs till it returns once more to Aries. This is due to the fact that the celestial equator is regularly slipping back in relation to the ecliptic; it does this at the rate of approximately 50″ a year, so that the complete cycle takes about twenty-six thousand years.

The times of the rising of the signs, which vary according to the geographical latitude of the observer as well as to the time of year, together with the position of the planets in relation to the signs, are all found by precise astronomical observation, and, when that is not possible, by mathematical calculation based on direct observations. Thus, for instance, if a map is being erected for someone born in the daytime, we still know what signs are rising and what planets are occupying the signs, even though we cannot see them, because signs and planets all move in regular paths, and once we know their position at any one time, as for instance at a moment at night when they are visible, we can calculate their precise position at any subsequent moment of time with relation to an observer placed at any desired position on the earth's surface. Nowadays, we erect our maps from special astrological tables called "ephemerides" which tabulate the position of the heavenly bodies from day to day. Earlier astrologers erected maps from the results of their own observations, which they made with primitive instruments such as the astrolabe; but nowadays we just look up the positions in an ephemeris, since these are based on observations made in the great astronomical observatories of the world with telescopes and clocks of a precision undreamed of by the earlier generations of astrologers. All the same, every astrologer remains an astronomer at heart, for without astronomy there can be no astrology.

Having now learned which are the houses, signs, and planets on the horoscope, we must next learn their significance, and we will accordingly start with that of the houses.

THE TWELVE HOUSES AND THEIR SIGNIFICANCE

As I have already stated, the order of houses remains invariable. Each house, moreover, has its own special significance, and in addition there are certain very important places in the horoscope, the cusps of the 1st and 10th houses, the ascendant or rising sign, and midheaven. And now a word of warning about the cusps. You must think of each cusp only in relation to its own house; because a planet is on the cusp of one house, you must not think that it can influence the adjacent house in any way.

The significances of the twelve houses are as follows:

1st house: The ascendant or rising sign. Personal appearance, character, ability; the self.
2nd house: Finance, movable property, peace, liberty, emotions.
3rd house: Relations, education, studies, literature, the nervous system; short journeys.
4th house: The home, inherited tendencies, the end of life, the father.
5th house: Pleasure, love affairs, children, speculation, amusements.
6th house: Domesticity, servants and inferiors, health, healing and nursing.
7th house: Marriage, partnerships and associations, communal life, open enemies, lawsuits.
8th house: Death and everything connected with it; inheritance and legacies.
9th house: Science, philosophy, religion, education. Long voyages. Dreams and visions.
10th house: The midheaven (*medium coeli*). The profession, honor, fame, and renown. The mother.
11th house: Friends, hopes, and wishes.
12th house: Trial, restriction, fear, sorrow, secret enemies; prisons, lunatic asylums, the "house of self-undoing."

THE TWELVE SIGNS AND THEIR SIGNIFICANCE

The most important sign is that rising on the ascendant; next to it in importance is that on the midheaven. But each of the twelve signs has its own special significance. Each sign has a ruling planet, the planet taking its color from the sign; and further each sign is distributed to one of the four elements: fire, earth, air, water. The significance of the signs may be tabulated as follows:

Aries, the Ram. Ruler: Mars. Fiery sign. Energetic, impulsive, positive. The pioneer sign.

Taurus, the Bull. Ruler: Venus. Earthy sign. Stubborn, dogmatic, kind-hearted, musical, not very intelligent.

Gemini, the Twins. Ruler: Mercury. Airy sign. Restless, versatile, clever, often superficial.

Cancer, the Crab. Ruler: the Moon. Watery sign. Sensitive, sympathetic, motherly, changeable, easily influenced.

272

♌ Leo, the Lion. Ruler: the Sun. Fiery sign. Proud, generous, energetic, domineering, authoritative.

♍ Virgo, the Virgin. Ruler: Mercury. Earthy sign. Exact, meticulous, painstaking, intelligent, chaste.

♎ Libra, the Balance. Ruler: Venus. Airy sign. Just, artistic, indolent, affectionate, sympathetic, honest.

♏ Scorpio, the Scorpion. Ruler: Mars. Watery sign. Ranges between the two extremes of saintly inspiration and criminal brutality. Energetic, passionate, jealous, mystical, proud, sensual.

♐ Sagittarius, the Archer. Ruler: Jupiter. Fiery sign. Impulsive, warmhearted, restless, impatient; love of nature, animals, and sport; candid and generous.

♑ Capricorn, the Goat. Ruler: Saturn. Earthy sign. Ambitious, persevering, tenacious, diplomatic, reserved, melancholy.

♒ Aquarius, the Water-bearer. Ruler: Uranus. Airy sign. Idealistic, artistic, intellectual, honest; easily influenced, popular yet solitary, often abnormal.

♓ Pisces, the Fishes. Ruler: Neptune. Watery sign. Gentle, kind, retiring, sensitive, unlucky, often melancholy.

To make the foregoing a little clearer, the following table groups the signs according to elements, or as it is known, to "triplicities"; they are:

Fiery Signs	♈	♌	♐	Airy Signs	♊	♎	♒
Earthy Signs	♉	♍	♑	Watery Signs	♋	♏	♓

You will notice that the signs of each triplicity are four signs apart; that is to say, they are in trine.

THE NINE PLANETS AND THEIR SIGNIFICANCE

You have already learned the names and symbols of the planets and how they are placed in the signs, their direction of movement on the map, and what is meant by "retrogradation." You must remember this last, as a "retrograde" planet is supposed to exercise a weaker influence. We are ignoring the newly discovered planet Pluto, as his influences are not sufficiently well known yet to be described in a popular work. The signficance of the planets may be tabulated as follows:

⊙ Sun: The male principle, honor, power, vitality, good fortune. Beneficent.

☽ Moon: The female principle; the passions, desires, and emotions. Health in general; all changes. Beneficent or the reverse, according to signs and aspects.

273

☿   Mercury: The intellect, the nervous system. The professions of literature, journalism, etc., or anything to do with them. Versatility. Varies in influence, the chameleon among planets.

♀   Venus: The love nature, pleasure, children, art, luck, wealth. Beneficent, the "Lesser Fortune" of the ancient.

♂   Mars: Courage, enthusiasm, war, wounds, fire. Malefic.

♃   Jupiter: Religion, philosophy, science, the law. Expansion, power, ceremony. Voyages and shipping. Beneficent. The "Greater Fortune" of the ancients.

♄   Saturn: Selfishness, reticence, diplomacy. Disappointments, delays, constriction in every respect. Hard work and perseverance. The earth, mines. Malefic.

♅   Uranus: Intellectual genius, inventiveness, eccentricity. New inventions. Sudden changes for good or evil, catastrophes or unexpected strokes of luck.

♆   Neptune: Emotional genius, art, poetry, mysticism, dreams, mediumism; if badly aspected, drunkenness, drugs, fraud.

It is important to remember that the action of every planet is modified by the action of the sign in which it is placed and by its aspects with other planets. A planet is more powerful in some signs than in others. A planet is very powerful for good or evil when it occupies its own sign, but is weak when placed in a sign opposite to its own. This latter position is called its "detriment." When it is placed in a sign nearly as powerful as its own sign, it is said to be in its "exaltation"; and when a planet is "exalted," it is more inclined to good than to evil. The sign opposite to its exaltation is called its "fall"; and when it is placed in its fall, a planet is weak and inclined to be evil. When two planets are placed in each other's signs they are said to be "in mutual reception."

The positions of the planets in the signs may be tabulated as follows:

PLANET	RULES	DETRIMENT	EXALTATION	FALL
☉	♌	♒	♈	♎
☽	♋	♑	♉	♏
☿	♊ ♍	♐ ♓	♍	♓
♀	♉ ♎	♏ ♈	♓	♍
♂	♈ ♏	♎ ♉	♑	♋

PLANET	RULES	DETRIMENT	EXALTATION	FALL
♃	♐ ♓	♊ ♍	♋	♑
♄	♑ ♒	♋ ♌	♎	♈

I have not included Uranus and Neptune in the tables, as doubts exist as to their houses and exaltations. But Uranus may be assumed at least to share the rulership of Aquarius with Saturn, and Neptune that of Pisces with Jupiter. And Uranus is said to have his exaltation in Sagittarius or Capricorn.

THE ASPECTS AND THEIR SIGNIFICANCE

As I have already remarked, aspects are calculated by signs and degrees in the signs and not in relation to the houses. The significance of the more important aspects is as follows:

   ☌ Conjunction (1° to 12° between Sun and Moon; 1° to 10° between planets). Good or bad, according to planets.
   △ Trine (120° or 4 signs). Very good.
   ✶ Sextile (60° or 2 signs). Good.
   □ Square (90° or 3 signs). Bad, an obstacle to overcome.
   ☍ Opposition (180° or 6 signs). Bad, a sudden disaster.

I must now explain what is meant by an "orb." You will see that the aspects as I have given them are exact to a degree. Now it is a matter of experience that the influence of the aspect starts before it is exact and continues for a little time after it has ceased to be exact. The amount of latitude permissible varies from about 7° to 11°, as follows:

   ☌ and ☍ about 10°, but between ☉ and ☽ 12°.
   △ and □ about 8°
   ✶ about 7°

INTERPRETATIONS OF THE HOROSCOPES OF NAPOLEON, WINSTON CHURCHILL, AND FRANKLIN D. ROOSEVELT

With the information I have just given, you should now be able to proceed to the next step, that is to say, judging a map; we proceed from analysis to synthesis. The best way to learn how this is done is for you to follow my analysis of specific horoscopes. So, in view of the maps which we shall be subsequently studying, I have first picked that of Napoleon, which is illustrated on p. 277. Before you read further take a good look at this and memorize the positions of the planets in the houses, their aspects, and the signs on the ascendant and midheaven. Now for the interpretation.

We find the sign Libra and the figure 17 on the upper line bounding the 1st house. Since both signs and planets progress counter-clockwise, the cusp of the 1st house falls on Libra 17°; in astrological terminology, "Libra is rising in the second decanate." On the cusp of the 2nd house we find Scorpio 14°, so the 1st house comprises not only the last 13° of Libra, but also the first 14° of Scorpio. Jupiter is on Scorpio 15° and is in the 2nd house; but, for example, had Jupiter been on 13° he would have fallen within the 1st house and his influence would have been different.

There is no planet near the ascendant, so we look to the midheaven or 10th house, which is most significantly tenanted. The Sun, Saturn, and Mercury are there. The Sun in the 10th house is always a sign of power and rulership, and furthermore he is in his own sign — Leo — which increases his influence a hundredfold. The qualities of the Lion are also enhanced. Mercury in Leo in the 10th house gives tremendous intellect, great self-confidence, and power. But close to the midheaven, and in conjunction with it is Saturn — the great enemy of mankind — in the melancholy sign Cancer. Saturn in the 10th house always signifies a rise to power through perseverance, but also, when badly aspected, a downfall as deep as the rise is high. And Saturn is in opposition to the Moon. Furthermore, the Moon and Saturn are in mutual reception, the Moon being in Capricorn, and Saturn in Cancer, and as a result of this the Moon becomes unfortunate. Moreover, in addition to being badly placed in this melancholy sign and with this catastrophic aspect from Saturn, she is in the 4th house (the end of life). So every novice can read the portents of utter downfall, and the slow, hopeless, pining away at St. Helena.

Napoleon was, above all else, a man of action and a public figure, so the study of the 10th house alone has already revealed the essential points of his fate. Let us continue with a methodical analysis of the planets.

Venus, the ruler of the ascendant, the planet of good fortune, in the 9th house signifies Napoleon's great intellectual qualities, his sympathetic attitude to religion, science, and higher education; Venus in Cancer shows his great love of family and offspring, and it was Venus in sextile to Neptune that made him a romantic in love, as his letters to Josephine reveal him to be.

Mars in Virgo gave him the great general's ability to think of every detail; Mars in the 11th house caused him to realize his hopes; Mars in trine to Uranus gave him his phenomenal luck in battle by sudden inspirations; and Mars in sextile to Jupiter was the source of his tremendous energy, as well as of his popularity with his men, for this aspect falls into the House of Friends.

Jupiter in Scorpio signifies pride and power, deep emotions, and a jealous nature, and also portends a tragic death. Jupiter's position in the 2nd house clearly indicates wealth, since the expansive influence of Jupiter is exerted on the house of finance. The very threatening aspect of Jupiter in opposition to Uranus is a sure sign of deep suffering and loss.

Uranus in Taurus gives that eccentric planet a background of earth-to-earth solidity; Uranus in the 7th house with the evil aspect from Jupiter clearly indicates disaster in marriage. Napoleon's first marriage was destroyed by legal considerations, and the second by the "powers and princes," which are symbolized by Jupiter.

Neptune in the 11th house is another indication of the emotional sway he held over his friends; moreover the 11th house also pertains to hopes and wishes, and Neptune being so well aspected by Venus is a great significator of success.

It is interesting to note that the cusp of the 10th house is in Cancer, though the house also comprises 24° of Leo. This shows that Napoleon's sense of family was all-important to him.

The foregoing should have shown you the method by which a natal horoscope is judged. Of

Bettmann Archive

Napoleon. Engraving after David.

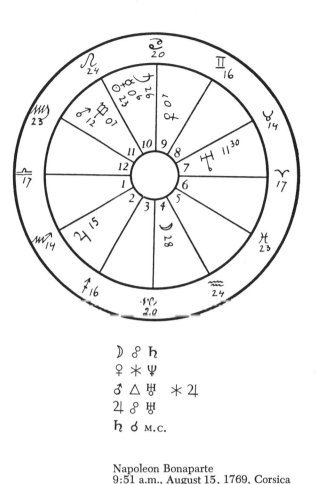

Napoleon Bonaparte
9:51 a.m., August 15, 1769, Corsica

course the full interpretation of a horoscope requires experience combined with knowledge, but the brief tabulation of the different significances of the houses, signs, and planets, gives you the basic facts on which even the most experienced horoscoper builds.

Winston Churchill's extremely powerful nativity indicates that the native will exercise great influence through the force of his intellect and the strength of his personality rather than dominate others through a particular profession.

In Mr. Churchill's map Scorpio is rising, and for a moment we are tempted to think it must be the dictator's sign! But a glance at Mr. Churchill's horoscope is enough to show why he could not be a dictator. His intelligence is too strong, and he lacks the necessary "one-track" mind. Mercury is conjunct the ascendant; the Mercurial sign Virgo is on the midheaven, strengthened by the Moon in conjunction; and the two mental houses are significantly tenanted, Saturn occupying the 3rd house and Uranus the 9th.

Sun in the 1st house gives the native his strength of personality, his huge vitality and energy, also dignity, authority, and self-reliance, while the position in Sagittarius gives great ambition, loyalty, generosity, and energy. The Sun does not agree with the Moon too well. She is in Virgo; this indicates that the native is likely to be subordinate to others in his profession, while the strong Sun and the ruler Mars indicate a constant desire for supreme authority. Also, Sun and Moon in square inevitably leads to frequent changes of opinion, making the character venturesome, egotistical, and intransigent. Losses through inferiors, and through over-confidence, are also indicated.

The changes of opinion referred to explain Mr. Churchill's secession from the Conservatives and joining of the Liberal Party in 1904 and his re-joining of the Conservative Party twenty years later. The losses through inferiors and over-confidence are borne out by the thwarting of Mr. Churchill's plans for the Dardanelles campaign during World War I. But fortunately the Sun is benefited by a sextile from Saturn, and this adds a strong sense of responsibility to the inherent authoritative traits, and brings honor and renown through official posts.

Moon conjunct the midheaven points to varying periods of great public prominence, while her position in the 9th house gives an ingenious mind, progressive ideas, and the ability to pursue deep studies; and the trine of Moon to Neptune adds a touch of imagination and artistic creativeness, personal charm, a sensitive nature, and great love of the sea.

The critical faculties of the Moon in Virgo are further enhanced by Mercury in Scorpio, which makes the mind extraordinarily shrewd and keen, extremely critical, and ever eager to gain new knowledge. Mercury in the 12th house points to a very subtle mind and a love of risks and dangerous adventures. Further, the mind is greatly benefited by Mercury's trine to Uranus, which makes it active, original, quick, and fertile.

Mars, the ruler of the horoscope, is in the 11th house, which is not auspicious for friendships; the rule here is "many acquaintances, few real friends." Mars in Libra is a fortunate position, giving an idealistic temperament and clear vision. This is good for domestic affairs and fortunate for marriage and children. Mars receives only good aspects; a trine from Venus, favoring finance and personal happiness, and a sextile from Uranus, which gives energy, impulse, an alert, decisive mind, originality, enterprise and resourcefulness, and also a predilection for sarcasm, irony, and destructive criticism.

Jupiter in the 11th house favors true friendship in itself; but as he is afflicted by Neptune, there will be frequent loss of friends, or alienation from them. A very fine influence, however, is the sextile from Venus, especially since Venus and Jupiter are in mutual reception, Venus being in Jupiter's sign Sagittarius, and Jupiter in Venus' sign Libra. This aspect will counterbalance the truculent and bellicose tendencies; it will also give genius in some form, and portends good fortune in public and domestic concerns.

The opposition Saturn-Uranus points to recurring lack of opportunity to exercise the inherent energy. This influence is similar in its effect to that of the square Sun-Moon discussed above, and therein we see the tragic side of Mr. Churchill's career. He has consistently foreseen danger and endeavored to forestall it, but he has been opposed — through no fault of his own — by the negative forces of timidity, superficiality, and procrastination.

Intellectuality and fiery energy are equally represented, four planets being in airy signs and four in fiery signs. The remaining planet, Mercury, is in the watery sign of Scorpio, which raises the imaginative powers to something akin to genius. Only the earthy element is missing — patience, tact, reserve! In another country, where such qualities are not so highly prized as in England, the native would have carried all before him.

278

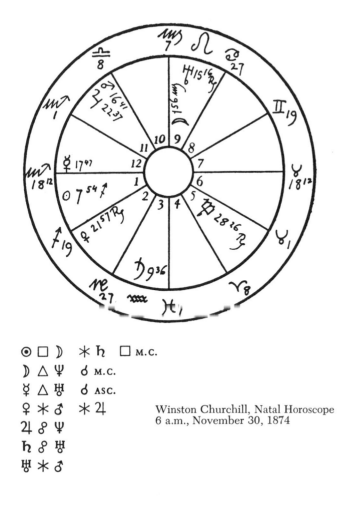

⊙ □ ☽ ✳ ♄ □ M.C.
☽ △ ♆ ♂ M.C.
☿ △ ♅ ♂ ASC.
♀ ✳ ♂ ✳ ♃
♃ ☍ ♆
♄ ☍ ♅
♅ ✳ ♂

Winston Churchill, Natal Horoscope
6 a.m., November 30, 1874

Franklin D. Roosevelt's horoscope shows the advanced ideas and ideals of the twentieth century. Virgo is rising — Virgo, the critical, detail-loving, restraining sign. But her influence is overshadowed since Uranus is conjunct the ascendant. For never yet have I found Uranus occupying a prominent position in a nativity without its manifesting some form of genius. All natives on a higher stage of development are favored by the vibrations from Uranus, though with the lower, unevolved type of man, Uranian influence tends toward the abnormal and the pathological. This is borne out by the aspects which Uranus receives. Thus, a strong and well-aspected Uranus gives great intuition, inspiration, and the inherent faculty of finding a way out of a situation which, to others, may well appear hopeless. President Roosevelt's National Recovery scheme may be ascribed to Uranus beneficially aspected. And Uranus is looked upon as the higher octave of Mercury, so he is well placed as the revolutionary genius, the pioneer and reformer among the planets, in Mercury's sign Virgo. Uranus receives a trine from Jupiter from the 9th house, and this is a clear indication that the mind is wide, humanitarian, and drawn to philosophical and scientific questions.

The ruler of the horoscope, Mercury, is in the 6th house (rather unfortunate for health) in Aquarius, the sign ruled by Uranus. So Uranus and Mercury are in mutual reception, which fur-

279

ther strengthens the intellectual originality and versatility. Aquarius also contains the Sun and Venus, who are in conjunction, so that the Aquarian characteristics are the most outstanding. President Roosevelt may be described as a true Aquarian.

Aquarians are often said to be the real representatives of our age, since the earth is moving into the sign Aquarius out of Pisces, the sign which she has been under for two thousand years. The exact year when this great cosmic event will be completed is a matter of conjecture and controversy, but the fact that many outstanding reformers, pioneers and leaders of modern science, thought, or art have been strongly influenced by Aquarius is undeniable. A few very dissimilar examples of men with Sun in Aquarius are Francis Bacon, Swedenborg, Edison, Darwin, and Charles Dickens. Besides genius and fame, they had one thing in common: utter disregard of existing traditions, the will to realize a Utopia of their minds. But it is often claimed that Aquarians, in spite of their high ideals, are unreliable and untrustworthy. This is probably due to the fact that fundamentally they are idealists; for the moment they lose touch with reality, they realize the wide discrepancy between the world as it is and their inner world of almost mathematical ideas.

The Sun, conjunct Venus in the 5th house, augurs well for personal happiness and domestic felicity. The native will have many children and enjoy society and personal popularity.

The Moon is in conjunction with Mars in the 10th house. The presence of either of the luminaries, Sun or Moon, in the 10th house almost inevitably favors prominence in the professions; and fame and publicity is especially influenced by the Moon. The Moon in Pisces indicates great activity and ambition, but extreme sensitivity. Mars in the 10th house is favorable, since he imparts energy, masterfulness, and ambition. The conjunction of Moon and Mars is not, in itself, a fortunate aspect, as it makes the native act rashly and imprudently, and often spurn tradition and convention, thus creating many violent enmities. On the other hand, it would not have been possible for President Roosevelt to overcome his physical disabilities in the wonderfully energetic way he did if there had not been this conjunction. Mars imparts energy to any planet or sign he touches; the Moon, as we know, symbolizes our subconscious and unconscious mind — and only when the subconscious is working hand in hand with the conscious mind is it possible to obtain mastery of the body. Mars in trine to Mercury gives a quick mind, sharp wit, and gifts of oratory.

Saturn, the restricting, disappointing, and moderating influence of our lives, does not play a prominent part in this nativity, but his sextile to the Moon is a good and steadying influence, indicating diplomacy, tact, the ability to influence others, and powers of organization. His square to the Sun is bad for health, and weakens character and courage; the latter can also be said of the square to Venus. Saturn in the 8th house points to bad luck with wills, legacies, and so on, and a slow death from some chronic ailment.

Jupiter and Neptune are in conjunction, and this refining influence gives true humanitarian ideals. Unfortunately, the fact that both planets are also in square to the Sun indicates a certain amount of moral vacillation, mistrustfulness, and duplicity; it also reacts adversely on physical health.

The Sun is in trine to the midheaven, a fine aspect for public success; and Jupiter trine the ascendant enriches the personality with helpful vibrations of power and expansion.

Looking on the nativity as a whole, we are struck by the fact that not a single planet is in a fiery sign; the element which stands for positive action is lacking. Five of the nine planets are in airy signs, and this points to an overwhelming predominance of speculation, idealism, even fantasy.

NORA WYDENBRUCK

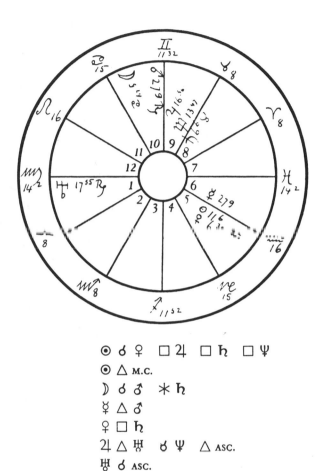

Franklin D. Roosevelt, Natal Horoscope
8 p.m., January 30, 1882, Hyde Park

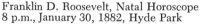

⊙ ♂ ♀   □ ♃   □ ♄   □ ♆
⊙ △ M.C.
☽ ♂ ♂   ⚹ ♄
☿ △ ♂
♀ □ ♄
♃ △ ♅   ♂ ♆   △ ASC.
♅ ♂ ASC.

[*Readers interested in making horoscopes will find "Raphael's Astronomical Ephemeris" handy. It is published in booklet form for each year, and gives the places of the planets in the twelve signs. They will also need Raphael's Table of Houses or Dalton's Table of Houses, which shows the rising sign for each four minutes of each day and the position of the signs for each house. Dalton's tables are published by Macoy, New York, and Raphael's are issued by David McKay of Philadelphia and W. Foulsham of London. Also recommended are such good basic textbooks as Alan Leo's* Astrology for All, *and his* Casting the Horoscope *and the* Key to Your Own Nativity.]

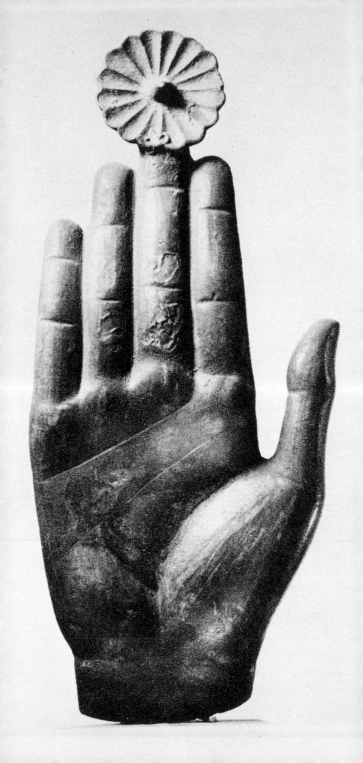

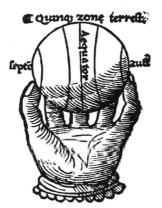

8. PALMISTRY AS RELATED TO ASTROLOGY

Nature has made the hand of man the principal organ and instrument of man's body.

ARISTOTLE

Why should the hand more than the other parts of the body reflect the forces from above? To this, the magus answers that since the world is a hierarchy, the miniature world — i.e., man — must necessarily be organized similarly. In the system of man, the hand fulfills a unique function, that of the mediator between the above and the below, between the intellectual microcosm, residing in the head, and the material microcosm, which dwells in the body. If the brain is comparable to the unmoved mover, the magi say, then the hand may be called the active force through which the mover manifests himself. For this reason, the hand occupies the second rank in the microcosmic hierarchy and is, after the head, the most worthy of investigation.

In the eighteenth century, when many magical traditions had been lost, over-zealous chiromancers believed it useful to investigate the *planets of the feet*, a ludicrous misconception. The feet are the most remote from the planets. Turned toward the earth, they receive the weakest light from above. They dwell, according to Fludd, in the microcosmic night, which is not tuned to the music of the spheres.

Chiromancy gathers from the heavenly imprints upon the hand two verities: character and destiny, a conclusion which all divinatory methods share. This is deductive as well as prophetic, rational and irrational. When reading his patient's hand, the chiromancer uses his reason and his

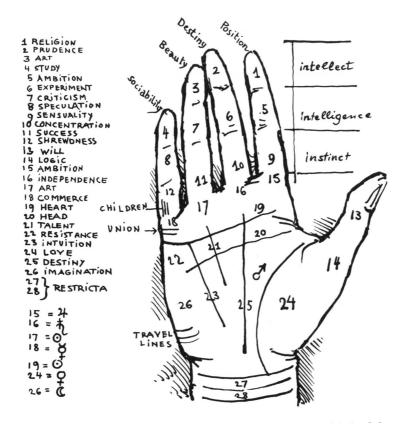

1 RELIGION
2 PRUDENCE
3 ART
4 STUDY
5 AMBITION
6 EXPERIMENT
7 CRITICISM
8 SPECULATION
9 SENSUALITY
10 CONCENTRATION
11 SUCCESS
12 SHREWDNESS
13 WILL
14 LOGIC
15 AMBITION
16 INDEPENDENCE
17 ART
18 COMMERCE
19 HEART
20 HEAD
21 TALENT
22 RESISTANCE
23 INTUITION
24 LOVE
25 DESTINY
26 IMAGINATION
27 } RESTRICTA
28 }

15 = ♃
16 = ♄
17 = ☉
18 = ☿
19 = ☉
24 = ♀
26 = ☽

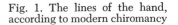

Fig. 1. The lines of the hand, according to modern chiromancy

divinatory gift. The lines whose significance was established by tradition are the scaffold upon which the magus sets his imagination. *Imagination* is the force which performs the marvel, as Agrippa, Paracelsus, and others have affirmed.

The chiromancers searched the Bible for verses that might prove the legitimacy of their art, for religion was believed to sanction magic, as in our days the occultist rashly relates his wisdom to true science. Thus, in the book of Job, 37:7, we read: "He seals up the hand of every man, that all men may know his work." And in Proverbs, 3:16: "Long life is given in her right hand. In her left are riches and honor."

It is not within the scope of these pages to explain the method of hand reading, on which there exists an extensive literature, but rather to give a few of the most striking illustrations of the periods when chiromancy was at the height of its popularity, i.e., the sixteenth and seventeenth centuries. It is useful, however, to compare these early schemes with that of modern palmistry. Figure 1 shows the modern demarcation of a left hand. Far more importance is given to the *fingers* today. They confirm the marks in the palm and add many interesting details to the more general information gathered from the palm. The upper phalanx of the thumb expresses will, the lower, logic. In the three phalanxes of the index finger reside religion, ambition, and sensuality. The middle finger contains prudence, the tendency to experiment, and concentration. The ring finger informs us of the individual's artistic gifts, his critical sense, and his successes. The little finger belongs to sociability; it is marked with the signs of study, speculation, and shrewdness. All the upper phalanxes give information concerning the subject's intellect; the middle phalanxes, of his intelligence; and the lowest phalanxes, of his instincts.

The most important lines of the palm are those of life, of destiny, of the heart, of the head, and of intuition. A shorter line that descends from the art or ring finger reveals artistic talents; and several parallel lines upon the wrist give supplementary information about the length of life.

Besides the lines of the hand, its "mounts" are important to the palmist. The hump of the thumb, called the mount of Venus, informs us about the individual's love; the mount of Jupiter, below the index finger, is marked by ambition; the mount of Saturn, below the middle finger, reveals man's independence; the mount of the Sun, below the annular finger, is that of Apollo, or art. And below the little finger, the mount of Mercury reveals commercial aptitudes. At the edge of the palm, opposed to the thumb, there are the mounts of Mars, denoting steadiness and resistance, and of the Moon containing the marks of imagination and melancholy.

Close by are the lines of travel, and above, in the mount of Mercury, those of union. Distant from the mount of love, in the realm of shrewdness (lowest phalanx of the little finger), is marked the number of children the person will beget or conceive.

To the question of whether the right or left hand or both should be inspected, no definite answer can be offered. From tradition, it has been accepted that in the left hand, which does not work as much as the right, the signs are preserved better and not distorted. Others say that in the left is inscribed the primitive destiny given by the stars at man's birth, whereas in the right hand are marked those changes which man causes daily by his will and work. This argument cannot be accepted lightly. If man's will is free, why should one inspect his left hand? If he modifies his destiny, the stars' original marks offer no valuable information. But if the stars are omnipotent, then there is no point in inspecting the right hand, for will, labor, and intelligence cannot overcome that which has been decided by the horoscope. This perennial strife as to whether man is free or not can certainly not be ended by the chiromancer. In his defense, one could say, however,

Fig. 2. The right hand, after Indagine   Fig. 3. The right hand, after Tricassus   Fig. 4. Chiromantic hand, after Cocle

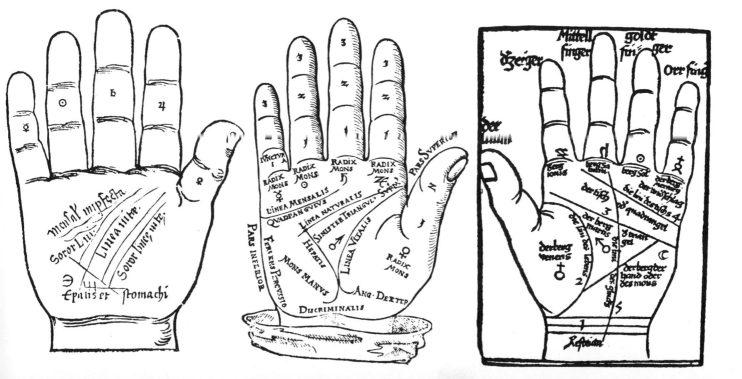

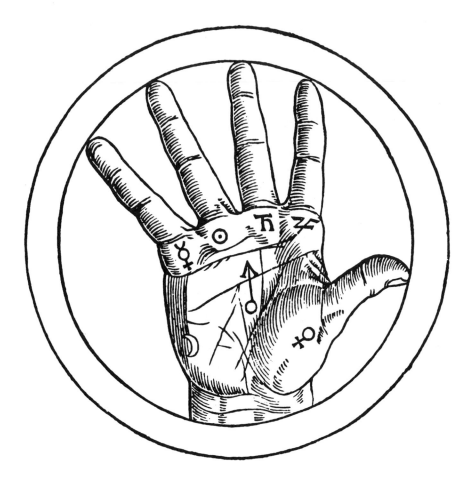

Fig. 5. Position of the planets on the right hand, after Agrippa

that in the left hand he reads man's natural disposition, whereas the right hand reveals to him what he has made with his gifts. Thus one may recognize whether the subject is living according to his inclinations, if his activities are in accord with the gifts bestowed upon him at birth, and the like. Accepting this, we can say that the stars influence but do not irretrievably decide our destiny.

The palmists or chiromancers render their judgment according to the various lengths of the lines, the depth of their engraving, their color, their continuity. They also consider whether the lines are doubled, like those in Indagine's woodcut (Fig. 2).

Indagine considers as the main lines the *linea mensalis*, identical with our line of the heart, the *linea media*, or middle line, the *linea vitae*, or life line, which he calls also line of the heart, and the *linea hepatis* or liver line, which reveals according to a few experts disturbances of the lower functions. The four mounts below the fingers correspond to those of modern palmistry.

The Dominican Tricasso de Cerasari (died 1550) shows a similar disposition of the principal lines in his treatise on chiromancy (Fig. 3).

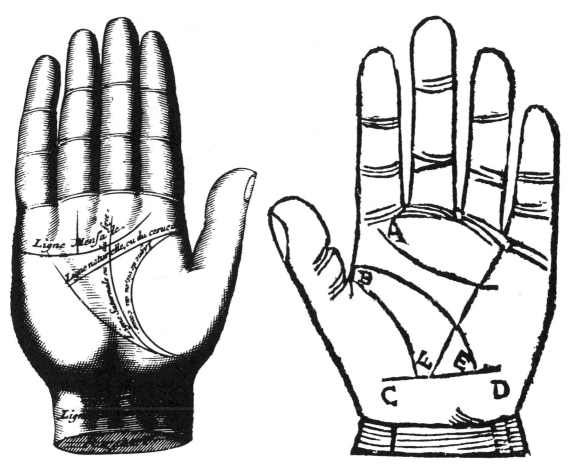

Fig. 6. Principal lines of
the hand, after Ronphyle

Fig. 7. Principal lines of
the left hand, after Indagine

"Four grooves," he says, "regulate and command the whole art of palmistry, and all the others depend on them. The life line must be divided into three parts — youth, maturity, and old age. From its length, we can recognize how long its owner has to live. When the heart line is short, without ramifications, it denotes mortal danger, conjured up by negligence. When the head line is stopped below the middle finger, this means that the individual will wound himself dangerously. When the liver line is very distant from the one of life, it denotes a vain or an insane being," and so on.

Neither Indagine nor Tricasso counts the line of Saturn, or destiny, among the important marks of the hand. The *linea Saturni* is, however, not a later invention for it is plainly marked in Bartolommeo Cocle's handsome woodcut (Fig. 4).

Agrippa's chiromantic hand (Fig. 5) shows the locations of the planets; they are not different from those of modern palmistry with the exception of the headquarters of Mars, which occupy the center of the palm.

In the seventeenth century, the number of principal lines was increased. The Parisian Ronphyle

Fig. 8. Lines of the thumb, after Indagine

adds to the older schemes the line of Saturn, which he also calls, arbitrarily, liver line, and the line of Apollo, that of artistic talents (Fig. 6).

As late as 1676, however, an English edition of Indagine's book clings still to the four lines of old (Fig. 7). To stress its conservatism, this book is printed in obsolete Gothic characters. The line of life, it says, has already been rightly judged by Pliny. Its length marks the boundaries of life. The middle line (E) reveals health and disease, the table line (A) informs us of our physical constitution and strength, of our temperament and mind. The wrist line (C, D) promises riches and felicity, when it is well colored. But when it reaches into the hill of the Moon, it signifies betrayal by women, and many storms in fortune. Special attention is given in this little treatise to the conformation of the thumb (Fig. 8). "If there be about the first joint of the thumb a crest like a ring going round about, and dividing the thumb, many do sternly judge and say, that this man shall be hanged. The which thing I have proved true in one man. But because I have seen many hanged who have lacked that mark, I leave it as uncertain."

A very instructive woodcut illustrates Jean Belot's treatise on chiromancy (Fig. 9). It shows a synthesis of many lines and districts. Moreover, Belot added to his scheme a novelty, introducing the *signs of the zodiac* into the four fingers. The index contains Ram, Bull, and Twins, the middle finger, Goat, Water Bearer, and Fishes, etc. Upon the thumb is marked the lost virginity: and the mount of Venus contains other items which apparently interested the abbot's contemporaries. In the hollow of the hand, in the region of Mars, we read: wounded in a duel, which shows that the occult sciences, like the true ones, adapt themselves to their epoch. Further down, in the triangle,

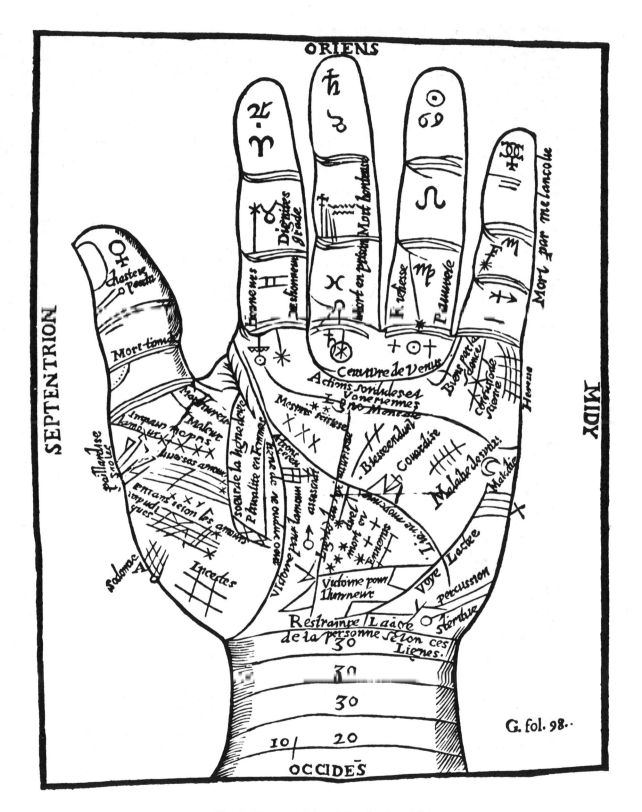

Fig. 9. Diagram of the left hand, after Belot

Fig. 10. Hand of an avaricious and
thoughtless man

Fig. 11. Hand of a stubborn and
iniquitous man

Fig. 12. Hand of an irascible and
evil man

Fig. 13. Wrist of a woman unsuited
for motherhood

formed by the middle line, that of the liver and the line of Saturn, we read about similar yet greater misfortunes: killed in a duel. Such sad predictions are separated only by a few millimeters from good news: close to the wrist, we read: victory in defense of honor. Below the mounts of the Sun and of Saturn reside sordid actions, and close by, upon the mount of Mercury, the good things brought to science. Between thumb and life line, finally, are the marks of polygamy; in the table of Mars, close to the life line, dwell success in love affairs, assassination, and insults received.

Belot's illustration suggests an ensemble of one hand. Innumerable other combinations are possible. They are as inexhaustible as those of human physiognomies. But this recognition should not discourage us from showing a few more instances of manual conformations, if only to give the reader an idea of the prodigious richness of the chiromantic literature.

An early treatise, signed by Andreas Corvus of Mirandola, another pseudonym for Cocle, reproduced numerous types of hands upon ever-changing backgrounds, in a rustic Renaissance style. Figure 10 represents an extended line of Saturn which is interpreted thus: "When you see this line of prosperity, going through the hand down to the wrist and being deeply engraven, it denotes prosperity and good business. If you find the contrary, it signifies an inventive man or woman, an innovator of science, yet shabby, greedy, etc."

A little triangle at the wrist, as in Figure 11, predicts a quiet life, the peace of the soul, honor, force of the mind and of the hand.

If the restricted lines at the root of the hand are formed as in Figure 12, they denote inventiveness, especially in evil matters; bad fortune, disobedience to one's father, and contempt.

If such lines diminish in strength toward the arm (Fig. 13), they predict increase up to the middle of life of wealth and honor, and afterwards a decrease in both.

It is remarkable how many of these combinations of lines are unfavorable omens, how little the palmists of old objected to communicating to others their inveterate pessimism, unlike the amiable disposition of modern palmists, who predict when paid well the good things to come, mingling with their ingratiating talk a few friendly warnings. In these old books, we read nothing about fatal dark-haired persons and favorable blonds, or of a letter that will change the course of our fate.

Palmistry of old was considered a science; the inspection of the hand was as grave as a doctor's visit is today; and the chiromancers were very serious about their craft. In his preface, Indagine describes the painstaking procedure necessary for efficacious investigation:

"I look upon the hand and therewithal behold the whole body, with the lineament and proportions of the same, which is called his physiognomy. Then I focus my mind upon the hour of nativity, month, day, or year, which I refer to the rules of natural astrology; I judge none of these by themselves sufficient, and think it better not to be rash or foolish in passing sentence. I gather all things and select those which I consider useful. Only then do I utter judgment, believing it madness to examine the hand and hastily interpret a life, and a body."

The chiromancer's verdict, pronounced with such strong conviction, was certainly endowed with a suggestive power. Sometimes it may have been based upon a general knowledge of man, on logical deductions, and the like, things which did not require much astrological calculation and chiromantic inspection. Indagine's statement that he can read the palm like a physiognomy is revealing: experience can produce a routine which may have, in serious cases, been more than idle fancy.

A Greek chiromancer predicted to Alessandro de' Medici that he was to suffer soon a violent death, which happened when he was assassinated by his cousin Lorenzo.

In the last century, the physician Bruhier reported the true story of a young man in whose hand a lady had read an evil future. "What a pity," she exclaimed, "that you have only one more month to live." Some time after, the youth went hunting, caught a fever, and died at the appointed date, as the amateur palmist had predicted.

A famous case of a chiromantic prophecy which came true is that of a M. Raillois who had been warned by a gypsy to beware of the scaffold. His whole life seemed to disprove this prediction made when Raillois was a boy. He would often mention in jest that he would suffer an ignominious death. He had a new house built on one of the fashionable Parisian boulevards. While inspecting the progress of the work, he stepped from a window upon the scaffold which, being fastened carelessly, collapsed. Raillois died from his fall.

Cocle read in the hand of Bentivoglio, ruler of Bologna, that he was to be exiled and would die in a battle. The angry Bentivoglio decided to have Cocle killed. He chose for this task a Bolognese nobleman to whom the palmist had predicted that he was going to commit an ignominious murder. He railed at the dying Cocle, saying that his prediction had now come true.

The earliest chiromancer of the Renaissance, Antioco Tiberto of Cesena, was stabbed by the tyrant of Rimini, Pandolfo Malatesta, to whom he had prophesied death in exile and poverty. Tiberto was a lively and intelligent scholar held in high esteem, even by those intellectuals who thought little of the chiromantic art.

Kurt Seligmann

Textue de Sphaera. Sacrobosco. 153*

Metropolitan Museum of Art

VRANIA   PTOLEMAEVS

TABLES OF ASCENDANTS

(Rising Signs)
Showing, approximately,
the Sign and Degree of the Zodiac
rising each hour of every fourth day in any year
These tables are calculated for 41° North Latitude

♈	Aries	♋	Cancer	♎	Libra	♑ Capricorn
♉	Taurus	♌	Leo	♏	Scorpio	♒ Aquarius
♊	Gemini	♍	Virgo	♐	Sagittarius	♓ Pisces

To ascertain the degree of the sign rising on any intermediate day or part of an hour, the proper proportion of increase should be taken.

JANUARY 1	JANUARY 5	JANUARY 9
A.M.	**A.M.**	**A.M.**

JANUARY 1 A.M.	JANUARY 5 A.M.	JANUARY 9 A.M.
At 1 o'clock, 20° of ♎ rises	At 1 o'clock, 23° of ♎ rises	At 1 o'clock, 26° of ♎ rises
" 2 " 1 " ♏ "	" 2 " 5 " ♏ "	" 2 " 8 " ♏ "
" 3 " 13 " ♏ "	" 3 " 16 " ♏ "	" 3 " 19 " ♏ "
" 4 " 25 " ♏ "	" 4 " 28 " ♏ "	" 4 " 1 " ♐ "
" 5 " 7 " ♐ "	" 5 " 10 " ♐ "	" 5 " 14 " ♐ "
" 6 " 19 " ♐ "	" 6 " 23 " ♐ "	" 6 " 26 " ♐ "
" 7 " 2 " ♑ "	" 7 " 7 " ♑ "	" 7 " 11 " ♑ "
" 8 " 18 " ♑ "	" 8 " 22 " ♑ "	" 8 " 27 " ♑ "
" 9 " 6 " ♒ "	" 9 " 11 " ♒ "	" 9 " 17 " ♒ "
" 10 " 27 " ♒ "	" 10 " 4 " ♓ "	" 10 " 9 " ♓ "
" 11 " 22 " ♓ "	" 11 " 29 " ♓ "	" 11 " 5 " ♈ "
" 12, Noon, 16 " ♈ "	" 12, Noon, 24 " ♈ "	" 12, Noon, 1 " ♉ "

JANUARY 1 P.M.	JANUARY 5 P.M.	JANUARY 9 P.M.
At 1 o'clock, 11° of ♉ rises	At 1 o'clock, 22° of ♉ rises	At 1 o'clock, 16° of ♉ rises
" 2 " 1 " ♊ "	" 2 " 10 " ♊ "	" 2 " 6 " ♊ "
" 3 " 17 " ♊ "	" 3 " 25 " ♊ "	" 3 " 21 " ♊ "
" 4 " 2 " ♋ "	" 4 " 8 " ♋ "	" 4 " 5 " ♋ "
" 5 " 15 " ♋ "	" 5 " 21 " ♋ "	" 5 " 18 " ♋ "
" 6 " 27 " ♋ "	" 6 " 3 " ♌ "	" 6 " 0 " ♌ "
" 7 " 9 " ♌ "	" 7 " 15 " ♌ "	" 7 " 12 " ♌ "
" 8 " 21 " ♌ "	" 8 " 27 " ♌ "	" 8 " 24 " ♌ "
" 9 " 2 " ♍ "	" 9 " 8 " ♍ "	" 9 " 6 " ♍ "
" 10 " 14 " ♍ "	" 10 " 20 " ♍ "	" 10 " 18 " ♍ "
" 11 " 26 " ♍ "	" 11 " 2 " ♎ "	" 11 " 29 " ♍ "
" 12, Midn't. 8 " ♎ "	" 12, Midn't. 14 " ♎ "	" 12, Midn't. 11 " ♎ "

294

JANUARY 13

A.M.

At 1 o'clock, 29° of ♎ rises
" 2 " 11 " ♏ "
" 3 " 23 " ♏ "
" 4 " 5 " ♐ "
" 5 " 17 " ♐ "
" 6 " 0 " ♑ "
" 7 " 15 " ♑ "
" 8 " 2 " ♒ "
" 9 " 22 " ♒ "
" 10 " 16 " ♓ "
" 11 " 13 " ♈ "
" 12, Noon, 7 " ♉ "

P.M.

At 1 o'clock, 27° of ♉ rises
" 2 " 14 " ♊ "
" 3 " 29 " ♊ "
" 4 " 12 " ♋ "
" 5 " 24 " ♋ "
" 6 " 7 " ♌ "
" 7 " 18 " ♌ "
" 8 " 0 " ♍ "
" 9 " 12 " ♍ "
" 10 " 24 " ♍ "
" 11 " 6 " ♎ "
" 12, Midn't 18 " ♎ "

JANUARY 21

A.M.

At 1 o'clock, 5° of ♏ rises
" 2 " 17 " ♏ "
" 3 " 29 " ♏ "
" 4 " 11 " ♐ "
" 5 " 24 " ♐ "
" 6 " 7 " ♑ "
" 7 " 23 " ♑ "
" 8 " 12 " ♒ "
" 9 " 5 " ♓ "
" 10 " 0 " ♈ "
" 11 " 25 " ♈ "
" 12, Noon, 18 " ♉ "

P.M.

At 1 o'clock, 7° of ♊ rises
" 2 " 22 " ♊ "
" 3 " 6 " ♋ "
" 4 " 19 " ♋ "
" 5 " 1 " ♌ "
" 6 " 12 " ♌ "
" 7 " 24 " ♌ "
" 8 " 6 " ♍ "
" 9 " 18 " ♍ "
" 10 " 0 " ♎ "
" 11 " 12 " ♎ "
" 12, Midn't, 24 " ♎ "

JANUARY 29

A.M.

At 1 o'clock, 12° of ♏ rises
" 2 " 23 " ♏ "
" 3 " 5 " ♐ "
" 4 " 17 " ♐ "
" 5 " 1 " ♑ "
" 6 " 15 " ♑ "
" 7 " 3 " ♒ "
" 8 " 24 " ♒ "
" 9 " 18 " ♓ "
" 10 " 13 " ♈ "
" 11 " 7 " ♉ "
" 12, Noon, 28 " ♉ "

P.M.

At 1 o'clock, 15° of ♊ rises
" 2 " 0 " ♋ "
" 3 " 13 " ♋ "
" 4 " 25 " ♋ "
" 5 " 7 " ♌ "
" 6 " 19 " ♌ "
" 7 " 0 " ♍ "
" 8 " 12 " ♍ "
" 9 " 24 " ♍ "
" 10 " 6 " ♎ "
" 11 " 18 " ♎ "
" 12, Midn't, 0 " ♏ "

JANUARY 17

A.M.

At 1 o'clock, 2° of ♏ rises
" 2 " 14 " ♏ "
" 3 " 26 " ♏ "
" 4 " 8 " ♐ "
" 5 " 20 " ♐ "
" 6 " 4 " ♑ "
" 7 " 19 " ♑ "
" 8 " 7 " ♒ "
" 9 " 29 " ♒ "
" 10 " 24 " ♓ "
" 11 " 20 " ♈ "
" 12, Noon, 13 " ♉ "

P.M.

At 1 o'clock, 2° of ♊ rises
" 2 " 18 " ♊ "
" 3 " 3 " ♋ "
" 4 " 15 " ♋ "
" 5 " 28 " ♋ "
" 6 " 10 " ♌ "
" 7 " 21 " ♌ "
" 8 " 3 " ♍ "
" 9 " 15 " ♍ "
" 10 " 27 " ♍ "
" 11 " 9 " ♎ "
" 12, Midn't 21 " ♎ "

JANUARY 25

A.M.

At 1 o'clock, 8° of ♏ rises
" 2 " 20 " ♏ "
" 3 " 2 " ♐ "
" 4 " 14 " ♐ "
" 5 " 27 " ♐ "
" 6 " 12 " ♑ "
" 7 " 28 " ♑ "
" 8 " 17 " ♒ "
" 9 " 11 " ♓ "
" 10 " 7 " ♈ "
" 11 " 2 " ♉ "
" 12, Noon, 23 " ♉ "

P.M.

At 1 o'clock, 11° of ♊ rises
" 2 " 26 " ♊ "
" 3 " 9 " ♋ "
" 4 " 22 " ♋ "
" 5 " 4 " ♌ "
" 6 " 16 " ♌ "
" 7 " 27 " ♌ "
" 8 " 9 " ♍ "
" 9 " 21 " ♍ "
" 10 " 3 " ♎ "
" 11 " 15 " ♎ "
" 12, Midn't. 27 " ♎ "

FEBRUARY 2

A.M.

At 1 o'clock, 15° of ♏ rises
" 2 " 26 " ♏ "
" 3 " 8 " ♐ "
" 4 " 21 " ♐ "
" 5 " 4 " ♑ "
" 6 " 20 " ♑ "
" 7 " 7 " ♒ "
" 8 " 0 " ♓ "
" 9 " 24 " ♓ "
" 10 " 20 " ♈ "
" 11 " 13 " ♉ "
" 12, Noon, 3 " ♊ "

P.M.

At 1 o'clock, 19° of ♊ rises
" 2 " 3 " ♋ "
" 3 " 16 " ♋ "
" 4 " 28 " ♋ "
" 5 " 10 " ♌ "
" 6 " 22 " ♌ "
" 7 " 4 " ♍ "
" 8 " 16 " ♍ "
" 9 " 27 " ♍ "
" 10 " 9 " ♎ "
" 11 " 21 " ♎ "
" 12, Midn't, 3 " ♏ "

FEBRUARY 6

A.M.

```
At 1 o'clock, 18° of ♏ rises
 " 2    "    29 "  ♏    "
 " 3    "    12 "  ♐    "
 " 4    "    24 "  ♐    "
 " 5    "     8 "  ♑    "
 " 6    "    24 "  ♑    "
 " 7    "    13 "  ♒    "
 " 8    "     5 "  ♓    "
 " 9    "     1 "  ♈    "
 " 10   "    27 "  ♈    "
 " 11   "    19 "  ♉    "
 " 12, Noon,   8 "  ♊    "
```

P.M.

```
At 1 o'clock, 23° of ♊ rises
 " 2    "     7 "  ♋    "
 " 3    "    19 "  ♋    "
 " 4    "     1 "  ♌    "
 " 5    "    13 "  ♌    "
 " 6    "    25 "  ♌    "
 " 7    "     7 "  ♍    "
 " 8    "    18 "  ♍    "
 " 9    "     0 "  ♎    "
 " 10   "    12 "  ♎    "
 " 11   "    24 "  ♎    "
 " 12, Midn't,  6 "  ♏    "
```

FEBRUARY 14

A.M.

```
At 1 o'clock, 24° of ♏ rises
 " 2    "     5 "  ♐    "
 " 3    "    18 "  ♐    "
 " 4    "     2 "  ♑    "
 " 5    "    16 "  ♑    "
 " 6    "     3 "  ♒    "
 " 7    "    24 "  ♒    "
 " 8    "    18 "  ♓    "
 " 9    "    15 "  ♈    "
 " 10   "     9 "  ♉    "
 " 11   "    29 "  ♉    "
 " 12, Noon,  16 "  ♊    "
```

P.M.

```
At 1 o'clock,  0° of ♋ rises
 " 2    "    13 "  ♋    "
 " 3    "    26 "  ♋    "
 " 4    "     8 "  ♌    "
 " 5    "    19 "  ♌    "
 " 6    "     1 "  ♍    "
 " 7    "    13 "  ♍    "
 " 8    "    25 "  ♍    "
 " 9    "     7 "  ♎    "
 " 10   "    18 "  ♎    "
 " 11   "     1 "  ♏    "
 " 12, Midn't, 12 "  ♏    "
```

FEBRUARY 22

A.M.

```
At 1 o'clock,  0° of ♐ rises
 " 2    "    12 "  ♐    "
 " 3    "    25 "  ♐    "
 " 4    "     9 "  ♑    "
 " 5    "    25 "  ♑    "
 " 6    "    14 "  ♒    "
 " 7    "     7 "  ♓    "
 " 8    "     3 "  ♈    "
 " 9    "    28 "  ♈    "
 " 10   "    20 "  ♉    "
 " 11   "     8 "  ♊    "
 " 12, Noon,  24 "  ♊    "
```

P.M.

```
At 1 o'clock,  8° of ♋ rises
 " 2    "    20 "  ♋    "
 " 3    "     2 "  ♌    "
 " 4    "    14 "  ♌    "
 " 5    "    25 "  ♌    "
 " 6    "     7 "  ♍    "
 " 7    "    19 "  ♍    "
 " 8    "     1 "  ♎    "
 " 9    "    13 "  ♎    "
 " 10   "    25 "  ♎    "
 " 11   "     6 "  ♏    "
 " 12, Midn't, 18 "  ♏    "
```

FEBRUARY 10

A.M.

```
At 1 o'clock, 21° of ♏ rises
 " 2    "     2 "  ♐    "
 " 3    "    15 "  ♐    "
 " 4    "    28 "  ♐    "
 " 5    "    12 "  ♑    "
 " 6    "    29 "  ♑    "
 " 7    "    19 "  ♒    "
 " 8    "    13 "  ♓    "
 " 9    "     9 "  ♈    "
 " 10   "     4 "  ♉    "
 " 11   "    24 "  ♉    "
 " 12, Noon,  12 "  ♊    "
```

P.M.

```
At 1 o'clock, 27° of ♊ rises
 " 2    "    10 "  ♋    "
 " 3    "    22 "  ♋    "
 " 4    "     5 "  ♌    "
 " 5    "    16 "  ♌    "
 " 6    "    28 "  ♌    "
 " 7    "    10 "  ♍    "
 " 8    "    22 "  ♍    "
 " 9    "     4 "  ♎    "
 " 10   "    15 "  ♎    "
 " 11   "    27 "  ♎    "
 " 12, Midn't.  9 "  ♏    "
```

FEBRUARY 18

A.M.

```
At 1 o'clock, 27° of ♏ rises
 " 2    "     9 "  ♐    "
 " 3    "    21 "  ♐    "
 " 4    "     5 "  ♑    "
 " 5    "    20 "  ♑    "
 " 6    "     9 "  ♒    "
 " 7    "     0 "  ♓    "
 " 8    "    26 "  ♓    "
 " 9    "    21 "  ♈    "
 " 10   "    15 "  ♉    "
 " 11   "     3 "  ♊    "
 " 12, Noon,  20 "  ♊    "
```

P.M.

```
At 1 o'clock,  4° of ♋ rises
 " 2    "    16 "  ♋    "
 " 3    "    29 "  ♋    "
 " 4    "    11 "  ♌    "
 " 5    "    22 "  ♌    "
 " 6    "     4 "  ♍    "
 " 7    "    16 "  ♍    "
 " 8    "    28 "  ♍    "
 " 9    "    10 "  ♎    "
 " 10   "    22 "  ♎    "
 " 11   "     3 "  ♏    "
 " 12, Midn't, 15 "  ♏    "
```

FEBRUARY 26

A.M.

```
At 1 o'clock,  3° of ♐ rises
 " 2    "    15 "  ♐    "
 " 3    "    29 "  ♐    "
 " 4    "    13 "  ♑    "
 " 5    "     0 "  ♒    "
 " 6    "    20 "  ♒    "
 " 7    "    14 "  ♓    "
 " 8    "    10 "  ♈    "
 " 9    "     4 "  ♉    "
 " 10   "    25 "  ♉    "
 " 11   "    13 "  ♊    "
 " 12, Noon,  28 "  ♊    "
```

P.M.

```
At 1 o'clock, 11° of ♋ rises
 " 2    "    23 "  ♋    "
 " 3    "     5 "  ♌    "
 " 4    "    17 "  ♌    "
 " 5    "    28 "  ♌    "
 " 6    "    11 "  ♍    "
 " 7    "    22 "  ♍    "
 " 8    "     4 "  ♎    "
 " 9    "    16 "  ♎    "
 " 10   "    28 "  ♎    "
 " 11   "    10 "  ♏    "
 " 12, Midn't, 21 "  ♏    "
```

MARCH 2

A.M.

At 1 o'clock, 7° of ♐ rises
" 2 " 20 " ♐ "
" 3 " 3 " ♑ "
" 4 " 18 " ♑ "
" 5 " 6 " ♒ "
" 6 " 28 " ♒ "
" 7 " 22 " ♓ "
" 8 " 18 " ♈ "
" 9 " 12 " ♉ "
" 10 " 1 " ♊ "
" 11 " 18 " ♊ "
" 12, Noon, 2 " ♋ "

P.M.

At 1 o'clock, 15° of ♋ rises
" 2 " 27 " ♋ "
" 3 " 9 " ♌ "
" 4 " 21 " ♌ "
" 5 " 2 " ♍ "
" 6 " 14 " ♍ "
" 7 " 26 " ♍ "
" 8 " 8 " ♎ "
" 9 " 20 " ♎ "
" 10 " 1 " ♏ "
" 11 " 13 " ♏ "
" 12, Midn't, 25 " ♏ "

MARCH 10

A.M.

At 1 o'clock, 14° of ♐ rises
" 2 " 26 " ♐ "
" 3 " 11 " ♑ "
" 4 " 27 " ♑ "
" 5 " 16 " ♒ "
" 6 " 10 " ♓ "
" 7 " 6 " ♈ "
" 8 " 1 " ♉ "
" 9 " 23 " ♉ "
" 10 " 10 " ♊ "
" 11 " 26 " ♊ "
" 12, Noon, 9 " ♋ "

P.M.

At 1 o'clock, 21° of ♋ rises
" 2 " 3 " ♌ "
" 3 " 15 " ♌ "
" 4 " 27 " ♌ "
" 5 " 9 " ♍ "
" 6 " 21 " ♍ "
" 7 " 2 " ♎ "
" 8 " 15 " ♎ "
" 9 " 27 " ♎ "
" 10 " 8 " ♏ "
" 11 " 20 " ♏ "
" 12, Midn't, 2 " ♐ "

MARCH 18

A.M.

At 1 o'clock, 20° of ♐ rises
" 2 " 4 " ♑ "
" 3 " 19 " ♑ "
" 4 " 7 " ♒ "
" 5 " 29 " ♒ "
" 6 " 24 " ♓ "
" 7 " 19 " ♈ "
" 8 " 13 " ♉ "
" 9 " 2 " ♊ "
" 10 " 18 " ♊ "
" 11 " 3 " ♋ "
" 12, Noon, 15 " ♋ "

P.M.

At 1 o'clock, 27° of ♋ rises
" 2 " 9 " ♌ "
" 3 " 21 " ♌ "
" 4 " 3 " ♍ "
" 5 " 15 " ♍ "
" 6 " 27 " ♍ "
" 7 " 9 " ♎ "
" 8 " 21 " ♎ "
" 9 " 2 " ♏ "
" 10 " 14 " ♏ "
" 11 " 26 " ♏ "
" 12, Midn't, 8 " ♐ "

MARCH 6

A.M.

At 1 o'clock, 11° of ♐ rises
" 2 " 23 " ♐ "
" 3 " 7 " ♑ "
" 4 " 22 " ♑ "
" 5 " 11 " ♒ "
" 6 " 4 " ♓ "
" 7 " 29 " ♓ "
" 8 " 25 " ♈ "
" 9 " 17 " ♉ "
" 10 " 6 " ♊ "
" 11 " 21 " ♊ "
" 12, Noon, 5 " ♋ "

P.M.

At 1 o'clock, 18° of ♋ rises
" 2 " 0 " ♌ "
" 3 " 12 " ♌ "
" 4 " 24 " ♌ "
" 5 " 6 " ♍ "
" 6 " 17 " ♍ "
" 7 " 29 " ♍ "
" 8 " 11 " ♎ "
" 9 " 23 " ♎ "
" 10 " 5 " ♏ "
" 11 " 17 " ♏ "
" 12, Midn't, 28 " ♏ "

MARCH 14

A.M.

At 1 o'clock, 17° of ♐ rises
" 2 " 1 " ♑ "
" 3 " 15 " ♑ "
" 4 " 2 " ♒ "
" 5 " 22 " ♒ "
" 6 " 16 " ♓ "
" 7 " 13 " ♈ "
" 8 " 7 " ♉ "
" 9 " 27 " ♉ "
" 10 " 14 " ♊ "
" 11 " 29 " ♊ "
" 12, Noon, 12 " ♋ "

P.M.

At 1 o'clock, 25° of ♋ rises
" 2 " 7 " ♌ "
" 3 " 18 " ♌ "
" 4 " 0 " ♍ "
" 5 " 12 " ♍ "
" 6 " 23 " ♍ "
" 7 " 6 " ♎ "
" 8 " 18 " ♎ "
" 9 " 29 " ♎ "
" 10 " 11 " ♏ "
" 11 " 23 " ♏ "
" 12, Midn't, 5 " ♐ "

MARCH 22

A.M.

At 1 o'clock, 24° of ♐ rises
" 2 " 8 " ♑ "
" 3 " 23 " ♑ "
" 4 " 12 " ♒ "
" 5 " 5 " ♓ "
" 6 " 0 " ♈ "
" 7 " 26 " ♈ "
" 8 " 18 " ♉ "
" 9 " 7 " ♊ "
" 10 " 22 " ♊ "
" 11 " 6 " ♋ "
" 12, Noon, 19 " ♋ "

P.M.

At 1 o'clock, 1° of ♌ rises
" 2 " 13 " ♌ "
" 3 " 24 " ♌ "
" 4 " 6 " ♍ "
" 5 " 18 " ♍ "
" 6 " 0 " ♎ "
" 7 " 12 " ♎ "
" 8 " 23 " ♎ "
" 9 " 5 " ♏ "
" 10 " 17 " ♏ "
" 11 " 29 " ♏ "
" 12, Midn't, 11 " ♐ "

MARCH 26

A.M.

At 1 o'clock, 27° of ♐ rises
" 2 " 12 " ♑ "
" 3 " 28 " ♑ "
" 4 " 17 " ♒ "
" 5 " 11 " ♓ "
" 6 " 7 " ♈ "
" 7 " 2 " ♉ "
" 8 " 23 " ♉ "
" 9 " 11 " ♊ "
" 10 " 26 " ♊ "
" 11 " 10 " ♋ "
" 12, Noon, 22 " ♋ "

P.M.

At 1 o'clock, 4° of ♌ rises
" 2 " 16 " ♌ "
" 3 " 28 " ♌ "
" 4 " 9 " ♍ "
" 5 " 21 " ♍ "
" 6 " 3 " ♎ "
" 7 " 15 " ♎ "
" 8 " 27 " ♎ "
" 9 " 9 " ♏ "
" 10 " 20 " ♏ "
" 11 " 2 " ♐ "
" 12, Midn't, 14 " ♐ "

APRIL 3

A.M.

At 1 o'clock, 5° of ♑ rises
" 2 " 20 " ♑ "
" 3 " 8 " ♒ "
" 4 " 0 " ♓ "
" 5 " 26 " ♓ "
" 6 " 20 " ♈ "
" 7 " 13 " ♉ "
" 8 " 3 " ♊ "
" 9 " 19 " ♊ "
" 10 " 3 " ♋ "
" 11 " 16 " ♋ "
" 12, Noon, 29 " ♋ "

P.M.

At 1 o'clock, 11° of ♌ rises
" 2 " 22 " ♌ "
" 3 " 4 " ♍ "
" 4 " 16 " ♍ "
" 5 " 28 " ♍ "
" 6 " 10 " ♎ "
" 7 " 21 " ♎ "
" 8 " 3 " ♏ "
" 9 " 15 " ♏ "
" 10 " 27 " ♏ "
" 11 " 8 " ♐ "
" 12, Midn't, 21 " ♐ "

APRIL 10

A.M.

At 1 o'clock, 11° of ♑ rises
" 2 " 28 " ♑ "
" 3 " 17 " ♒ "
" 4 " 11 " ♓ "
" 5 " 7 " ♈ "
" 6 " 2 " ♉ "
" 7 " 23 " ♉ "
" 8 " 11 " ♊ "
" 9 " 26 " ♊ "
" 10 " 9 " ♋ "
" 11 " 22 " ♋ "
" 12, Noon, 4 " ♌ "

P.M.

At 1 o'clock, 16° of ♌ rises
" 2 " 28 " ♌ "
" 3 " 9 " ♍ "
" 4 " 21 " ♍ "
" 5 " 3 " ♎ "
" 6 " 15 " ♎ "
" 7 " 27 " ♎ "
" 8 " 9 " ♏ "
" 9 " 20 " ♏ "
" 10 " 2 " ♐ "
" 11 " 14 " ♐ "
" 12, Midn't, 27 " ♐ "

MARCH 30

A.M.

At 1 o'clock, 1° of ♑ rises
" 2 " 16 " ♑ "
" 3 " 3 " ♒ "
" 4 " 24 " ♒ "
" 5 " 18 " ♓ "
" 6 " 15 " ♈ "
" 7 " 9 " ♉ "
" 8 " 28 " ♉ "
" 9 " 15 " ♊ "
" 10 " 0 " ♋ "
" 11 " 13 " ♋ "
" 12, Noon, 25 " ♋ "

P.M.

At 1 o'clock, 7° of ♌ rises
" 2 " 19 " ♌ "
" 3 " 1 " ♍ "
" 4 " 12 " ♍ "
" 5 " 24 " ♍ "
" 6 " 6 " ♎ "
" 7 " 18 " ♎ "
" 8 " 0 " ♏ "
" 9 " 12 " ♏ "
" 10 " 24 " ♏ "
" 11 " 5 " ♐ "
" 12, Midn't. 17 " ♐ "

APRIL 7

A.M.

At 1 o'clock, 8° of ♑ rises
" 2 " 24 " ♑ "
" 3 " 13 " ♒ "
" 4 " 5 " ♓ "
" 5 " 1 " ♈ "
" 6 " 27 " ♈ "
" 7 " 19 " ♉ "
" 8 " 8 " ♊ "
" 9 " 23 " ♊ "
" 10 " 7 " ♋ "
" 11 " 19 " ♋ "
" 12, Noon, 2 " ♌ "

P.M.

At 1 o'clock, 13° of ♌ rises
" 2 " 25 " ♌ "
" 3 " 7 " ♍ "
" 4 " 18 " ♍ "
" 5 " 0 " ♎ "
" 6 " 12 " ♎ "
" 7 " 24 " ♎ "
" 8 " 6 " ♏ "
" 9 " 18 " ♏ "
" 10 " 29 " ♏ "
" 11 " 12 " ♐ "
" 12, Midn't, 25 " ♐ "

APRIL 14

A.M.

At 1 o'clock, 15° of ♑ rises
" 2 " 3 " ♒ "
" 3 " 24 " ♒ "
" 4 " 18 " ♓ "
" 5 " 14 " ♈ "
" 6 " 8 " ♉ "
" 7 " 28 " ♉ "
" 8 " 15 " ♊ "
" 9 " 29 " ♊ "
" 10 " 13 " ♋ "
" 11 " 25 " ♋ "
" 12, Noon, 7 " ♌ "

P.M.

At 1 o'clock, 19° of ♌ rises
" 2 " 1 " ♍ "
" 3 " 12 " ♍ "
" 4 " 24 " ♍ "
" 5 " 6 " ♎ "
" 6 " 18 " ♎ "
" 7 " 0 " ♏ "
" 8 " 12 " ♏ "
" 9 " 24 " ♏ "
" 10 " 5 " ♐ "
" 11 " 17 " ♐ "
" 12, Midn't. 1 " ♑ "

APRIL 18

A.M.

At 1 o'clock, 20° of ♑ rises
" 2 " 7 " ♒ "
" 3 " 0 " ♓ "
" 4 " 26 " ♓ "
" 5 " 20 " ♈ "
" 6 " 13 " ♉ "
" 7 " 3 " ♊ "
" 8 " 19 " ♊ "
" 9 " 3 " ♋ "
" 10 " 16 " ♋ "
" 11 " 28 " ♋ "
" 12, Noon, 10 " ♌

P.M.

At 1 o'clock, 22° of ♌ rises
" 2 " 4 " ♍ "
" 3 " 16 " ♍ "
" 4 " 28 " ♍ "
" 5 " 9 " ♎ "
" 6 " 22 " ♎ "
" 7 " 3 " ♏ "
" 8 " 15 " ♏ "
" 9 " 27 " ♏ "
" 10 " 8 " ♐ "
" 11 " 21 " ♐ "
" 12, Midn't, 5 " ♑

APRIL 26

A.M.

At 1 o'clock, 28° of ♑ rises
" 2 " 19 " ♒ "
" 3 " 13 " ♓ "
" 4 " 9 " ♈ "
" 5 " 3 " ♉ "
" 6 " 24 " ♉ "
" 7 " 12 " ♊ "
" 8 " 27 " ♊ "
" 9 " 10 " ♋ "
" 10 " 23 " ♋ "
" 11 " 5 " ♌ "
" 12, Noon, 16 " ♌

P.M.

At 1 o'clock, 28° of ♌ rises
" 2 " 10 " ♍ "
" 3 " 22 " ♍ "
" 4 " 4 " ♎ "
" 5 " 16 " ♎ "
" 6 " 27 " ♎ "
" 7 " 9 " ♏ "
" 8 " 21 " ♏ "
" 9 " 2 " ♐ "
" 10 " 14 " ♐ "
" 11 " 28 " ♐ "
" 12, Midn't, 12 " ♑

MAY 4

A.M.

At 1 o'clock, 9° of ♒ rises
" 2 " 0 " ♓ "
" 3 " 26 " ♓ "
" 4 " 22 " ♈ "
" 5 " 15 " ♉ "
" 6 " 4 " ♊ "
" 7 " 20 " ♊ "
" 8 " 4 " ♋ "
" 9 " 17 " ♋ "
" 10 " 29 " ♋ "
" 11 " 11 " ♌ "
" 12, Noon, 22 " ♌

P.M.

At 1 o'clock, 4° of ♍ rises
" 2 " 16 " ♍ "
" 3 " 28 " ♍ "
" 4 " 10 " ♎ "
" 5 " 22 " ♎ "
" 6 " 4 " ♏ "
" 7 " 15 " ♏ "
" 8 " 27 " ♏ "
" 9 " 9 " ♐ "
" 10 " 21 " ♐ "
" 11 " 5 " ♑ "
" 12, Midn't. 20 " ♑

APRIL 22

A.M.

At 1 o'clock, 23° of ♑ rises
" 2 " 13 " ♒ "
" 3 " 5 " ♓ "
" 4 " 1 " ♈ "
" 5 " 27 " ♈ "
" 6 " 19 " ♉ "
" 7 " 7 " ♊ "
" 8 " 23 " ♊ "
" 9 " 7 " ♋ "
" 10 " 19 " ♋ "
" 11 " 1 " ♌ "
" 12, Noon, 13 " ♌

P.M.

At 1 o'clock, 26° of ♌ rises
" 2 " 7 " ♍ "
" 3 " 18 " ♍ "
" 4 " 0 " ♎ "
" 5 " 12 " ♎ "
" 6 " 24 " ♎ "
" 7 " 5 " ♏ "
" 8 " 18 " ♏ "
" 9 " 29 " ♏ "
" 10 " 11 " ♐ "
" 11 " 24 " ♐ "
" 12, Midn't, 8 " ♑

APRIL 30

A.M.

At 1 o'clock, 3° of ♒ rises
" 2 " 25 " ♒ "
" 3 " 18 " ♓ "
" 4 " 15 " ♈ "
" 5 " 9 " ♉ "
" 6 " 29 " ♉ "
" 7 " 16 " ♊ "
" 8 " 0 " ♋ "
" 9 " 14 " ♋ "
" 10 " 26 " ♋ "
" 11 " 8 " ♌ "
" 12, Noon, 19 " ♌

P.M.

At 1 o'clock, 1° of ♍ rises
" 2 " 13 " ♍ "
" 3 " 24 " ♍ "
" 4 " 7 " ♎ "
" 5 " 19 " ♎ "
" 6 " 1 " ♏ "
" 7 " 12 " ♏ "
" 8 " 24 " ♏ "
" 9 " 6 " ♐ "
" 10 " 18 " ♐ "
" 11 " 2 " ♑ "
" 12, Midn't. 16 " ♑

MAY 8

A.M.

At 1 o'clock, 14° of ♒ rises
" 2 " 7 " ♓ "
" 3 " 3 " ♈ "
" 4 " 29 " ♈ "
" 5 " 20 " ♉ "
" 6 " 8 " ♊ "
" 7 " 24 " ♊ "
" 8 " 8 " ♋ "
" 9 " 20 " ♋ "
" 10 " 2 " ♌ "
" 11 " 14 " ♌ "
" 12, Noon, 25 " ♌

P.M.

At 1 o'clock, 7° of ♍ rises
" 2 " 19 " ♍ "
" 3 " 1 " ♎ "
" 4 " 13 " ♎ "
" 5 " 25 " ♎ "
" 6 " 7 " ♏ "
" 7 " 18 " ♏ "
" 8 " 0 " ♐ "
" 9 " 12 " ♐ "
" 10 " 25 " ♐ "
" 11 " 9 " ♑ "
" 12, Midn't. 25 " ♑

299

A.M.

At 1 o'clock, 19° of ♒ rises
" 2 " 13 " ♓ "
" 3 " 9 " ♈ "
" 4 " 4 " ♉ "
" 5 " 25 " ♉ "
" 6 " 12 " ♊ "
" 7 " 28 " ♊ "
" 8 " 11 " ♋ "
" 9 " 23 " ♋ "
" 10 " 5 " ♌ "
" 11 " 17 " ♌ "
" 12, Noon, 28 " ♌ "

P.M.

At 1 o'clock, 11° of ♍ rises
" 2 " 23 " ♍ "
" 3 " 4 " ♎ "
" 4 " 16 " ♎ "
" 5 " 28 " ♎ "
" 6 " 10 " ♏ "
" 7 " 21 " ♏ "
" 8 " 3 " ♐ "
" 9 " 16 " ♐ "
" 10 " 29 " ♐ "
" 11 " 13 " ♑ "
" 12, Midn't. 0 " ♒ "

A.M.

At 1 o'clock, 2° of ♓ rises
" 2 " 28 " ♓ "
" 3 " 23 " ♈ "
" 4 " 16 " ♉ "
" 5 " 6 " ♊ "
" 6 " 21 " ♊ "
" 7 " 5 " ♋ "
" 8 " 18 " ♋ "
" 9 " 0 " ♌ "
" 10 " 11 " ♌ "
" 11 " 23 " ♌ "
" 12, Noon, 5 " ♍ "

P.M.

At 1 o'clock, 17° of ♍ rises
" 2 " 29 " ♍ "
" 3 " 11 " ♎ "
" 4 " 23 " ♎ "
" 5 " 4 " ♏ "
" 6 " 16 " ♏ "
" 7 " 27 " ♏ "
" 8 " 10 " ♐ "
" 9 " 22 " ♐ "
" 10 " 6 " ♑ "
" 11 " 21 " ♑ "
" 12, Midn't, 10 " ♒ "

A.M.

At 1 o'clock, 14° of ♓ rises
" 2 " 11 " ♈ "
" 3 " 5 " ♉ "
" 4 " 26 " ♉ "
" 5 " 13 " ♊ "
" 6 " 28 " ♊ "
" 7 " 12 " ♋ "
" 8 " 24 " ♋ "
" 9 " 5 " ♌ "
" 10 " 17 " ♌ "
" 11 " 29 " ♌ "
" 12, Noon, 11 " ♍ "

P.M.

At 1 o'clock, 23° of ♍ rises
" 2 " 5 " ♎ "
" 3 " 17 " ♎ "
" 4 " 28 " ♎ "
" 5 " 10 " ♏ "
" 6 " 22 " ♏ "
" 7 " 3 " ♐ "
" 8 " 16 " ♐ "
" 9 " 29 " ♐ "
" 10 " 14 " ♑ "
" 11 " 1 " ♒ "
" 12, Midn't, 20 " ♒ "

A.M.

At 1 o'clock, 25° of ♒ rises
" 2 " 20 " ♓ "
" 3 " 16 " ♈ "
" 4 " 10 " ♉ "
" 5 " 1 " ♊ "
" 6 " 16 " ♊ "
" 7 " 1 " ♋ "
" 8 " 14 " ♋ "
" 9 " 26 " ♋ "
" 10 " 8 " ♌ "
" 11 " 20 " ♌ "
" 12, Noon, 2 " ♍ "

P.M.

At 1 o'clock, 14° of ♍ rises
" 2 " 25 " ♍ "
" 3 " 7 " ♎ "
" 4 " 19 " ♎ "
" 5 " 1 " ♏ "
" 6 " 13 " ♏ "
" 7 " 24 " ♏ "
" 8 " 7 " ♐ "
" 9 " 19 " ♐ "
" 10 " 2 " ♑ "
" 11 " 17 " ♑ "
" 12, Midn't. 5 " ♒ "

A.M.

At 1 o'clock, 9° of ♓ rises
" 2 " 4 " ♈ "
" 3 " 29 " ♈ "
" 4 " 22 " ♉ "
" 5 " 9 " ♊ "
" 6 " 25 " ♊ "
" 7 " 8 " ♋ "
" 8 " 21 " ♋ "
" 9 " 2 " ♌ "
" 10 " 14 " ♌ "
" 11 " 26 " ♌ "
" 12, Noon, 8 " ♍ "

P.M.

At 1 o'clock, 20 of ♍ rises
" 2 " 2 " ♎ "
" 3 " 14 " ♎ "
" 4 " 26 " ♎ "
" 5 " 7 " ♏ "
" 6 " 19 " ♏ "
" 7 " 0 " ♐ "
" 8 " 13 " ♐ "
" 9 " 26 " ♐ "
" 10 " 10 " ♑ "
" 11 " 26 " ♑ "
" 12, Midn't, 16 " ♒ "

A.M.

At 1 o'clock, 22° of ♓ rises
" 2 " 18 " ♈ "
" 3 " 12 " ♉ "
" 4 " 1 " ♊ "
" 5 " 17 " ♊ "
" 6 " 2 " ♋ "
" 7 " 15 " ♋ "
" 8 " 27 " ♋ "
" 9 " 9 " ♌ "
" 10 " 21 " ♌ "
" 11 " 2 " ♍ "
" 12, Noon, 14 " ♍ "

P.M.

At 1 o'clock, 26° of ♍ rises
" 2 " 8 " ♎ "
" 3 " 20 " ♎ "
" 4 " 1 " ♏ "
" 5 " 13 " ♏ "
" 6 " 25 " ♏ "
" 7 " 7 " ♐ "
" 8 " 19 " ♐ "
" 9 " 2 " ♑ "
" 10 " 18 " ♑ "
" 11 " 6 " ♒ "
" 12, Midn't. 27 " ♒ "

JUNE 5

A.M.

At 1 o'clock, 27° of ♓ rises
" 2   "   22 " ♈ "
" 3   "   15 " ♉ "
" 4   "   4 " ♊ "
" 5   "   20 " ♊ "
" 6   "   4 " ♋ "
" 7   "   17 " ♋ "
" 8   "   0 " ♌ "
" 9   "   11 " ♌ "
" 10   "   23 " ♌ "
" 11   "   5 " ♍ "
" 12, Noon, 17 " ♍ "

P.M.

At 1 o'clock, 29° of ♍ rises
" 2   "   10 " ♎ "
" 3   "   22 " ♎ "
" 4   "   4 " ♏ "
" 5   "   15 " ♏ "
" 6   "   27 " ♏ "
" 7   "   0 " ♐ "
" 8   "   22 " ♐ "
" 9   "   6 " ♑ "
" 10   "   21 " ♑ "
" 11   "   10 " ♒ "
" 12, Midn't. 2 " ♓ "

JUNE 13

A.M.

At 1 o'clock, 11° of ♈ rises
" 2   "   4 " ♉ "
" 3   "   26 " ♉ "
" 4   "   13 " ♊ "
" 5   "   28 " ♊ "
" 6   "   12 " ♋ "
" 7   "   24 " ♋ "
" 8   "   5 " ♌ "
" 9   "   23 " ♌ "
" 10   "   29 " ♌ "
" 11   "   11 " ♍ "
" 12, Noon, 23 " ♍ "

P.M.

At 1 o'clock, 5° of ♎ rises
" 2   "   17 " ♎ "
" 3   "   28 " ♎ "
" 4   "   10 " ♏ "
" 5   "   21 " ♏ "
" 6   "   3 " ♐ "
" 7   "   10 " ♐ "
" 8   "   20 " ♐ "
" 9   "   14 " ♑ "
" 10   "   1 " ♒ "
" 11   "   20 " ♒ "
" 12, Midn't. 14 " ♓ "

JUNE 21

A.M.

At 1 o'clock, 24° of ♈ rises
" 2   "   16 " ♉ "
" 3   "   6 " ♊ "
" 4   "   21 " ♊ "
" 5   "   5 " ♋ "
" 6   "   18 " ♋ "
" 7   "   0 " ♌ "
" 8   "   11 " ♌ "
" 9   "   23 " ♌ "
" 10   "   5 " ♍ "
" 11   "   17 " ♍ "
" 12, Noon, 29 " ♍ "

P.M.

At 1 o'clock, 11° of ♎ rises
" 2   "   23 " ♎ "
" 3   "   5 " ♏ "
" 4   "   16 " ♏ "
" 5   "   28 " ♏ "
" 6   "   10 " ♐ "
" 7   "   23 " ♐ "
" 8   "   6 " ♑ "
" 9   "   22 " ♑ "
" 10   "   11 " ♒ "
" 11   "   4 " ♓ "
" 12, Midn't, 28 " ♓ "

JUNE 9

A.M.

At 1 o'clock, 3° of ♈ rises
" 2   "   29 " ♈ "
" 3   "   20 " ♉ "
" 4   "   9 " ♊ "
" 5   "   24 " ♊ "
" 6   "   8 " ♋ "
" 7   "   20 " ♋ "
" 8   "   2 " ♌ "
" 9   "   14 " ♌ "
" 10   "   26 " ♌ "
" 11   "   8 " ♍ "
" 12, Noon, 20 " ♍ "

P.M.

At 1 o'clock, 2° of ♎ rises
" 2   "   14 " ♎ "
" 3   "   25 " ♎ "
" 4   "   7 " ♏ "
" 5   "   19 " ♏ "
" 6   "   1 " ♐ "
" 7   "   13 " ♐ "
" 8   "   26 " ♐ "
" 9   "   10 " ♑ "
" 10   "   26 " ♑ "
" 11   "   16 " ♒ "
" 12, Midn't. 9 " ♓ "

JUNE 17

A.M.

At 1 o'clock, 16° of ♈ rises
" 2   "   11 " ♉ "
" 3   "   1 " ♊ "
" 4   "   17 " ♊ "
" 5   "   2 " ♋ "
" 6   "   15 " ♋ "
" 7   "   27 " ♋ "
" 8   "   8 " ♌ "
" 9   "   21 " ♌ "
" 10   "   2 " ♍ "
" 11   "   14 " ♍ "
" 12, Noon, 26 " ♍ "

P.M.

At 1 o'clock, 7° of ♎ rises
" 2   "   20 " ♎ "
" 3   "   1 " ♏ "
" 4   "   13 " ♏ "
" 5   "   25 " ♏ "
" 6   "   7 " ♐ "
" 7   "   19 " ♐ "
" 8   "   3 " ♑ "
" 9   "   18 " ♑ "
" 10   "   6 " ♒ "
" 11   "   27 " ♒ "
" 12, Midn't. 22 " ♓ "

JUNE 25

A.M.

At 1 o'clock, 0° of ♉ rises
" 2   "   22 " ♉ "
" 3   "   10 " ♊ "
" 4   "   25 " ♊ "
" 5   "   8 " ♋ "
" 6   "   21 " ♋ "
" 7   "   3 " ♌ "
" 8   "   15 " ♌ "
" 9   "   26 " ♌ "
" 10   "   8 " ♍ "
" 11   "   20 " ♍ "
" 12, Noon, 2 " ♎ "

P.M.

At 1 o'clock, 14° of ♎ rises
" 2   "   26 " ♎ "
" 3   "   8 " ♏ "
" 4   "   19 " ♏ "
" 5   "   1 " ♐ "
" 6   "   14 " ♐ "
" 7   "   26 " ♐ "
" 8   "   11 " ♑ "
" 9   "   27 " ♑ "
" 10   "   16 " ♒ "
" 11   "   9 " ♓ "
" 12, Midn't, 5 " ♈ "

JUNE 29

A.M.

At 1 o'clock,   6° of ♉ rises
" 2   "   27 " ♉ "
" 3   "   14 " ♊ "
" 4   "   28 " ♊ "
" 5   "   12 " ♋ "
" 6   "   24 " ♋ "
" 7   "   6 " ♌ "
" 8   "   18 " ♌ "
" 9   "   0 " ♍ "
" 10   "   12 " ♍ "
" 11   "   23 " ♍ "
" 12, Noon,   5 " ♎ "

P.M.

At 1 o'clock, 17° of ♎ rises
" 2   "   29 " ♎ "
" 3   "   11 " ♏ "
" 4   "   23 " ♏ "
" 5   "   5 " ♐ "
" 6   "   17 " ♐ "
" 7   "   0 " ♑ "
" 8   "   15 " ♑ "
" 9   "   2 " ♒ "
" 10   "   22 " ♒ "
" 11   "   16 " ♓ "
" 12, Midn't, 13 " ♈ "

JULY 7

A.M.

At 1 o'clock, 18° of ♉ rises
" 2   "   6 " ♊ "
" 3   "   22 " ♊ "
" 4   "   6 " ♋ "
" 5   "   18 " ♋ "
" 6   "   0 " ♌ "
" 7   "   12 " ♌ "
" 8   "   24 " ♌ "
" 9   "   6 " ♍ "
" 10   "   17 " ♍ "
" 11   "   29 " ♍ "
" 12, Noon,   12 " ♎ "

P.M.

At 1 o'clock, 23° of ♎ rises
" 2   "   5 " ♏ "
" 3   "   17 " ♏ "
" 4   "   29 " ♏ "
" 5   "   11 " ♐ "
" 6   "   23 " ♐ "
" 7   "   7 " ♑ "
" 8   "   23 " ♑ "
" 9   "   11 " ♒ "
" 10   "   4 " ♓ "
" 11   "   0 " ♈ "
" 12, Midn't. 25 " ♈ "

JULY 14

A.M.

At 1 o'clock, 26° of ♉ rises
" 2   "   14 " ♊ "
" 3   "   28 " ♊ "
" 4   "   12 " ♋ "
" 5   "   24 " ♋ "
" 6   "   6 " ♌ "
" 7   "   17 " ♌ "
" 8   "   29 " ♌ "
" 9   "   12 " ♍ "
" 10   "   23 " ♍ "
" 11   "   5 " ♎ "
" 12, Noon,   17 " ♎ "

P.M.

At 1 o'clock, 29° of ♎ rises
" 2   "   11 " ♏ "
" 3   "   22 " ♏ "
" 4   "   5 " ♐ "
" 5   "   17 " ♐ "
" 6   "   0 " ♑ "
" 7   "   15 " ♑ "
" 8   "   2 " ♒ "
" 9   "   22 " ♒ "
" 10   "   16 " ♓ "
" 11   "   13 " ♈ "
" 12, Midn't. 6 " ♉ "

JULY 3

A.M.

At 1 o'clock, 12° of ♉ rises
" 2   "   2 " ♊ "
" 3   "   17 " ♊ "
" 4   "   2 " ♋ "
" 5   "   15 " ♋ "
" 6   "   27 " ♋ "
" 7   "   9 " ♌ "
" 8   "   21 " ♌ "
" 9   "   2 " ♍ "
" 10   "   14 " ♍ "
" 11   "   26 " ♍ "
" 12, Noon,   8 " ♎ "

P.M.

At 1 o'clock, 20° of ♎ rises
" 2   "   2 " ♏ "
" 3   "   14 " ♏ "
" 4   "   25 " ♏ "
" 5   "   7 " ♐ "
" 6   "   20 " ♐ "
" 7   "   3 " ♑ "
" 8   "   18 " ♑ "
" 9   "   6 " ♒ "
" 10   "   27 " ♒ "
" 11   "   22 " ♓ "
" 12, Midn't, 19 " ♈ "

JULY 11

A.M.

At 1 o'clock, 22° of ♉ rises
" 2   "   10 " ♊ "
" 3   "   26 " ♊ "
" 4   "   9 " ♋ "
" 5   "   21 " ♋ "
" 6   "   3 " ♌ "
" 7   "   15 " ♌ "
" 8   "   27 " ♌ "
" 9   "   9 " ♍ "
" 10   "   21 " ♍ "
" 11   "   2 " ♎ "
" 12, Noon,   14 " ♎ "

P.M.

At 1 o'clock, 26° of ♎ rises
" 2   "   8 " ♏ "
" 3   "   20 " ♏ "
" 4   "   2 " ♐ "
" 5   "   14 " ♐ "
" 6   "   27 " ♐ "
" 7   "   11 " ♑ "
" 8   "   28 " ♑ "
" 9   "   17 " ♒ "
" 10   "   11 " ♓ "
" 11   "   7 " ♈ "
" 12, Midn't. 2 " ♉ "

JULY 18

A.M.

At 1 o'clock,   1° of ♊ rises
" 2   "   17 " ♊ "
" 3   "   2 " ♋ "
" 4   "   15 " ♋ "
" 5   "   27 " ♋ "
" 6   "   9 " ♌ "
" 7   "   21 " ♌ "
" 8   "   2 " ♍ "
" 9   "   14 " ♍ "
" 10   "   26 " ♍ "
" 11   "   8 " ♎ "
" 12, Noon,   20 " ♎ "

P.M.

At 1 o'clock,   1° of ♏ rises
" 2   "   13 " ♏ "
" 3   "   25 " ♏ "
" 4   "   7 " ♐ "
" 5   "   20 " ♐ "
" 6   "   3 " ♑ "
" 7   "   19 " ♑ "
" 8   "   6 " ♒ "
" 9   "   28 " ♒ "
" 10   "   22 " ♓ "
" 11   "   18 " ♈ "
" 12, Midn't. 12 " ♉ "

JULY 22

A.M.

At 1 o'clock,	6° of ♊ rises
" 2 "	22 " ♊ "
" 3 "	5 " ♋ "
" 4 "	18 " ♋ "
" 5 "	0 " ♌ "
" 6 "	12 " ♌ "
" 7 "	24 " ♌ "
" 8 "	6 " ♍ "
" 9 "	17 " ♍ "
" 10 "	29 " ♍ "
" 11 "	12 " ♎ "
" 12, Noon,	23 " ♎ "

P.M.

At 1 o'clock,	5° of ♏ rises
" 2 "	16 " ♏ "
" 3 "	28 " ♏ "
" 4 "	11 " ♐ "
" 5 "	23 " ♐ "
" 6 "	7 " ♑ "
" 7 "	22 " ♑ "
" 8 "	11 " ♒ "
" 9 "	4 " ♓ "
" 10 "	29 " ♓ "
" 11 "	24 " ♈ "
" 12, Midn't,	17 " ♉ "

JULY 30

A.M.

At 1 o'clock,	14° of ♊ rises
" 2 "	29 " ♊ "
" 3 "	12 " ♋ "
" 4 "	24 " ♋ "
" 5 "	7 " ♌ "
" 6 "	18 " ♌ "
" 7 "	0 " ♍ "
" 8 "	12 " ♍ "
" 9 "	23 " ♍ "
" 10 "	6 " ♎ "
" 11 "	18 " ♎ "
" 12, Noon,	29 " ♎ "

P.M.

At 1 o'clock,	11° of ♏ rises
" 2 "	23 " ♏ "
" 3 "	5 " ♐ "
" 4 "	17 " ♐ "
" 5 "	0 " ♑ "
" 6 "	15 " ♑ "
" 7 "	2 " ♒ "
" 8 "	22 " ♒ "
" 9 "	16 " ♓ "
" 10 "	13 " ♈ "
" 11 "	7 " ♉ "
" 12, Midn't,	27 " ♉ "

AUGUST 7

A.M.

At 1 o'clock,	22° of ♊ rises
" 2 "	6 " ♋ "
" 3 "	19 " ♋ "
" 4 "	1 " ♌ "
" 5 "	13 " ♌ "
" 6 "	24 " ♌ "
" 7 "	7 " ♍ "
" 8 "	18 " ♍ "
" 9 "	0 " ♎ "
" 10 "	12 " ♎ "
" 11 "	24 " ♎ "
" 12, Noon,	6 " ♏ "

P.M.

At 1 o'clock,	18° of ♏ rises
" 2 "	29 " ♏ "
" 3 "	11 " ♐ "
" 4 "	25 " ♐ "
" 5 "	8 " ♑ "
" 6 "	21 " ♑ "
" 7 "	17 " ♒ "
" 8 "	5 " ♓ "
" 9 "	1 " ♈ "
" 10 "	27 " ♈ "
" 11 "	19 " ♉ "
" 12, Midn't.	8 " ♊ "

JULY 26

A.M.

At 1 o'clock,	10° of ♊ rises
" 2 "	25 " ♊ "
" 3 "	9 " ♋ "
" 4 "	21 " ♋ "
" 5 "	3 " ♌ "
" 6 "	15 " ♌ "
" 7 "	27 " ♌ "
" 8 "	9 " ♍ "
" 9 "	20 " ♍ "
" 10 "	2 " ♎ "
" 11 "	14 " ♎ "
" 12, Noon,	26 " ♎ "

P.M.

At 1 o'clock,	8° of ♏ rises
" 2 "	20 " ♏ "
" 3 "	2 " ♐ "
" 4 "	14 " ♐ "
" 5 "	26 " ♐ "
" 6 "	11 " ♑ "
" 7 "	27 " ♑ "
" 8 "	16 " ♒ "
" 9 "	10 " ♓ "
" 10 "	5 " ♈ "
" 11 "	0 " ♉ "
" 12, Midn't,	23 " ♉ "

AUGUST 3

A.M.

At 1 o'clock,	18° of ♊ rises
" 2 "	3 " ♋ "
" 3 "	15 " ♋ "
" 4 "	28 " ♋ "
" 5 "	10 " ♌ "
" 6 "	21 " ♌ "
" 7 "	3 " ♍ "
" 8 "	15 " ♍ "
" 9 "	27 " ♍ "
" 10 "	9 " ♎ "
" 11 "	21 " ♎ "
" 12, Noon,	2 " ♏ "

P.M.

At 1 o'clock,	14° of ♏ rises
" 2 "	26 " ♏ "
" 3 "	8 " ♐ "
" 4 "	21 " ♐ "
" 5 "	4 " ♑ "
" 6 "	20 " ♑ "
" 7 "	7 " ♒ "
" 8 "	29 " ♒ "
" 9 "	24 " ♓ "
" 10 "	20 " ♈ "
" 11 "	13 " ♉ "
" 12, Midn't.	3 " ♊ "

AUGUST 11

A.M.

At 1 o'clock,	26° of ♊ rises
" 2 "	9 " ♋ "
" 3 "	22 " ♋ "
" 4 "	4 " ♌ "
" 5 "	16 " ♌ "
" 6 "	28 " ♌ "
" 7 "	10 " ♍ "
" 8 "	21 " ♍ "
" 9 "	3 " ♎ "
" 10 "	15 " ♎ "
" 11 "	27 " ♎ "
" 12, Noon,	9 " ♏ "

P.M.

At 1 o'clock,	21° of ♏ rises
" 2 "	2 " ♐ "
" 3 "	14 " ♐ "
" 4 "	28 " ♐ "
" 5 "	12 " ♑ "
" 6 "	28 " ♑ "
" 7 "	19 " ♒ "
" 8 "	13 " ♓ "
" 9 "	7 " ♈ "
" 10 "	2 " ♉ "
" 11 "	24 " ♉ "
" 12, Midn't.	12 " ♊ "

AUGUST 15

A.M.
At 1 o'clock, 0° of ♋ rises
" 2 " 13 " ♋ "
" 3 " 25 " ♋ "
" 4 " 7 " ♌ "
" 5 " 19 " ♌ "
" 6 " 1 " ♍ "
" 7 " 12 " ♍ "
" 8 " 24 " ♍ "
" 9 " 6 " ♎ "
" 10 " 18 " ♎ "
" 11 " 0 " ♏ "
" 12, Noon, 12 " ♏ "

P.M.
At 1 o'clock, 24° of ♏ rises
" 2 " 5 " ♐ "
" 3 " 18 " ♐ "
" 4 " 2 " ♑ "
" 5 " 16 " ♑ "
" 6 " 3 " ♒ "
" 7 " 24 " ♒ "
" 8 " 18 " ♓ "
" 9 " 15 " ♈ "
" 10 " 9 " ♉ "
" 11 " 29 " ♉ "
" 12, Midn't. 16 " ♊ "

AUGUST 23

A.M.
At 1 o'clock, 7° of ♋ rises
" 2 " 19 " ♋ "
" 3 " 1 " ♌ "
" 4 " 13 " ♌ "
" 5 " 24 " ♌ "
" 6 " 7 " ♍ "
" 7 " 18 " ♍ "
" 8 " 0 " ♎ "
" 9 " 12 " ♎ "
" 10 " 24 " ♎ "
" 11 " 6 " ♏ "
" 12, Noon, 18 " ♏ "

P.M.
At 1 o'clock, 0° of ♐ rises
" 2 " 12 " ♐ "
" 3 " 25 " ♐ "
" 4 " 9 " ♑ "
" 5 " 25 " ♑ "
" 6 " 14 " ♒ "
" 7 " 7 " ♓ "
" 8 " 3 " ♈ "
" 9 " 27 " ♈ "
" 10 " 20 " ♉ "
" 11 " 8 " ♊ "
" 12, Midn't, 24 " ♊ "

AUGUST 31

A.M.
At 1 o'clock, 14° of ♋ rises
" 2 " 26 " ♋ "
" 3 " 8 " ♌ "
" 4 " 19 " ♌ "
" 5 " 1 " ♍ "
" 6 " 13 " ♍ "
" 7 " 25 " ♍ "
" 8 " 7 " ♎ "
" 9 " 19 " ♎ "
" 10 " 1 " ♏ "
" 11 " 12 " ♏ "
" 12, Noon, 24 " ♏ "

P.M.
At 1 o'clock, 6° of ♐ rises
" 2 " 19 " ♐ "
" 3 " 2 " ♑ "
" 4 " 17 " ♑ "
" 5 " 5 " ♒ "
" 6 " 25 " ♒ "
" 7 " 20 " ♓ "
" 8 " 16 " ♈ "
" 9 " 10 " ♉ "
" 10 " 0 " ♊ "
" 11 " 17 " ♊ "
" 12, Midn't, 1 " ♋ "

AUGUST 19

A.M.
At 1 o'clock, 3° of ♋ rises
" 2 " 16 " ♋ "
" 3 " 28 " ♋ "
" 4 " 10 " ♌ "
" 5 " 22 " ♌ "
" 6 " 4 " ♍ "
" 7 " 16 " ♍ "
" 8 " 28 " ♍ "
" 9 " 9 " ♎ "
" 10 " 22 " ♎ "
" 11 " 3 " ♏ "
" 12, Noon, 15 " ♏ "

P.M.
At 1 o'clock, 27° of ♏ rises
" 2 " 9 " ♐ "
" 3 " 21 " ♐ "
" 4 " 5 " ♑ "
" 5 " 20 " ♑ "
" 6 " 9 " ♒ "
" 7 " 0 " ♓ "
" 8 " 26 " ♓ "
" 9 " 22 " ♈ "
" 10 " 15 " ♉ "
" 11 " 4 " ♊ "
" 12, Midn't. 20 " ♊ "

AUGUST 27

A.M.
At 1 o'clock, 10° of ♋ rises
" 2 " 22 " ♋ "
" 3 " 5 " ♌ "
" 4 " 16 " ♌ "
" 5 " 28 " ♌ "
" 6 " 10 " ♍ "
" 7 " 22 " ♍ "
" 8 " 4 " ♎ "
" 9 " 16 " ♎ "
" 10 " 27 " ♎ "
" 11 " 9 " ♏ "
" 12, Noon, 21 " ♏ "

P.M.
At 1 o'clock, 2° of ♐ rises
" 2 " 15 " ♐ "
" 3 " 28 " ♐ "
" 4 " 13 " ♑ "
" 5 " 29 " ♑ "
" 6 " 20 " ♒ "
" 7 " 13 " ♓ "
" 8 " 9 " ♈ "
" 9 " 4 " ♉ "
" 10 " 24 " ♉ "
" 11 " 12 " ♊ "
" 12, Midn't, 28 " ♊ "

SEPTEMBER 4

A.M.
At 1 o'clock, 17° of ♋ rises
" 2 " 29 " ♋ "
" 3 " 11 " ♌ "
" 4 " 23 " ♌ "
" 5 " 4 " ♍ "
" 6 " 17 " ♍ "
" 7 " 28 " ♍ "
" 8 " 10 " ♎ "
" 9 " 22 " ♎ "
" 10 " 4 " ♏ "
" 11 " 15 " ♏ "
" 12, Noon, 27 " ♏ "

P.M.
At 1 o'clock, 9° of ♐ rises
" 2 " 22 " ♐ "
" 3 " 6 " ♑ "
" 4 " 21 " ♑ "
" 5 " 10 " ♒ "
" 6 " 2 " ♓ "
" 7 " 28 " ♓ "
" 8 " 24 " ♈ "
" 9 " 16 " ♉ "
" 10 " 4 " ♊ "
" 11 " 20 " ♊ "
" 12, Midn't. 5 " ♋ "

SEPTEMBER 8

A.M.

At 1 o'clock, 20° of ♋ rises
" 2 " 2 " ♌ "
" 3 " 14 " ♌ "
" 4 " 25 " ♌ "
" 5 " 7 " ♍ "
" 6 " 19 " ♍ "
" 7 " 1 " ♎ "
" 8 " 13 " ♎ "
" 9 " 25 " ♎ "
" 10 " 7 " ♏ "
" 11 " 18 " ♏ "
" 12, Noon, 0 " ♐ "

P.M.

At 1 o'clock, 12° of ♐ rises
" 2 " 25 " ♐ "
" 3 " 9 " ♑ "
" 4 " 25 " ♑ "
" 5 " 15 " ♒ "
" 6 " 7 " ♓ "
" 7 " ? " ♈ "
" 8 " 29 " ♈ "
" 9 " 21 " ♉ "
" 10 " 9 " ♊ "
" 11 " 24 " ♊ "
" 12, Midn't. 8 " ♋ "

SEPTEMBER 16

A.M.

At 1 o'clock, 27° of ♋ rises
" 2 " 8 " ♌ "
" 3 " 20 " ♌ "
" 4 " 2 " ♍ "
" 5 " 13 " ♍ "
" 6 " 25 " ♍ "
" 7 " 7 " ♎ "
" 8 " 19 " ♎ "
" 9 " 1 " ♏ "
" 10 " 13 " ♏ "
" 11 " 24 " ♏ "
" 12, Noon, 7 " ♐ "

P.M.

At 1 o'clock, 19° of ♐ rises
" 2 " 2 " ♑ "
" 3 " 18 " ♑ "
" 4 " 6 " ♒ "
" 5 " 27 " ♒ "
" 6 " 22 " ♓ "
" 7 " 17 " ♈ "
" 8 " 12 " ♉ "
" 9 " 1 " ♊ "
" 10 " 17 " ♊ "
" 11 " 2 " ♋ "
" 12, Midn't. 15 " ♋ "

SEPTEMBER 24

A.M.

At 1 o'clock, 2° of ♌ rises
" 2 " 14 " ♌ "
" 3 " 26 " ♌ "
" 4 " 8 " ♍ "
" 5 " 20 " ♍ "
" 6 " 2 " ♎ "
" 7 " 14 " ♎ "
" 8 " 26 " ♎ "
" 9 " 8 " ♏ "
" 10 " 19 " ♏ "
" 11 " 1 " ♐ "
" 12, Noon, 13 " ♐ "

P.M.

At 1 o'clock, 26° of ♑ rises
" 2 " 11 " ♑ "
" 3 " 27 " ♑ "
" 4 " 16 " ♒ "
" 5 " 9 " ♓ "
" 6 " 5 " ♈ "
" 7 " 0 " ♉ "
" 8 " 22 " ♉ "
" 9 " 10 " ♊ "
" 10 " 25 " ♊ "
" 11 " 9 " ♋ "
" 12, Midn't, 21 " ♋ "

SEPTEMBER 12

A.M.

At 1 o'clock, 23° of ♋ rises
" 2 " 5 " ♌ "
" 3 " 17 " ♌ "
" 4 " 28 " ♌ "
" 5 " 11 " ♍ "
" 6 " 22 " ♍ "
" 7 " 4 " ♎ "
" 8 " 16 " ♎ "
" 9 " 27 " ♎ "
" 10 " 10 " ♏ "
" 11 " 21 " ♏ "
" 12, Noon, 3 " ♐ "

P.M.

At 1 o'clock, 15° of ♐ rises
" 2 " 29 " ♐ "
" 3 " 14 " ♑ "
" 4 " 1 " ♒ "
" 5 " 20 " ♒ "
" 6 " 15 " ♓ "
" 7 " 11 " ♈ "
" 8 " 5 " ♉ "
" 9 " 26 " ♉ "
" 10 " 13 " ♊ "
" 11 " 28 " ♊ "
" 12, Midn't. 12 " ♋ "

SEPTEMBER 20

A.M.

At 1 o'clock, 0° of ♌ rises
" 2 " 11 " ♌ "
" 3 " 23 " ♌ "
" 4 " 5 " ♍ "
" 5 " 17 " ♍ "
" 6 " 29 " ♍ "
" 7 " 11 " ♎ "
" 8 " 23 " ♎ "
" 9 " 4 " ♏ "
" 10 " 16 " ♏ "
" 11 " 28 " ♏ "
" 12, Noon, 10 " ♐ "

P.M.

At 1 o'clock, 22° of ♐ rises
" 2 " 6 " ♑ "
" 3 " 22 " ♑ "
" 4 " 11 " ♒ "
" 5 " 4 " ♓ "
" 6 " 29 " ♓ "
" 7 " 24 " ♈ "
" 8 " 16 " ♉ "
" 9 " 6 " ♊ "
" 10 " 21 " ♊ "
" 11 " 5 " ♋ "
" 12, Midn't. 18 " ♋ "

SEPTEMBER 28

A.M.

At 1 o'clock, 6° of ♌ rises
" 2 " 17 " ♌ "
" 3 " 29 " ♌ "
" 4 " 11 " ♍ "
" 5 " 23 " ♍ "
" 6 " 5 " ♎ "
" 7 " 17 " ♎ "
" 8 " 29 " ♎ "
" 9 " 11 " ♏ "
" 10 " 22 " ♏ "
" 11 " 4 " ♐ "
" 12, Noon, 16 " ♐ "

P.M.

At 1 o'clock, 0° of ♑ rises
" 2 " 14 " ♑ "
" 3 " 2 " ♒ "
" 4 " 22 " ♒ "
" 5 " 16 " ♓ "
" 6 " 12 " ♈ "
" 7 " 7 " ♉ "
" 8 " 27 " ♉ "
" 9 " 14 " ♊ "
" 10 " 29 " ♊ "
" 11 " 12 " ♋ "
" 12, Midn't, 24 " ♋ "

OCTOBER 2

A.M.

At 1 o'clock, 9° of ♌ rises
" 2 " 21 " ♌ "
" 3 " 2 " ♍ "
" 4 " 14 " ♍ "
" 5 " 26 " ♍ "
" 6 " 8 " ♎ "
" 7 " 20 " ♎ "
" 8 " 2 " ♏ "
" 9 " 13 " ♏ "
" 10 " 25 " ♏ "
" 11 " 7 " ♐ "
" 12, Noon, 19 " ♐ "

P.M.

At 1 o'clock, 3° of ♑ rises
" 2 " 18 " ♑ "
" 3 " 6 " ♒ "
" 4 " 27 " ♒ "
" 5 " 22 " ♓ "
" 6 " 18 " ♈ "
" 7 " 12 " ♉ "
" 8 " 2 " ♊ "
" 9 " 18 " ♊ "
" 10 " 2 " ♋ "
" 11 " 15 " ♋ "
" 12, Midn't, 27 " ♋ "

OCTOBER 10

A.M.

At 1 o'clock, 15° of ♌ rises
" 2 " 27 " ♌ "
" 3 " 8 " ♍ "
" 4 " 20 " ♍ "
" 5 " 2 " ♎ "
" 6 " 14 " ♎ "
" 7 " 27 " ♎ "
" 8 " 9 " ♏ "
" 9 " 19 " ♏ "
" 10 " 2 " ♐ "
" 11 " 14 " ♐ "
" 12, Noon, 26 " ♐ "

P.M.

At 1 o'clock, 11° of ♑ rises
" 2 " 27 " ♑ "
" 3 " 17 " ♒ "
" 4 " 11 " ♓ "
" 5 " 7 " ♈ "
" 6 " 2 " ♉ "
" 7 " 23 " ♉ "
" 8 " 11 " ♊ "
" 9 " 26 " ♊ "
" 10 " 9 " ♋ "
" 11 " 22 " ♋ "
" 12, Midn't. 4 " ♌ "

OCTOBER 18

A.M.

At 1 o'clock, 21° of ♌ rises
" 2 " 3 " ♍ "
" 3 " 15 " ♍ "
" 4 " 27 " ♍ "
" 5 " 9 " ♎ "
" 6 " 20 " ♎ "
" 7 " 2 " ♏ "
" 8 " 14 " ♏ "
" 9 " 26 " ♏ "
" 10 " 8 " ♐ "
" 11 " 21 " ♐ "
" 12, Noon, 4 " ♑ "

P.M.

At 1 o'clock, 19° of ♑ rises
" 2 " 7 " ♒ "
" 3 " 29 " ♒ "
" 4 " 24 " ♓ "
" 5 " 20 " ♈ "
" 6 " 13 " ♉ "
" 7 " 3 " ♊ "
" 8 " 19 " ♊ "
" 9 " 3 " ♋ "
" 10 " 16 " ♋ "
" 11 " 28 " ♋ "
" 12, Midn't. 10 " ♌ "

OCTOBER 6

A.M.

At 1 o'clock, 12° of ♌ rises
" 2 " 24 " ♌ "
" 3 " 6 " ♍ "
" 4 " 17 " ♍ "
" 5 " 29 " ♍ "
" 6 " 11 " ♎ "
" 7 " 23 " ♎ "
" 8 " 5 " ♏ "
" 9 " 16 " ♏ "
" 10 " 28 " ♏ "
" 11 " 11 " ♐ "
" 12, Noon, 23 " ♐ "

P.M.

At 1 o'clock, 7° of ♑ rises
" 2 " 23 " ♑ "
" 3 " 13 " ♒ "
" 4 " 5 " ♓ "
" 5 " 0 " ♈ "
" 6 " 25 " ♈ "
" 7 " 18 " ♉ "
" 8 " 6 " ♊ "
" 9 " 22 " ♊ "
" 10 " 6 " ♋ "
" 11 " 18 " ♋ "
" 12, Midn't. 1 " ♌ "

OCTOBER 14

A.M.

At 1 o'clock, 18° of ♌ rises
" 2 " 0 " ♍ "
" 3 " 12 " ♍ "
" 4 " 23 " ♍ "
" 5 " 6 " ♎ "
" 6 " 18 " ♎ "
" 7 " 29 " ♎ "
" 8 " 11 " ♏ "
" 9 " 22 " ♏ "
" 10 " 5 " ♐ "
" 11 " 17 " ♐ "
" 12, Noon, 0 " ♑ "

P.M.

At 1 o'clock, 15° of ♑ rises
" 2 " 2 " ♒ "
" 3 " 22 " ♒ "
" 4 " 16 " ♓ "
" 5 " 13 " ♈ "
" 6 " 7 " ♉ "
" 7 " 27 " ♉ "
" 8 " 15 " ♊ "
" 9 " 29 " ♊ "
" 10 " 12 " ♋ "
" 11 " 25 " ♋ "
" 12, Midn't. 7 " ♌ "

OCTOBER 22

A.M.

At 1 o'clock, 24° of ♌ rises
" 2 " 6 " ♍ "
" 3 " 18 " ♍ "
" 4 " 0 " ♎ "
" 5 " 12 " ♎ "
" 6 " 24 " ♎ "
" 7 " 5 " ♏ "
" 8 " 17 " ♏ "
" 9 " 29 " ♏ "
" 10 " 11 " ♐ "
" 11 " 24 " ♐ "
" 12, Noon, 7 " ♑ "

P.M.

At 1 o'clock, 24° of ♑ rises
" 2 " 13 " ♒ "
" 3 " 5 " ♓ "
" 4 " 1 " ♈ "
" 5 " 27 " ♈ "
" 6 " 19 " ♉ "
" 7 " 7 " ♊ "
" 8 " 23 " ♊ "
" 9 " 7 " ♋ "
" 10 " 19 " ♋ "
" 11 " 1 " ♌ "
" 12, Midn't. 13 " ♌ "

OCTOBER 26

A.M.
At 1 o'clock, 28° of ♌ rises
" 2 " 9 " ♍ "
" 3 " 21 " ♍ "
" 4 " 3 " ♎ "
" 5 " 15 " ♎ "
" 6 " 27 " ♎ "
" 7 " 9 " ♏ "
" 8 " 20 " ♏ "
" 9 " 2 " ♐ "
" 10 " 14 " ♐ "
" 11 " 27 " ♐ "
" 12, Noon, 12 " ♑ "

P.M.
At 1 o'clock, 28° of ♑ rises
" 2 " 19 " ♒ "
" 3 " 13 " ♓ "
" 4 " 8 " ♈ "
" 5 " 2 " ♉ "
" 6 " 24 " ♉ "
" 7 " 11 " ♊ "
" 8 " 27 " ♊ "
" 9 " 10 " ♋ "
" 10 " 22 " ♋ "
" 11 " 5 " ♌ "
" 12, Midn't, 16 " ♌ "

NOVEMBER 3

A.M.
At 1 o'clock, 3° of ♍ rises
" 2 " 15 " ♍ "
" 3 " 27 " ♍ "
" 4 " 9 " ♎ "
" 5 " 21 " ♎ "
" 6 " 3 " ♏ "
" 7 " 15 " ♏ "
" 8 " 27 " ♏ "
" 9 " 8 " ♐ "
" 10 " 21 " ♐ "
" 11 " 4 " ♑ "
" 12, Noon, 20 " ♑ "

P.M.
At 1 o'clock, 9° of ♒ rises
" 2 " 0 " ♓ "
" 3 " 26 " ♓ "
" 4 " 22 " ♈ "
" 5 " 14 " ♉ "
" 6 " 3 " ♊ "
" 7 " 19 " ♊ "
" 8 " 3 " ♋ "
" 9 " 16 " ♋ "
" 10 " 29 " ♋ "
" 11 " 11 " ♌ "
" 12, Midn't, 22 " ♌ "

NOVEMBER 11

A.M.
At 1 o'clock, 10° of ♍ rises
" 2 " 22 " ♍ "
" 3 " 4 " ♎ "
" 4 " 16 " ♎ "
" 5 " 27 " ♎ "
" 6 " 9 " ♏ "
" 7 " 21 " ♏ "
" 8 " 2 " ♐ "
" 9 " 15 " ♐ "
" 10 " 28 " ♐ "
" 11 " 12 " ♑ "
" 12, Noon, 29 " ♑ "

P.M.
At 1 o'clock, 20° of ♒ rises
" 2 " 13 " ♓ "
" 3 " 9 " ♈ "
" 4 " 4 " ♉ "
" 5 " 25 " ♉ "
" 6 " 12 " ♊ "
" 7 " 28 " ♊ "
" 8 " 11 " ♋ "
" 9 " 23 " ♋ "
" 10 " 5 " ♌ "
" 11 " 17 " ♌ "
" 12, Midn't. 28 " ♌ "

OCTOBER 30

A.M.
At 1 o'clock, 1° of ♍ rises
" 2 " 12 " ♍ "
" 3 " 24 " ♍ "
" 4 " 6 " ♎ "
" 5 " 18 " ♎ "
" 6 " 0 " ♏ "
" 7 " 12 " ♏ "
" 8 " 23 " ♏ "
" 9 " 5 " ♐ "
" 10 " 17 " ♐ "
" 11 " 1 " ♑ "
" 12, Noon, 16 " ♑ "

P.M.
At 1 o'clock, 3° of ♒ rises
" 2 " 24 " ♒ "
" 3 " 19 " ♓ "
" 4 " 15 " ♈ "
" 5 " 9 " ♉ "
" 6 " 29 " ♉ "
" 7 " 16 " ♊ "
" 8 " 0 " ♋ "
" 9 " 13 " ♋ "
" 10 " 26 " ♋ "
" 11 " 8 " ♌ "
" 12, Midn't, 19 " ♌ "

NOVEMBER 7

A.M.
At 1 o'clock, 7° of ♍ rises
" 2 " 18 " ♍ "
" 3 " 0 " ♎ "
" 4 " 12 " ♎ "
" 5 " 24 " ♎ "
" 6 " 6 " ♏ "
" 7 " 18 " ♏ "
" 8 " 29 " ♏ "
" 9 " 12 " ♐ "
" 10 " 25 " ♐ "
" 11 " 8 " ♑ "
" 12, Noon, 25 " ♑ "

P.M.
At 1 o'clock, 13° of ♒ rises
" 2 " 7 " ♓ "
" 3 " 2 " ♈ "
" 4 " 27 " ♈ "
" 5 " 20 " ♉ "
" 6 " 8 " ♊ "
" 7 " 23 " ♊ "
" 8 " 7 " ♋ "
" 9 " 20 " ♋ "
" 10 " 2 " ♌ "
" 11 " 14 " ♌ "
" 12, Midn't. 25 " ♌ "

NOVEMBER 15

A.M.
At 1 o'clock, 13° of ♍ rises
" 2 " 25 " ♍ "
" 3 " 6 " ♎ "
" 4 " 19 " ♎ "
" 5 " 1 " ♏ "
" 6 " 12 " ♏ "
" 7 " 24 " ♏ "
" 8 " 6 " ♐ "
" 9 " 18 " ♐ "
" 10 " 2 " ♑ "
" 11 " 17 " ♑ "
" 12, Noon, 5 " ♒ "

P.M.
At 1 o'clock, 25° of ♒ rises
" 2 " 20 " ♓ "
" 3 " 16 " ♈ "
" 4 " 10 " ♉ "
" 5 " 0 " ♊ "
" 6 " 16 " ♊ "
" 7 " 1 " ♋ "
" 8 " 14 " ♋ "
" 9 " 26 " ♋ "
" 10 " 8 " ♌ "
" 11 " 20 " ♌ "
" 12, Midn't. 2 " ♍ "

NOVEMBER 19

A.M.
At 1 o'clock, 16° of ♍ rises
" 2 " 28 " ♍ "
" 3 " 10 " ♎ "
" 4 " 22 " ♎ "
" 5 " 4 " ♏ "
" 6 " 15 " ♏ "
" 7 " 27 " ♏ "
" 8 " 9 " ♐ "
" 9 " 21 " ♐ "
" 10 " 5 " ♑ "
" 11 " 20 " ♑ "
" 12, Noon, 9 " ♒ "

P.M.
At 1 o'clock, 2° of ♓ rises
" 2 " 27 " ♓ "
" 3 " 23 " ♈ "
" 4 " 15 " ♉ "
" 5 " 4 " ♊ "
" 6 " 20 " ♊ "
" 7 " 4 " ♋ "
" 8 " 17 " ♋ "
" 9 " 29 " ♋ "
" 10 " 11 " ♌ "
" 11 " 23 " ♌ "
" 12, Midn't. 5 " ♍ "

NOVEMBER 27

A.M.
At 1 o'clock, 22° of ♍ rises
" 2 " 4 " ♎ "
" 3 " 16 " ♎ "
" 4 " 28 " ♎ "
" 5 " 10 " ♏ "
" 6 " 21 " ♏ "
" 7 " 3 " ♐ "
" 8 " 15 " ♐ "
" 9 " 29 " ♐ "
" 10 " 14 " ♑ "
" 11 " 0 " ♒ "
" 12, Noon, 20 " ♒ "

P.M.
At 1 o'clock, 14° of ♓ rises
" 2 " 11 " ♈ "
" 3 " 8 " ♉ "
" 4 " 26 " ♉ "
" 5 " 13 " ♊ "
" 6 " 28 " ♊ "
" 7 " 13 " ♋ "
" 8 " 24 " ♋ "
" 9 " 5 " ♌ "
" 10 " 17 " ♌ "
" 11 " 29 " ♌ "
" 12, Midn't, 11 " ♍ "

DECEMBER 5

A.M.
At 1 o'clock, 28° of ♍ rises
" 2 " 10 " ♎ "
" 3 " 21 " ♎ "
" 4 " 3 " ♏ "
" 5 " 15 " ♏ "
" 6 " 27 " ♏ "
" 7 " 9 " ♐ "
" 8 " 21 " ♐ "
" 9 " 5 " ♑ "
" 10 " 20 " ♑ "
" 11 " 9 " ♒ "
" 12, Noon, 0 " ♓ "

P.M.
At 1 o'clock, 26° of ♓ rises
" 2 " 22 " ♈ "
" 3 " 15 " ♉ "
" 4 " 4 " ♊ "
" 5 " 20 " ♊ "
" 6 " 4 " ♋ "
" 7 " 17 " ♋ "
" 8 " 29 " ♋ "
" 9 " 11 " ♌ "
" 10 " 22 " ♌ "
" 11 " 4 " ♍ "
" 12, Midn't, 16 " ♍ "

NOVEMBER 23

A.M.
At 1 o'clock, 19° of ♍ rises
" 2 " 1 " ♎ "
" 3 " 13 " ♎ "
" 4 " 25 " ♎ "
" 5 " 7 " ♏ "
" 6 " 18 " ♏ "
" 7 " 0 " ♐ "
" 8 " 12 " ♐ "
" 9 " 25 " ♐ "
" 10 " 9 " ♑ "
" 11 " 25 " ♑ "
" 12, Noon, 14 " ♒ "

P.M.
At 1 o'clock, 8° of ♓ rises
" 2 " 3 " ♈ "
" 3 " 29 " ♈ "
" 4 " 20 " ♉ "
" 5 " 9 " ♊ "
" 6 " 24 " ♊ "
" 7 " 8 " ♋ "
" 8 " 20 " ♋ "
" 9 " 2 " ♌ "
" 10 " 14 " ♌ "
" 11 " 26 " ♌ "
" 12, Midn't. 7 " ♍ "

DECEMBER 1

A.M.
At 1 o'clock, 25° of ♍ rises
" 2 " 7 " ♎ "
" 3 " 19 " ♎ "
" 4 " 1 " ♏ "
" 5 " 13 " ♏ "
" 6 " 25 " ♏ "
" 7 " 7 " ♐ "
" 8 " 19 " ♐ "
" 9 " 2 " ♑ "
" 10 " 17 " ♑ "
" 11 " 5 " ♒ "
" 12, Noon, 27 " ♒ "

P.M.
At 1 o'clock, 21° of ♓ rises
" 2 " 16 " ♈ "
" 3 " 10 " ♉ "
" 4 " 1 " ♊ "
" 5 " 17 " ♊ "
" 6 " 2 " ♋ "
" 7 " 15 " ♋ "
" 8 " 27 " ♋ "
" 9 " 9 " ♌ "
" 10 " 21 " ♌ "
" 11 " 2 " ♍ "
" 12, Midn't, 14 " ♍ "

DECEMBER 9

A.M.
At 1 o'clock, 2° of ♎ rises
" 2 " 14 " ♎ "
" 3 " 25 " ♎ "
" 4 " 8 " ♏ "
" 5 " 19 " ♏ "
" 6 " 1 " ♐ "
" 7 " 13 " ♐ "
" 8 " 26 " ♐ "
" 9 " 10 " ♑ "
" 10 " 26 " ♑ "
" 11 " 16 " ♒ "
" 12, Noon, 9 " ♓ "

P.M.
At 1 o'clock, 5° of ♈ rises
" 2 " 0 " ♉ "
" 3 " 22 " ♉ "
" 4 " 10 " ♊ "
" 5 " 25 " ♊ "
" 6 " 9 " ♋ "
" 7 " 21 " ♋ "
" 8 " 3 " ♌ "
" 9 " 15 " ♌ "
" 10 " 27 " ♌ "
" 11 " 8 " ♍ "
" 12, Midn't. 20 " ♍ "

308

DECEMBER 13

A.M.
At 1 o'clock, 5° of ♎ rises
" 2 " 17 " ♎ "
" 3 " 28 " ♎ "
" 4 " 10 " ♏ "
" 5 " 22 " ♏ "
" 6 " 4 " ♐ "
" 7 " 16 " ♐ "
" 8 " 29 " ♐ "
" 9 " 14 " ♑ "
" 10 " 1 " ♒ "
" 11 " 21 " ♒ "
" 12, Noon, 15 " ♓ "

P.M.
At 1 o'clock, 12° of ♈ rises
" 2 " 6 " ♉ "
" 3 " 27 " ♉ "
" 4 " 14 " ♊ "
" 5 " 29 " ♊ "
" 6 " 12 " ♋ "
" 7 " 24 " ♋ "
" 8 " 6 " ♌ "
" 9 " 18 " ♌ "
" 10 " 0 " ♍ "
" 11 " 12 " ♍ "
" 12, Midn't. 23 " ♍ "

DECEMBER 23

A.M.
At 1 o'clock, 12° of ♎ rises
" 2 " 24 " ♎ "
" 3 " 6 " ♏ "
" 4 " 18 " ♏ "
" 5 " 0 " ♐ "
" 6 " 12 " ♐ "
" 7 " 25 " ♐ "
" 8 " 9 " ♑ "
" 9 " 25 " ♑ "
" 10 " 14 " ♒ "
" 11 " 7 " ♓ "
" 12, Noon, 2 " ♈ "

P.M.
At 1 o'clock, 28° of ♈ rises
" 2 " 20 " ♉ "
" 3 " 9 " ♊ "
" 4 " 24 " ♊ "
" 5 " 8 " ♋ "
" 6 " 20 " ♋ "
" 7 " 2 " ♌ "
" 8 " 14 " ♌ "
" 9 " 26 " ♌ "
" 10 " 7 " ♍ "
" 11 " 19 " ♍ "
" 12, Midn't. 1 " ♎ "

DECEMBER 18

A.M.
At 1 o'clock, 9° of ♎ rises
" 2 " 21 " ♎ "
" 3 " 2 " ♏ "
" 4 " 14 " ♏ "
" 5 " 26 " ♏ "
" 6 " 8 " ♐ "
" 7 " 21 " ♐ "
" 8 " 4 " ♑ "
" 9 " 19 " ♑ "
" 10 " 7 " ♒ "
" 11 " 29 " ♒ "
" 12, Noon, 24 " ♓ "

P.M.
At 1 o'clock, 20° of ♈ rises
" 2 " 13 " ♉ "
" 3 " 3 " ♊ "
" 4 " 19 " ♊ "
" 5 " 3 " ♋ "
" 6 " 16 " ♋ "
" 7 " 28 " ♋ "
" 8 " 10 " ♌ "
" 9 " 22 " ♌ "
" 10 " 4 " ♍ "
" 11 " 16 " ♍ "
" 12, Midn't. 27 " ♍ "

DECEMBER 28

A.M.
At 1 o'clock, 16° of ♎ rises
" 2 " 28 " ♎ "
" 3 " 10 " ♏ "
" 4 " 22 " ♏ "
" 5 " 4 " ♐ "
" 6 " 16 " ♐ "
" 7 " 29 " ♐ "
" 8 " 14 " ♑ "
" 9 " 1 " ♒ "
" 10 " 21 " ♒ "
" 11 " 14 " ♓ "
" 12, Noon, 11 " ♈ "

P.M.
At 1 o'clock, 5° of ♉ rises
" 2 " 26 " ♉ "
" 3 " 13 " ♊ "
" 4 " 28 " ♊ "
" 5 " 12 " ♋ "
" 6 " 24 " ♋ "
" 7 " 6 " ♌ "
" 8 " 17 " ♌ "
" 9 " 0 " ♍ "
" 10 " 12 " ♍ "
" 11 " 23 " ♍ "
" 12, Midn't. 6 " ♎ "

EPHEMERIDES OF THE MOON (1900–1974)

The following tables enable the reader to find the zodiacal sign and degree for the moon's position for the date of any birth between 1900 and 1974. The number indicates the degree of the zodiacal sign which is given in the same column.

The zodiac is divided into twelve equal parts of 30 degrees each and the moon's average motion is one degree every two hours in its passage through the zodiac. These tables are calculated for Greenwich Mean Time at zero hour in the morning. And finding out where the moon was at any other hour is a matter of simple arithmetic. First convert your zone time into Greenwich Mean Time (hereafter referred to as GMT). For example, if you were born at six a.m. on February 15, 1930, in New York City, the time of your birth in GMT is eleven a.m., since GMT is five hours later than Eastern Standard Time. The moon's position at zero hour is given as 19 degrees in Virgo; therefore you would have the moon in Virgo. If you were born at six a.m. a day later—on February 16, 1930—in New York City, a further interpolation would have to be made. The chart shows the days of odd number (only every other day being given, to save space), so in this case the moon's movement during the forty-eight hours between zero hour of the fifteenth and zero hour of the seventeenth must be found. On the fifteenth the moon was in 19 degrees of Virgo. You will note that out of 30 degrees (which every sign has), 11 degrees in Virgo are remaining in this instance. On the seventeenth the moon was in 17 degrees of Libra. (Libra follows Virgo in the order of the constellations.) To arrive at the calculation add the eleven remaining degrees of Virgo (30 minus 19) to the 17 degrees of Libra; this makes a total of 28 degrees. A movement of 28 degrees has occurred in forty-eight hours. And to get the GMT at zero hour on the day between—namely, the sixteenth—divide the 28 degrees in half. The result is 14 degrees, which means that the moon has moved 14 degrees in twenty-four hours. Since there are 11 degrees of Virgo remaining (30 minus 19) the moon's position at zero hour on the sixteenth is 3 degrees of Libra, which means that if you were born on February 16, 1930, the moon was in Libra. Similar calculations must be made for all even-numbered days. Let us take another example. The Greenwich Mean Time of the birth may occur on a day after that of the given date of birth. For example, ten p.m. Eastern Standard Time, February 15, 1930, becomes (through the addition of five hours) three a.m., February 16, 1930, GMT. The same calculations for the moon's average movement must be made. We have, of course, 3 degrees of Libra at zero hour of the sixteenth, GMT. We add three hours to find the moon's position at three a.m. In three hours it has moved 1½ degrees, giving us 4½ degrees of Libra, which in this example again shows the moon was in Libra.

1900

	Jan.	Feb.	Mar.	April	May	June	July	Aug.	Sep.	Oct.	Nov.	Dec.
1	2 ♑	25 ♒	3 ♓	27 ♈	4 ♊	22 ♋	25 ♌	9 ♎	23 ♏	27 ♐	16 ♑	25 ♒
3	2 ♒	25 ♓	4 ♈	26 ♉	1 ♋	17 ♌	19 ♍	2 ♏	18 ♐	23 ♑	15 ♒	24 ♓
5	1 ♓	24 ♈	3 ♉	23 ♊	26 ♋	12 ♍	12 ♎	27 ♏	14 ♐	21 ♒	15 ♓	22 ♈
7	0 ♈	22 ♉	1 ♊	18 ♋	21 ♌	4 ♎	7 ♏	23 ♐	13 ♑	21 ♒	15 ♈	22 ♉
9	28 ♈	18 ♊	27 ♊	12 ♌	15 ♍	28 ♎	2 ♐	20 ♑	13 ♒	22 ♓	14 ♉	19 ♊
11	25 ♉	12 ♋	22 ♌	6 ♍	8 ♎	22 ♏	28 ♐	19 ♒	13 ♓	20 ♈	12 ♊	15 ♋
13	21 ♊	7 ♌	16 ♌	0 ♎	3 ♏	20 ♐	26 ♑	19 ♓	13 ♈	20 ♉	8 ♋	10 ♌
15	15 ♋	1 ♍	9 ♍	24 ♎	28 ♏	18 ♑	25 ♒	18 ♈	12 ♉	16 ♊	2 ♌	4 ♍
17	10 ♌	24 ♍	3 ♎	19 ♏	24 ♐	17 ♒	24 ♓	17 ♉	7 ♊	11 ♋	26 ♌	28 ♍
19	4 ♍	18 ♎	27 ♎	14 ♐	21 ♑	17 ♓	24 ♈	16 ♊	27 ♋	6 ♌	20 ♍	22 ♎
21	27 ♍	12 ♏	22 ♏	10 ♑	18 ♒	17 ♈	23 ♉	10 ♋	21 ♌	23 ♍	14 ♎	17 ♏
23	21 ♏	8 ♐	17 ♐	7 ♒	17 ♓	16 ♉	20 ♊	5 ♌	20 ♍	17 ♎	8 ♐	13 ♐
25	16 ♐	4 ♑	14 ♑	6 ♓	15 ♈	13 ♊	13 ♋	0 ♍	14 ♎	11 ♏	4 ♑	10 ♑
27	12 ♐	3 ♒	12 ♒	6 ♈	14 ♉	10 ♋	8 ♌	23 ♍	6 ♏	11 ♐	0 ♒	8 ♒
29	10 ♑		11 ♓	5 ♉	12 ♊	4 ♌	3 ♍	17 ♎	6 ♐	6 ♑	6 ♓	6 ♓
31	10 ♒		12 ♈		9 ♋		27 ♍	11 ♏		3 ♒		4 ♉

1901

	Jan.	Feb.	Mar.	April	May	June	July	Aug.	Sep.	Oct.	Nov.	Dec.
1	18 ♉	10 ♋	20 ♋	7 ♍	10 ♎	24 ♏	27 ♐	15 ♒	7 ♈	16 ♉	9 ♋	15 ♌
3	16 ♊	6 ♌	15 ♌	1 ♍	4 ♏	18 ♐	18 ♑	11 ♓	4 ♉	13 ♊	6 ♌	11 ♍
5	14 ♋	1 ♍	10 ♍	25 ♍	27 ♏	13 ♑	19 ♒	11 ♈	2 ♊	13 ♋	2 ♍	6 ♎
7	10 ♌	26 ♍	4 ♎	18 ♎	21 ♐	9 ♒	16 ♓	13 ♉	29 ♊	9 ♌	27 ♍	0 ♏
9	6 ♍	20 ♎	28 ♎	12 ♏	16 ♑	6 ♓	14 ♈	13 ♊	25 ♋	5 ♍	21 ♎	23 ♏
11	0 ♎	13 ♏	22 ♏	7 ♐	11 ♒	4 ♈	13 ♉	11 ♋	21 ♌	1 ♎	15 ♏	17 ♐
13	24 ♎	7 ♐	16 ♐	3 ♑	8 ♓	3 ♉	11 ♊	7 ♌	15 ♍	26 ♎	8 ♐	11 ♑
15	17 ♏	3 ♑	11 ♑	0 ♒	8 ♈	3 ♊	10 ♋	2 ♍	9 ♎	18 ♏	2 ♑	6 ♒
17	12 ♐	0 ♒	7 ♒	29 ♒	8 ♉	4 ♋	7 ♌	27 ♍	3 ♏	11 ♐	26 ♑	2 ♓
19	8 ♑	28 ♒	6 ♓	0 ♈	8 ♊	4 ♌	4 ♍	19 ♎	27 ♏	5 ♑	19 ♒	28 ♓
21	5 ♒	28 ♓	6 ♈	0 ♉	7 ♋	2 ♍	29 ♍	13 ♏	22 ♐	0 ♒	17 ♓	25 ♈
23	4 ♓	27 ♈	6 ♉	29 ♉	5 ♌	27 ♍	23 ♎	7 ♐	17 ♑	26 ♒	17 ♈	25 ♉
25	3 ♈	26 ♉	6 ♊	26 ♊	2 ♍	22 ♎	17 ♏	2 ♑	14 ♒	24 ♓	17 ♉	25 ♊
27	1 ♉	23 ♊	4 ♋	22 ♋	28 ♍	16 ♏	11 ♐	27 ♑	16 ♓	16 ♈	17 ♊	23 ♋
29	29 ♉		3 ♌	16 ♌	24 ♎	9 ♐	6 ♑	24 ♒	16 ♈	24 ♉	17 ♊	20 ♌
31	26 ♊		25 ♌		12 ♏		3 ♐	22 ♓		24 ♊		20 ♍

1902

	Jan.	Feb.	Mar.	April	May	June	July	Aug.	Sep.	Oct.	Nov.	Dec.
1	2 ♎	16 ♏	24 ♏	7 ♑	10 ♒	28 ♓	5 ♉	28 ♊	22 ♌	28 ♍	15 ♏	18 ♐
3	26 ♎	10 ♐	18 ♐	2 ♒	6 ♓	26 ♈	4 ♊	28 ♋	20 ♍	24 ♎	9 ♐	12 ♑
5	20 ♏	4 ♑	12 ♑	28 ♒	3 ♈	25 ♉	4 ♋	27 ♌	16 ♎	19 ♏	3 ♑	5 ♒
7	14 ♐	29 ♑	7 ♒	25 ♓	2 ♉	26 ♊	4 ♌	25 ♍	11 ♏	13 ♐	27 ♑	29 ♒
9	8 ♑	25 ♒	3 ♓	24 ♈	2 ♊	26 ♋	3 ♍	21 ♎	5 ♐	7 ♑	21 ♒	21 ♓
11	3 ♒	22 ♓	1 ♈	28 ♉	2 ♋	24 ♌	0 ♎	15 ♏	29 ♐	1 ♒	16 ♓	21 ♈
13	29 ♒	19 ♈	29 ♈	23 ♊	1 ♌	25 ♍	25 ♎	9 ♐	23 ♑	26 ♒	13 ♈	20 ♉
15	25 ♓	17 ♉	28 ♉	21 ♋	29 ♌	16 ♎	19 ♏	3 ♑	18 ♒	22 ♓	12 ♉	20 ♊
17	22 ♈	15 ♊	26 ♊	20 ♌	24 ♍	10 ♏	13 ♐	27 ♑	14 ♓	19 ♈	12 ♊	20 ♋
19	21 ♉	14 ♋	24 ♋	15 ♍	19 ♎	4 ♐	6 ♑	22 ♒	11 ♈	18 ♉	11 ♋	20 ♌
21	19 ♊	12 ♌	22 ♌	10 ♎	13 ♏	28 ♐	1 ♒	18 ♓	8 ♉	17 ♊	11 ♌	18 ♍
23	19 ♋	9 ♍	20 ♍	4 ♏	7 ♐	22 ♑	26 ♒	15 ♈	5 ♊	16 ♋	8 ♍	14 ♎
25	17 ♌	5 ♎	13 ♎	28 ♏	1 ♑	16 ♒	21 ♓	12 ♉	5 ♋	14 ♌	4 ♎	9 ♏
27	14 ♍	0 ♏	8 ♏	22 ♐	25 ♑	11 ♓	18 ♈	10 ♊	3 ♌	11 ♍	29 ♎	3 ♐
29	10 ♎		2 ♐	16 ♑	19 ♒	7 ♈	15 ♉	10 ♋	1 ♍	7 ♎	24 ♏	27 ♐
31	4 ♏		25 ♐		15 ♓		14 ♊	7 ♌		3 ♏		20 ♑

1903

	Jan.	Feb.	Mar.	April	May	June	July	Aug.	Sep.	Oct.	Nov.	Dec.
1	2 ♒	18 ♓	27 ♓	17 ♉	25 ♊	19 ♌	27 ♍	16 ♏	1 ♑	3 ♒	17 ♓	20 ♈
3	26 ♒	13 ♈	23 ♈	15 ♊	24 ♋	17 ♍	23 ♎	11 ♐	25 ♑	27 ♒	12 ♈	17 ♉
5	21 ♓	10 ♉	20 ♉	13 ♋	22 ♌	14 ♎	19 ♏	5 ♑	19 ♒	22 ♓	9 ♉	15 ♊
7	17 ♈	7 ♊	18 ♊	11 ♌	20 ♍	9 ♏	13 ♐	29 ♑	15 ♓	17 ♈	6 ♊	14 ♋
9	14 ♉	7 ♋	16 ♋	10 ♍	17 ♎	4 ♐	8 ♑	22 ♒	11 ♈	13 ♉	4 ♋	13 ♌
11	13 ♊	7 ♌	16 ♌	7 ♎	13 ♏	29 ♐	1 ♒	16 ♓	8 ♉	10 ♊	3 ♌	12 ♍
13	13 ♋	6 ♍	15 ♍	4 ♏	8 ♐	23 ♑	26 ♒	11 ♈	6 ♊	8 ♋	2 ♍	9 ♎
15	14 ♌	5 ♎	12 ♎	0 ♐	2 ♑	17 ♒	21 ♓	6 ♉	27 ♋	8 ♌	29 ♍	5 ♏
17	13 ♍	1 ♏	8 ♏	24 ♐	26 ♑	11 ♓	16 ♈	4 ♊	27 ♌	8 ♍	26 ♎	1 ♐
19	10 ♎	26 ♏	4 ♐	18 ♑	20 ♒	5 ♈	13 ♉	2 ♋	25 ♍	3 ♎	21 ♏	27 ♐
21	6 ♏	20 ♐	28 ♐	12 ♒	14 ♓	1 ♉	10 ♊	1 ♌	24 ♍	28 ♎	15 ♐	22 ♑
23	0 ♐	14 ♑	22 ♑	6 ♓	10 ♈	29 ♉	8 ♋	1 ♍	20 ♎	23 ♏	7 ♑	15 ♒
25	24 ♐	8 ♒	16 ♒	2 ♈	7 ♉	29 ♊	8 ♌	29 ♍	15 ♏	18 ♐	1 ♒	9 ♓
27	17 ♑	2 ♓	11 ♓	28 ♈	5 ♊	29 ♋	8 ♍	28 ♎	10 ♑	11 ♑	25 ♒	4 ♈
29	11 ♒		6 ♈	26 ♉	5 ♋	29 ♌	6 ♎	25 ♏		11 ♒		28 ♈
31	6 ♓		3 ♉		4 ♌		3 ♏	19 ♐		5 ♓		24 ♉

1904

	Jan.	Feb.	Mar.	April	May	June	July	Aug.	Sep.	Oct.	Nov.	Dec.
1	9 ♊	1 ♌	24 ♌	17 ♎	24 ♏	12 ♑	15 ♒	29 ♓	13 ♉	18 ♊	9 ♌	17 ♍
3	8 ♋	1 ♍	24 ♍	16 ♏	21 ♐	6 ♒	8 ♓	22 ♈	9 ♊	15 ♋	7 ♍	16 ♎
5	8 ♌	1 ♎	24 ♎	13 ♐	16 ♑	0 ♓	2 ♈	17 ♉	5 ♋	13 ♌	6 ♎	14 ♏
7	8 ♍	29 ♎	22 ♏	8 ♑	11 ♒	24 ♓	26 ♈	13 ♊	4 ♌	12 ♍	5 ♏	12 ♐
9	6 ♎	26 ♏	18 ♐	3 ♒	4 ♓	18 ♈	21 ♉	11 ♋	4 ♍	12 ♎	4 ♐	10 ♑
11	3 ♏	21 ♐	12 ♑	26 ♒	28 ♓	13 ♉	18 ♊	10 ♌	4 ♎	12 ♏	2 ♑	5 ♒
13	29 ♏	15 ♑	6 ♒	20 ♓	23 ♈	10 ♊	17 ♋	10 ♍	4 ♏	10 ♐	28 ♑	0 ♓
15	24 ♐	9 ♒	0 ♓	14 ♈	18 ♉	8 ♋	16 ♌	9 ♎	2 ♐	6 ♑	23 ♒	23 ♓
17	18 ♑	3 ♓	23 ♓	9 ♉	15 ♊	7 ♌	16 ♍	9 ♏	28 ♐	2 ♒	16 ♓	17 ♈
19	12 ♒	26 ♓	18 ♈	5 ♊	13 ♋	6 ♍	15 ♎	7 ♐	23 ♑	26 ♒	9 ♈	12 ♉
21	6 ♓	21 ♈	12 ♉	2 ♋	11 ♌	4 ♎	12 ♏	1 ♑	17 ♒	19 ♓	4 ♉	7 ♊
23	29 ♓	15 ♉	8 ♊	0 ♌	9 ♍	2 ♏	9 ♐	26 ♑	11 ♓	13 ♈	29 ♉	4 ♋
25	24 ♈	12 ♊	5 ♋	28 ♌	7 ♎	29 ♏	4 ♑	20 ♒	2 ♈	7 ♉	22 ♊	2 ♌
27	19 ♉	9 ♋	3 ♌	27 ♍	5 ♏	25 ♐	29 ♑	14 ♓	28 ♈	2 ♊	22 ♋	0 ♍
29	17 ♊	9 ♌	3 ♍	26 ♎	2 ♐	20 ♑	23 ♒	7 ♈	23 ♉	0 ♋	19 ♌	28 ♍
31	16 ♋		3 ♎		29 ♐		17 ♓	1 ♉		25 ♋		26 ♎

1905	Jan.	Feb.	Mar.	April	May	June	July	Aug.	Sep.	Oct.	Nov.	Dec.
1	10 ♏	1 ♉	11 ♉	27 ♋	6 ♌	14 ♍	18 ♎	6 ♐	28 ♑	7 ♓	0 ♉	6 ♋
3	8 ♐	27 ♉	6 ♋	21 ♌	24 ♌	9 ♎	14 ♏	4 ♑	27 ♒	6 ♈	27 ♉	1 ♌
5	5 ♑	22 ♊	0 ♋	15 ♍	9 ♍	4 ♏	11 ♐	3 ♒	26 ♓	4 ♊	23 ♋	26 ♌
7	1 ♒	16 ♋	24 ♋	9 ♎	2 ♎	1 ♐	8 ♑	2 ♓	24 ♈	1 ♋	19 ♌	20 ♍
9	25 ♒	9 ♈	18 ♌	3 ♏	27 ♎	28 ♐	6 ♒	0 ♈	21 ♉	26 ♋	14 ♍	13 ♎
11	19 ♓	3 ♉	12 ♍	27 ♏	22 ♏	25 ♑	5 ♓	28 ♈	16 ♊	20 ♌	9 ♎	7 ♏
13	13 ♈	27 ♉	6 ♎	24 ♐	19 ♐	24 ♒	3 ♈	24 ♉	11 ♋	14 ♍	2 ♏	2 ♐
15	7 ♉	23 ♊	1 ♏	23 ♑	23 ♑	20 ♓	1 ♉	20 ♊	5 ♌	8 ♎	27 ♏	27 ♐
17	2 ♊	20 ♋	28 ♏	22 ♒	20 ♒	17 ♈	28 ♉	15 ♋	29 ♌	2 ♏	22 ♐	23 ♑
19	28 ♊	19 ♌	27 ♐	20 ♓	20 ♓	13 ♉	24 ♊	9 ♌	23 ♎	26 ♏	18 ♑	20 ♒
21	26 ♋	19 ♍	27 ♑	20 ♈	28 ♈	9 ♊	16 ♋	3 ♍	17 ♏	21 ♐	15 ♒	18 ♓
23	25 ♌	19 ♎	27 ♒	20 ♉	25 ♉	5 ♋	11 ♌	27 ♍	12 ♐	17 ♑	14 ♓	17 ♈
25	24 ♎	18 ♏	27 ♓	18 ♊	21 ♊	0 ♌	6 ♍	21 ♎	8 ♑	14 ♒	8 ♈	17 ♉
27	23 ♎	15 ♐	25 ♈	12 ♋	15 ♋	28 ♌	1 ♎	17 ♏	7 ♒	14 ♓	8 ♉	16 ♊
29	21 ♏		21 ♉	6 ♌	8 ♌	23 ♍	26 ♎	14 ♐	6 ♓	15 ♈	8 ♊	13 ♋
31	18 ♐		15 ♊		2 ♍		22 ♏	13 ♑		15 ♉		9 ♌

1906	Jan.	Feb.	Mar.	April	May	June	July	Aug.	Sep.	Oct.	Nov.	Dec.
1	22 ♓	6 ♉	13 ♉	27 ♊	0 ♌	19 ♍	27 ♎	20 ♐	13 ♒	19 ♓	5 ♉	8 ♊
3	16 ♈	29 ♉	7 ♊	22 ♋	26 ♌	14 ♎	26 ♏	19 ♑	10 ♓	14 ♈	0 ♊	2 ♋
5	10 ♉	24 ♊	1 ♋	18 ♌	24 ♍	11 ♏	26 ♐	18 ♒	6 ♈	9 ♉	23 ♊	26 ♋
7	4 ♊	19 ♋	27 ♋	15 ♍	15 ♎	9 ♐	25 ♑	15 ♓	1 ♉	3 ♊	17 ♋	20 ♌
9	28 ♊	15 ♌	23 ♌	12 ♎	15 ♏	7 ♑	23 ♒	11 ♈	25 ♉	27 ♊	11 ♌	15 ♍
11	24 ♋	11 ♍	22 ♍	21 ♏	15 ♐	7 ♒	20 ♓	5 ♉	19 ♊	21 ♋	6 ♍	11 ♎
13	20 ♌	9 ♎	21 ♎	15 ♐	23 ♑	6 ♓	16 ♈	29 ♉	13 ♋	15 ♌	4 ♎	11 ♏
15	17 ♍	8 ♏	19 ♏	13 ♑	20 ♒	6 ♈	9 ♉	23 ♊	8 ♌	12 ♍	0 ♏	11 ♐
17	15 ♎	8 ♐	17 ♐	10 ♒	10 ♓	3 ♉	3 ♊	17 ♋	2 ♍	10 ♎	3 ♐	11 ♑
19	13 ♏	6 ♑	17 ♑	6 ♓	10 ♈	24 ♉	27 ♊	12 ♌	28 ♍	9 ♏	3 ♑	11 ♒
21	12 ♐	3 ♒	6 ♒	25 ♓	27 ♈	18 ♊	21 ♋	6 ♍	25 ♎	9 ♐	5 ♒	9 ♓
23	10 ♑	0 ♓	9 ♓	25 ♈	21 ♉	12 ♋	16 ♌	2 ♎	23 ♏	9 ♑	5 ♓	5 ♈
25	8 ♒	25 ♓	5 ♈	18 ♉	15 ♊	7 ♌	12 ♍	28 ♎	25 ♐	6 ♒	3 ♈	29 ♈
27	4 ♓	20 ♈	28 ♈	12 ♊	9 ♋	6 ♍	9 ♎	25 ♏	25 ♑	3 ♓	29 ♈	23 ♉
29	29 ♓		22 ♉	6 ♋	3 ♌	6 ♎	7 ♏	1 ♐	23 ♒	28 ♈	14 ♉	17 ♊
31	24 ♈		15 ♊		5 ♍		29 ♏	29 ♑		23 ♈		11 ♋

1907	Jan.	Feb.	Mar.	April	May	June	July	Aug.	Sep.	Oct.	Nov.	Dec.
1	23 ♋	9 ♍	18 ♍	9 ♏	17 ♐	11 ♒	18 ♓	6 ♉	21 ♊	23 ♋	7 ♍	10 ♎
3	17 ♌	5 ♎	15 ♎	7 ♐	16 ♑	8 ♓	15 ♈	1 ♊	15 ♋	17 ♌	2 ♎	7 ♏
5	12 ♍	2 ♏	2 ♏	6 ♑	14 ♒	5 ♈	10 ♉	25 ♊	9 ♌	11 ♍	29 ♎	6 ♐
7	8 ♎	0 ♐	11 ♐	4 ♒	12 ♓	0 ♉	4 ♊	18 ♋	3 ♍	7 ♎	26 ♏	5 ♑
9	5 ♏	28 ♐	9 ♑	28 ♒	8 ♈	25 ♉	28 ♊	12 ♌	28 ♍	4 ♏	25 ♐	4 ♒
11	4 ♐	28 ♑	7 ♒	28 ♓	3 ♉	19 ♊	21 ♋	7 ♍	23 ♎	2 ♐	25 ♑	4 ♓
13	4 ♑	27 ♒	5 ♓	24 ♈	28 ♉	13 ♋	15 ♌	1 ♎	19 ♏	0 ♑	23 ♒	1 ♈
15	4 ♒	24 ♓	3 ♈	20 ♉	22 ♊	6 ♌	9 ♍	25 ♎	17 ♐	28 ♑	23 ♓	28 ♈
17	3 ♓	21 ♈	29 ♈	14 ♊	16 ♋	0 ♍	25 ♍	17 ♏	17 ♑	26 ♒	18 ♈	23 ♉
19	0 ♈	16 ♉	24 ♉	9 ♋	9 ♌	25 ♍	1 ♎	19 ♐	24 ♒	14 ♓	9 ♉	18 ♊
21	26 ♈	10 ♊	18 ♊	1 ♌	4 ♍	22 ♎	19 ♎	19 ♑	23 ♓	14 ♈	9 ♊	12 ♋
23	20 ♉	4 ♋	12 ♋	26 ♌	20 ♍	20 ♏	28 ♏	22 ♒	13 ♈	10 ♉	5 ♋	5 ♌
25	14 ♊	28 ♋	6 ♌	21 ♍	0 ♏	20 ♐	28 ♑	21 ♓	8 ♉	7 ♊	21 ♋	29 ♌
27	7 ♋	22 ♌	0 ♍	19 ♎	26 ♏	20 ♑	26 ♒	19 ♈	5 ♊	7 ♋	21 ♌	23 ♍
29	2 ♌		27 ♍	27 ♏	26 ♐	20 ♒	27 ♓	15 ♉	29 ♊		15 ♍	18 ♎
31	26 ♌		24 ♎		26 ♑		24 ♈	9 ♊		25 ♌		15 ♏

1908	Jan.	Feb.	Mar.	April	May	June	July	Aug.	Sep.	Oct.	Nov.	Dec.
1	29 ♏	21 ♑	15 ♒	8 ♈	15 ♉	2 ♋	4 ♌	19 ♍	4 ♏	9 ♐	0 ♒	10 ♓
3	28 ♐	21 ♒	14 ♓	6 ♉	11 ♊	26 ♋	26 ♌	13 ♎	0 ♐	6 ♑	29 ♒	6 ♈
5	29 ♑	22 ♓	14 ♈	3 ♊	6 ♋	20 ♌	22 ♍	7 ♏	26 ♐	4 ♒	28 ♓	6 ♉
7	29 ♒	20 ♈	12 ♉	28 ♊	0 ♌	14 ♍	16 ♎	3 ♐	24 ♑	3 ♓	27 ♈	3 ♊
9	27 ♓	17 ♉	8 ♊	22 ♋	24 ♌	8 ♎	12 ♏	1 ♑	24 ♒	3 ♈	22 ♉	0 ♋
11	25 ♈	12 ♊	2 ♋	16 ♌	18 ♍	4 ♏	9 ♐	1 ♒	24 ♓	3 ♉	22 ♊	25 ♋
13	20 ♉	6 ♋	26 ♋	10 ♍	13 ♎	1 ♐	8 ♑	1 ♓	23 ♈	1 ♊	17 ♋	13 ♌
15	15 ♊	29 ♋	19 ♌	4 ♎	7 ♏	29 ♐	7 ♒	0 ♈	23 ♉	27 ♊	11 ♌	7 ♍
17	9 ♋	23 ♌	14 ♍	0 ♏	6 ♐	7 ♑	7 ♓	0 ♉	13 ♊	21 ♋	5 ♍	1 ♎
19	2 ♌	17 ♍	8 ♎	27 ♏	4 ♑	3 ♒	5 ♈	28 ♉	15 ♋	29 ♍	1 ♎	27 ♎
21	26 ♌	11 ♎	4 ♏	22 ♐	1 ♒	24 ♓	2 ♉	22 ♊	7 ♌	9 ♎	19 ♏	24 ♐
23	20 ♍	7 ♏	0 ♐	22 ♑	1 ♓	24 ♈	25 ♊	16 ♋	3 ♍	28 ♏	16 ♐	23 ♑
25	14 ♎	3 ♐	27 ♐	20 ♒	29 ♓	20 ♉	25 ♋	10 ♌	25 ♍	28 ♐	16 ♑	23 ♒
27	10 ♏	1 ♑	25 ♑	19 ♓	27 ♈	16 ♊	11 ♌	7 ♎	19 ♎	20 ♑	15 ♒	21 ♓
29	7 ♐	0 ♒	24 ♒	17 ♈	27 ♉	10 ♋	13 ♍	28 ♏	14 ♏	20 ♒	11 ♓	21 ♈
31	6 ♑		24 ♓		19 ♊		7 ♎	22 ♐		17 ♑		19 ♈

1909	Jan.	Feb.	Mar.	April	May	June	July	Aug.	Sep.	Oct.	Nov.	Dec.
1	3 ♉	22 ♊	2 ♋	18 ♌	20 ♍	4 ♏	7 ♐	26 ♑	19 ♓	28 ♈	20 ♊	25 ♋
3	0 ♊	17 ♋	27 ♋	11 ♍	14 ♎	29 ♏	4 ♑	25 ♒	19 ♈	28 ♉	17 ♋	21 ♌
5	26 ♊	11 ♌	21 ♌	5 ♎	9 ♏	28 ♐	1 ♒	25 ♓	19 ♉	26 ♊	11 ♌	16 ♍
7	21 ♋	6 ♍	14 ♍	29 ♎	3 ♐	22 ♑	0 ♓	24 ♈	16 ♊	22 ♋	5 ♍	10 ♎
9	15 ♌	29 ♍	8 ♎	24 ♏	29 ♐	22 ♒	29 ♓	22 ♉	12 ♋	17 ♌	1 ♎	3 ♏
11	9 ♍	23 ♎	2 ♏	19 ♐	25 ♑	18 ♓	27 ♈	19 ♊	7 ♌	11 ♍	25 ♎	27 ♏
13	3 ♎	18 ♏	27 ♏	15 ♑	23 ♒	16 ♈	25 ♉	15 ♋	2 ♍	4 ♎	19 ♏	22 ♐
15	27 ♎	13 ♐	23 ♐	12 ♒	21 ♓	15 ♉	23 ♊	9 ♌	26 ♍	28 ♎	13 ♐	18 ♑
17	22 ♏	10 ♑	19 ♑	11 ♓	21 ♈	20 ♊	0 ♑	6 ♍	9 ♎	24 ♐	12 ♑	15 ♒
19	18 ♐	10 ♒	18 ♒	11 ♈	20 ♉	10 ♋	16 ♌	0 ♎	22 ♎	7 ♑	4 ♒	15 ♓
21	17 ♑	10 ♓	18 ♓	11 ♉	18 ♊	0 ♌	8 ♍	22 ♎	11 ♐	2 ♒	2 ♈	12 ♈
23	16 ♒	10 ♈	18 ♈	10 ♊	13 ♋	16 ♍	0 ♎	16 ♏	8 ♑	0 ♓	9 ♈	9 ♉
25	16 ♓	9 ♉	18 ♉	7 ♋	8 ♌	24 ♍	26 ♎	11 ♐	29 ♑	29 ♈	29 ♈	8 ♊
27	15 ♈	6 ♊	15 ♊	2 ♌	4 ♍	18 ♎	20 ♏	7 ♑	27 ♒	6 ♉	29 ♉	6 ♋
29	13 ♉		11 ♋	26 ♌	28 ♍	12 ♏	15 ♐	4 ♒	27 ♓	6 ♊	28 ♊	2 ♌
31	10 ♊		6 ♌		22 ♎		12 ♑	4 ♓		6 ♋		29 ♌

1910	Jan.	Feb.	Mar.	April	May	June	July	Aug.	Sep.	Oct.	Nov.	Dec.
1	12♍	25♎	3♏	17♐	21♑	10♓	19♈	12♊	4♌	10♍	26♎	28♏
3	6♎	19♏	27♏	12♑	17♒	9♈	18♉	10♋	1♍	5♎	20♏	22♐
5	29♎	13♐	21♐	8♒	15♓	8♉	8♊	8♌	26♍	29♎	13♐	16♑
7	23♏	6♑	16♑	6♓	14♈	7♊	15♋	8♍	21♎	23♏	1♑	11♒
9	18♐	6♒	14♒	6♈	14♉	7♋	13♌	0♎	15♏	16♐	1♒	6♓
11	14♑	4♓	13♓	6♉	14♊	10♌	10♍	25♎	10♐	10♑	27♒	3♈
13	11♒	3♈	12♈	6♊	13♋	8♍	5♎	18♏	5♑	5♒	24♓	2♉
15	9♓	2♉	11♉	6♋	10♌	27♍	29♎	12♐	2♒	3♓	23♈	2♊
17	7♈	0♊	11♊	1♌	6♍	21♎	22♏	7♑	24♓	1♈	24♉	2♋
19	6♉	28♊	8♋	0♎	1♎	14♏	16♐	0♒	19♈	0♉	24♊	29♋
21	4♊	24♋	4♌	21♍	24♏	8♐	11♑	0♓	16♉	0♊	23♋	29♌
23	1♋	20♌	0♍	15♎	17♏	2♑	7♒	28♓	13♊	21♊	21♌	25♍
25	28♋	15♍	18♍	9♏	11♐	26♑	24♒	25♈	10♋	24♋	16♎	13♎
27	24♌	10♎	18♎	2♐	6♑	21♒	24♓	23♉	17♌	24♌	11♏	13♏
29	19♍		12♎	26♐	1♒	21♓	23♈	23♊	14♍	19♎	5♐	7♐
31	13♎		5♐		27♒		28♉	20♋		14♏		1♑

1911	Jan.	Feb.	Mar.	April	May	June	July	Aug.	Sep.	Oct.	Nov.	Dec.
1	13♑	0♓	9♓	0♉	8♊	2♌	9♍	27♎	11♐	13♑	27♒	0♈
3	8♒	27♓	8♈	29♉	6♋	0♍	5♎	5♐	7♑	7♒	27♓	0♉
5	3♓	24♈	4♉	28♊	6♌	26♍	0♏	15♐	29♑	2♓	19♈	26♉
7	0♈	22♉	3♊	26♋	3♍	21♎	24♏	18♑	18♒	28♓	18♉	23♊
9	27♈	20♊	1♋	23♌	29♍	15♏	18♐	3♒	19♓	25♈	18♊	27♋
11	26♉	19♋	29♋	19♍	24♎	9♐	12♑	27♒	16♈	24♉	17♋	26♌
13	25♊	17♌	27♌	15♎	18♏	3♑	6♒	23♓	13♊	22♊	16♌	23♍
15	25♋	15♍	23♍	10♏	12♐	27♑	1♓	19♈	11♋	21♋	13♍	19♎
17	23♌	11♎	19♎	4♐	6♑	22♒	26♓	16♉	10♌	19♌	9♎	14♏
19	20♍	6♏	14♏	27♐	0♒	16♓	22♈	15♊	10♍	16♎	4♏	8♐
21	16♎	0♐	7♐	21♑	24♒	11♈	19♉	13♋	13♍	13♏	29♏	2♑
23	10♏	23♐	1♑	16♒	20♓	8♉	19♊	13♌	4♎	8♐	22♐	26♑
25	3♐	17♑	25♑	12♓	18♈	10♊	19♋	12♍	0♏	3♑	17♑	19♒
27	27♐	13♒	21♒	9♈	17♉	9♋	17♌	9♎	27♏	27♑	11♒	15♓
29	22♑		17♓	8♉	17♊	11♌	16♍	5♏	19♐	20♒	5♓	9♈
31	17♒		15♈		17♋		14♎	29♏		14♓		5♉

1912	Jan.	Feb.	Mar.	April	May	June	July	Aug.	Sep.	Oct.	Nov.	Dec.
1	19♉	12♋	6♌	29♍	5♏	22♐	25♑	9♉	25♈	1♊	23♋	2♍
3	19♊	13♌	6♍	27♎	1♐	16♑	18♒	3♊	21♉	28♊	21♌	0♎
5	20♋	13♍	5♎	23♏	26♐	10♒	12♓	28♊	20♊	26♋	20♍	26♎
7	20♌	11♎	2♏	18♐	20♑	4♓	6♈	24♋	18♌	25♌	18♎	24♏
9	19♍	7♏	28♏	12♑	15♒	28♓	2♉	22♌	16♍	24♍	13♐	19♐
11	16♎	2♐	22♐	6♒	8♓	23♈	29♉	22♍	16♎	21♎	7♑	15♑
13	11♏	26♐	16♑	0♓	2♈	21♉	28♊	22♌	15♏	20♏	7♒	9♒
15	5♐	19♑	10♒	25♓	29♈	20♊	29♋	20♍	13♐	16♐	1♓	4♓
17	29♐	13♒	4♓	21♈	27♉	20♋	29♌	21♎	9♑	11♑	25♓	26♓
19	23♑	8♓	29♓	18♉	26♊	20♌	28♍	18♏	3♒	5♒	13♈	17♈
21	16♒	2♈	25♈	16♊	25♋	18♍	25♎	12♐	27♒	29♒	13♈	17♉
23	11♓	28♈	22♉	14♋	24♌	15♎	21♏	6♑	21♓	23♓	9♉	15♊
25	5♈	25♉	19♊	13♌	22♍	11♏	16♐	0♒	15♈	18♈	6♊	14♋
27	1♉	23♊	18♋	11♍	18♎	6♐	10♑	24♒	9♈	14♉	5♋	14♌
29	28♉	22♋	16♌	8♎	14♏	1♑	3♒	18♓	5♉	11♊	4♌	14♍
31	27♊		15♍		9♐		27♒	13♈		9♋		11♎

1913	Jan.	Feb.	Mar.	April	May	June	July	Aug.	Sep.	Oct.	Nov.	Dec.
1	25♎	13♐	22♐	8♒	10♓	24♈	27♉	17♋	10♍	18♎	10♐	16♑
3	21♏	8♑	17♑	2♓	4♈	19♉	24♋	16♌	9♎	8♐	11♑	11♒
5	16♐	2♒	11♒	25♓	28♈	16♊	23♌	16♍	16♏	16♐	5♒	5♓
7	11♑	26♒	5♓	19♈	24♉	14♋	22♍	3♎	16♐	12♑	28♒	29♓
9	5♒	20♓	29♓	14♉	20♊	12♌	21♍	14♏	3♑	7♒	21♓	23♈
11	29♒	13♈	23♈	10♊	17♋	10♍	10♎	6♑	22♒	1♓	15♈	17♉
13	23♓	8♉	17♉	7♋	15♌	9♎	9♏	6♑	22♓	25♓	9♉	13♊
15	17♈	4♊	13♊	4♌	14♍	6♏	13♐	1♒	16♈	18♈	4♊	9♋
17	12♉	1♋	10♋	3♍	12♎	6♏	13♐	0♓	12♉	12♉	0♋	8♌
19	9♊	0♌	9♌	2♎	10♏	0♑	4♒	19♈	9♊	7♊	26♋	5♍
21	7♋	1♍	9♍	2♏	9♐	26♑	22♒	16♉	6♋	23♋	22♌	1♎
23	7♌	1♎	9♎	0♐	5♑	20♒	6♈	6♊	23♋	23♌	22♍	1♏
25	8♍	0♏	8♏	27♐	0♒	14♓	9♈	10♉	28♌	28♍	21♎	29♏
27	7♎	27♏	6♐	22♑	24♒	8♈	10♉	27♊	18♎	27♎	20♏	27♐
29	5♏		2♑	16♒	18♓	2♉	5♊	25♋	18♍	27♏	18♐	24♑
31	1♐		26♑		12♈		3♋	25♌		26♏		19♒

1914	Jan.	Feb.	Mar.	April	May	June	July	Aug.	Sep.	Oct.	Nov.	Dec.
1	1♓	15♈	23♈	8♊	12♋	2♍	11♎	4♐	26♑	1♓	16♈	19♉
3	25♓	9♉	17♉	3♋	8♌	0♎	9♏	2♑	21♒	25♓	10♉	13♊
5	19♈	3♊	11♊	27♋	6♍	29♎	8♐	29♑	16♓	19♈	19♊	7♋
7	13♉	29♊	7♋	27♌	5♎	29♏	6♑	25♒	11♈	13♉	13♋	1♌
9	8♊	26♋	4♌	24♍	5♏	28♐	4♒	20♓	4♉	7♊	7♌	22♌
11	4♋	25♌	3♍	27♍	5♐	26♑	0♓	14♈	28♉	1♌	18♍	25♍
13	2♌	25♍	3♎	27♎	4♑	22♒	24♓	8♉	22♊	26♌	15♎	23♎
15	1♍	24♎	3♏	27♏	1♒	16♓	18♈	2♊	18♋	22♍	14♏	23♏
17	29♍	22♏	2♐	22♐	26♒	10♈	12♉	27♊	14♌	21♎	14♐	23♐
19	28♎	20♐	0♑	17♑	20♓	4♉	6♊	22♋	13♍	21♏	15♑	22♑
21	26♏	16♑	26♑	12♒	14♈	28♉	2♋	20♌	13♎	21♐	14♒	19♒
23	23♐	11♒	20♒	6♓	8♉	23♊	28♋	19♍	13♏	21♑	11♓	15♓
25	19♑	6♓	14♓	29♓	2♊	19♋	25♌	18♎	12♐	19♒	7♈	10♈
27	15♒	29♓	8♈	23♈	27♊	16♌	23♍	17♐	9♑	16♓	1♉	3♉
29	9♓		2♉	17♉	22♋	13♍	22♎	15♑	6♒	10♈	25♉	27♉
31	3♈		26♉		19♌		20♏	12♒		4♉		21♊

🙲 *Horizontis recti, typus, & po-sitio.*

🙲 *Varietatis Finito-rum imago.*

1915	Jan.	Feb.	Mar.	April	May	June	July	Aug.	Sep.	Oct.	Nov.	Dec.
1	4 ♋	21 ♌	29 ♌	21 ♎	0 ♐	23 ♑	29 ♒	16 ♈	1 ♊	2 ♋	17 ♌	20 ♍
3	29 ♋	18 ♍	27 ♍	21 ♏	0 ♐	21 ♑	26 ♒	11 ♉	24 ♊	26 ♋	12 ♌	18 ♍
5	25 ♌	16 ♎	26 ♎	20 ♏	28 ♐	17 ♒	20 ♓	5 ♊	18 ♋	21 ♌	10 ♎	17 ♏
7	22 ♌	14 ♏	25 ♏	18 ♐	25 ♐	12 ♒	14 ♓	8 ♋	13 ♌	18 ♍	9 ♏	15 ♐
9	19 ♎	13 ♐	24 ♐	15 ♑	20 ♑	6 ♓	8 ♈	23 ♋	10 ♍	16 ♎	9 ♐	15 ♑
11	18 ♏	11 ♑	23 ♑	11 ♒	15 ♒	0 ♈	2 ♉	18 ♌	7 ♎	15 ♏	9 ♑	15 ♒
13	17 ♐	8 ♒	18 ♒	5 ♓	9 ♓	23 ♈	26 ♉	14 ♍	5 ♏	14 ♐	7 ♒	14 ♓
15	16 ♑	5 ♓	14 ♓	0 ♈	4 ♈	17 ♉	21 ♊	11 ♎	2 ♐	13 ♑	4 ♓	10 ♈
17	14 ♒	1 ♈	9 ♈	24 ♈	26 ♈	12 ♊	17 ♋	9 ♏	0 ♑	11 ♒	0 ♈	4 ♉
19	10 ♓	25 ♈	3 ♉	17 ♉	20 ♉	7 ♋	14 ♌	6 ♐	27 ♑	7 ♓	25 ♈	28 ♉
21	5 ♈	19 ♉	27 ♉	11 ♊	15 ♊	4 ♌	12 ♍	6 ♑	27 ♒	20 ♓	20 ♉	22 ♊
23	29 ♈	13 ♊	21 ♊	6 ♋	11 ♋	2 ♍	11 ♎	4 ♒	23 ♓	28 ♈	13 ♊	16 ♋
25	23 ♉	7 ♋	15 ♋	2 ♌	8 ♌	1 ♎	10 ♏	0 ♓	20 ♈	22 ♉	7 ♋	10 ♌
27	17 ♊	3 ♌	10 ♌	0 ♍	7 ♍	1 ♏	9 ♐	29 ♓	15 ♉	17 ♊	1 ♌	4 ♎
29	12 ♋		7 ♍	29 ♍	8 ♎	1 ♐	7 ♑	24 ♈	9 ♋	10 ♌	25 ♌	0 ♎
31	8 ♌		6 ♎		8 ♏		4 ♒	19 ♉		4 ♌		27 ♏

1916	Jan.	Feb.	Mar.	April	May	June	July	Aug.	Sep.	Oct.	Nov.	Dec.
1	11 ♏	4 ♑	28 ♑	20 ♒	26 ♈	12 ♊	15 ♋	29 ♌	16 ♎	23 ♏	15 ♑	24 ♒
3	10 ♐	4 ♒	27 ♒	17 ♓	21 ♉	6 ♋	8 ♌	24 ♍	20 ♏	20 ♐	14 ♒	22 ♓
5	11 ♑	3 ♓	25 ♓	13 ♈	16 ♊	0 ♌	2 ♍	19 ♎	10 ♐	19 ♑	12 ♓	19 ♈
7	11 ♒	29 ♓	22 ♈	7 ♉	9 ♋	23 ♌	27 ♍	16 ♏	8 ♑	17 ♒	9 ♈	15 ♉
9	9 ♓	27 ♈	17 ♉	2 ♊	3 ♌	18 ♍	23 ♎	14 ♐	7 ♒	15 ♓	6 ♉	11 ♊
11	6 ♈	22 ♉	12 ♊	25 ♊	27 ♌	14 ♎	20 ♏	13 ♑	6 ♓	11 ♈	2 ♊	5 ♋
13	1 ♉	16 ♊	5 ♋	22 ♋	22 ♍	11 ♏	19 ♐	13 ♒	3 ♈	8 ♉	27 ♊	29 ♋
15	25 ♉	9 ♋	29 ♋	14 ♌	19 ♎	11 ♐	19 ♑	13 ♓	0 ♉	2 ♊	21 ♋	22 ♌
17	19 ♊	3 ♌	24 ♌	9 ♍	17 ♏	11 ♑	20 ♒	11 ♈	26 ♉	26 ♊	14 ♌	16 ♍
19	13 ♋	28 ♌	19 ♍	9 ♏	17 ♐	11 ♒	19 ♓	8 ♉	20 ♊	23 ♋	8 ♍	11 ♎
21	7 ♌	23 ♍	16 ♎	8 ♐	17 ♑	10 ♓	16 ♈	3 ♊	17 ♋	18 ♌	3 ♎	7 ♏
23	1 ♍	20 ♎	14 ♏	9 ♑	16 ♒	7 ♈	12 ♉	27 ♊	11 ♌	13 ♍	0 ♏	5 ♐
25	27 ♍	17 ♏	12 ♐	5 ♒	13 ♓	2 ♉	6 ♊	21 ♋	5 ♍	9 ♎	5 ♐...	5 ♑
27	23 ♎	15 ♐	10 ♑	0 ♓	10 ♈	27 ♉	0 ♋	14 ♌	0 ♎	5 ♏	26 ♐	5 ♒
29	20 ♏	14 ♑	8 ♒	0 ♈	5 ♉	21 ♊	24 ♋	8 ♍	26 ♎		26 ♑	4 ♓
31	19 ♐		6 ♓		0 ♊		17 ♌	3 ♎		1 ♑		3 ♈

1917	Jan.	Feb.	Mar.	April	May	June	July	Aug.	Sep.	Oct.	Nov.	Dec.
1	16 ♈	4 ♊	13 ♊	28 ♋	29 ♌	14 ♎	18 ♏	7 ♑	1 ♓	9 ♈	1 ♊	6 ♋
3	12 ♉	29 ♊	8 ♋	21 ♌	23 ♍	10 ♏	15 ♐	7 ♒	1 ♈	9 ♉	28 ♊	1 ♌
5	7 ♊	22 ♋	1 ♌	15 ♍	18 ♎	7 ♐	14 ♑	7 ♓	7 ♉	23 ♊	23 ♋	25 ♌
7	2 ♋	16 ♌	25 ♌	10 ♎	14 ♏	5 ♑	13 ♒	7 ♈	2 ♊	17 ♋	17 ♌	19 ♍
9	26 ♋	10 ♍	19 ♍	5 ♏	12 ♐	4 ♒	13 ♓	5 ♉	27 ♊	11 ♌	11 ♍	13 ♎
11	19 ♌	4 ♎	13 ♎	2 ♐	9 ♑	3 ♓	12 ♈	2 ♊	21 ♋	5 ♍	5 ♎	7 ♏
13	13 ♍	29 ♎	9 ♏	29 ♐	7 ♒	1 ♈	9 ♉	27 ♊	15 ♌	29 ♍	3 ♏	3 ♐
15	7 ♎	24 ♏	5 ♐	27 ♑	6 ♓	28 ♈	5 ♊	21 ♋	9 ♍	25 ♎	0 ♐	28 ♐
17	2 ♏	22 ♐	3 ♑	25 ♒	4 ♈	25 ♉	0 ♋	15 ♌	0 ♎	21 ♏	26 ♐	25 ♑
19	29 ♏	21 ♑	0 ♒	24 ♓	2 ♉	21 ♊	24 ♋	9 ♍	24 ♎	18 ♐	0 ♒...	23 ♒
21	28 ♐	21 ♒	0 ♓	23 ♈	29 ♉	16 ♋	18 ♌	3 ♎	21 ♏	16 ♑	28 ♑	21 ♓
23	28 ♑	21 ♓	29 ♓	20 ♉	25 ♊	10 ♌	12 ♍	29 ♎	18 ♐	16 ♒	0 ♈	21 ♈
25	28 ♒	20 ♈	28 ♈	17 ♊	20 ♋	3 ♍	6 ♎	22 ♏	16 ♑	18 ♓	28 ♈	20 ♉
27	28 ♓	18 ♉	26 ♉	12 ♋	14 ♌	27 ♍	0 ♏	18 ♐	9 ♒	18 ♈	27 ♉	18 ♊
29	26 ♈		22 ♊	6 ♌	7 ♍	22 ♎	22 ♏	16 ♑	9 ♓	18 ♉	25 ♊	14 ♋
31	22 ♉		16 ♋		1 ♎		23 ♐	15 ♒		17 ♈		9 ♌

1918	Jan.	Feb.	Mar.	April	May	June	July	Aug.	Sep.	Oct.	Nov.	Dec.
1	21 ♌	5 ♎	13 ♎	29 ♏	3 ♑	24 ♒	4 ♈	27 ♉	17 ♍	21 ♎	7 ♑	9 ♒
3	15 ♍	29 ♎	7 ♏	24 ♐	0 ♒	2 ♓	2 ♉	24 ♊	12 ♎	16 ♏	0 ♒	3 ♓
5	8 ♎	23 ♏	2 ♐	20 ♑	28 ♒	21 ♓	0 ♊	20 ♋	7 ♏	10 ♐	24 ♒	28 ♓
7	3 ♏	19 ♐	27 ♐	18 ♒	27 ♓	20 ♈	27 ♊	15 ♌	1 ♐	3 ♑	18 ♓	23 ♈
9	28 ♏	16 ♑	24 ♑	17 ♓	26 ♈	16 ♉	22 ♋	10 ♍	24 ♐	13 ♒	13 ♈	19 ♉
11	25 ♐	16 ♒	24 ♒	18 ♈	26 ♉	16 ♊	19 ♌	4 ♎	18 ♑	21 ♓	9 ♉	17 ♊
13	24 ♑	16 ♓	24 ♓	18 ♉	24 ♊	14 ♋	14 ♎	28 ♎	12 ♒	16 ♈	6 ♊	14 ♋
15	22 ♒	16 ♈	25 ♈	16 ♊	21 ♋	6 ♍	9 ♏	22 ♐	13 ♓	12 ♉	5 ♋	13 ♌
17	20 ♓	14 ♉	22 ♉	13 ♋	16 ♌	2 ♎	2 ♐	16 ♑	12 ♈	5 ♊	4 ♌	13 ♍
19	20 ♈	11 ♊	21 ♊	8 ♌	10 ♍	24 ♎	26 ♐	11 ♒	12 ♉	5 ♋	4 ♍	12 ♎
21	18 ♉	7 ♋	16 ♋	2 ♍	4 ♎	18 ♏	21 ♑	11 ♓	12 ♊	4 ♌	4 ♎	9 ♏
23	14 ♊	2 ♌	11 ♌	25 ♍	28 ♎	13 ♐	16 ♒	10 ♈	10 ♋	12 ♌	1 ♏	5 ♐
25	10 ♋	26 ♌	5 ♍	19 ♎	22 ♏	8 ♑	16 ♓	9 ♉	10 ♌	6 ♍...	27 ♏	29 ♐
27	5 ♌	20 ♍	28 ♍	13 ♏	17 ♐	3 ♒	17 ♈	7 ♊	1 ♎	6 ♎	21 ♐	23 ♑
29	29 ♌		22 ♎	8 ♐	13 ♑	5 ♓	14 ♉	4 ♋	27 ♎	1 ♏	15 ♑	17 ♒
31	23 ♍		16 ♏		10 ♒		13 ♊	4 ♌		25 ♏		11 ♓

1919	Jan.	Feb.	Mar.	April	May	June	July	Aug.	Sep.	Oct.	Nov.	Dec.
1	24 ♐	12 ♒	20 ♒	12 ♈	21 ♉	13 ♋	19 ♌	6 ♎	20 ♏	22 ♑	7 ♒	11 ♓
3	19 ♑	10 ♓	19 ♓	12 ♉	20 ♊	11 ♌	16 ♍	0 ♏	14 ♐	16 ♒	3 ♓	9 ♈
5	16 ♒	8 ♈	18 ♈	12 ♊	19 ♋	7 ♍	10 ♎	24 ♏	8 ♑	11 ♓	0 ♈	8 ♉
7	14 ♓	7 ♉	17 ♉	10 ♋	15 ♌	2 ♎	4 ♏	18 ♐	3 ♒	8 ♈	0 ♉	8 ♊
9	12 ♈	5 ♊	16 ♊	6 ♌	11 ♍	26 ♎	28 ♏	12 ♑	0 ♓	6 ♉	0 ♊	7 ♋
11	10 ♉	2 ♋	13 ♋	2 ♍	6 ♎	20 ♏	22 ♐	8 ♒	27 ♓	6 ♊	0 ♋	5 ♌
13	8 ♊	29 ♋	9 ♌	26 ♍	29 ♎	13 ♐	17 ♑	5 ♓	26 ♈	6 ♋	29 ♋	1 ♍
15	7 ♋	25 ♌	4 ♍	20 ♎	23 ♏	8 ♑	12 ♒	3 ♈	26 ♉	5 ♌	26 ♌	25 ♍
17	4 ♌	21 ♍	29 ♍	14 ♏	16 ♐	2 ♒	9 ♓	2 ♉	25 ♊	5 ♍	21 ♍	19 ♎
19	0 ♍	15 ♎	23 ♎	7 ♐	11 ♑	29 ♒	6 ♈	29 ♉	22 ♋	29 ♍	16 ♎	12 ♏
21	25 ♍	9 ♏	17 ♏	1 ♑	6 ♒	24 ♓	4 ♉	25 ♊	18 ♌	25 ♎	4 ♐...	6 ♐
23	19 ♎	3 ♐	11 ♐	26 ♑	2 ♓	24 ♈	3 ♊	20 ♋	15 ♍	19 ♏	4 ♐	0 ♑
25	13 ♏	27 ♐	5 ♑	22 ♒	29 ♓	22 ♉	0 ♋	15 ♌	10 ♎	13 ♐	27 ♐	25 ♑
27	7 ♐	22 ♑	0 ♒	20 ♓	29 ♈	22 ♊	29 ♋	11 ♍	4 ♏	7 ♑	21 ♑	21 ♒
29	2 ♑		28 ♒	20 ♈	29 ♉	21 ♋	28 ♌	14 ♎	28 ♏	0 ♒	16 ♒	21 ♓
31	28 ♑		27 ♓		29 ♊		24 ♍	8 ♏		24 ♑		18 ♈

Horizontis obliqui pictura, & positio.

Horizontes mutari ab Aquilone in Austrū eundo, & contrà.

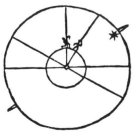

A table of the positions of the Sun in the zodiac, 1920–1924.

1920

	Jan.	Feb.	Mar.	April	May	June	July	Aug.	Sep.	Oct.	Nov.	Dec.
1	2 ♉	25 ♊	20 ♋	11 ♍	17 ♎	2 ♐	5 ♑	20 ♒	8 ♈	15 ♉	7 ♋	17 ♌
3	1 ♊	24 ♋	23 ♌	3 ♏	5 ♐	26 ♐	20 ♑	23 ♒	4 ♉	11 ♊	4 ♌	14 ♍
5	0 ♋	23 ♌	21 ♍	27 ♏	29 ♐	20 ♑	18 ♒	27 ♒	2 ♊	9 ♋	2 ♍	6 ♎
7	0 ♌	17 ♍	7 ♎	21 ♐	23 ♑	9 ♒	5 ♓	1 ♈	29 ♊	9 ♌	9 ♎	1 ♏
9	26 ♍	11 ♎	7 ♏	21 ♑	23 ♒	9 ♓	4 ♈	4 ♉	26 ♋	5 ♍	27 ♎	25 ♏
11	21 ♍	5 ♏	25 ♏	15 ♒	17 ♓	4 ♈	10 ♉	4 ♊	26 ♌	5 ♎	16 ♏	19 ♐
13	15 ♎	29 ♏	19 ♐	15 ♓	10 ♈	3 ♉	10 ♊	3 ♋	23 ♍	26 ♎	10 ♐	13 ♑
15	9 ♏	23 ♐	14 ♑	4 ♈	10 ♉	2 ♊	10 ♋	3 ♌	23 ♎	4 ♏	7 ♑	7 ♒
17	3 ♐	18 ♑	10 ♒	0 ♉	8 ♊	8 ♋	2 ♌	28 ♎	13 ♐	14 ♑	28 ♒	1 ♓
19	27 ♐	14 ♒	7 ♓	7 ♊	8 ♋	8 ♌	28 ♎	23 ♏	13 ♑	8 ♒	22 ♓	25 ♓
21	22 ♑	11 ♓	5 ♈	7 ♋	8 ♌	7 ♍	22 ♎	17 ♐	0 ♒	3 ♓	20 ♈	25 ♈
23	18 ♒	9 ♈	4 ♉	7 ♌	28 ♍	23 ♎	28 ♐	10 ♑	20 ♒	3 ♈	20 ♉	26 ♉
25	15 ♓	9 ♉	4 ♊	28 ♌	27 ♎	21 ♐	20 ♑	5 ♒	20 ♓	26 ♈	26 ♊	26 ♊
27	12 ♈	7 ♊	2 ♋	27 ♍	23 ♏	17 ♑	14 ♒	2 ♓	17 ♈	24 ♉	26 ♋	26 ♋
29	12 ♉	6 ♋	29 ♋	21 ♎	26 ♐	11 ♒	14 ♓	29 ♓	17 ♉	24 ♊	17 ♌	26 ♌
31	11 ♊		28 ♌		20 ♐		8 ♈	25 ♈		23 ♋		24 ♍

1921

	Jan.	Feb.	Mar.	April	May	June	July	Aug.	Sep.	Oct.	Nov.	Dec.
1	8 ♉	25 ♏	3 ♐	17 ♒	19 ♓	4 ♉	8 ♋	28 ♊	22 ♌	0 ♎	21 ♏	25 ♐
3	3 ♍	19 ♐	27 ♐	11 ♓	13 ♈	29 ♈	5 ♊	28 ♋	22 ♍	29 ♎	17 ♐	21 ♑
5	3 ♍	13 ♑	13 ♑	5 ♈	8 ♉	26 ♉	4 ♋	28 ♌	18 ♎	22 ♏	13 ♑	15 ♒
7	22 ♍	6 ♒	15 ♒	0 ♉	8 ♊	26 ♊	4 ♌	28 ♍	14 ♐	7 ♐	1 ♒	8 ♓
9	9 ♎	0 ♓	9 ♓	26 ♉	1 ♋	25 ♋	3 ♍	23 ♎	9 ♑	11 ♑	24 ♒	2 ♈
11	9 ♏	25 ♓	4 ♈	23 ♊	1 ♌	25 ♌	0 ♎	18 ♏	9 ♒	5 ♒	19 ♓	27 ♈
13	3 ♐	20 ♈	0 ♉	21 ♋	0 ♍	23 ♍	26 ♎	12 ♐	2 ♓	5 ♓	23 ♈	21 ♉
15	28 ♐	16 ♉	26 ♉	19 ♌	26 ♍	20 ♎	21 ♐	6 ♑	20 ♓	24 ♈	23 ♉	20 ♊
17	23 ♈	13 ♊	24 ♊	17 ♍	26 ♎	16 ♏	21 ♑	6 ♒	20 ♈	24 ♉	12 ♊	20 ♋
19	18 ♉	12 ♋	22 ♋	16 ♎	23 ♏	11 ♐	15 ♒	0 ♓	19 ♉	19 ♊	10 ♋	20 ♌
21	18 ♊	12 ♌	21 ♌	14 ♏	19 ♐	6 ♑	9 ♓	23 ♓	10 ♊	16 ♋	9 ♌	18 ♍
23	19 ♋	12 ♍	19 ♍	11 ♐	15 ♑	0 ♒	2 ♈	26 ♈	6 ♋	14 ♌	7 ♍	12 ♎
25	19 ♌	11 ♎	19 ♎	6 ♑	9 ♒	24 ♒	26 ♈	26 ♉	6 ♌	14 ♍	5 ♎	12 ♏
27	19 ♍	8 ♏	16 ♏	1 ♒	3 ♓	17 ♓	21 ♉	9 ♊	5 ♍	10 ♎	2 ♏	9 ♐
29	19 ♎		11 ♐	27 ♒	25 ♓	12 ♈	16 ♊	7 ♋	9 ♎	7 ♏	29 ♐	4 ♑
31	12 ♏		6 ♑		21 ♈		14 ♋	7 ♌		7 ♐		29 ♒

1922

	Jan.	Feb.	Mar.	April	May	June	July	Aug.	Sep.	Oct.	Nov.	Dec.
1	11 ♒	25 ♓	4 ♈	19 ♉	25 ♊	17 ♌	26 ♍	18 ♏	8 ♑	12 ♒	27 ♓	28 ♈
3	5 ♓	19 ♈	28 ♈	15 ♊	22 ♋	15 ♍	24 ♎	15 ♐	3 ♒	6 ♓	20 ♈	23 ♉
5	28 ♓	13 ♉	22 ♉	11 ♋	20 ♌	13 ♎	21 ♏	11 ♑	27 ♒	0 ♈	14 ♉	18 ♊
7	22 ♈	9 ♊	18 ♊	9 ♌	18 ♍	11 ♏	18 ♐	6 ♒	21 ♓	23 ♈	9 ♊	15 ♋
9	18 ♉	7 ♋	15 ♋	9 ♍	17 ♎	9 ♐	14 ♑	0 ♓	14 ♈	17 ♉	5 ♋	12 ♌
11	15 ♊	7 ♌	15 ♌	9 ♎	16 ♏	5 ♑	10 ♒	24 ♓	8 ♉	12 ♊	1 ♌	9 ♍
13	14 ♋	7 ♍	15 ♍	8 ♏	14 ♐	1 ♒	4 ♓	18 ♈	12 ♋	8 ♋	0 ♍	7 ♎
15	14 ♌	7 ♎	14 ♎	6 ♐	11 ♑	26 ♒	28 ♓	12 ♉	28 ♋	5 ♌	27 ♍	6 ♏
17	13 ♍	7 ♏	14 ♏	3 ♑	6 ♒	20 ♓	22 ♈	7 ♊	25 ♌	3 ♍	26 ♎	4 ♐
19	12 ♎	2 ♐	11 ♐	28 ♑	0 ♓	13 ♈	16 ♉	3 ♋	24 ♍	3 ♎	26 ♏	3 ♑
21	9 ♏	28 ♐	7 ♑	22 ♒	23 ♓	17 ♉	8 ♊	0 ♌	24 ♎	3 ♏	24 ♐	29 ♑
23	6 ♐	22 ♑	1 ♒	15 ♓	17 ♈	3 ♊	8 ♋	0 ♍	24 ♏	0 ♐	22 ♑	19 ♒
25	1 ♑	16 ♒	25 ♒	9 ♈	12 ♉	8 ♋	0 ♌	0 ♎	24 ♐	26 ♑	17 ♒	13 ♓
27	25 ♑	10 ♓	19 ♓	4 ♉	8 ♊	8 ♌	29 ♌	0 ♏	22 ♑	21 ♒	13 ♓	9 ♈
29	19 ♒		13 ♈	29 ♉	8 ♋	6 ♍	29 ♍	18 ♐	18 ♒	15 ♓	5 ♈	6 ♉
31	13 ♓		7 ♉		3 ♌		25 ♐			15 ♈		6 ♊

1923

	Jan.	Feb.	Mar.	April	May	June	July	Aug.	Sep.	Oct.	Nov.	Dec.
1	14 ♊	2 ♌	10 ♌	2 ♎	11 ♏	4 ♑	10 ♒	26 ♓	10 ♉	12 ♊	27 ♋	3 ♍
3	10 ♋	1 ♍	9 ♍	3 ♏	11 ♐	2 ♒	6 ♓	20 ♈	4 ♊	6 ♋	23 ♌	0 ♎
5	8 ♌	28 ♍	0 ♎	3 ♐	10 ♑	0 ♓	0 ♈	14 ♉	28 ♊	1 ♌	20 ♍	29 ♎
7	6 ♍	28 ♎	9 ♎	1 ♑	6 ♒	22 ♓	24 ♈	8 ♊	20 ♋	20 ♌	20 ♎	29 ♏
9	4 ♎	27 ♏	9 ♏	28 ♑	0 ♓	16 ♈	18 ♉	3 ♋	20 ♌	19 ♍	21 ♏	29 ♐
11	2 ♏	24 ♐	5 ♐	22 ♒	25 ♓	9 ♉	12 ♊	29 ♋	19 ♍	21 ♎	21 ♐	28 ♑
13	0 ♐	21 ♑	1 ♑	17 ♓	19 ♈	4 ♊	7 ♋	26 ♌	18 ♎	27 ♏	20 ♑	21 ♒
15	25 ♐	16 ♒	20 ♒	10 ♈	13 ♉	0 ♋	3 ♌	24 ♍	18 ♏	27 ♐	15 ♒	15 ♓
17	20 ♑	11 ♓	20 ♓	4 ♉	7 ♊	23 ♋	0 ♍	24 ♎	24 ♐	12 ♑	15 ♓	9 ♈
19	20 ♒	5 ♈	7 ♈	2 ♊	20 ♋	28 ♌	27 ♍	24 ♏	10 ♑	15 ♒	9 ♈	2 ♊
21	15 ♓	28 ♈	7 ♉	22 ♊	27 ♌	17 ♍	25 ♎	23 ♐	10 ♒	0 ♓	9 ♉	21 ♊
23	9 ♈	22 ♉	1 ♊	23 ♋	23 ♍	15 ♎	25 ♏	17 ♑	4 ♓	9 ♈	18 ♊	21 ♋
25	2 ♉	17 ♊	25 ♊	23 ♌	14 ♎	15 ♏	23 ♐	11 ♒	29 ♓	18 ♉	21 ♋	21 ♌
27	26 ♉	13 ♋	21 ♋	13 ♍	14 ♏	14 ♐	21 ♑	5 ♓	24 ♈	27 ♊	21 ♌	13 ♍
29	22 ♊		18 ♌	13 ♎	20 ♐	14 ♑	18 ♒	29 ♓	2 ♉	27 ♋	13 ♍	13 ♎
31	18 ♋		17 ♍		19 ♑		13 ♓	28 ♈		15 ♌		10 ♏

1924

	Jan.	Feb.	Mar.	April	May	June	July	Aug.	Sep.	Oct.	Nov.	Dec.
1	24 ♎	17 ♐	12 ♑	3 ♓	7 ♈	23 ♉	25 ♊	11 ♌	29 ♍	6 ♏	0 ♑	8 ♒
3	23 ♏	16 ♑	10 ♒	28 ♓	2 ♉	16 ♊	19 ♋	6 ♍	26 ♎	5 ♐	28 ♑	6 ♓
5	22 ♐	14 ♒	6 ♓	23 ♈	26 ♉	10 ♋	14 ♌	2 ♎	24 ♏	4 ♑	26 ♒	2 ♈
7	21 ♑	11 ♓	27 ♓	17 ♉	19 ♊	4 ♌	9 ♍	22 ♎	22 ♐	2 ♒	22 ♓	27 ♈
9	20 ♒	6 ♈	27 ♈	11 ♊	12 ♋	29 ♌	5 ♎	21 ♏	21 ♑	29 ♒	18 ♈	22 ♉
11	16 ♓	1 ♉	21 ♉	5 ♋	7 ♌	25 ♍	3 ♏	16 ♐	19 ♒	25 ♓	12 ♉	15 ♊
13	11 ♈	7 ♉	15 ♊	9 ♌	3 ♍	21 ♎	1 ♐	16 ♑	13 ♓	21 ♈	7 ♊	9 ♋
15	5 ♉	3 ♊	8 ♋	10 ♍	0 ♎	22 ♏	1 ♑	24 ♒	16 ♈	16 ♉	3 ♋	3 ♌
17	29 ♉	3 ♋	3 ♌	0 ♎	20 ♎	29 ♐	21 ♑	17 ♓	2 ♉	11 ♊	22 ♋	22 ♌
19	23 ♊	9 ♌	0 ♍	29 ♎	23 ♏	29 ♑	23 ♓	23 ♈	26 ♊	4 ♋	22 ♌	13 ♍
21	18 ♋	9 ♍	28 ♍	21 ♏	29 ♐	29 ♒	22 ♓	22 ♉	20 ♋	28 ♌	13 ♍	18 ♎
23	12 ♌	7 ♎	25 ♎	21 ♐	29 ♑	18 ♓	22 ♈	6 ♊	20 ♌	22 ♍	10 ♎	16 ♏
25	10 ♍	5 ♏	26 ♏	19 ♑	26 ♒	14 ♈	16 ♉	0 ♋	15 ♍	18 ♎	8 ♏	16 ♐
27	7 ♎	2 ♐	23 ♐	19 ♒	19 ♓	8 ♉	2 ♊	24 ♋	15 ♎	10 ♏	8 ♐	17 ♑
29	5 ♏	28 ♐	23 ♑	12 ♓	17 ♈	2 ♊	4 ♋	19 ♌	8 ♐	15 ♐	8 ♑	17 ♒
31	3 ♐		20 ♒		11 ♉		28 ♋	15 ♍		15 ♑		15 ♓

1925	Jan.	Feb.	Mar.	April	May	June	July	Aug.	Sep.	Oct.	Nov.	Dec.
1	28 ♓	15 ♉	23 ♉	7 ♋	9 ♌	23 ♍	28 ♎	19 ♐	13 ♒	21 ♓	12 ♉	16 ♊
3	24 ♈	9 ♊	17 ♊	1 ♌	26 ♌	11 ♎	25 ♏	19 ♑	12 ♓	19 ♈	8 ♊	10 ♋
5	19 ♉	3 ♋	11 ♋	25 ♌	28 ♍	18 ♏	25 ♐	19 ♒	11 ♈	17 ♉	2 ♋	4 ♌
7	12 ♊	27 ♋	5 ♌	20 ♍	20 ♎	16 ♐	25 ♑	19 ♓	9 ♉	12 ♊	26 ♋	28 ♌
9	6 ♋	21 ♌	29 ♌	17 ♎	17 ♏	16 ♑	17 ♒	17 ♈	4 ♊	7 ♋	20 ♌	22 ♍
11	0 ♌	16 ♍	25 ♍	15 ♏	16 ♐	17 ♒	24 ♓	13 ♉	29 ♊	1 ♌	14 ♍	17 ♎
13	24 ♌	11 ♎	21 ♎	13 ♐	17 ♑	22 ♓	8 ♈	8 ♊	22 ♋	24 ♌	9 ♎	13 ♏
15	19 ♍	8 ♏	19 ♏	12 ♑	21 ♒	21 ♈	17 ♉	2 ♋	16 ♌	19 ♍	6 ♏	11 ♐
17	14 ♎	6 ♐	16 ♐	10 ♒	9 ♓	2 ♉	11 ♊	26 ♋	10 ♍	14 ♎	3 ♐	10 ♑
19	11 ♏	4 ♑	15 ♑	7 ♓	15 ♈	2 ♊	5 ♋	19 ♌	5 ♎	11 ♏	3 ♑	11 ♒
21	10 ♐	5 ♒	13 ♒	1 ♈	26 ♈	26 ♊	29 ♋	14 ♍	2 ♏	8 ♐	5 ♒	10 ♓
23	10 ♑	3 ♓	11 ♓	1 ♉	5 ♊	20 ♋	22 ♌	9 ♎	1 ♐	8 ♑	4 ♓	7 ♈
25	9 ♒	28 ♓	7 ♈	27 ♉	13 ♊	13 ♌	16 ♍	4 ♏	1 ♑	6 ♒	4 ♈	4 ♉
27	9 ♓	—	6 ♉	21 ♊	23 ♋	7 ♍	11 ♎	1 ♐	23 ♑	4 ♓	24 ♈	0 ♊
29	7 ♈	—	1 ♊	15 ♋	17 ♌	2 ♎	7 ♏	29 ♐	22 ♒	0 ♈	20 ♉	25 ♊
31	3 ♉	—	25 ♊	—	11 ♍	—	5 ♐	28 ♑	—	28 ♈	—	19 ♋

1926	Jan.	Feb.	Mar.	April	May	June	July	Aug.	Sep.	Oct.	Nov.	Dec.
1	1 ♌	15 ♍	24 ♍	10 ♏	17 ♐	9 ♒	18 ♓	10 ♉	29 ♊	2 ♌	16 ♍	18 ♎
3	24 ♌	9 ♎	18 ♎	7 ♐	14 ♑	7 ♓	16 ♈	7 ♊	23 ♋	26 ♌	10 ♎	13 ♏
5	18 ♍	4 ♏	13 ♏	5 ♑	14 ♒	3 ♈	2 ♉	0 ♋	17 ♌	20 ♍	5 ♏	9 ♐
7	12 ♎	0 ♐	9 ♐	3 ♒	10 ♓	5 ♉	10 ♊	26 ♋	11 ♍	14 ♎	0 ♐	9 ♑
9	8 ♏	28 ♐	6 ♑	1 ♓	7 ♈	9 ♊	26 ♋	20 ♌	5 ♎	9 ♏	28 ♐	9 ♒
11	5 ♐	27 ♑	6 ♒	29 ♓	7 ♉	26 ♊	0 ♌	14 ♍	29 ♎	3 ♐	23 ♑	10 ♓
13	4 ♑	28 ♒	6 ♓	26 ♈	8 ♊	21 ♋	24 ♌	8 ♎	29 ♏	20 ♐	0 ♒	0 ♈
15	4 ♒	28 ♓	5 ♈	26 ♉	1 ♋	15 ♌	18 ♍	2 ♏	24 ♐	29 ♑	18 ♓	9 ♈
17	4 ♓	27 ♈	5 ♉	23 ♊	25 ♋	9 ♍	11 ♎	27 ♏	24 ♑	19 ♒	18 ♈	26 ♈
19	3 ♈	23 ♉	2 ♊	17 ♋	19 ♌	2 ♎	6 ♏	22 ♐	15 ♒	24 ♈	15 ♉	19 ♊
21	1 ♉	19 ♊	27 ♊	11 ♌	13 ♍	28 ♎	2 ♐	22 ♑	15 ♓	23 ♉	11 ♊	14 ♋
23	27 ♉	13 ♋	21 ♋	5 ♍	7 ♎	24 ♏	29 ♐	22 ♒	15 ♈	23 ♊	6 ♋	8 ♌
25	22 ♊	6 ♌	15 ♌	29 ♍	3 ♏	21 ♐	28 ♑	22 ♓	15 ♉	16 ♋	0 ♌	2 ♍
27	16 ♋	0 ♍	9 ♍	24 ♎	29 ♏	20 ♑	29 ♒	22 ♈	12 ♊	11 ♌	1 ♎	26 ♍
29	9 ♌	—	3 ♎	20 ♏	28 ♐	20 ♒	20 ♓	20 ♉	7 ♋	5 ♍	—	26 ♎
31	3 ♍	—	28 ♎	—	24 ♑	—	16 ♈	8 ♊	—	5 ♎	—	21 ♏

1927	Jan.	Feb.	Mar.	April	May	June	July	Aug.	Sep.	Oct.	Nov.	Dec.
1	4 ♐	23 ♑	0 ♒	23 ♓	2 ♉	24 ♊	0 ♌	16 ♍	0 ♏	2 ♐	18 ♑	24 ♒
3	1 ♑	22 ♒	0 ♓	21 ♈	10 ♉	17 ♋	25 ♌	26 ♎	18 ♐	14 ♑	14 ♒	20 ♓
5	29 ♑	22 ♓	0 ♈	22 ♉	2 ♊	27 ♋	13 ♍	3 ♏	18 ♐	22 ♑	12 ♓	20 ♈
7	28 ♒	21 ♈	0 ♉	18 ♊	27 ♊	6 ♌	13 ♎	22 ♐	11 ♑	18 ♒	11 ♈	20 ♉
9	26 ♓	19 ♉	29 ♉	13 ♋	21 ♋	6 ♍	2 ♎	19 ♑	11 ♓	18 ♓	12 ♉	18 ♊
11	25 ♈	16 ♊	26 ♊	6 ♌	15 ♌	29 ♍	2 ♐	19 ♒	10 ♈	18 ♈	12 ♊	18 ♋
13	22 ♉	12 ♋	20 ♋	1 ♍	3 ♎	19 ♎	24 ♐	16 ♓	10 ♉	7 ♉	11 ♋	11 ♌
15	19 ♊	7 ♌	16 ♌	1 ♎	1 ♏	19 ♐	24 ♑	16 ♈	10 ♊	7 ♊	5 ♌	5 ♍
17	15 ♋	1 ♍	9 ♍	1 ♏	1 ♐	3 ♑	20 ♒	14 ♉	6 ♋	9 ♋	0 ♍	29 ♍
19	10 ♌	25 ♍	4 ♎	18 ♏	22 ♐	12 ♒	10 ♓	9 ♊	6 ♌	11 ♌	27 ♍	29 ♎
21	4 ♍	19 ♎	21 ♎	8 ♑	15 ♑	18 ♓	10 ♈	12 ♋	1 ♎	6 ♍	8 ♎	23 ♏
23	28 ♍	12 ♏	16 ♏	5 ♒	13 ♒	15 ♈	17 ♉	2 ♌	26 ♎	24 ♎	4 ♏	17 ♐
25	22 ♎	7 ♐	12 ♐	5 ♓	13 ♓	7 ♉	15 ♊	29 ♌	21 ♏	4 ♐	8 ♐	12 ♑
27	16 ♏	3 ♑	9 ♑	2 ♈	11 ♈	8 ♊	8 ♋	4 ♍	15 ♐	11 ♑	5 ♒	8 ♒
29	12 ♐	—	9 ♒	2 ♉	11 ♉	3 ♋	8 ♌	24 ♍	11 ♑	1 ♒	28 ♒	5 ♓
31	8 ♑	—	8 ♓	—	10 ♊	—	3 ♍	18 ♎	—	5 ♓	—	2 ♈

1928	Jan.	Feb.	Mar.	April	May	June	July	Aug.	Sep.	Oct.	Nov.	Dec.
1	16 ♈	9 ♊	4 ♋	24 ♌	28 ♍	13 ♏	15 ♐	1 ♒	20 ♓	28 ♈	21 ♊	29 ♋
3	15 ♉	7 ♋	1 ♌	19 ♍	22 ♎	7 ♐	9 ♑	27 ♒	18 ♈	24 ♉	20 ♋	27 ♌
5	14 ♊	3 ♌	13 ♌	13 ♎	17 ♏	3 ♑	0 ♒	24 ♓	18 ♉	24 ♊	18 ♌	23 ♍
7	12 ♋	28 ♌	22 ♍	7 ♏	10 ♐	25 ♑	22 ♒	23 ♈	14 ♊	24 ♋	14 ♍	18 ♎
9	10 ♌	26 ♍	11 ♍	25 ♐	17 ♑	25 ♒	20 ♓	13 ♉	9 ♋	20 ♌	9 ♎	12 ♏
11	6 ♍	21 ♎	4 ♎	25 ♐	28 ♑	17 ♓	25 ♈	23 ♊	5 ♌	10 ♍	3 ♏	6 ♐
13	1 ♎	14 ♏	4 ♏	4 ♑	19 ♒	15 ♈	23 ♉	17 ♋	0 ♎	27 ♍	29 ♏	29 ♐
15	25 ♎	8 ♐	14 ♐	12 ♒	20 ♓	13 ♉	22 ♊	12 ♌	28 ♎	6 ♎	23 ♐	23 ♑
17	19 ♏	3 ♑	12 ♑	10 ♓	20 ♈	9 ♊	16 ♋	6 ♍	0 ♐	23 ♎	18 ♑	13 ♒
19	13 ♐	26 ♑	18 ♒	7 ♈	20 ♉	12 ♋	2 ♌	29 ♍	18 ♐	4 ♐	8 ♒	13 ♓
21	7 ♑	26 ♒	18 ♓	2 ♉	17 ♊	9 ♌	7 ♍	24 ♎	18 ♑	14 ♑	0 ♈	6 ♈
23	1 ♒	24 ♓	18 ♈	10 ♊	11 ♋	6 ♍	20 ♎	19 ♏	9 ♒	3 ♒	29 ♈	7 ♉
25	1 ♓	22 ♈	18 ♉	10 ♋	5 ♌	0 ♎	14 ♏	14 ♐	9 ♓	8 ♓	29 ♉	7 ♊
27	29 ♓	18 ♉	17 ♊	8 ♌	28 ♌	24 ♎	9 ♐	9 ♑	1 ♈	6 ♈	29 ♊	7 ♋
29	25 ♈	20 ♊	11 ♋	1 ♍	22 ♍	18 ♏	6 ♑	9 ♒	—	6 ♉	—	7 ♌
31	25 ♉	—	11 ♌	—	1 ♎	—	6 ♒	6 ♓	—	6 ♊	—	6 ♍

1929	Jan.	Feb.	Mar.	April	May	June	July	Aug.	Sep.	Oct.	Nov.	Dec.
1	19 ♍	5 ♏	13 ♏	27 ♐	28 ♑	14 ♓	19 ♈	10 ♊	4 ♌	12 ♍	2 ♏	6 ♐
3	15 ♎	29 ♏	7 ♐	22 ♑	10 ♒	10 ♈	11 ♉	10 ♋	3 ♍	10 ♎	28 ♏	0 ♑
5	9 ♏	23 ♐	1 ♑	15 ♒	10 ♓	10 ♉	11 ♊	10 ♌	0 ♎	6 ♏	22 ♐	24 ♑
7	3 ♐	16 ♑	25 ♑	10 ♓	7 ♈	14 ♊	8 ♋	6 ♍	27 ♎	1 ♐	16 ♑	18 ♒
9	26 ♐	11 ♒	19 ♒	7 ♈	14 ♉	8 ♋	16 ♌	0 ♎	24 ♏	7 ♑	10 ♒	12 ♓
11	20 ♑	7 ♓	15 ♓	6 ♉	14 ♊	8 ♌	15 ♍	24 ♎	18 ♐	20 ♑	4 ♓	12 ♈
13	15 ♒	0 ♈	15 ♈	4 ♊	12 ♋	3 ♍	7 ♎	18 ♏	22 ♑	0 ♒	4 ♈	8 ♉
15	10 ♓	0 ♈	10 ♉	4 ♋	6 ♌	27 ♍	1 ♏	22 ♐	6 ♒	26 ♒	4 ♉	2 ♊
17	6 ♈	28 ♈	7 ♊	0 ♌	0 ♍	20 ♎	22 ♏	26 ♐	4 ♓	4 ♈	2 ♊	28 ♊
19	3 ♉	27 ♉	7 ♋	29 ♌	22 ♍	25 ♐	19 ♐	22 ♑	26 ♈	4 ♉	23 ♋	2 ♌
21	1 ♊	23 ♊	5 ♌	1 ♍	1 ♏	16 ♑	19 ♒	4 ♒	29 ♉	23 ♊	2 ♌	2 ♍
23	1 ♋	24 ♋	3 ♍	21 ♏	0 ♐	7 ♑	17 ♓	22 ♈	29 ♋	23 ♋	16 ♍	26 ♍
25	0 ♌	21 ♌	0 ♎	17 ♏	4 ♑	3 ♓	20 ♈	17 ♉	27 ♌	22 ♌	11 ♎	20 ♎
27	27 ♌	18 ♍	26 ♎	19 ♐	7 ♑	29 ♓	20 ♉	15 ♊	22 ♍	19 ♍	16 ♏	15 ♐
29	23 ♍	—	21 ♏	5 ♑	23 ♒	29 ♈	20 ♊	13 ♋	—	5 ♎	11 ♐	9 ♑
31	23 ♎	—	15 ♐	—	1 ♓	—	26 ♋	19 ♌	—	19 ♏	—	9 ♒

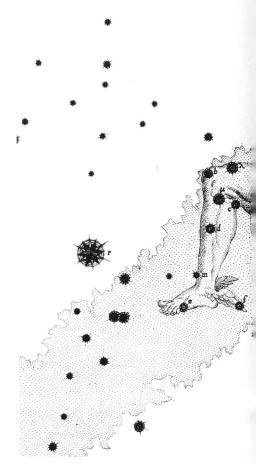

1930

	Jan.	Feb.	Mar.	April	May	June	July	Aug.	Sep.	Oct.	Nov.	Dec.
1	21 ♑	6 ♓	15 ♓	1 ♉	8 ♊	1 ♌	10 ♍	2 ♏	19 ♐	22 ♑	6 ♓	8 ♈
3	15 ♒	0 ♈	9 ♈	28 ♉	6 ♋	0 ♍	8 ♍	28 ♏	2 ♑	16 ♒	0 ♈	29 ♈
5	8 ♓	25 ♈	5 ♉	25 ♊	4 ♌	28 ♍	5 ♏	23 ♐	8 ♒	10 ♓	25 ♈	27 ♉
7	3 ♈	21 ♉	1 ♊	23 ♋	3 ♍	25 ♎	1 ♐	17 ♑	25 ♒	4 ♈	21 ♉	25 ♊
9	28 ♈	19 ♊	28 ♊	22 ♌	1 ♎	21 ♏	25 ♐	11 ♒	4 ♓	29 ♈	17 ♊	25 ♋
11	26 ♉	18 ♋	27 ♋	21 ♍	28 ♎	16 ♐	20 ♑	4 ♓	14 ♈	28 ♉	16 ♋	22 ♌
13	25 ♊	18 ♌	27 ♌	18 ♎	25 ♏	11 ♑	14 ♒	28 ♓	22 ♈	20 ♊	16 ♌	20 ♍
15	25 ♋	19 ♍	27 ♍	16 ♏	20 ♐	5 ♒	7 ♓	22 ♈	10 ♊	18 ♋	14 ♍	16 ♎
17	26 ♌	17 ♎	25 ♎	12 ♐	15 ♑	29 ♒	1 ♈	18 ♉	8 ♋	7 ♌	10 ♎	14 ♏
19	25 ♍	14 ♏	22 ♏	7 ♑	9 ♒	23 ♓	26 ♈	14 ♊	7 ♌	16 ♍	8 ♏	11 ♐
21	22 ♎	9 ♐	17 ♐	1 ♒	3 ♓	17 ♈	22 ♉	13 ♋	6 ♍	6 ♎	5 ♐	6 ♑
23	18 ♏	3 ♑	11 ♑	25 ♒	27 ♓	13 ♉	19 ♊	13 ♌	6 ♎	13 ♏	4 ♑	0 ♒
25	12 ♐	27 ♑	5 ♒	19 ♓	22 ♈	11 ♊	19 ♋	13 ♍	5 ♏	13 ♐	0 ♒	22 ♒
27	6 ♑	20 ♒	29 ♒	14 ♈	19 ♉	11 ♋	20 ♌	13 ♎	2 ♐	6 ♑	20 ♒	22 ♓
29	0 ♒		23 ♓	10 ♉	19 ♊	11 ♌	20 ♍	11 ♏	28 ♐	1 ♒	14 ♓	16 ♈
31	24 ♒		18 ♈		16 ♋		18 ♎	7 ♐		24 ♒		11 ♉

1931

	Jan.	Feb.	Mar.	April	May	June	July	Aug.	Sep.	Oct.	Nov.	Dec.
1	24 ♉	13 ♋	21 ♋	14 ♍	23 ♎	15 ♐	20 ♑	6 ♓	20 ♈	22 ♉	9 ♋	16 ♌
3	21 ♊	13 ♌	21 ♌	15 ♎	22 ♏	12 ♑	15 ♒	29 ♓	13 ♉	17 ♊	6 ♌	14 ♍
5	20 ♋	13 ♍	21 ♍	14 ♏	20 ♐	7 ♒	9 ♓	23 ♈	8 ♊	10 ♋	2 ♍	11 ♎
7	19 ♌	13 ♎	21 ♎	12 ♐	17 ♑	1 ♓	3 ♈	17 ♉	4 ♋	10 ♌	2 ♎	9 ♏
9	19 ♍	11 ♏	20 ♏	8 ♑	11 ♒	25 ♓	27 ♈	12 ♊	1 ♌	9 ♍	2 ♏	9 ♐
11	17 ♎	7 ♐	17 ♐	3 ♒	5 ♓	19 ♈	21 ♉	8 ♋	1 ♍	9 ♎	2 ♐	5 ♑
13	14 ♏	3 ♑	12 ♑	27 ♒	29 ♓	13 ♉	16 ♊	7 ♌	1 ♎	8 ♏	1 ♑	1 ♒
15	10 ♐	27 ♑	6 ♒	21 ♓	23 ♈	9 ♊	13 ♋	7 ♍	1 ♏	8 ♐	27 ♑	25 ♒
17	6 ♑	21 ♒	0 ♓	14 ♈	18 ♉	6 ♋	13 ♌	7 ♎	0 ♐	6 ♑	23 ♒	25 ♓
19	0 ♒	15 ♓	24 ♓	9 ♉	13 ♊	4 ♌	13 ♍	7 ♏	27 ♐	20 ♑	17 ♓	12 ♈
21	25 ♒	9 ♈	18 ♈	4 ♊	10 ♋	2 ♍	13 ♎	4 ♐	23 ♑	26 ♒	10 ♈	8 ♉
23	18 ♓	3 ♉	13 ♉	2 ♋	8 ♌	0 ♎	11 ♏	0 ♑	17 ♒	14 ♓	28 ♈	7 ♊
25	12 ♈	27 ♉	7 ♊	27 ♋	5 ♍	28 ♎	7 ♐	26 ♑	11 ♓	4 ♈	24 ♉	7 ♋
27	6 ♉	23 ♊	3 ♋	25 ♌	4 ♎	26 ♏	29 ♑	14 ♈	5 ♈	27 ♈	20 ♊	7 ♌
29	1 ♊		0 ♌	24 ♍	2 ♏	24 ♐	29 ♒	14 ♓	27 ♈	27 ♉	22 ♋	27 ♌
31	29 ♊		0 ♍		1 ♐		24 ♓	8 ♈		27 ♊		25 ♍

1932

	Jan.	Feb.	Mar.	April	May	June	July	Aug.	Sep.	Oct.	Nov.	Dec.
1	9 ♎	2 ♐	26 ♐	15 ♒	19 ♓	3 ♉	5 ♊	21 ♌	11 ♎	18 ♏	12 ♑	18 ♒
3	7 ♏	29 ♐	22 ♑	10 ♓	13 ♈	27 ♉	0 ♋	18 ♍	9 ♏	18 ♐	11 ♒	14 ♓
5	5 ♐	26 ♑	18 ♒	4 ♈	6 ♉	21 ♊	26 ♋	15 ♎	8 ♐	16 ♑	5 ♓	8 ♈
7	3 ♑	20 ♒	12 ♓	21 ♈	27 ♉	16 ♋	24 ♌	14 ♏	5 ♑	12 ♒	29 ♓	2 ♉
9	0 ♒	16 ♓	7 ♈	21 ♉	24 ♊	12 ♌	19 ♍	5 ♐	8 ♒	23 ♓	9 ♈	26 ♉
11	26 ♒	4 ♈	0 ♉	9 ♊	15 ♋	6 ♍	15 ♎	8 ♑	2 ♈	8 ♈	16 ♉	20 ♊
13	20 ♓	4 ♉	24 ♉	9 ♋	15 ♌	6 ♎	15 ♏	8 ♒	28 ♈	0 ♈	16 ♊	14 ♋
15	14 ♈	28 ♉	18 ♊	5 ♌	12 ♍	3 ♏	14 ♐	6 ♓	23 ♈	26 ♈	16 ♋	8 ♌
17	8 ♉	23 ♊	13 ♋	2 ♍	9 ♎	1 ♐	10 ♑	27 ♓	12 ♉	14 ♉	9 ♌	4 ♍
19	2 ♊	19 ♋	10 ♌	2 ♎	7 ♏	4 ♑	10 ♒	27 ♈	12 ♊	16 ♊	4 ♍	9 ♎
21	28 ♊	17 ♌	9 ♍	2 ♏	7 ♐	3 ♒	10 ♓	15 ♉	29 ♊	3 ♋	28 ♍	29 ♎
23	24 ♋	16 ♍	9 ♎	2 ♐	7 ♑	0 ♓	24 ♓	9 ♊	26 ♋	27 ♋	22 ♎	28 ♏
25	21 ♌	15 ♎	8 ♏	3 ♑	3 ♒	24 ♓	18 ♈	4 ♋	21 ♌	21 ♌	20 ♏	28 ♐
27	21 ♍	14 ♏	8 ♐	29 ♑	3 ♓	18 ♈	12 ♉	0 ♌	21 ♍	21 ♍	20 ♐	28 ♑
29	20 ♎	12 ♐	6 ♑	24 ♒	27 ♓	11 ♉	8 ♊	29 ♌	19 ♍	19 ♍	20 ♐	28 ♒
31	18 ♏		2 ♒		21 ♈		8 ♋	27 ♌		27 ♍		26 ♓

1933

	Jan.	Feb.	Mar.	April	May	June	July	Aug.	Sep.	Oct.	Nov.	Dec.
1	9 ♓	25 ♈	2 ♉	16 ♊	18 ♋	4 ♍	10 ♎	2 ♐	26 ♑	4 ♓	23 ♎	27 ♐
3	5 ♈	19 ♉	26 ♉	10 ♋	13 ♌	0 ♎	8 ♏	1 ♑	24 ♒	1 ♈	18 ♏	21 ♑
5	29 ♈	12 ♊	20 ♊	4 ♌	8 ♍	29 ♎	7 ♐	0 ♒	19 ♓	22 ♈	12 ♐	14 ♒
7	22 ♉	7 ♋	14 ♋	0 ♍	6 ♎	28 ♏	7 ♑	0 ♓	14 ♈	16 ♉	6 ♑	9 ♓
9	16 ♊	1 ♌	8 ♌	27 ♍	5 ♏	29 ♐	6 ♒	26 ♓	8 ♉	10 ♊	0 ♒	27 ♓
11	11 ♋	27 ♌	6 ♍	27 ♎	5 ♐	29 ♑	6 ♓	23 ♈	8 ♊	10 ♋	24 ♒	27 ♈
13	6 ♌	24 ♍	3 ♎	26 ♏	4 ♑	26 ♒	3 ♈	26 ♉	26 ♊	28 ♋	16 ♓	23 ♉
15	1 ♍	20 ♎	2 ♏	26 ♐	4 ♒	22 ♓	28 ♈	22 ♊	6 ♋	20 ♌	10 ♈	23 ♊
17	28 ♍	19 ♏	1 ♐	24 ♑	1 ♓	18 ♈	13 ♉	16 ♋	20 ♌	24 ♍	15 ♉	23 ♋
19	25 ♎	19 ♐	27 ♑	21 ♒	27 ♓	11 ♉	7 ♊	11 ♌	13 ♍	21 ♎	15 ♊	23 ♌
21	23 ♏	17 ♑	27 ♑	17 ♓	22 ♈	7 ♊	1 ♋	9 ♍	15 ♎	15 ♏	23 ♊	21 ♍
23	23 ♐	15 ♒	24 ♒	12 ♈	16 ♉	0 ♋	0 ♎	17 ♎	15 ♐	11 ♑	23 ♋	21 ♎
25	22 ♑	12 ♓	20 ♓	7 ♉	10 ♊	24 ♋	28 ♎	15 ♏	19 ♑	17 ♒	11 ♍	11 ♏
27	20 ♒	8 ♈	16 ♈	1 ♊	3 ♋	18 ♌	15 ♐	8 ♑	17 ♒	17 ♓	7 ♎	6 ♐
29	17 ♓		10 ♉	25 ♊	27 ♋	13 ♍	18 ♑	11 ♒	13 ♈	14 ♈	2 ♏	29 ♐
31	12 ♈		4 ♊		22 ♌		18 ♏	11 ♓		10 ♈		29 ♑

1934

	Jan.	Feb.	Mar.	April	May	June	July	Aug.	Sep.	Oct.	Nov.	Dec.
1	11 ♋	26 ♌	5 ♍	22 ♎	29 ♏	23 ♑	1 ♓	23 ♈	10 ♊	12 ♋	26 ♌	28 ♍
3	5 ♌	21 ♍	0 ♎	20 ♏	28 ♐	22 ♒	0 ♈	19 ♉	4 ♋	6 ♌	20 ♍	23 ♎
5	29 ♌	16 ♎	26 ♎	18 ♐	27 ♑	20 ♓	26 ♈	13 ♊	28 ♋	0 ♍	15 ♎	20 ♏
7	24 ♍	13 ♏	23 ♏	16 ♑	25 ♒	17 ♈	21 ♉	7 ♋	21 ♌	24 ♍	11 ♏	18 ♐
9	19 ♎	10 ♐	21 ♐	14 ♒	23 ♓	12 ♉	16 ♊	1 ♌	15 ♍	19 ♎	9 ♐	17 ♑
11	17 ♏	10 ♑	19 ♑	13 ♓	19 ♈	7 ♊	10 ♋	25 ♌	10 ♎	16 ♏	9 ♑	16 ♒
13	16 ♐	9 ♒	18 ♒	9 ♈	15 ♉	1 ♋	4 ♌	19 ♍	13 ♏	10 ♐	5 ♒	14 ♓
15	16 ♑	9 ♓	17 ♓	7 ♉	9 ♊	25 ♋	27 ♌	13 ♎	2 ♏	10 ♑	4 ♓	12 ♈
17	16 ♒	7 ♈	15 ♈	3 ♊	3 ♋	19 ♌	21 ♍	9 ♏	7 ♏	9 ♒	12 ♈	9 ♉
19	15 ♓	4 ♉	12 ♉	27 ♊	29 ♋	13 ♍	17 ♎	7 ♐	28 ♏	8 ♓	21 ♉	5 ♊
21	13 ♈	29 ♉	7 ♊	21 ♋	22 ♌	8 ♎	14 ♏	7 ♑	27 ♐	4 ♈	21 ♊	0 ♋
23	8 ♉	23 ♊	1 ♋	14 ♌	16 ♍	4 ♏	13 ♐	4 ♒	27 ♑	4 ♉	16 ♋	24 ♋
25	3 ♊	17 ♋	25 ♋	9 ♍	12 ♎	2 ♐	13 ♑	4 ♓	25 ♒	1 ♊	10 ♌	18 ♌
27	26 ♊	10 ♌	18 ♌	4 ♎	9 ♏	2 ♑	13 ♒	3 ♈	23 ♓	26 ♊	4 ♍	12 ♍
29	20 ♋		13 ♍	1 ♏	8 ♐	2 ♒	12 ♓	1 ♉	18 ♈	20 ♋	4 ♎	6 ♎
31	14 ♌		9 ♎		8 ♑		9 ♈	27 ♉		14 ♌		1 ♏

1935	Jan.	Feb.	Mar.	April	May	June	July	Aug.	Sep.	Oct.	Nov.	Dec.
1	14 ♏	4 ♑	12 ♑	5 ♓	14 ♈	6 ♊	10 ♋	25 ♌	10 ♎	13 ♏	1 ♑	8 ♒
3	11 ♐	4 ♒	12 ♒	5 ♈	13 ♉	2 ♋	5 ♌	19 ♍	4 ♏	8 ♐	27 ♑	6 ♓
5	11 ♐	4 ♒	12 ♒	5 ♈	8 ♊	27 ♋	23 ♌	7 ♎	24 ♐	1 ♒	24 ♒	4 ♈
7	11 ♒	4 ♓	12 ♈	2 ♉	6 ♊	21 ♌	21 ♍	7 ♏	24 ♐	1 ♒	24 ♒	3 ♈
9	10 ♓	2 ♈	11 ♉	29 ♉	1 ♋	15 ♍	17 ♎	2 ♐	0 ♑	0 ♓	24 ♓	2 ♉
11	9 ♈	29 ♈	8 ♊	23 ♊	25 ♋	9 ♎	11 ♏	29 ♐	21 ♑	0 ♈	23 ♈	29 ♉
13	6 ♉	24 ♉	3 ♋	18 ♋	13 ♌	3 ♏	8 ♐	28 ♑	21 ♒	0 ♉	21 ♉	25 ♊
15	2 ♊	18 ♊	27 ♋	10 ♍	13 ♍	29 ♏	5 ♑	28 ♒	22 ♈	29 ♉	20 ♊	20 ♋
17	27 ♊	12 ♌	20 ♌	5 ♎	8 ♏	27 ♐	4 ♒	28 ♓	21 ♉	27 ♊	12 ♋	14 ♍
19	21 ♋	5 ♍	14 ♍	29 ♎	4 ♐	25 ♑	4 ♓	28 ♈	18 ♊	22 ♋	6 ♌	9 ♎
21	15 ♌	29 ♍	8 ♎	25 ♏	2 ♑	25 ♒	4 ♈	25 ♉	13 ♋	16 ♌	0 ♎	2 ♏
23	8 ♎	23 ♎	3 ♏	21 ♐	1 ♒	25 ♓	3 ♉	21 ♊	8 ♌	10 ♎	24 ♎	27 ♏
25	2 ♎	18 ♏	28 ♏	19 ♑	28 ♒	21 ♈	29 ♉	16 ♋	1 ♎	4 ♏	19 ♏	23 ♐
27	26 ♎	15 ♐	24 ♐	17 ♒	24 ♓	18 ♉	24 ♊	10 ♌	25 ♎	28 ♏	14 ♐	20 ♑
29	22 ♏		22 ♑	15 ♓	24 ♈	15 ♊	19 ♋	4 ♍	19 ♏	23 ♐	11 ♑	18 ♒
31	19 ♐		21 ♒		22 ♉		14 ♌	28 ♍		18 ♑		17 ♓

1936	Jan.	Feb.	Mar.	April	May	June	July	Aug.	Sep.	Oct.	Nov.	Dec.
1	1 ♈	24 ♉	18 ♊	6 ♌	9 ♍	23 ♎	25 ♏	11 ♑	1 ♓	9 ♈	3 ♊	10 ♋
3	29 ♈	21 ♊	14 ♋	0 ♍	3 ♎	17 ♏	20 ♐	8 ♒	1 ♈	10 ♉	2 ♋	8 ♌
5	27 ♉	17 ♋	9 ♌	24 ♍	26 ♎	12 ♐	16 ♑	7 ♓	1 ♉	9 ♊	0 ♌	4 ♍
7	24 ♊	12 ♌	3 ♍	18 ♎	20 ♏	7 ♑	13 ♒	8 ♈	29 ♊	7 ♋	25 ♌	29 ♍
9	20 ♋	6 ♍	27 ♍	11 ♏	15 ♐	3 ♒	9 ♓	9 ♉	27 ♋	3 ♌	20 ♍	22 ♎
11	16 ♌	0 ♎	21 ♎	6 ♐	11 ♑	0 ♓	9 ♈	8 ♊	23 ♌	28 ♌	14 ♎	16 ♏
13	10 ♍	24 ♎	14 ♏	0 ♑	6 ♒	28 ♓	8 ♉	6 ♋	19 ♍	23 ♎	7 ♏	10 ♐
15	4 ♎	18 ♏	9 ♐	27 ♑	4 ♓	27 ♈	6 ♊	2 ♌	14 ♎	17 ♏	1 ♐	5 ♑
17	28 ♎	13 ♐	4 ♑	24 ♒	2 ♈	26 ♉	4 ♋	28 ♌	8 ♏	10 ♐	25 ♐	0 ♒
19	22 ♏	9 ♑	1 ♒	23 ♓	2 ♉	25 ♊	1 ♌	23 ♍	2 ♏	4 ♑	20 ♑	26 ♒
21	18 ♐	7 ♒	29 ♒	23 ♈	0 ♊	18 ♋	27 ♌	19 ♎	25 ♏	0 ♒	16 ♒	23 ♓
23	15 ♑	6 ♓	29 ♓	23 ♉	0 ♋	18 ♌	13 ♍	15 ♏	19 ♐	24 ♒	13 ♓	21 ♈
25	13 ♒	7 ♈	0 ♈	19 ♊	23 ♋	13 ♍	15 ♎	9 ♐	14 ♑	19 ♓	11 ♈	20 ♉
27	13 ♓	6 ♉	0 ♉	19 ♋	23 ♌	7 ♎	9 ♏	3 ♑	11 ♒	18 ♈	11 ♉	19 ♊
29	12 ♈	4 ♊	27 ♉	15 ♌	17 ♍	1 ♏	3 ♐	19 ♑	9 ♓	18 ♉	11 ♊	18 ♋
31	10 ♉		23 ♊		11 ♎		28 ♐	17 ♒		16 ♊		16 ♌

1937	Jan.	Feb.	Mar.	April	May	June	July	Aug.	Sep.	Oct.	Nov.	Dec.
1	29 ♌	14 ♎	22 ♎	6 ♐	9 ♑	25 ♒	2 ♈	24 ♉	18 ♋	25 ♌	14 ♎	17 ♏
3	24 ♍	8 ♏	16 ♏	0 ♑	3 ♒	22 ♓	0 ♉	23 ♊	15 ♌	22 ♍	8 ♏	11 ♐
5	19 ♎	2 ♐	10 ♐	25 ♑	29 ♒	20 ♈	0 ♊	20 ♋	9 ♍	17 ♎	2 ♐	4 ♑
7	12 ♏	26 ♐	4 ♑	20 ♒	27 ♓	19 ♉	28 ♊	20 ♌	9 ♎	12 ♏	26 ♐	28 ♑
9	6 ♐	21 ♑	29 ♑	18 ♓	26 ♈	20 ♊	28 ♋	17 ♍	4 ♏	6 ♐	19 ♑	23 ♒
11	1 ♑	18 ♒	26 ♒	18 ♈	26 ♉	19 ♋	26 ♌	13 ♎	28 ♏	29 ♐	14 ♒	18 ♓
13	26 ♑	16 ♓	25 ♓	18 ♉	26 ♊	18 ♌	23 ♍	8 ♏	21 ♐	23 ♑	9 ♓	13 ♈
15	22 ♒	14 ♈	24 ♈	17 ♊	25 ♋	14 ♍	18 ♎	1 ♐	15 ♑	18 ♒	5 ♈	13 ♉
17	20 ♓	13 ♉	23 ♉	16 ♋	22 ♌	9 ♎	12 ♏	25 ♐	10 ♒	15 ♓	5 ♉	13 ♊
19	18 ♈	11 ♊	22 ♊	14 ♌	18 ♍	4 ♏	7 ♐	19 ♑	7 ♓	6 ♈	6 ♉	14 ♋
21	16 ♉	9 ♋	19 ♋	8 ♍	12 ♎	27 ♏	24 ♑	15 ♒	4 ♈	6 ♉	7 ♊	11 ♌
23	14 ♊	6 ♌	16 ♌	3 ♎	6 ♏	24 ♐	19 ♑	12 ♓	4 ♉	6 ♊	7 ♋	7 ♎
25	13 ♋	2 ♍	11 ♍	27 ♎	0 ♐	15 ♑	15 ♒	9 ♈	2 ♊	11 ♋	4 ♌	2 ♏
27	10 ♌	28 ♍	6 ♎	21 ♏	24 ♐	9 ♒	15 ♓	9 ♉	0 ♋	0 ♌	28 ♌	26 ♏
29	7 ♍		1 ♏	15 ♐	18 ♑	5 ♓	5 ♈	5 ♊	28 ♋	0 ♍	23 ♍	26 ♐
31	2 ♎		24 ♏		12 ♒		10 ♉	3 ♋		1 ♎		20 ♐

1938	Jan.	Feb.	Mar.	April	May	June	July	Aug.	Sep.	Oct.	Nov.	Dec.
1	1 ♑	16 ♒	25 ♒	13 ♈	20 ♉	14 ♋	22 ♌	13 ♎	0 ♐	2 ♑	16 ♒	17 ♓
3	25 ♑	12 ♓	21 ♓	11 ♉	20 ♊	13 ♌	21 ♍	9 ♏	24 ♐	26 ♑	10 ♓	13 ♈
5	20 ♒	8 ♈	18 ♈	10 ♊	19 ♋	14 ♍	17 ♎	3 ♐	18 ♑	20 ♒	5 ♈	10 ♉
7	15 ♓	5 ♉	15 ♉	9 ♋	17 ♌	12 ♎	12 ♏	27 ♐	14 ♒	10 ♓	0 ♉	8 ♊
9	11 ♈	2 ♊	11 ♊	6 ♌	15 ♍	3 ♏	7 ♐	21 ♑	6 ♈	0 ♈	8 ♊	8 ♋
11	8 ♉	0 ♋	11 ♋	1 ♎	6 ♎	1 ♐	24 ♑	27 ♒	5 ♉	28 ♉	7 ♋	7 ♌
13	7 ♊	0 ♌	10 ♌	1 ♎	6 ♏	21 ♐	24 ♒	9 ♓	27 ♉	26 ♊	4 ♌	4 ♎
15	7 ♋	29 ♌	8 ♍	1 ♏	1 ♐	15 ♑	18 ♒	4 ♈	24 ♊	3 ♋	0 ♎	4 ♏
17	7 ♌	27 ♍	2 ♎	2 ♏	16 ♐	12 ♒	7 ♓	27 ♈	20 ♋	29 ♋	21 ♎	26 ♏
19	6 ♍	24 ♎	2 ♏	16 ♐	18 ♑	3 ♓	7 ♈	20 ♉	29 ♌	21 ♎	14 ♏	20 ♑
21	3 ♎	19 ♏	20 ♐	4 ♑	7 ♒	24 ♓	1 ♉	25 ♊	25 ♎	24 ♏	11 ♐	14 ♒
23	29 ♎	13 ♐	14 ♑	28 ♑	2 ♓	24 ♈	1 ♊	25 ♋	18 ♏	21 ♐	11 ♑	8 ♓
25	23 ♏	6 ♑	14 ♒	24 ♒	0 ♈	22 ♉	1 ♋	24 ♌	16 ♐	16 ♑	6 ♒	2 ♈
27	16 ♐	1 ♒	9 ♓	24 ♓	0 ♉	22 ♊	1 ♌	24 ♍	12 ♑	16 ♒	0 ♓	2 ♉
29	10 ♑		3 ♈	0 ♈	29 ♊	23 ♋	1 ♍	21 ♎	8 ♐	10 ♑	23 ♒	26 ♓
31	4 ♒		0 ♈		29 ♊		17 ♏			3 ♒		21 ♈

1939	Jan.	Feb.	Mar.	April	May	June	July	Aug.	Sep.	Oct.	Nov.	Dec.
1	4 ♉	24 ♊	3 ♋	27 ♌	6 ♎	26 ♏	1 ♐	16 ♒	0 ♈	4 ♉	22 ♊	0 ♌
3	2 ♊	24 ♋	3 ♌	26 ♍	4 ♏	22 ♐	25 ♑	10 ♓	24 ♈	29 ♉	20 ♋	29 ♌
5	1 ♋	25 ♌	3 ♍	22 ♎	0 ♐	19 ♑	20 ♒	15 ♈	26 ♉	25 ♊	18 ♌	25 ♍
7	1 ♌	24 ♍	1 ♎	17 ♏	24 ♐	13 ♒	15 ♓	6 ♉	24 ♊	22 ♋	16 ♍	20 ♎
9	1 ♍	21 ♎	28 ♎	11 ♐	18 ♑	7 ♓	9 ♈	3 ♊	21 ♋	20 ♌	13 ♎	14 ♏
11	0 ♎	19 ♏	23 ♏	5 ♑	11 ♒	1 ♈	3 ♉	0 ♋	20 ♌	13 ♍	7 ♏	10 ♐
13	27 ♎	14 ♐	17 ♐	29 ♑	5 ♓	26 ♈	0 ♊	28 ♋	19 ♍	11 ♎	1 ♐	4 ♑
15	23 ♏	8 ♑	11 ♑	23 ♒	0 ♈	22 ♉	28 ♊	27 ♌	16 ♎	6 ♏	25 ♐	0 ♒
17	17 ♐	2 ♒	5 ♒	17 ♓	25 ♈	19 ♊	25 ♋	25 ♍	11 ♏	0 ♐	19 ♑	4 ♓
19	11 ♑	26 ♒	29 ♒	16 ♈	21 ♉	16 ♋	25 ♌	23 ♎	6 ♐	20 ♑	14 ♒	22 ♈
21	5 ♒	20 ♓	24 ♓	13 ♉	21 ♊	15 ♌	23 ♍	18 ♏	0 ♑	14 ♒	9 ♓	17 ♉
23	29 ♒	14 ♈	24 ♈	11 ♊	21 ♋	15 ♍	23 ♎	12 ♐	24 ♑	8 ♓	11 ♈	11 ♊
25	23 ♓	9 ♉	19 ♉	11 ♋	21 ♌	13 ♎	20 ♏	15 ♑	18 ♒	18 ♈	5 ♉	8 ♋
27	17 ♈	6 ♊		16 ♋	18 ♍	10 ♏	15 ♐	1 ♒	15 ♓	18 ♉	5 ♊	11 ♌
29	13 ♉		14 ♋	7 ♌	16 ♎	6 ♐	10 ♑	25 ♒	9 ♈	13 ♊	2 ♋	10 ♍
31	10 ♊		13 ♍		13 ♏		4 ♒	18 ♓		9 ♋		9 ♍

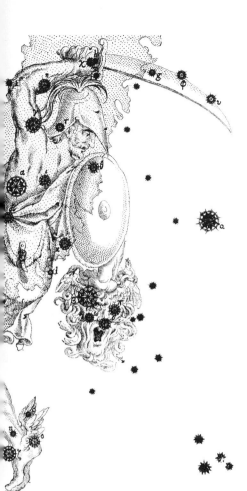

1940	Jan.	Feb.	Mar.	April	May	June	July	Aug.	Sep.	Oct.	Nov.	Dec.
1	24 ♍	16 ♏	9 ♐	26 ♑	29 ♒	13 ♈	15 ♉	1 ♋	22 ♌	0 ♎	24 ♏	1 ♑
3	22 ♎	12 ♐	5 ♑	21 ♒	23 ♓	7 ♉	10 ♊	29 ♊	22 ♍	1 ♏	23 ♐	28 ♑
5	19 ♏	8 ♑	29 ♑	14 ♓	16 ♈	2 ♊	2 ♋	28 ♌	22 ♎	0 ♐	20 ♑	24 ♒
7	15 ♐	2 ♒	23 ♒	8 ♈	11 ♉	28 ♊	28 ♋	27 ♍	21 ♏	28 ♐	16 ♒	18 ♓
9	11 ♑	27 ♒	17 ♓	2 ♉	5 ♊	25 ♋	25 ♌	27 ♎	18 ♐	24 ♑	10 ♓	12 ♈
11	6 ♒	21 ♓	11 ♈	26 ♉	1 ♋	23 ♌	2 ♍	25 ♏	15 ♑	19 ♒	4 ♈	6 ♉
13	0 ♓	14 ♈	5 ♉	21 ♊	28 ♋	21 ♍	21 ♎	22 ♐	10 ♒	13 ♓	27 ♈	0 ♊
15	24 ♓	9 ♉	29 ♉	18 ♋	26 ♌	19 ♎	17 ♏	18 ♑	4 ♓	7 ♈	21 ♉	25 ♊
17	17 ♈	3 ♊	25 ♊	15 ♌	24 ♎	17 ♏	15 ♐	13 ♒	28 ♓	1 ♉	16 ♊	21 ♋
19	12 ♉	29 ♊	22 ♋	14 ♍	23 ♏	15 ♐	12 ♑	7 ♓	22 ♈	24 ♉	11 ♋	18 ♌
21	7 ♊	27 ♋	20 ♌	14 ♎	22 ♐	12 ♑	12 ♒	1 ♈	17 ♉	19 ♊	7 ♌	15 ♍
23	4 ♋	27 ♌	21 ♍	14 ♏	21 ♑	7 ♒	11 ♓	25 ♈	13 ♊	15 ♋	4 ♍	13 ♎
25	4 ♌	28 ♍	20 ♎	13 ♐	17 ♒	3 ♓	5 ♈	19 ♉	9 ♋	13 ♌	3 ♎	12 ♏
27	4 ♍	27 ♎	20 ♏	9 ♑	13 ♓	27 ♓	29 ♈	15 ♊	8 ♌	11 ♍	2 ♏	10 ♐
29	4 ♎	26 ♏	18 ♐	5 ♒	7 ♈	21 ♈	23 ♉	10 ♋	8 ♍	9 ♎	2 ♐	9 ♑
31	2 ♏		14 ♑		1 ♈		18 ♊	7 ♌		7 ♏		6 ♒

1941	Jan.	Feb.	Mar.	April	May	June	July	Aug.	Sep.	Oct.	Nov.	Dec.
1	19 ♒	4 ♈	12 ♈	26 ♉	29 ♊	16 ♌	24 ♍	16 ♏	10 ♑	17 ♒	4 ♈	7 ♉
3	14 ♓	28 ♈	6 ♉	20 ♊	24 ♋	13 ♍	21 ♎	15 ♐	7 ♒	13 ♓	28 ♈	1 ♊
5	8 ♈	21 ♉	29 ♉	15 ♋	20 ♌	11 ♎	20 ♏	13 ♑	3 ♓	7 ♈	22 ♉	25 ♊
7	2 ♉	16 ♊	24 ♊	11 ♌	17 ♍	10 ♏	19 ♐	11 ♒	29 ♓	2 ♉	16 ♊	19 ♋
9	26 ♉	11 ♋	19 ♋	9 ♍	16 ♎	10 ♐	18 ♑	8 ♓	23 ♈	25 ♉	10 ♋	14 ♌
11	21 ♊	9 ♌	16 ♌	8 ♎	17 ♏	10 ♑	16 ♒	3 ♈	17 ♉	19 ♊	4 ♌	9 ♍
13	17 ♋	7 ♍	15 ♍	9 ♏	17 ♐	8 ♒	13 ♓	27 ♈	11 ♊	13 ♋	0 ♍	6 ♎
15	14 ♌	6 ♎	15 ♎	9 ♐	16 ♑	4 ♓	8 ♈	21 ♉	5 ♋	8 ♌	27 ♍	4 ♏
17	12 ♍	5 ♏	15 ♏	7 ♑	13 ♒	29 ♓	2 ♉	15 ♊	0 ♌	5 ♍	26 ♎	4 ♐
19	10 ♎	3 ♐	14 ♐	4 ♒	9 ♓	23 ♈	25 ♉	10 ♋	27 ♌	3 ♎	26 ♏	5 ♑
21	8 ♏	1 ♑	11 ♑	29 ♒	3 ♈	17 ♉	19 ♊	5 ♌	25 ♍	3 ♏	27 ♐	4 ♒
23	6 ♐	27 ♑	7 ♒	24 ♓	26 ♈	11 ♊	14 ♋	2 ♍	24 ♎	4 ♐	26 ♑	2 ♓
25	4 ♑	23 ♒	2 ♓	18 ♈	20 ♉	5 ♋	10 ♌	29 ♍	24 ♏	4 ♑	23 ♒	28 ♓
27	1 ♒	18 ♓	27 ♓	11 ♉	14 ♊	1 ♌	7 ♍	29 ♎	23 ♐	3 ♒	19 ♓	22 ♈
29	27 ♒		21 ♈	5 ♊	8 ♋	27 ♌	4 ♎	28 ♏	20 ♑	0 ♓	13 ♈	16 ♉
31	22 ♓		14 ♉		4 ♌		2 ♏	26 ♐		22 ♓		10 ♊

1942	Jan.	Feb.	Mar.	April	May	June	July	Aug.	Sep.	Oct.	Nov.	Dec.
1	22 ♊	7 ♌	15 ♌	4 ♎	11 ♏	5 ♑	13 ♒	3 ♈	20 ♉	22 ♊	5 ♌	7 ♍
3	16 ♋	3 ♍	12 ♍	2 ♏	11 ♐	5 ♒	12 ♓	29 ♈	14 ♊	15 ♋	0 ♍	3 ♎
5	11 ♌	29 ♍	9 ♎	2 ♐	11 ♑	3 ♓	7 ♈	24 ♉	7 ♋	9 ♌	25 ♍	0 ♏
7	6 ♍	27 ♎	7 ♏	1 ♑	9 ♒	29 ♓	3 ♉	17 ♊	1 ♌	4 ♍	22 ♎	29 ♏
9	2 ♎	25 ♏	6 ♐	29 ♑	6 ♓	24 ♈	27 ♉	11 ♋	26 ♌	0 ♎	21 ♏	29 ♐
11	28 ♎	23 ♐	4 ♑	26 ♒	2 ♈	18 ♉	21 ♊	5 ♌	22 ♍	28 ♎	21 ♐	28 ♑
13	28 ♏	22 ♑	2 ♒	22 ♓	27 ♈	12 ♊	14 ♋	0 ♍	18 ♎	26 ♏	21 ♑	26 ♒
15	28 ♐	20 ♒	29 ♒	17 ♈	21 ♉	6 ♋	8 ♌	25 ♍	16 ♏	25 ♐	18 ♒	26 ♓
17	28 ♑	18 ♓	26 ♓	12 ♉	15 ♊	0 ♌	3 ♍	22 ♎	14 ♐	24 ♑	15 ♓	21 ♈
19	26 ♒	13 ♈	21 ♈	6 ♊	8 ♋	24 ♌	28 ♍	19 ♏	13 ♑	21 ♒	12 ♈	16 ♉
21	23 ♓	8 ♉	16 ♉	0 ♋	2 ♌	19 ♍	25 ♎	17 ♐	11 ♒	2 ♓	7 ♉	11 ♊
23	18 ♈	2 ♊	10 ♊	24 ♋	27 ♌	15 ♎	23 ♏	15 ♑	9 ♓	26 ♓	1 ♊	5 ♋
25	12 ♉	26 ♊	4 ♋	18 ♌	23 ♍	13 ♏	22 ♐	16 ♒	4 ♈	20 ♈	26 ♊	28 ♋
27	6 ♊	20 ♋	28 ♋	14 ♍	20 ♎	13 ♐	22 ♑	14 ♓	29 ♈	14 ♉	20 ♋	22 ♌
29	0 ♋		23 ♌	12 ♎	19 ♏	14 ♑	22 ♒	11 ♈	23 ♉	8 ♊	13 ♌	16 ♍
31	24 ♋		20 ♍		20 ♐		20 ♓	7 ♉		23 ♋		11 ♎

1943	Jan.	Feb.	Mar.	April	May	June	July	Aug.	Sep.	Oct.	Nov.	Dec.
1	25 ♎	16 ♐	26 ♐	19 ♒	27 ♓	17 ♉	21 ♊	6 ♌	21 ♍	25 ♎	14 ♐	22 ♑
3	22 ♏	15 ♑	25 ♑	18 ♓	24 ♈	12 ♊	15 ♋	20 ♌	15 ♎	21 ♏	12 ♑	21 ♒
5	22 ♐	16 ♒	24 ♒	15 ♈	21 ♉	7 ♋	9 ♌	24 ♍	11 ♏	17 ♐	10 ♒	19 ♓
7	23 ♑	15 ♓	23 ♓	12 ♉	16 ♊	0 ♌	3 ♍	18 ♎	7 ♐	15 ♑	8 ♓	17 ♈
9	23 ♒	13 ♈	21 ♈	8 ♊	10 ♋	24 ♌	27 ♍	11 ♏	3 ♑	13 ♒	4 ♈	14 ♉
11	21 ♓	10 ♉	18 ♉	2 ♋	4 ♌	18 ♍	22 ♎	10 ♐	3 ♒	12 ♓	4 ♉	10 ♊
13	18 ♈	4 ♊	13 ♊	26 ♋	28 ♌	13 ♎	18 ♏	10 ♑	3 ♓	1 ♈	0 ♊	5 ♋
15	13 ♉	28 ♊	7 ♋	20 ♌	22 ♍	16 ♏	16 ♐	7 ♒	10 ♈	27 ♈	24 ♊	29 ♋
17	8 ♊	22 ♋	0 ♌	14 ♍	18 ♎	8 ♐	8 ♑	6 ♓	2 ♉	7 ♉	22 ♋	23 ♌
19	2 ♋	16 ♌	24 ♌	10 ♎	15 ♏	6 ♑	8 ♒	7 ♈	29 ♉	24 ♊	16 ♌	11 ♍
21	25 ♋	10 ♍	19 ♍	7 ♏	14 ♐	6 ♒	8 ♓	16 ♎	24 ♊	26 ♋	9 ♍	5 ♎
23	19 ♌	5 ♎	14 ♎	5 ♐	13 ♑	7 ♓	7 ♈	14 ♏	3 ♌	18 ♌	3 ♎	4 ♏
25	13 ♍	1 ♏	11 ♏	3 ♑	12 ♒	5 ♈	5 ♉	11 ♐	27 ♌	13 ♍	29 ♎	4 ♐
27	8 ♎	28 ♏	8 ♐	2 ♒	10 ♓	1 ♉	6 ♊	21 ♑	5 ♎	8 ♏	26 ♐	2 ♒
29	4 ♏		6 ♑	0 ♓	8 ♈	27 ♉	0 ♋	15 ♒	0 ♐	4 ♐	24 ♑	1 ♓
31	1 ♐		5 ♒		4 ♉		24 ♋	9 ♍		0 ♑		1 ♓

1944	Jan.	Feb.	Mar.	April	May	June	July	Aug.	Sep.	Oct.	Nov.	Dec.
1	15 ♓	7 ♉	0 ♊	17 ♋	19 ♌	2 ♎	5 ♏	22 ♑	12 ♓	21 ♈	14 ♉	21 ♊
3	14 ♈	4 ♊	26 ♊	10 ♌	12 ♍	27 ♎	0 ♐	20 ♒	13 ♈	21 ♉	13 ♊	18 ♋
5	11 ♉	29 ♊	20 ♋	4 ♍	6 ♎	22 ♏	27 ♐	19 ♓	13 ♉	21 ♊	10 ♋	14 ♌
7	7 ♊	23 ♋	14 ♌	28 ♍	1 ♏	19 ♐	26 ♑	19 ♈	12 ♊	19 ♋	6 ♌	8 ♍
9	2 ♋	17 ♌	7 ♍	22 ♎	27 ♏	16 ♑	25 ♒	18 ♉	10 ♋	15 ♌	0 ♍	2 ♎
11	26 ♋	10 ♍	1 ♎	17 ♏	24 ♐	15 ♒	25 ♓	17 ♊	6 ♌	10 ♍	24 ♍	26 ♎
13	20 ♌	4 ♎	25 ♎	13 ♐	22 ♑	15 ♓	22 ♈	13 ♋	1 ♍	3 ♎	18 ♎	20 ♏
15	13 ♍	28 ♎	20 ♏	10 ♑	18 ♒	11 ♈	9 ♉	9 ♌	25 ♍	28 ♎	12 ♏	16 ♐
17	7 ♎	23 ♏	16 ♐	7 ♒	16 ♓	9 ♉	6 ♊	2 ♍	18 ♎	21 ♏	7 ♐	12 ♑
19	2 ♏	20 ♐	13 ♑	6 ♓	15 ♈	7 ♊	2 ♋	28 ♍	12 ♏	15 ♐	3 ♑	9 ♒
21	26 ♏	18 ♑	11 ♒	5 ♈	13 ♉	3 ♋	7 ♌	21 ♎	6 ♐	10 ♑	29 ♑	7 ♓
23	26 ♐	18 ♒	11 ♓	5 ♉	11 ♊	28 ♋	1 ♍	15 ♏	10 ♑	6 ♒	26 ♒	4 ♈
25	25 ♑	18 ♓	11 ♈	4 ♊	8 ♋	23 ♌	25 ♍	9 ♐	4 ♒	0 ♓	24 ♓	4 ♉
27	25 ♒	18 ♈	11 ♉	0 ♋	3 ♌	16 ♍	18 ♎	4 ♑	23 ♒	0 ♈	24 ♈	2 ♊
29	25 ♓	17 ♉	8 ♊	25 ♋	27 ♌	10 ♎	13 ♏	0 ♒	29 ♓	23 ♈		0 ♋
31	24 ♈		4 ♋		20 ♍		8 ♐	28 ♑		0 ♉		26 ♋

❧ Meridianos varios ac fugaces, à polis mundi per locorum vertices procedere.

❧ Meridianorum diuersitas.

Meridiani, Æquato-
ris, & Zodiaci positio.

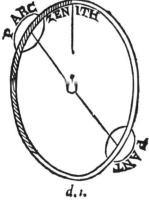

Nud° meridiani, &
poli eiusdem situs, ac
pictura.

d. 1.

1945	Jan.	Feb.	Mar.	April	May	June	July	Aug.	Sep.	Oct.	Nov.	Dec.
1	9 ♌	24 ♍	2 ♎	16 ♏	20 ♐	8 ♒	16 ♓	9 ♈	28 ♉	3 ♋	25 ♌	28 ♎
3	4 ♍	17 ♎	26 ♎	11 ♐	15 ♑	5 ♓	14 ♈	7 ♉	28 ♊	0 ♌	19 ♍	21 ♏
5	28 ♍	11 ♏	20 ♏	5 ♑	11 ♒	3 ♈	12 ♉	5 ♊	24 ♋	28 ♌	13 ♎	15 ♐
7	21 ♎	6 ♐	14 ♐	1 ♒	9 ♓	2 ♉	11 ♊	2 ♋	19 ♌	22 ♍	6 ♏	9 ♑
9	16 ♏	1 ♑	9 ♑	29 ♒	8 ♈	2 ♊	9 ♋	28 ♋	13 ♍	16 ♎	0 ♐	4 ♒
11	11 ♐	29 ♑	7 ♒	29 ♓	8 ♉	0 ♋	6 ♌	24 ♌	7 ♎	9 ♏	25 ♐	0 ♓
13	7 ♑	28 ♒	6 ♓	0 ♉	8 ♊	28 ♋	2 ♍	17 ♍	1 ♐	3 ♐	20 ♑	28 ♓
15	5 ♒	27 ♓	6 ♈	0 ♊	6 ♋	25 ♌	27 ♍	11 ♎	25 ♐	28 ♐	18 ♒	26 ♈
17	3 ♓	27 ♈	6 ♉	28 ♊	3 ♌	19 ♍	21 ♎	5 ♐	20 ♑	25 ♑	17 ♓	26 ♉
19	2 ♈	25 ♉	5 ♊	25 ♋	29 ♌	13 ♎	15 ♏	29 ♐	17 ♒	23 ♒	18 ♈	25 ♊
21	1 ♉	22 ♊	2 ♋	20 ♌	23 ♍	7 ♏	9 ♐	25 ♑	16 ♓	24 ♓	18 ♉	24 ♋
23	29 ♉	18 ♋	28 ♋	14 ♍	16 ♎	1 ♐	4 ♑	23 ♒	16 ♈	24 ♈	17 ♊	22 ♌
25	26 ♊	14 ♌	23 ♌	8 ♎	10 ♏	26 ♐	0 ♒	22 ♓	14 ♉	22 ♉	14 ♋	18 ♍
27	22 ♋	8 ♍	17 ♍	2 ♏	4 ♐	21 ♑	28 ♒	21 ♈	15 ♊	22 ♊	9 ♌	12 ♎
29	17 ♌		11 ♎	26 ♏	29 ♐	18 ♒	26 ♓	21 ♉	12 ♋	18 ♌	4 ♍	6 ♏
31	12 ♍		5 ♏		25 ♑		25 ♈	18 ♊		13 ♍		0 ♐

1946	Jan.	Feb.	Mar.	April	May	June	July	Aug.	Sep.	Oct.	Nov.	Dec.
1	12 ♐	27 ♑	5 ♒	24 ♓	2 ♉	26 ♊	4 ♌	23 ♍	9 ♏	11 ♐	25 ♑	28 ♒
3	6 ♑	23 ♒	2 ♓	24 ♈	2 ♊	25 ♋	2 ♍	19 ♎	3 ♐	5 ♐	19 ♒	23 ♓
5	1 ♒	21 ♓	0 ♈	24 ♉	2 ♋	23 ♌	28 ♍	13 ♏	27 ♐	29 ♐	15 ♓	21 ♈
7	27 ♒	19 ♈	29 ♈	21 ♊	0 ♌	20 ♍	23 ♎	7 ♐	21 ♑	21 ♑	12 ♈	20 ♉
9	24 ♓	17 ♉	28 ♉	21 ♋	27 ♌	14 ♎	17 ♏	1 ♑	16 ♒	21 ♒	12 ♉	20 ♊
11	22 ♈	15 ♊	26 ♊	17 ♌	23 ♍	8 ♏	11 ♐	25 ♑	12 ♓	19 ♓	12 ♊	20 ♋
13	21 ♉	13 ♋	24 ♋	13 ♍	17 ♎	2 ♐	4 ♑	20 ♒	11 ♈	18 ♈	11 ♋	19 ♌
15	19 ♊	11 ♌	20 ♌	8 ♎	11 ♏	26 ♐	29 ♑	17 ♓	10 ♉	17 ♉	10 ♌	17 ♍
17	18 ♋	8 ♍	16 ♍	2 ♏	5 ♐	20 ♑	24 ♒	14 ♈	8 ♊	16 ♊	6 ♍	13 ♎
19	16 ♌	3 ♎	12 ♎	26 ♏	29 ♐	14 ♒	20 ♓	12 ♉	5 ♋	13 ♋	3 ♎	7 ♏
21	13 ♍	28 ♎	6 ♏	20 ♐	23 ♑	10 ♓	17 ♈	10 ♊	2 ♌	10 ♌	28 ♎	1 ♐
23	8 ♎	22 ♏	0 ♐	14 ♑	17 ♒	7 ♈	15 ♉	8 ♋	0 ♍	6 ♍	22 ♏	25 ♐
25	2 ♏	15 ♐	23 ♐	8 ♒	13 ♓	5 ♉	14 ♊	7 ♌	27 ♍	1 ♎	16 ♐	18 ♑
27	26 ♏	10 ♑	18 ♑	5 ♓	11 ♈	5 ♊	13 ♋	4 ♍	23 ♎	25 ♎	9 ♑	12 ♒
29	20 ♐		13 ♒	3 ♈	11 ♉	4 ♋	12 ♌	2 ♎	17 ♏	19 ♐	3 ♒	7 ♓
31	14 ♑		10 ♓		11 ♊		10 ♍	27 ♎		13 ♑		2 ♈

1947	Jan.	Feb.	Mar.	April	May	June	July	Aug.	Sep.	Oct.	Nov.	Dec.
1	16 ♈	7 ♊	18 ♊	11 ♌	19 ♍	8 ♏	12 ♐	26 ♑	11 ♈	16 ♉	5 ♋	14 ♌
3	13 ♉	6 ♋	16 ♋	9 ♍	16 ♎	3 ♐	5 ♑	20 ♒	6 ♉	12 ♊	4 ♌	13 ♍
5	13 ♊	6 ♌	15 ♌	5 ♎	11 ♏	27 ♐	14 ♒	9 ♓	3 ♊	9 ♋	2 ♍	9 ♎
7	13 ♋	6 ♍	14 ♍	3 ♏	6 ♐	20 ♑	23 ♒	9 ♈	29 ♋	7 ♌	29 ♍	3 ♏
9	13 ♌	4 ♎	11 ♎	28 ♏	0 ♑	14 ♒	17 ♓	5 ♉	26 ♌	6 ♍	25 ♎	5 ♐
11	12 ♍	0 ♏	8 ♏	22 ♐	24 ♑	8 ♓	13 ♈	2 ♊	25 ♍	4 ♎	22 ♏	25 ♐
13	9 ♎	24 ♏	2 ♐	16 ♑	18 ♒	3 ♈	9 ♉	1 ♋	25 ♎	3 ♏	17 ♐	19 ♑
15	4 ♏	18 ♐	26 ♐	10 ♒	12 ♓	0 ♉	7 ♊	1 ♌	24 ♎	0 ♐	11 ♑	13 ♒
17	28 ♏	12 ♑	20 ♑	4 ♓	8 ♈	29 ♉	7 ♋	0 ♍	26 ♏	26 ♐	5 ♒	7 ♓
19	22 ♐	6 ♒	14 ♒	0 ♈	6 ♉	28 ♊	7 ♌	0 ♎	18 ♐	13 ♐	1 ♓	1 ♈
21	15 ♑	1 ♓	9 ♓	28 ♈	5 ♊	29 ♋	7 ♍	27 ♎	15 ♑	15 ♑	29 ♓	24 ♈
23	9 ♒	26 ♓	5 ♈	26 ♉	5 ♋	28 ♌	5 ♎	23 ♏	9 ♒	9 ♒	27 ♈	23 ♉
25	4 ♓	23 ♈	3 ♉	25 ♊	4 ♌	25 ♍	2 ♏	17 ♐	1 ♓	3 ♓	24 ♉	23 ♊
27	29 ♓	20 ♉	0 ♊	24 ♋	2 ♍	22 ♎	27 ♏	11 ♑	25 ♒	28 ♓	23 ♊	23 ♋
29	26 ♈		29 ♊	23 ♌	0 ♎	17 ♏	21 ♐	5 ♒	20 ♓	24 ♈	22 ♋	
31	23 ♉		27 ♋		25 ♎		14 ♑	29 ♒		22 ♉		23 ♌

1948	Jan.	Feb.	Mar.	April	May	June	July	Aug.	Sep.	Oct.	Nov.	Dec.
1	7 ♍	29 ♎	20 ♏	6 ♑	8 ♒	22 ♓	24 ♈	12 ♊	3 ♌	12 ♍	5 ♏	11 ♐
3	6 ♎	26 ♏	16 ♐	0 ♒	2 ♓	18 ♈	20 ♉	10 ♋	4 ♍	12 ♎	3 ♐	8 ♑
5	2 ♏	19 ♐	10 ♑	24 ♒	26 ♓	14 ♉	17 ♊	10 ♌	4 ♎	11 ♏	0 ♑	3 ♒
7	28 ♏	13 ♑	4 ♒	18 ♓	21 ♈	12 ♊	16 ♋	10 ♍	3 ♏	9 ♐	26 ♑	28 ♒
9	22 ♐	7 ♒	28 ♒	13 ♈	17 ♉	8 ♋	16 ♌	8 ♎	26 ♏	5 ♑	20 ♒	21 ♓
11	16 ♑	1 ♓	22 ♓	8 ♉	14 ♊	6 ♌	16 ♍	5 ♏	26 ♐	0 ♒	14 ♓	15 ♈
13	10 ♒	25 ♓	16 ♈	4 ♊	12 ♋	6 ♍	14 ♎	4 ♈	21 ♑	24 ♒	10 ♈	10 ♉
15	4 ♓	19 ♈	11 ♉	1 ♋	10 ♌	6 ♎	11 ♏	7 ♉	15 ♒	19 ♓	6 ♉	6 ♊
17	28 ♓	14 ♉	6 ♊	0 ♌	9 ♍	5 ♏	7 ♐	1 ♊	9 ♈	11 ♉	4 ♊	6 ♋
19	22 ♈	11 ♊	5 ♋	28 ♌	7 ♎	1 ♐	28 ♐	2 ♊	7 ♉	6 ♊	1 ♋	0 ♌
21	18 ♉	9 ♋	3 ♌	27 ♍	5 ♏	23 ♐	23 ♑	5 ♋	27 ♉	1 ♌	0 ♌	
23	15 ♊	9 ♌	2 ♍	23 ♎	1 ♐	27 ♑	15 ♒	29 ♋	21 ♊	17 ♍	17 ♍	
25	15 ♋	9 ♍	2 ♎	23 ♏	27 ♐	6 ♒	15 ♓	29 ♌	24 ♋	14 ♎	24 ♎	24 ♐
27	16 ♌	9 ♎	1 ♏	19 ♐	22 ♑	6 ♓	8 ♈	7 ♍	21 ♌	14 ♏	16 ♏	20 ♑
29	16 ♍	7 ♏	28 ♏	14 ♑	16 ♒	0 ♈	3 ♉	3 ♎	18 ♍	12 ♐	14 ♐	16 ♒
31	15 ♎		24 ♐		10 ♓		28 ♉	19 ♏		21 ♑		16 ♓

1949	Jan.	Feb.	Mar.	April	May	June	July	Aug.	Sep.	Oct.	Nov.	Dec.
1	29 ♑	14 ♓	22 ♓	7 ♉	11 ♊	0 ♌	8 ♍	1 ♏	23 ♐	29 ♑	15 ♈	18 ♉
3	23 ♒	7 ♈	16 ♈	1 ♊	6 ♋	27 ♌	6 ♎	29 ♏	20 ♑	24 ♒	9 ♉	11 ♊
5	17 ♓	1 ♉	10 ♉	26 ♊	3 ♌	25 ♍	4 ♏	26 ♐	15 ♒	18 ♓	3 ♊	5 ♋
9	5 ♉	21 ♊	0 ♊	21 ♌	0 ♍	23 ♏	0 ♐	18 ♑	4 ♈	6 ♉	21 ♋	26 ♌
11	0 ♊	19 ♋	27 ♋	20 ♍	29 ♍	20 ♐	18 ♑	13 ♓	27 ♈	29 ♉	16 ♌	22 ♍
13	29 ♊	19 ♌	27 ♌	20 ♎	28 ♎	18 ♑	15 ♒	7 ♈	21 ♉	24 ♊	12 ♍	20 ♎
15	26 ♋	19 ♍	27 ♍	19 ♏	26 ♐	14 ♒	10 ♓	0 ♉	15 ♊	19 ♋	10 ♎	18 ♏
17	25 ♌	17 ♎	27 ♎	16 ♐	23 ♑	9 ♓	4 ♈	24 ♉	11 ♋	15 ♌	8 ♏	16 ♐
19	25 ♍	14 ♏	23 ♏	11 ♑	15 ♒	3 ♈	28 ♈	18 ♊	7 ♌	15 ♍	8 ♐	16 ♑
21	23 ♎	10 ♐	19 ♐	4 ♒	6 ♓	27 ♈	22 ♉	13 ♋	6 ♎	15 ♎	7 ♑	15 ♒
23	20 ♏	4 ♑	13 ♑	28 ♒	0 ♈	20 ♉	16 ♊	11 ♌	6 ♏	15 ♏	4 ♒	8 ♓
25	17 ♐	29 ♑	8 ♒	22 ♓	25 ♈	16 ♊	12 ♋	9 ♍	6 ♐	15 ♑	0 ♓	2 ♈
27	13 ♑	29 ♒	2 ♓	16 ♈	20 ♉	12 ♋	9 ♌	8 ♎	3 ♑	9 ♒	24 ♓	
29	7 ♒		1 ♈	9 ♉	15 ♊	10 ♌	9 ♍	3 ♏		9 ♓	26 ♈	26 ♉
31	2 ♓		25 ♈		16 ♋		17 ♍	10 ♐		3 ♈		19 ♉

1950	Jan.	Feb.	Mar.	April	May	June	July	Aug.	Sep.	Oct.	Nov.	Dec.
1	1 ♊	17 ♋	25 ♋	15 ♍	23 ♎	17 ♐	24 ♑	14 ♓	29 ♈	1 ♊	15 ♋	18 ♌
3	26 ♊	15 ♌	23 ♌	15 ♎	23 ♏	16 ♑	16 ♒	22 ♓	23 ♉	23 ♊	10 ♌	14 ♍
5	22 ♋	13 ♍	21 ♍	15 ♏	23 ♐	14 ♒	18 ♓	3 ♈	16 ♊	19 ♋	5 ♍	11 ♎
7	19 ♌	11 ♎	21 ♎	14 ♐	22 ♑	10 ♓	13 ♈	27 ♈	11 ♋	14 ♌	3 ♎	10 ♏
9	17 ♍	10 ♏	20 ♏	12 ♑	19 ♒	5 ♈	7 ♉	21 ♉	6 ♌	11 ♍	3 ♏	11 ♐
11	14 ♍	8 ♐	18 ♐	9 ♒	14 ♓	28 ♈	0 ♊	15 ♊	3 ♍	9 ♎	3 ♐	11 ♑
13	13 ♏	5 ♑	16 ♑	4 ♓	8 ♈	22 ♉	25 ♊	11 ♌	0 ♎	9 ♏	3 ♑	10 ♒
15	11 ♐	2 ♒	12 ♒	29 ♓	1 ♉	16 ♊	19 ♋	8 ♍	0 ♏	9 ♐	2 ♒	8 ♓
17	9 ♑	28 ♒	8 ♓	25 ♈	25 ♉	10 ♋	15 ♌	5 ♎	27 ♏	5 ♑	29 ♒	3 ♈
19	7 ♒	23 ♓	2 ♈	16 ♉	19 ♊	5 ♌	12 ♍	4 ♏	27 ♐	5 ♒	24 ♓	27 ♈
21	3 ♓	18 ♈	27 ♈	10 ♊	13 ♋	2 ♍	9 ♎	4 ♐	25 ♑	1 ♓	18 ♈	21 ♉
23	28 ♓	11 ♉	19 ♉	4 ♋	8 ♌	28 ♍	7 ♏	2 ♑	22 ♒	27 ♓	12 ♉	15 ♊
25	22 ♉	5 ♊	13 ♊	29 ♋	2 ♍	26 ♎	4 ♐	26 ♒	13 ♓	21 ♈	6 ♊	9 ♋
27	15 ♉	29 ♊	7 ♋	25 ♌	1 ♎	25 ♏	3 ♑	22 ♓	7 ♈	15 ♉	0 ♋	3 ♌
29	9 ♊		3 ♌	23 ♍	1 ♏	25 ♐	3 ♒	17 ♈	7 ♉	9 ♊	24 ♋	28 ♌
31	4 ♋		1 ♍		1 ♐		0 ♓			3 ♋		24 ♍

1951	Jan.	Feb.	Mar.	April	May	June	July	Aug.	Sep.	Oct.	Nov.	Dec.
1	7 ♎	29 ♏	10 ♐	3 ♒	11 ♓	29 ♈	2 ♊	16 ♋	2 ♍	6 ♎	27 ♏	5 ♑
3	5 ♏	28 ♐	9 ♑	1 ♓	7 ♈	23 ♉	26 ♊	10 ♌	27 ♍	3 ♏	26 ♐	5 ♒
5	4 ♐	28 ♑	7 ♒	27 ♓	2 ♉	17 ♊	20 ♋	5 ♍	23 ♎	1 ♐	25 ♑	3 ♓
7	4 ♑	26 ♒	5 ♓	23 ♈	26 ♉	11 ♋	13 ♌	0 ♎	21 ♏	0 ♑	23 ♒	0 ♈
9	4 ♒	24 ♓	1 ♈	18 ♉	20 ♊	4 ♌	8 ♍	27 ♎	18 ♐	28 ♑	19 ♓	26 ♈
11	2 ♓	19 ♈	27 ♈	12 ♊	14 ♋	29 ♌	3 ♎	24 ♏	17 ♑	26 ♒	16 ♈	21 ♉
13	29 ♓	14 ♉	22 ♉	5 ♋	8 ♌	24 ♍	0 ♏	22 ♐	16 ♒	24 ♓	12 ♉	16 ♊
15	24 ♈	8 ♊	16 ♊	29 ♋	2 ♍	20 ♎	28 ♏	22 ♑	15 ♓	20 ♈	7 ♊	10 ♋
17	18 ♉	2 ♋	9 ♋	24 ♌	28 ♍	19 ♏	28 ♐	22 ♒	12 ♈	16 ♉	1 ♋	3 ♌
19	12 ♊	26 ♋	4 ♌	20 ♍	26 ♎	19 ♐	28 ♑	20 ♓	7 ♉	11 ♊	25 ♋	27 ♌
21	5 ♋	21 ♌	29 ♌	18 ♎	26 ♏	20 ♑	28 ♒	17 ♈	3 ♊	5 ♋	19 ♌	21 ♍
23	0 ♌	17 ♍	26 ♍	17 ♏	26 ♐	19 ♒	26 ♓	13 ♉	7 ♋	23 ♌	9 ♎	14 ♏
25	25 ♌	14 ♎	24 ♎	17 ♐	26 ♑	17 ♓	22 ♈	7 ♊	21 ♋	23 ♎	9 ♏	13 ♐
27	21 ♍	12 ♏	22 ♏	16 ♑	24 ♒	13 ♈	17 ♉	1 ♋	15 ♌	18 ♏	6 ♐	13 ♑
29	17 ♎		21 ♐	14 ♒	21 ♓	8 ♉	11 ♊	25 ♋	10 ♍	14 ♐	5 ♑	14 ♒
31	15 ♏		20 ♑		16 ♈		5 ♋	19 ♌		12 ♏		14 ♓

1952	Jan.	Feb.	Mar.	April	May	June	July	Aug.	Sep.	Oct.	Nov.	Dec.
1	29 ♒	19 ♈	10 ♉	26 ♊	28 ♋	11 ♍	14 ♎	3 ♐	24 ♑	3 ♓	26 ♈	2 ♊
3	27 ♓	15 ♉	4 ♊	20 ♋	22 ♌	6 ♎	8 ♏	1 ♑	24 ♒	2 ♈	24 ♉	28 ♊
5	23 ♈	10 ♊	0 ♋	14 ♌	16 ♍	2 ♏	5 ♐	1 ♒	24 ♓	29 ♈	20 ♊	23 ♋
7	18 ♉	4 ♋	24 ♋	8 ♍	11 ♎	0 ♐	4 ♑	1 ♓	21 ♈	25 ♉	15 ♋	17 ♌
9	13 ♊	27 ♋	18 ♌	3 ♎	7 ♏	29 ♐	4 ♒	29 ♓	17 ♉	20 ♊	9 ♌	11 ♍
11	7 ♋	21 ♌	12 ♍	29 ♎	5 ♐	29 ♑	7 ♓	26 ♈	11 ♊	14 ♋	3 ♍	5 ♎
13	0 ♌	15 ♍	7 ♎	26 ♏	4 ♑	28 ♒	6 ♈	22 ♉	5 ♋	8 ♌	27 ♍	0 ♏
15	24 ♌	10 ♎	3 ♏	24 ♐	3 ♒	26 ♓	3 ♉	20 ♊	29 ♋	2 ♍	22 ♎	26 ♏
17	18 ♍	6 ♏	29 ♏	22 ♑	1 ♓	23 ♈	29 ♊	14 ♋	23 ♌	26 ♍	18 ♏	24 ♐
19	13 ♎	2 ♐	27 ♐	20 ♒	29 ♓	19 ♉	23 ♋	8 ♌	23 ♍	26 ♎	16 ♐	23 ♑
21	9 ♏	1 ♑	25 ♑	18 ♓	26 ♈	14 ♊	17 ♌	2 ♍	26 ♎	19 ♏	11 ♑	20 ♒
23	7 ♐	0 ♒	24 ♒	16 ♈	22 ♉	8 ♋	11 ♍	26 ♍	9 ♐	16 ♐	9 ♒	18 ♓
25	6 ♑	0 ♓	23 ♓	13 ♉	18 ♊	2 ♌	5 ♎	20 ♎	9 ♑	16 ♑	7 ♓	18 ♈
27	7 ♒	29 ♓	21 ♈	9 ♊	12 ♋	26 ♌	0 ♏	15 ♏	6 ♒	14 ♒	7 ♈	11 ♉
29	7 ♓	27 ♈	18 ♉	4 ♋	6 ♌	20 ♍	23 ♏	12 ♐	4 ♓	13 ♓	6 ♉	11 ♊
31	5 ♈		14 ♊		0 ♍		19 ♐	10 ♑		12 ♈		7 ♋

1953	Jan.	Feb.	Mar.	April	May	June	July	Aug.	Sep.	Oct.	Nov.	Dec.
1	19 ♋	4 ♍	12 ♍	27 ♎	2 ♐	21 ♑	0 ♓	24 ♈	15 ♊	20 ♋	5 ♍	7 ♎
3	13 ♌	27 ♍	6 ♎	22 ♏	28 ♐	19 ♒	29 ♓	21 ♉	11 ♋	15 ♌	29 ♍	1 ♎
5	7 ♍	21 ♎	0 ♏	18 ♐	18 ♑	18 ♓	27 ♈	18 ♊	6 ♌	9 ♍	23 ♎	26 ♏
7	1 ♎	16 ♏	26 ♏	14 ♑	18 ♒	16 ♈	25 ♉	14 ♋	0 ♍	3 ♎	17 ♏	21 ♐
9	25 ♎	12 ♐	23 ♐	11 ♒	16 ♓	14 ♉	22 ♊	3 ♌	17 ♍	20 ♏	14 ♐	14 ♑
11	20 ♏	10 ♑	18 ♑	11 ♓	20 ♈	12 ♊	9 ♋	2 ♍	26 ♍	11 ♐	15 ♑	12 ♒
13	18 ♐	9 ♒	17 ♒	11 ♈	19 ♉	9 ♋	12 ♌	26 ♍	15 ♐	15 ♑	4 ♒	12 ♓
15	16 ♑	10 ♓	18 ♓	11 ♉	9 ♊	4 ♌	6 ♍	20 ♎	1 ♐	7 ♒	9 ♓	9 ♈
17	16 ♒	10 ♈	18 ♈	9 ♊	13 ♋	28 ♌	0 ♎	14 ♏	1 ♐	7 ♓	7 ♈	5 ♉
19	16 ♓	8 ♉	17 ♉	6 ♋	7 ♌	22 ♍	6 ♏	5 ♐	27 ♒	6 ♈	7 ♉	2 ♊
21	15 ♈	5 ♊	14 ♊	0 ♌	2 ♍	16 ♎	18 ♐	14 ♑	4 ♈	29 ♈	20 ♊	27 ♊
23	12 ♉	1 ♋	10 ♋	24 ♌	18 ♍	6 ♐	14 ♑	4 ♒	28 ♈	24 ♉	20 ♋	27 ♋
25	8 ♊	25 ♋	4 ♌	18 ♍	20 ♎	6 ♑	10 ♒	4 ♓	28 ♉	5 ♊	20 ♌	21 ♍
27	4 ♋	19 ♌	28 ♌	12 ♎	15 ♏	3 ♒	1 ♓	4 ♈	27 ♊	3 ♋	20 ♎	15 ♏
29	28 ♋		21 ♍	6 ♏	1 ♐	1 ♓	10 ♈	2 ♉	25 ♋	25 ♌	14 ♏	9 ♐
31	22 ♌		15 ♎		8 ♑		9 ♈	2 ♊		23 ♌		3 ♑

1954	Jan.	Feb.	Mar.	April	May	June	July	Aug.	Sep.	Oct.	Nov.	Dec.
1	21 ♏	7 ♑	15 ♑	5 ♓	14 ♈	8 ♊	15 ♋	3 ♍	19 ♎	21 ♏	5 ♑	9 ♒
3	17 ♐	5 ♒	13 ♒	5 ♈	14 ♉	7 ♋	12 ♌	28 ♍	14 ♏	0 ♐	0 ♒	3 ♓
5	13 ♑	4 ♓	12 ♓	6 ♉	14 ♊	4 ♌	8 ♍	23 ♎	6 ♐	9 ♑	26 ♒	3 ♈
7	10 ♒	3 ♈	12 ♈	6 ♊	12 ♋	0 ♍	3 ♎	16 ♏	1 ♑	4 ♒	24 ♓	2 ♉
9	8 ♓	2 ♉	12 ♉	4 ♋	9 ♌	24 ♍	27 ♎	10 ♐	26 ♑	1 ♓	23 ♈	2 ♊
11	7 ♈	0 ♊	10 ♊	0 ♌	4 ♍	18 ♎	20 ♏	5 ♑	23 ♒	0 ♈	24 ♉	2 ♋
13	5 ♉	27 ♊	7 ♋	25 ♌	28 ♍	12 ♏	15 ♐	1 ♒	21 ♓	0 ♉	23 ♊	28 ♋
15	3 ♊	23 ♋	3 ♌	19 ♍	22 ♎	6 ♐	10 ♑	29 ♒	21 ♈	1 ♊	23 ♋	28 ♌
17	1 ♋	19 ♌	28 ♌	13 ♎	16 ♏	3 ♑	6 ♒	27 ♓	20 ♉	0 ♋	19 ♌	23 ♍
19	27 ♋	13 ♍	22 ♍	7 ♏	10 ♐	27 ♑	3 ♓	26 ♈	20 ♊	27 ♋	15 ♍	18 ♎
21	23 ♌	7 ♎	16 ♎	1 ♐	4 ♑	20 ♒	29 ♓	23 ♉	18 ♋	23 ♌	9 ♎	11 ♏
23	17 ♍	1 ♏	10 ♏	25 ♐	0 ♒	19 ♓	29 ♈	20 ♊	13 ♌	18 ♍	27 ♏	5 ♐
25	11 ♎	25 ♏	4 ♐	20 ♑	26 ♒	19 ♈	19 ♉	18 ♋	8 ♍	12 ♎	27 ♐	29 ♐
27	5 ♏	19 ♐	28 ♐	16 ♒	24 ♓	17 ♉	17 ♊	4 ♌	27 ♎	0 ♐	14 ♑	19 ♑
29	29 ♏		24 ♑	14 ♓	23 ♈	17 ♊		24 ♌		23 ♐		19 ♒
31	24 ♐		21 ♒		23 ♉		20 ♌	7 ♍		23 ♑		15 ♓

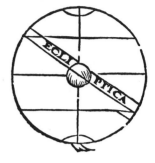

1955	Jan.	Feb.	Mar.	April	May	June	July	Aug.	Sep.	Oct.	Nov.	Dec.
1	29 ♓	22 ♉	3 ♊	25 ♊	2 ♍	19 ♎	22 ♏	6 ♑	22 ♒	27 ♓	18 ♉	26 ♊
3	27 ♈	20 ♊	1 ♊	28 ♍	22 ♍	14 ♏	16 ♐	1 ♒	18 ♓	25 ♈	18 ♊	26 ♋
5	26 ♉	19 ♋	28 ♊	18 ♍	22 ♎	7 ♐	10 ♑	26 ♒	15 ♈	23 ♉	17 ♋	25 ♌
7	25 ♊	17 ♌	25 ♌	13 ♎	16 ♏	1 ♑	4 ♒	22 ♓	13 ♉	22 ♊	15 ♌	22 ♍
9	24 ♋	13 ♍	22 ♍	10 ♏	10 ♐	25 ♑	29 ♒	19 ♈	11 ♊	20 ♋	12 ♍	18 ♎
11	22 ♌	9 ♎	17 ♎	2 ♐	4 ♑	19 ♒	25 ♓	16 ♉	9 ♋	18 ♌	8 ♎	12 ♏
13	19 ♍	4 ♏	12 ♏	25 ♐	29 ♑	15 ♓	22 ♈	15 ♊	8 ♌	15 ♍	3 ♏	6 ♐
15	14 ♎	27 ♏	5 ♐	19 ♑	23 ♒	12 ♈	20 ♉	13 ♋	5 ♍	11 ♎	27 ♏	0 ♑
17	8 ♏	21 ♐	29 ♐	14 ♒	19 ♓	10 ♉	19 ♊	12 ♌	2 ♎	7 ♏	21 ♐	23 ♑
19	1 ♐	16 ♑	23 ♑	10 ♓	17 ♈	10 ♊	19 ♋	10 ♍	28 ♎	1 ♐	15 ♑	17 ♒
21	25 ♐	11 ♒	19 ♒	9 ♈	17 ♉	11 ♋	18 ♌	7 ♎	23 ♏	25 ♐	8 ♒	12 ♓
23	20 ♑	8 ♓	16 ♓	8 ♉	17 ♊	12 ♌	16 ♍	3 ♏	17 ♐	18 ♑	3 ♓	8 ♈
25	16 ♒	6 ♈	15 ♈	8 ♊	17 ♋	12 ♍	12 ♎	27 ♏	10 ♑	12 ♒	29 ♓	5 ♉
27	12 ♓	4 ♉	14 ♉	8 ♋	15 ♌	8 ♎	7 ♏	21 ♐	5 ♒	8 ♓	26 ♈	4 ♊
29	10 ♈		13 ♊	6 ♌	12 ♍	28 ♎	1 ♐	14 ♑	0 ♓	5 ♈	26 ♉	4 ♋
31	8 ♉		12 ♋		7 ♎		24 ♐	9 ♒		3 ♉		5 ♌

1956	Jan.	Feb.	Mar.	April	May	June	July	Aug.	Sep.	Oct.	Nov.	Dec.
1	19 ♌	10 ♎	1 ♏	16 ♐	17 ♑	1 ♓	5 ♈	24 ♉	16 ♋	25 ♌	17 ♎	23 ♏
3	18 ♍	5 ♏	26 ♏	10 ♑	11 ♒	26 ♓	1 ♉	22 ♊	15 ♌	24 ♍	14 ♏	18 ♐
5	14 ♎	0 ♐	20 ♐	3 ♒	6 ♓	29 ♈	29 ♉	21 ♋	13 ♍	22 ♎	10 ♐	13 ♑
7	9 ♏	24 ♐	13 ♑	28 ♒	1 ♈	20 ♉	28 ♊	20 ♌	11 ♎	19 ♏	5 ♑	7 ♒
9	3 ♐	17 ♑	7 ♒	23 ♓	28 ♈	20 ♊	28 ♋	18 ♍	7 ♏	15 ♐	29 ♑	1 ♓
11	27 ♐	11 ♒	2 ♓	20 ♈	26 ♉	20 ♋	27 ♌	16 ♎	1 ♐	9 ♑	23 ♒	25 ♓
13	20 ♑	6 ♓	28 ♓	17 ♉	26 ♊	19 ♌	24 ♍	11 ♏	25 ♐	3 ♒	17 ♓	20 ♈
15	14 ♒	1 ♈	24 ♈	16 ♊	25 ♋	18 ♍	21 ♎	5 ♐	19 ♑	27 ♒	12 ♈	16 ♉
17	9 ♓	27 ♈	21 ♉	14 ♋	23 ♌	14 ♎	17 ♏	28 ♐	12 ♒	21 ♓	8 ♉	14 ♊
19	4 ♈	24 ♉	19 ♊	12 ♌	21 ♍	10 ♏	14 ♐	22 ♑	6 ♓	17 ♈	6 ♊	14 ♋
21	0 ♉	22 ♊	17 ♋	10 ♍	17 ♎	5 ♐	8 ♑	15 ♒	1 ♈	13 ♉	6 ♋	14 ♌
23	28 ♉	21 ♋	16 ♌	8 ♎	13 ♏	29 ♐	2 ♒	9 ♓	26 ♈	11 ♊	4 ♌	13 ♍
25	27 ♊	21 ♌	14 ♍	4 ♏	8 ♐	22 ♑	25 ♒	4 ♈	22 ♉	9 ♋	2 ♍	10 ♎
27	27 ♋	20 ♍	12 ♎	29 ♏	2 ♑	16 ♒	19 ♓	0 ♉	28 ♊	7 ♌	0 ♎	7 ♏
29	27 ♌	17 ♎	9 ♏	24 ♐	26 ♑	10 ♓	14 ♈	26 ♉		5 ♍	27 ♎	2 ♐
31	26 ♍		4 ♐		19 ♒		10 ♉	1 ♋		3 ♎		27 ♐

1957	Jan.	Feb.	Mar.	April	May	June	July	Aug.	Sep.	Oct.	Nov.	Dec.
1	9 ♑	24 ♒	3 ♓	18 ♈	22 ♉	13 ♋	22 ♌	15 ♎	6 ♐	11 ♑	25 ♒	27 ♓
3	3 ♒	18 ♓	27 ♓	13 ♉	19 ♊	12 ♌	21 ♍	13 ♏	2 ♑	5 ♒	19 ♓	21 ♈
5	27 ♒	12 ♈	21 ♈	9 ♊	17 ♋	10 ♍	19 ♎	9 ♐	29 ♑	29 ♒	13 ♈	16 ♉
7	21 ♓	6 ♉	16 ♉	6 ♋	15 ♌	8 ♎	16 ♏	4 ♑	23 ♒	23 ♓	7 ♉	11 ♊
9	15 ♈	2 ♊	11 ♊	4 ♌	13 ♍	6 ♏	12 ♐	29 ♑	14 ♓	17 ♈	3 ♊	8 ♋
11	11 ♉	0 ♋	9 ♋	2 ♍	11 ♎	3 ♐	8 ♑	23 ♒	11 ♈	11 ♉	29 ♋	6 ♌
13	8 ♊	0 ♌	9 ♌	2 ♎	10 ♏	29 ♐	3 ♒	17 ♓	2 ♉	6 ♊	26 ♌	4 ♍
15	7 ♋	1 ♍	9 ♍	1 ♏	7 ♐	24 ♑	26 ♒	11 ♈	26 ♉	2 ♋	3 ♍	1 ♎
17	7 ♌	1 ♎	9 ♎	29 ♏	3 ♑	18 ♒	20 ♓	5 ♉	22 ♊	29 ♋	22 ♎	1 ♏
19	7 ♎	29 ♎	7 ♏	25 ♐	28 ♑	12 ♓	14 ♈	0 ♊	18 ♋	27 ♍	21 ♏	29 ♏
21	7 ♎	26 ♏	4 ♐	20 ♑	22 ♒	6 ♈	8 ♉	26 ♊	18 ♌	27 ♎	20 ♐	26 ♐
23	4 ♏	21 ♐	0 ♑	14 ♒	16 ♓	0 ♉	4 ♊	24 ♋	19 ♎	26 ♏	17 ♑	22 ♑
25	0 ♐	15 ♑	24 ♑	8 ♓	10 ♈	26 ♉	2 ♋	25 ♌	19 ♏	26 ♐	14 ♒	17 ♒
27	24 ♐	9 ♒	18 ♒	2 ♈	5 ♉	23 ♊	1 ♍	25 ♎	18 ♐	19 ♑	9 ♓	11 ♓
29	18 ♑		11 ♓	27 ♈	1 ♊	22 ♋	1 ♎	25 ♏	15 ♑	13 ♒	5 ♈	5 ♈
31	12 ♒		6 ♈		29 ♊		1 ♎	23 ♏		13 ♓		29 ♈

1958	Jan.	Feb.	Mar.	April	May	June	July	Aug.	Sep.	Oct.	Nov.	Dec.
1	11 ♉	27 ♊	5 ♋	26 ♋	5 ♍	28 ♎	24 ♐	9 ♈	11 ♉	26 ♊	1 ♌
3	6 ♊	25 ♋	3 ♌	26 ♍	5 ♎	27 ♐	2 ♑	18 ♓	5 ♊	21 ♋	27 ♌
5	3 ♋	25 ♌	3 ♍	27 ♎	4 ♐	24 ♑	28 ♒	12 ♈	29 ♊	17 ♌	24 ♍
7	1 ♌	25 ♍	3 ♎	26 ♏	2 ♑	20 ♒	26 ♓	6 ♉	29 ♋	15 ♍	23 ♎
9	1 ♍	24 ♎	3 ♏	24 ♐	29 ♑	14 ♓	10 ♈	0 ♊	16 ♌	22 ♍	23 ♏
11	29 ♍	22 ♏	2 ♐	21 ♑	24 ♒	8 ♈	10 ♉	25 ♊	13 ♍	21 ♎	22 ♐
13	28 ♎	19 ♐	29 ♐	16 ♒	18 ♓	2 ♉	4 ♊	22 ♋	13 ♎	21 ♏	21 ♑
15	25 ♏	14 ♑	25 ♑	10 ♓	12 ♈	26 ♉	0 ♋	20 ♌	12 ♏	20 ♐	18 ♒
17	22 ♐	9 ♒	19 ♒	3 ♈	6 ♉	21 ♊	29 ♋	19 ♍	20 ♐	18 ♑	5 ♓
19	18 ♑	4 ♓	13 ♓	27 ♈	0 ♊	18 ♋	25 ♌	18 ♎	11 ♐	18 ♑	5 ♒
21	13 ♒	28 ♓	6 ♈	21 ♉	26 ♊	13 ♌	22 ♎	14 ♐	4 ♑	14 ♒	29 ♈
23	7 ♓	21 ♈	0 ♉	15 ♊	21 ♋	13 ♎	14 ♐	4 ♑	8 ♓	23 ♓	25 ♉
25	1 ♈	15 ♉	24 ♉	11 ♋	19 ♌	11 ♏	9 ♑	5 ♒	2 ♈	17 ♈	19 ♊
27	25 ♈	9 ♊	18 ♊	8 ♌	16 ♍	9 ♐	18 ♒	2 ♓	26 ♈	11 ♉	15 ♋
29	19 ♉		14 ♋	6 ♍	14 ♎	8 ♐	15 ♓	2 ♈	20 ♉	5 ♊	11 ♌
31	14 ♊		12 ♌		14 ♏		11 ♈	27 ♈		14 ♊		8 ♍

1959	Jan.	Feb.	Mar.	April	May	June	July	Aug.	Sep.	Oct.	Nov.	Dec.
1	21 ♍	14 ♏	25 ♏	17 ♑	24 ♒	10 ♈	12 ♉	26 ♊	12 ♌	17 ♍	9 ♏	17 ♐
3	19 ♎	12 ♐	23 ♐	14 ♒	19 ♓	4 ♉	6 ♊	21 ♋	9 ♍	15 ♎	9 ♐	17 ♑
5	16 ♏	9 ♑	20 ♑	10 ♓	13 ♈	28 ♉	1 ♋	18 ♌	8 ♎	14 ♏	7 ♑	13 ♒
7	13 ♐	6 ♒	17 ♒	4 ♈	7 ♉	21 ♊	25 ♋	13 ♍	5 ♏	14 ♐	7 ♒	8 ♓
9	15 ♑	2 ♓	12 ♓	28 ♈	0 ♊	16 ♋	20 ♌	8 ♏	3 ♐	10 ♑	29 ♒	3 ♈
11	13 ♒	29 ♓	7 ♈	21 ♉	24 ♊	10 ♌	16 ♍	8 ♏	1 ♑	6 ♒	23 ♓	26 ♈
13	9 ♓	23 ♈	1 ♉	15 ♊	18 ♋	6 ♍	12 ♎	7 ♐	27 ♑	0 ♓	20 ♈	20 ♉
15	3 ♈	17 ♉	25 ♉	9 ♋	13 ♌	2 ♎	10 ♏	27 ♐		2 ♈	17 ♉	14 ♊
17	27 ♈	11 ♊	19 ♊	4 ♌	10 ♍	1 ♏	11 ♐	4 ♒	23 ♓	27 ♈	11 ♊	8 ♋
19	21 ♉	5 ♋	13 ♋	0 ♍	8 ♎	1 ♐	8 ♑	12 ♈	18 ♉	22 ♉	5 ♋	3 ♌
21	15 ♊	1 ♌	9 ♌	29 ♍	8 ♏	1 ♑	27 ♒	9 ♈	13 ♊	15 ♊	29 ♋	29 ♌
23	10 ♋	27 ♌	6 ♍	29 ♎	8 ♑	6 ♓	17 ♓	28 ♉	23 ♋	19 ♋	17 ♎	29 ♍
25	7 ♌	26 ♍	6 ♎	29 ♏	28 ♑	24 ♓	17 ♈	22 ♊	17 ♌	25 ♍	17 ♎	26 ♏
27	4 ♍	26 ♎	6 ♏	29 ♐	24 ♒	27 ♈	10 ♉	18 ♋	24 ♎	20 ♎	17 ♏	25 ♐
29	2 ♎		5 ♐	27 ♑	19 ♓	14 ♉	29 ♊		20 ♏	17 ♐	25 ♑
31	0 ♏		4 ♑		28 ♓		14 ♊	29 ♋		24 ♎		26 ♑

1960	Jan.	Feb.	Mar.	April	May	June	July	Aug.	Sep.	Oct.	Nov.	Dec.
1	10 ♒	0 ♈	20 ♈	5 ♊	7 ♋	22 ♌	25 ♍	15 ♏	8 ♑	17 ♒	8 ♈	14 ♉
3	8 ♓	25 ♈	15 ♉	29 ♊	23 ♋	16 ♍	21 ♎	13 ♐	7 ♒	15 ♓	13 ♉	9 ♊
5	5 ♈	20 ♉	9 ♊	23 ♋	25 ♌	11 ♎	19 ♐	13 ♑	6 ♓	13 ♈	0 ♊	3 ♋
7	29 ♈	13 ♊	3 ♋	17 ♌	21 ♍	11 ♏	19 ♐	13 ♒	4 ♈	9 ♉	25 ♊	27 ♋
9	27 ♉	7 ♋	27 ♋	18 ♍	11 ♏	11 ♐	19 ♑	10 ♓	1 ♉	5 ♊	20 ♋	20 ♌
11	17 ♊	1 ♌	20 ♌	8 ♎	17 ♏	11 ♑	18 ♒	6 ♈	8 ♊	21 ♋	14 ♌	14 ♍
13	11 ♋	27 ♌	15 ♍	8 ♏	17 ♐	18 ♒	16 ♓	6 ♉	11 ♋	23 ♌	8 ♍	9 ♎
15	5 ♌	22 ♍	8 ♎	8 ♐	17 ♑	17 ♓	9 ♈	1 ♊	15 ♌	16 ♍	2 ♎	6 ♏
17	0 ♍	19 ♎	8 ♏	8 ♐	17 ♒	10 ♈	5 ♉	9 ♋	9 ♍	11 ♎	0 ♐	5 ♐
19	26 ♍	16 ♏	11 ♐	8 ♑	13 ♓	5 ♉	4 ♊	18 ♋	3 ♎	7 ♏	26 ♐	5 ♑
21	22 ♎	15 ♐	10 ♑	5 ♒	2 ♈	9 ♊	25 ♊	28 ♋	28 ♎	4 ♐	26 ♑	5 ♒
23	20 ♏	13 ♑	8 ♒	4 ♓	28 ♈	28 ♊	13 ♋	16 ♌	7 ♐	2 ♑	24 ♒	2 ♓
25	19 ♐	12 ♒	6 ♓	24 ♓	24 ♉	19 ♋	16 ♌	10 ♍	2 ♑	1 ♒	22 ♓	28 ♓
27	2 ♑	10 ♓	2 ♈	19 ♈	19 ♊	13 ♌	8 ♍	2 ♎	20 ♑	29 ♒	18 ♈	23 ♈
29	18 ♒	7 ♈	28 ♈	13 ♉	16 ♋	5 ♍	1 ♎	25 ♎	18 ♒	27 ♓	—	18 ♉
31	16 ♓		23 ♉		10 ♌		23 ♏	1 ♏		25 ♈		18 ♊

1961	Jan.	Feb.	Mar.	April	May	June	July	Aug.	Sept.	Oct.	Nov.	Dec.
1	0 ♋	14 ♌	23 ♌	8 ♎	13 ♐	5 ♒	13 ♓	7 ♈	27 ♉	1 ♋	15 ♌	16 ♍
3	24 ♋	8 ♍	17 ♍	4 ♏	11 ♑	4 ♓	13 ♈	4 ♉	22 ♊	25 ♋	9 ♍	10 ♎
5	17 ♌	2 ♎	12 ♎	3 ♐	9 ♒	2 ♈	11 ♉	1 ♊	17 ♋	19 ♌	3 ♎	6 ♏
7	11 ♍	27 ♎	7 ♏	28 ♐	8 ♓	0 ♉	8 ♊	25 ♊	10 ♌	12 ♍	29 ♎	3 ♐
9	5 ♎	24 ♏	4 ♐	26 ♑	6 ♈	27 ♉	3 ♋	20 ♋	4 ♍	6 ♎	23 ♏	2 ♑
11	0 ♐	22 ♐	2 ♑	25 ♒	4 ♉	24 ♊	28 ♋	13 ♌	28 ♍	1 ♏	20 ♐	28 ♑
13	28 ♐	21 ♑	2 ♒	23 ♓	1 ♊	19 ♋	22 ♌	7 ♍	23 ♎	27 ♏	18 ♑	26 ♒
15	28 ♑	21 ♒	0 ♓	19 ♈	28 ♊	14 ♌	16 ♍	1 ♎	17 ♏	23 ♐	16 ♒	25 ♓
17	28 ♒	20 ♓	29 ♓	14 ♉	23 ♋	8 ♍	10 ♎	25 ♎	14 ♐	21 ♑	16 ♓	23 ♈
19	28 ♓	20 ♈	27 ♈	10 ♊	18 ♌	2 ♎	4 ♏	20 ♏	11 ♑	19 ♒	15 ♈	20 ♉
21	27 ♈	16 ♉	24 ♉	5 ♋	11 ♍	25 ♎	28 ♏	17 ♐	9 ♒	18 ♓	11 ♉	17 ♊
23	25 ♉	11 ♊	20 ♊	4 ♌	5 ♎	20 ♏	24 ♐	15 ♑	9 ♓	17 ♈	8 ♊	12 ♋
25	20 ♊	6 ♋	14 ♋	7 ♍	25 ♎	16 ♐	22 ♑	15 ♒	9 ♈	16 ♉	4 ♋	7 ♌
27	15 ♋	29 ♋	7 ♌	21 ♍	25 ♏	13 ♑	22 ♒	15 ♓	8 ♉	13 ♊	29 ♋	1 ♍
29	9 ♌		1 ♍	17 ♎	22 ♐	14 ♒	22 ♓	15 ♈	5 ♊	9 ♋	23 ♌	24 ♍
31	2 ♍		26 ♍		20 ♐		22 ♈	13 ♉		9 ♌		18 ♎

1962	Jan.	Feb.	Mar.	April	May	June	July	Aug.	Sept.	Oct.	Nov.	Dec.
1	1 ♏	18 ♐	26 ♐	17 ♒	26 ♓	20 ♉	26 ♊	14 ♌	28 ♍	1 ♏	17 ♐	22 ♑
3	26 ♏	16 ♑	24 ♑	17 ♓	25 ♈	17 ♊	22 ♋	8 ♍	22 ♎	25 ♏	12 ♑	19 ♒
5	24 ♐	15 ♒	23 ♒	17 ♈	23 ♉	18 ♋	18 ♌	2 ♎	16 ♏	20 ♐	8 ♒	16 ♓
7	23 ♑	16 ♓	24 ♓	17 ♉	23 ♊	10 ♌	12 ♍	25 ♎	11 ♐	15 ♑	6 ♓	15 ♈
9	22 ♒	15 ♈	23 ♈	11 ♊	19 ♋	4 ♍	5 ♎	20 ♏	6 ♑	12 ♒	5 ♈	14 ♉
11	21 ♓	13 ♉	23 ♉	11 ♋	14 ♌	27 ♍	29 ♎	15 ♐	4 ♒	11 ♓	5 ♉	13 ♊
13	20 ♈	10 ♊	20 ♊	11 ♌	8 ♍	21 ♎	24 ♏	12 ♑	4 ♓	12 ♈	5 ♊	11 ♋
15	17 ♉	5 ♋	15 ♋	29 ♌	2 ♎	16 ♏	20 ♐	10 ♒	4 ♈	12 ♉	4 ♋	8 ♌
17	13 ♊	0 ♌	9 ♌	3 ♍	25 ♎	10 ♐	17 ♑	10 ♓	4 ♉	11 ♊	0 ♌	3 ♍
19	8 ♋	24 ♌	3 ♍	17 ♎	20 ♏	6 ♑	16 ♒	9 ♈	3 ♊	9 ♋	25 ♌	27 ♍
21	3 ♌	17 ♍	26 ♍	11 ♏	16 ♐	5 ♒	15 ♓	9 ♉	0 ♋	4 ♌	19 ♍	21 ♎
23	27 ♌	11 ♎	20 ♎	4 ♐	13 ♑	5 ♓	14 ♈	6 ♊	25 ♋	29 ♌	13 ♎	15 ♏
25	21 ♍	5 ♏	14 ♏	14 ♑	10 ♒	5 ♈	12 ♉	3 ♋	20 ♌	22 ♍	7 ♏	10 ♐
27	14 ♎	0 ♐	10 ♐	10 ♒	8 ♓	5 ♉	10 ♊	28 ♋	14 ♍	16 ♎	1 ♐	5 ♑
29	9 ♏		6 ♑	6 ♓	9 ♈	1 ♊	6 ♋	23 ♌	7 ♎	10 ♏	26 ♐	2 ♒
31	4 ♐		3 ♒		5 ♉		1 ♌	17 ♍		4 ♐		29 ♒

1963	Jan.	Feb.	Mar.	April	May	June	July	Aug.	Sept.	Oct.	Nov.	Dec.
1	13 ♓	6 ♉	17 ♉	9 ♋	14 ♌	0 ♎	2 ♏	16 ♐	2 ♒	7 ♓	29 ♈	8 ♊
3	11 ♈	5 ♊	15 ♊	5 ♌	9 ♍	24 ♎	26 ♏	11 ♑	29 ♒	6 ♈	0 ♉	8 ♋
5	10 ♉	2 ♋	12 ♋	0 ♍	17 ♎	20 ♏	20 ♐	7 ♒	27 ♓	6 ♉	0 ♊	7 ♌
7	8 ♊	28 ♋	8 ♌	24 ♍	27 ♎	12 ♐	15 ♑	4 ♓	28 ♈	6 ♊	28 ♊	3 ♍
9	6 ♋	24 ♌	3 ♍	18 ♎	21 ♏	6 ♑	11 ♒	2 ♈	24 ♉	20 ♋	23 ♋	29 ♍
11	3 ♌	19 ♍	27 ♍	12 ♏	15 ♐	1 ♒	8 ♓	1 ♉	20 ♊	27 ♌	14 ♌	17 ♎
13	28 ♌	13 ♎	21 ♎	6 ♐	9 ♑	27 ♒	6 ♈	29 ♉	18 ♋	21 ♍	10 ♍	10 ♏
15	17 ♍	7 ♏	15 ♏	0 ♑	4 ♒	4 ♓	3 ♉	27 ♊	13 ♌	17 ♎	4 ♎	4 ♐
17	17 ♎	1 ♐	9 ♐	25 ♑	1 ♓	1 ♈	3 ♊	21 ♋	17 ♍	11 ♏	29 ♎	1 ♑
19	11 ♏	25 ♐	3 ♑	21 ♒	29 ♓	23 ♉	23 ♊	17 ♌	5 ♎	5 ♐	24 ♐	20 ♑
21	5 ♐	21 ♑	29 ♑	20 ♓	28 ♈	22 ♊	22 ♋	12 ♍	26 ♎	29 ♐	20 ♑	17 ♒
23	1 ♑	19 ♒	26 ♒	20 ♈	28 ♉	21 ♋	26 ♌	6 ♎	20 ♏	24 ♑	20 ♒	16 ♓
25	27 ♑	18 ♓	26 ♓	20 ♉	28 ♊	18 ♌	22 ♍	0 ♐	14 ♐	20 ♒	17 ♓	16 ♈
27	25 ♒	18 ♈	27 ♈	20 ♊	27 ♋	14 ♍	16 ♎	24 ♐	14 ♑	18 ♓	16 ♈	16 ♉
29	23 ♓		27 ♉	18 ♋	23 ♌	8 ♎	10 ♏	19 ♑	12 ♒	15 ♈	16 ♉	16 ♊
31	22 ♈		25 ♊		18 ♍		4 ♐	19 ♒		14 ♉		16 ♋

1964	Jan.	Feb.	Mar.	April	May	June	July	Aug.	Sept.	Oct.	Nov.	Dec.
1	1 ♌	19 ♍	10 ♎	25 ♏	27 ♐	12 ♒	16 ♓	7 ♉	0 ♌	9 ♍	0 ♎	5 ♏
3	28 ♌	15 ♎	5 ♏	19 ♐	21 ♑	7 ♓	5 ♈	5 ♊	28 ♌	6 ♎	25 ♎	29 ♏
5	24 ♍	9 ♏	29 ♏	13 ♑	15 ♒	4 ♈	4 ♉	3 ♋	27 ♍	3 ♏	20 ♐	23 ♑
7	19 ♎	3 ♐	23 ♐	7 ♒	11 ♓	1 ♉	3 ♊	25 ♋	25 ♎	29 ♏	15 ♑	17 ♒
9	13 ♏	27 ♐	17 ♑	3 ♓	9 ♈	0 ♊	1 ♋	21 ♌	24 ♐	24 ♑	8 ♒	10 ♓
11	7 ♐	21 ♑	12 ♒	1 ♈	9 ♉	1 ♋	0 ♌	16 ♍	21 ♑	18 ♒	2 ♓	4 ♈
13	1 ♑	17 ♒	8 ♓	0 ♉	8 ♊	1 ♌	26 ♌	10 ♎	17 ♒	12 ♓	26 ♓	0 ♉
15	25 ♑	13 ♓	6 ♈	29 ♉	8 ♋	0 ♍	21 ♍	4 ♏	13 ♓	8 ♈	23 ♈	27 ♉
17	21 ♒	11 ♈	6 ♉	29 ♊	7 ♌	26 ♍	14 ♎	28 ♏	9 ♈	6 ♉	1 ♉	25 ♊
19	17 ♓	9 ♉	4 ♊	27 ♋	4 ♍	21 ♎	8 ♏	23 ♐	19 ♉	4 ♊	18 ♊	25 ♋
21	14 ♈	7 ♊	2 ♋	20 ♌	29 ♍	24 ♏	2 ♐	18 ♑	27 ♊	4 ♋	20 ♋	26 ♌
23	12 ♉	5 ♋	0 ♌	20 ♍	24 ♎	9 ♐	26 ♐	12 ♒	27 ♋	3 ♌	20 ♌	25 ♍
25	11 ♊	3 ♌	27 ♌	15 ♎	18 ♏	3 ♑	20 ♑	8 ♓	24 ♌	23 ♍	16 ♍	21 ♎
27	10 ♋	1 ♍	23 ♍	10 ♏	12 ♐	6 ♒	14 ♒	4 ♈	22 ♍	19 ♎	13 ♎	14 ♏
29	8 ♌	27 ♍	18 ♎	4 ♐	6 ♑	0 ♓	10 ♓	2 ♉	19 ♎	14 ♏	10 ♏	8 ♐
31	6 ♍		13 ♏		0 ♒		8 ♈	0 ♊		11 ♐		1 ♑

1965

	Jan.	Feb.	Mar.	April	May	June	July	Aug.	Sept.	Oct.	Nov.	Dec.
1	20 ♐	4 ♒	13 ♒	29 ♓	4 ♉	26 ♊	4 ♌	28 ♍	17 ♏	21 ♐	5 ♒	6 ♓
3	14 ♑	29 ♒	7 ♓	25 ♈	2 ♊	25 ♋	4 ♍	25 ♎	12 ♐	15 ♑	28 ♒	0 ♈
5	7 ♑	23 ♓	3 ♈	23 ♉	2 ♋	24 ♌	21 ♍	21 ♏	7 ♑	9 ♒	23 ♓	26 ♈
7	1 ♒	19 ♈	29 ♈	20 ♊	30 ♋	22 ♍	16 ♎	16 ♐	0 ♒	2 ♓	18 ♈	22 ♉
9	26 ♒	15 ♉	26 ♉	20 ♋	29 ♌	24 ♎	16 ♏	10 ♑	22 ♒	28 ♓	12 ♉	20 ♊
11	22 ♓	13 ♊	24 ♊	17 ♌	25 ♍	15 ♏	19 ♐	3 ♒	18 ♓	22 ♈	12 ♊	20 ♋
13	19 ♈	12 ♋	22 ♋	15 ♍	12 ♎	6 ♐	19 ♑	21 ♒	9 ♈	15 ♉	11 ♋	19 ♌
15	18 ♉	12 ♌	21 ♌	13 ♎	18 ♏	4 ♑	6 ♒	21 ♓	9 ♉	15 ♊	8 ♌	15 ♍
17	19 ♊	12 ♍	20 ♍	9 ♏	28 ♐	0 ♒	5 ♓	12 ♈	2 ♊	5 ♋	5 ♍	12 ♎
19	19 ♋	10 ♎	18 ♎	5 ♐	7 ♑	21 ♒	3 ♈	8 ♉	2 ♋	11 ♌	5 ♎	7 ♐
21	18 ♌	7 ♏	14 ♏	0 ♑	25 ♑	10 ♓	25 ♈	7 ♊	0 ♌	9 ♍	28 ♎	2 ♑
23	15 ♍	1 ♐	9 ♐	23 ♑	15 ♒	10 ♈	25 ♉	7 ♋	30 ♍	9 ♎	24 ♏	27 ♑
25	11 ♎	25 ♐	3 ♑	19 ♒	19 ♓	7 ♉	13 ♊	6 ♌	7 ♏	7 ♐	20 ♐	20 ♒
27	5 ♐	19 ♑	27 ♑	13 ♓	19 ♈	6 ♊	13 ♋	6 ♍	28 ♏	3 ♑	14 ♑	14 ♓
29	29 ♐		21 ♒	9 ♈	15 ♉	5 ♋	13 ♌	4 ♎	23 ♐	28 ♑	12 ♒	8 ♈
31	22 ♑		16 ♓		11 ♊		13 ♍	4 ♏		23 ♒		8 ♈

1966

	Jan.	Feb.	Mar.	April	May	June	July	Aug.	Sept.	Oct.	Nov.	Dec.
1	21 ♈	8 ♊	17 ♊	9 ♌	18 ♍	11 ♏	17 ♐	4 ♒	19 ♓	22 ♈	8 ♊	14 ♋
3	16 ♉	6 ♋	15 ♋	8 ♍	17 ♎	8 ♐	13 ♑	28 ♒	13 ♈	16 ♉	8 ♋	11 ♌
5	14 ♊	6 ♌	14 ♌	7 ♎	13 ♏	2 ♑	8 ♒	23 ♓	7 ♉	11 ♊	6 ♌	9 ♍
7	13 ♋	7 ♍	15 ♍	7 ♏	13 ♐	26 ♑	2 ♓	16 ♈	1 ♊	6 ♋	4 ♍	6 ♎
9	13 ♌	7 ♎	13 ♎	1 ♐	24 ♐	20 ♒	10 ♈	19 ♉	5 ♋	4 ♌	0 ♎	6 ♏
11	13 ♍	5 ♏	10 ♏	26 ♐	9 ♑	4 ♓	17 ♉	5 ♊	25 ♋	4 ♍	26 ♎	4 ♐
13	12 ♎	1 ♐	5 ♐	20 ♑	6 ♒	10 ♈	10 ♊	5 ♋	25 ♌	3 ♎	23 ♏	17 ♑
15	9 ♏	26 ♐	29 ♐	13 ♒	21 ♓	6 ♉	2 ♋	5 ♌	25 ♍	2 ♏	17 ♐	28 ♑
17	4 ♐	20 ♑	23 ♑	7 ♓	16 ♈	2 ♊	1 ♌	5 ♍	25 ♎	2 ♐	20 ♑	17 ♒
19	29 ♐	14 ♒	17 ♒	2 ♈	7 ♉	28 ♊	1 ♍	23 ♎	20 ♏	25 ♐	9 ♒	11 ♓
21	23 ♑	8 ♓	11 ♓	7 ♉	7 ♊	28 ♋	7 ♎	20 ♏	25 ♐	19 ♑	5 ♓	11 ♈
23	17 ♒	2 ♈	5 ♈	20 ♉	26 ♊	6 ♌	4 ♏	24 ♐	10 ♑	13 ♒	29 ♓	26 ♈
25	11 ♓	26 ♈	1 ♉	1 ♋	26 ♋	2 ♍	24 ♏	18 ♑	4 ♒	9 ♓	27 ♈	26 ♉
27	5 ♈	21 ♉	27 ♉	29 ♋	21 ♌	0 ♎	18 ♐	13 ♒	28 ♓	0 ♈	17 ♉	23 ♊
29	29 ♈		25 ♊	19 ♌	21 ♍	27 ♎	13 ♑	7 ♓		17 ♈		23 ♋
31	25 ♉		25 ♋		27 ♎		22 ♒	3 ♈		25 ♉		21 ♌

1967

	Jan.	Feb.	Mar.	April	May	June	July	Aug.	Sept.	Oct.	Nov.	Dec.
1	6 ♍	29 ♎	9 ♏	30 ♐	5 ♒	20 ♓	22 ♈	6 ♊	22 ♋	28 ♌	20 ♎	29 ♏
3	4 ♎	27 ♏	7 ♐	26 ♑	0 ♓	14 ♈	16 ♉	1 ♋	20 ♌	27 ♍	21 ♏	29 ♐
5	2 ♏	23 ♐	3 ♑	21 ♒	24 ♓	7 ♉	10 ♊	27 ♋	19 ♍	27 ♎	21 ♐	24 ♑
7	0 ♐	19 ♑	29 ♑	15 ♓	17 ♈	2 ♊	2 ♋	24 ♌	18 ♎	26 ♏	15 ♑	19 ♒
9	27 ♐	13 ♒	24 ♒	8 ♈	11 ♉	27 ♊	2 ♌	24 ♍	26 ♏	15 ♐	9 ♒	13 ♓
11	23 ♑	9 ♓	18 ♓	2 ♉	5 ♊	20 ♋	28 ♌	21 ♎	19 ♐	4 ♑	3 ♓	7 ♈
13	18 ♒	3 ♈	13 ♈	26 ♉	3 ♋	20 ♌	21 ♍	16 ♐	13 ♑	19 ♒	0 ♈	2 ♉
15	13 ♓	26 ♈	5 ♉	20 ♊	20 ♋	17 ♍	15 ♎	16 ♑	9 ♒	4 ♓	25 ♈	26 ♉
17	7 ♈	20 ♉	29 ♉	16 ♋	23 ♌	15 ♎	16 ♏	9 ♒	4 ♓	22 ♈	20 ♉	20 ♊
19	0 ♉	15 ♊	24 ♊	13 ♌	21 ♍	14 ♏	13 ♐	23 ♒	22 ♈	16 ♉	20 ♊	16 ♋
21	24 ♉	11 ♋	20 ♋	11 ♍	19 ♎	11 ♐	11 ♑	16 ♓	16 ♊	10 ♊	12 ♋	14 ♌
23	20 ♊	10 ♌	18 ♌	9 ♎	19 ♏	8 ♑	5 ♒	10 ♈	10 ♋	5 ♌	12 ♌	12 ♍
25	17 ♋	10 ♍	18 ♍	9 ♏	17 ♐	4 ♒	0 ♓	5 ♉	5 ♌	2 ♍	10 ♎	8 ♎
27	16 ♌	10 ♎	18 ♎	7 ♐	13 ♑	29 ♒	24 ♓	0 ♊	4 ♍	9 ♎	2 ♏	8 ♏
29	16 ♍		18 ♏	3 ♑	8 ♒	23 ♓	14 ♈	25 ♋	4 ♎	6 ♏	29 ♏	7 ♐
31	15 ♎		16 ♐		28 ♒		23 ♉	6 ♌		6 ♐		7 ♑

1968

	Jan.	Feb.	Mar.	April	May	June	July	Aug.	Sept.	Oct.	Nov.	Dec.
1	21 ♑	10 ♓	0 ♈	15 ♉	17 ♊	3 ♌	8 ♍	29 ♎	22 ♐	1 ♒	21 ♓	26 ♈
3	19 ♒	5 ♈	25 ♈	9 ♊	11 ♋	4 ♍	4 ♎	27 ♏	27 ♐	24 ♒	16 ♈	20 ♉
5	15 ♓	29 ♈	19 ♉	2 ♋	8 ♌	24 ♍	26 ♎	24 ♐	18 ♑	24 ♓	11 ♉	13 ♊
7	9 ♈	23 ♉	13 ♊	27 ♋	23 ♌	15 ♎	15 ♐	18 ♑	11 ♒	5 ♈	4 ♊	7 ♋
9	3 ♉	16 ♊	6 ♋	22 ♌	29 ♍	22 ♏	22 ♐	20 ♒	6 ♓	8 ♉	28 ♊	1 ♌
11	27 ♉	11 ♋	1 ♌	21 ♍	28 ♎	22 ♐	22 ♑	20 ♓	6 ♈	22 ♉	22 ♋	25 ♌
13	21 ♊	7 ♌	5 ♍	20 ♎	29 ♏	22 ♑	16 ♒	20 ♈	26 ♉	16 ♊	17 ♌	17 ♍
15	16 ♋	5 ♍	27 ♍	20 ♏	25 ♐	20 ♒	10 ♓	24 ♉	26 ♊	10 ♋	12 ♍	17 ♎
17	12 ♌	5 ♎	26 ♎	20 ♐	20 ♑	18 ♓	4 ♈	28 ♊	13 ♋	5 ♌	8 ♎	16 ♏
19	9 ♍	5 ♏	1 ♐	26 ♑	19 ♒	2 ♈	28 ♈	4 ♌	8 ♍	8 ♍	9 ♏	16 ♐
21	6 ♎	4 ♐	22 ♐	11 ♒	5 ♓	26 ♈	6 ♉	29 ♌	9 ♎	8 ♎	9 ♐	14 ♑
23	4 ♏	28 ♐	22 ♑	22 ♓	5 ♈	6 ♊	26 ♉	26 ♍	7 ♏	6 ♐	8 ♑	14 ♒
25	3 ♐	22 ♑	17 ♒	14 ♈	6 ♉	26 ♊	18 ♊	14 ♎	6 ♐	15 ♑	5 ♒	10 ♓
27	1 ♑	16 ♒	14 ♓	6 ♉	2 ♊	9 ♋	17 ♋	14 ♏	5 ♑	14 ♒	1 ♓	5 ♈
29	29 ♑	18 ♓	9 ♈	24 ♉	26 ♊		12 ♌	18 ♐	4 ♒	14 ♓		0 ♉
31	27 ♒		9 ♉		20 ♊		15 ♍	8 ♑		8 ♈		28 ♉

1969

	Jan.	Feb.	Mar.	April	May	June	July	Aug.	Sept.	Oct.	Nov.	Dec.
1	10 ♊	25 ♋	3 ♌	19 ♍	24 ♎	17 ♐	26 ♑	18 ♓	7 ♉	10 ♊	24 ♋	26 ♌
3	4 ♋	19 ♌	28 ♌	16 ♎	23 ♏	17 ♑	26 ♒	16 ♈	2 ♊	5 ♋	18 ♌	20 ♍
5	28 ♋	14 ♍	23 ♍	14 ♏	22 ♐	18 ♒	24 ♓	11 ♉	26 ♊	0 ♌	12 ♍	15 ♎
7	22 ♌	10 ♎	20 ♎	13 ♐	22 ♑	16 ♓	20 ♈	6 ♊	20 ♋	24 ♌	8 ♎	12 ♏
9	17 ♍	7 ♏	18 ♏	13 ♑	20 ♒	10 ♈	15 ♉	0 ♋	14 ♌	18 ♍	4 ♏	11 ♐
11	13 ♎	5 ♐	17 ♐	11 ♒	9 ♓	6 ♉	9 ♊	25 ♋	9 ♍	14 ♎	3 ♐	11 ♑
13	11 ♏	5 ♑	17 ♑	7 ♓	4 ♈	26 ♉	3 ♋	18 ♌	4 ♎	9 ♏	3 ♑	11 ♒
15	10 ♐	5 ♒	16 ♒	4 ♈	0 ♉	21 ♊	27 ♋	18 ♍	1 ♏	7 ♐	3 ♒	9 ♓
17	10 ♑	4 ♓	12 ♓	0 ♉	25 ♉	15 ♋	18 ♌	18 ♎	27 ♏	5 ♑	1 ♓	5 ♈
19	9 ♒	0 ♈	8 ♈	25 ♉	20 ♊	21 ♋	21 ♌	0 ♏	23 ♐	4 ♒	28 ♓	0 ♉
21	9 ♓	26 ♈	4 ♉	19 ♊	15 ♋	21 ♍	0 ♎	28 ♏	22 ♑	3 ♓	19 ♈	24 ♉
23	6 ♈	1 ♉	29 ♉	23 ♋	15 ♌	15 ♎	27 ♎	28 ♐	21 ♒	0 ♈	14 ♉	17 ♊
25	1 ♉	1 ♊	23 ♊	29 ♋	15 ♍	9 ♏	4 ♐	28 ♑	19 ♓	27 ♈	8 ♊	11 ♋
27	25 ♉	19 ♋	17 ♋	5 ♍	9 ♎	4 ♐	4 ♑	25 ♒	15 ♈	23 ♉	2 ♋	5 ♌
29	19 ♊		11 ♌	2 ♎	5 ♏	1 ♑	4 ♒	21 ♓	9 ♉	18 ♊	19 ♋	0 ♍
31	13 ♋		6 ♍		2 ♐		24 ♒	15 ♈		12 ♋		28 ♍

1970	Jan.	Feb.	Mar.	April	May	June	July	Aug.	Sept.	Oct.	Nov.	Dec.
1	11 ♎	29 ♏	9 ♐	1 ♒	10 ♓	2 ♉	8 ♊	25 ♋	9 ♍	12 ♎	29 ♏	5 ♑
3	7 ♏	27 ♐	7 ♑	0 ♓	8 ♈	29 ♊	29 ♋	18 ♌	25 ♎	6 ♏	25 ♑	3 ♒
5	4 ♐	27 ♑	6 ♒	29 ♓	6 ♉	6 ♋	12 ♌	28 ♍	27 ♎	4 ♐	22 ♒	1 ♓
7	4 ♑	27 ♒	28 ♒	3 ♈	19 ♉	22 ♋	15 ♍	0 ♏	18 ♐	26 ♐	20 ♓	27 ♓
9	5 ♒	27 ♓	5 ♓	25 ♈	29 ♊	7 ♌	4 ♏	18 ♎	26 ♑	24 ♑	19 ♈	27 ♈
11	5 ♓	26 ♈	22 ♓	0 ♊	21 ♊	23 ♌	4 ♏	26 ♎	16 ♒	24 ♒	16 ♉	22 ♉
13	5 ♈	22 ♉	0 ♉	15 ♊	17 ♋	7 ♍	11 ♐	4 ♐	25 ♓	25 ♓	18 ♊	18 ♊
15	3 ♉	17 ♊	25 ♉	9 ♋	9 ♌	11 ♎	26 ♐	22 ♐	22 ♈	22 ♈	18 ♋	13 ♋
17	25 ♉	11 ♋	19 ♊	19 ♋	3 ♍	1 ♏	11 ♑	22 ♑	22 ♉	14 ♉	6 ♌	0 ♍
19	20 ♊	4 ♌	13 ♋	27 ♌	27 ♍	1 ♐	20 ♒	28 ♒	22 ♊	19 ♊	5 ♍	8 ♎
21	14 ♋	28 ♌	7 ♌	1 ♏	28 ♎	20 ♐	19 ♓	28 ♓	19 ♋	11 ♋	15 ♎	16 ♏
23	8 ♌	22 ♍	1 ♎	26 ♎	24 ♏	19 ♑	28 ♈	28 ♈	11 ♌	9 ♌	22 ♏	24 ♐
25	1 ♍	17 ♎	26 ♎	24 ♏	16 ♐	16 ♒	26 ♉	10 ♉	1 ♍	26 ♍	11 ♐	19 ♑
27	25 ♍	12 ♏	22 ♏	14 ♐	23 ♑	16 ♓	23 ♊	5 ♋	24 ♍	26 ♎	11 ♑	16 ♒
29	20 ♎		19 ♐	12 ♑	21 ♒	12 ♈	19 ♋	18 ♌	18 ♍	16 ♏	8 ♒	14 ♓
31	15 ♏		17 ♑		19 ♓		13 ♌	27 ♍		16 ♐		13 ♈

1971	Jan.	Feb.	Mar.	April	May	June	July	Aug.	Sept.	Oct.	Nov.	Dec.
1	27 ♒	21 ♈	0 ♉	21 ♊	26 ♋	11 ♍	12 ♎	26 ♏	13 ♑	19 ♒	11 ♈	20 ♉
3	26 ♓	18 ♉	28 ♉	17 ♋	20 ♌	4 ♎	6 ♏	21 ♐	10 ♒	18 ♓	11 ♉	19 ♊
5	24 ♈	15 ♊	25 ♊	14 ♌	28 ♍	28 ♎	1 ♐	18 ♑	10 ♓	18 ♈	11 ♊	18 ♋
7	22 ♉	11 ♋	20 ♋	6 ♍	29 ♎	22 ♏	26 ♐	17 ♒	9 ♈	17 ♉	10 ♋	15 ♌
9	18 ♊	6 ♌	15 ♌	29 ♍	1 ♐	18 ♑	24 ♑	16 ♓	8 ♉	14 ♊	6 ♌	10 ♍
11	14 ♋	0 ♍	9 ♍	23 ♎	26 ♐	14 ♒	22 ♒	15 ♈	8 ♊	10 ♋	1 ♍	4 ♎
13	9 ♌	25 ♍	3 ♎	17 ♏	20 ♑	11 ♓	20 ♓	11 ♉	5 ♋	5 ♌	25 ♍	27 ♎
15	3 ♍	17 ♎	26 ♎	12 ♐	17 ♒	9 ♈	19 ♈	7 ♊	1 ♌	29 ♌	19 ♎	21 ♏
17	27 ♍	11 ♏	20 ♏	7 ♑	13 ♓	6 ♉	17 ♉	4 ♋	25 ♌	22 ♍	13 ♏	16 ♐
19	21 ♎	6 ♐	15 ♐	4 ♒	11 ♈	6 ♊	14 ♊	29 ♋	13 ♎	16 ♏	7 ♐	11 ♑
21	15 ♏	6 ♑	11 ♑	2 ♓	11 ♉	4 ♋	11 ♋	24 ♌	13 ♏	16 ♐	1 ♑	7 ♒
23	11 ♐	6 ♒	9 ♒	2 ♈	10 ♊	29 ♋	7 ♌	17 ♍	7 ♐	4 ♑	23 ♑	4 ♓
25	8 ♑	0 ♓	9 ♓	2 ♉	10 ♋	23 ♌	2 ♍	10 ♎	21 ♐	0 ♒	21 ♒	1 ♈
27	7 ♒	7 ♈	9 ♈	2 ♊	8 ♌	17 ♍	27 ♍	4 ♐	27 ♑	27 ♒	20 ♓	29 ♈
29	7 ♓		9 ♉	1 ♋	4 ♍	20 ♎	20 ♎	4 ♐	20 ♑		21 ♈	29 ♉
31	6 ♈		7 ♊		29 ♍		14 ♏	29 ♐		26 ♓		28 ♊

1972	Jan.	Feb.	Mar.	April	May	June	July	Aug.	Sept.	Oct.	Nov.	Dec.
1	12 ♋	0 ♍	21 ♍	6 ♏	8 ♑	24 ♒	0 ♓	21 ♈	14 ♊	23 ♋	13 ♍	17 ♎
3	9 ♌	25 ♍	16 ♎	29 ♏	2 ♒	19 ♓	26 ♓	19 ♉	12 ♋	20 ♌	7 ♎	11 ♏
5	5 ♍	19 ♎	13 ♏	9 ♐	27 ♒	16 ♈	24 ♈	18 ♊	10 ♌	16 ♍	2 ♏	5 ♐
7	0 ♎	13 ♏	8 ♐	18 ♑	23 ♓	14 ♉	23 ♉	14 ♋	6 ♍	11 ♎	25 ♏	28 ♐
9	24 ♎	7 ♐	27 ♐	14 ♒	20 ♈	13 ♊	22 ♊	11 ♌	2 ♎	5 ♏	19 ♐	22 ♑
11	17 ♏	2 ♑	20 ♑	11 ♓	20 ♉	13 ♋	21 ♋	6 ♍	25 ♎	29 ♏	12 ♑	17 ♒
13	11 ♐	29 ♑	18 ♒	11 ♈	20 ♊	11 ♌	16 ♌	1 ♎	19 ♏	22 ♐	7 ♒	9 ♓
15	7 ♑	26 ♒	18 ♓	11 ♉	20 ♋	7 ♍	11 ♍	25 ♎	13 ♐	17 ♑	3 ♓	9 ♈
17	3 ♒	24 ♓	18 ♈	11 ♊	19 ♌	2 ♎	8 ♎	20 ♏	8 ♑	11 ♒	0 ♈	7 ♉
19	1 ♓	23 ♈	17 ♉	10 ♋	16 ♍	27 ♎	3 ♏	5 ♐	4 ♒	7 ♓	29 ♈	7 ♊
21	28 ♓	22 ♉	16 ♊	7 ♌	12 ♎	21 ♏	28 ♏	28 ♐	0 ♓	5 ♈	29 ♉	8 ♋
23	26 ♈	20 ♊	14 ♋	2 ♍	6 ♏	14 ♐	17 ♐	23 ♑	27 ♓	5 ♉	0 ♋	5 ♌
25	23 ♉	17 ♋	10 ♌	5 ♎	0 ♐	9 ♑	17 ♑	5 ♒	26 ♈	6 ♊	0 ♌	1 ♍
27	23 ♊	13 ♌	5 ♍	21 ♎	23 ♐	4 ♒	9 ♒	26 ♓	26 ♉	6 ♋	29 ♌	26 ♍
29	21 ♋	9 ♍	0 ♎	15 ♏	17 ♑	4 ♓	4 ♓	26 ♈	25 ♊	6 ♌	25 ♍	19 ♎
31	17 ♌		24 ♎		12 ♒		10 ♈	0 ♊		0 ♍		

1973	Jan.	Feb.	Mar.	April	May	June	July	Aug.	Sept.	Oct.	Nov.	Dec.
1	1 ♐	16 ♑	24 ♑	10 ♓	15 ♈	8 ♊	17 ♋	9 ♍	28 ♎	1 ♐	15 ♑	17 ♒
3	25 ♐	10 ♒	19 ♒	7 ♈	14 ♉	8 ♋	16 ♌	2 ♎	23 ♏	25 ♐	9 ♒	11 ♓
5	19 ♑	6 ♓	15 ♓	5 ♉	14 ♊	8 ♌	15 ♍	27 ♎	17 ♐	19 ♑	3 ♓	5 ♈
7	14 ♒	2 ♈	12 ♈	4 ♊	14 ♋	6 ♍	11 ♎	21 ♏	11 ♑	13 ♒	28 ♓	2 ♉
9	9 ♓	0 ♉	10 ♉	4 ♋	12 ♌	2 ♎	6 ♏	15 ♐	5 ♒	8 ♓	24 ♈	0 ♊
11	5 ♈	27 ♉	8 ♊	1 ♌	9 ♍	27 ♎	0 ♐	9 ♑	1 ♓	5 ♈	22 ♉	0 ♋
13	2 ♉	25 ♊	6 ♋	28 ♌	5 ♎	21 ♏	24 ♐	3 ♒	28 ♓	3 ♉	22 ♊	1 ♌
15	1 ♊	23 ♋	4 ♌	25 ♍	0 ♏	15 ♐	18 ♑	29 ♒	27 ♈	3 ♊	22 ♋	0 ♍
17	1 ♋	23 ♌	2 ♍	20 ♎	24 ♏	9 ♑	13 ♒	26 ♓	26 ♉	3 ♋	22 ♌	28 ♍
19	1 ♌	21 ♍	29 ♍	15 ♏	18 ♐	4 ♒	9 ♓	24 ♈	26 ♊	3 ♌	20 ♍	23 ♎
21	29 ♌	17 ♎	24 ♎	9 ♐	12 ♑	0 ♓	6 ♈	23 ♉	25 ♋	1 ♍	15 ♎	20 ♏
23	26 ♍	12 ♏	19 ♏	3 ♑	6 ♒	26 ♓	3 ♉	22 ♊	22 ♌	27 ♍	10 ♏	14 ♐
25	22 ♎	6 ♐	14 ♐	27 ♑	2 ♓	24 ♈	2 ♊	21 ♋	19 ♍	23 ♎	5 ♐	8 ♑
27	16 ♏	29 ♐	7 ♑	22 ♒	28 ♓	22 ♉	1 ♋	19 ♌	14 ♎	18 ♏	29 ♐	2 ♒
29	10 ♐		1 ♒	18 ♓	26 ♈	23 ♊	1 ♌	17 ♍	9 ♏	12 ♐	23 ♑	25 ♒
31	3 ♑		27 ♒		25 ♉		0 ♍	15 ♎		6 ♑		19 ♓

1974	Jan.	Feb.	Mar.	April	May	June	July	Aug.	Sept.	Oct.	Nov.	Dec.
1	14 ♈	4 ♊	14 ♊	7 ♌	16 ♍	7 ♏	12 ♐	28 ♑	12 ♓	15 ♈	3 ♊	11 ♋
3	11 ♉	3 ♋	13 ♋	6 ♍	14 ♎	3 ♐	7 ♑	21 ♒	6 ♈	11 ♉	1 ♋	9 ♌
5	10 ♊	3 ♌	12 ♌	3 ♎	11 ♏	28 ♐	1 ♒	15 ♓	2 ♉	9 ♊	0 ♌	8 ♍
7	10 ♋	3 ♍	11 ♍	2 ♏	7 ♐	22 ♑	24 ♒	9 ♈	27 ♉	7 ♋	27 ♌	6 ♎
9	11 ♌	2 ♎	8 ♎	29 ♏	1 ♑	16 ♒	18 ♓	4 ♉	23 ♊	7 ♌	24 ♍	3 ♏
11	10 ♍	0 ♏	5 ♏	24 ♐	26 ♑	9 ♓	12 ♈	0 ♊	21 ♋	7 ♍	21 ♎	26 ♏
13	8 ♎	25 ♏	0 ♐	18 ♑	20 ♒	3 ♈	8 ♉	28 ♊	21 ♌	5 ♎	16 ♏	21 ♐
15	4 ♏	20 ♐	24 ♐	12 ♒	14 ♓	28 ♈	4 ♊	28 ♋	20 ♍	3 ♏	10 ♐	15 ♑
17	29 ♏	14 ♑	18 ♑	6 ♓	8 ♈	25 ♉	2 ♋	28 ♌	18 ♎	29 ♏	7 ♑	9 ♒
19	23 ♐	7 ♒	12 ♒	0 ♈	4 ♉	23 ♊	4 ♌	26 ♍	15 ♏	24 ♐	1 ♒	3 ♓
21	17 ♑	1 ♓	5 ♓	26 ♈	0 ♊	23 ♋	4 ♍	23 ♎	10 ♐	18 ♑	25 ♒	28 ♓
23	10 ♒	26 ♓	0 ♈	24 ♉	0 ♋	23 ♌	3 ♎	18 ♏	5 ♑	12 ♒	19 ♓	23 ♈
25	4 ♓	21 ♈	26 ♈	22 ♊	0 ♌	22 ♍	0 ♏	13 ♐	29 ♑	5 ♓	14 ♈	20 ♉
27	29 ♓	17 ♉	23 ♉	20 ♋	29 ♌	21 ♎	27 ♏	7 ♑	23 ♒	0 ♈	13 ♉	20 ♊
29	23 ♈		21 ♊	18 ♌	29 ♍	16 ♏	21 ♐	1 ♒	17 ♓	24 ♈	13 ♊	20 ♋
31	20 ♉		23 ♋		24 ♎		16 ♑	26 ♒		20 ♉		19 ♌

INSTRVMĒTVM VERI LOCI
LVNE IN ZODIACO·

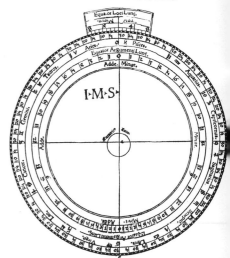